A Stitch in Time:

a baseball chronology, 1845-2000

by

Gene Elston

Halcyon Press, Ltd
www.halcyon-press.com

Published by Halcyon Press, Ltd. http://www.halcyon-press.com

For information, write:

Halcyon Press, Ltd.
6065 Hillcroft Suite 525
Houston, TX 77081

David J. Raley, Editor
Photos courtesy of Gene Elston
Cover by Chris Henderson

Printed in the United States of America

Library of Congress Cataloging-in-Publication Data

Elston, Gene, 1922-
A stitch in time : a baseball chronology, 1845-2000 / Gene Elston.
p. cm.
Includes index.
ISBN 0-9706054-1-2 (paperback).—ISBN 0-9706054-5-5 (hardcover)
1. Baseball--History--Chronology. 2. Baseball--Miscellanea. I. Title.
GV862.5 .E58 2000
796.357'09--dc21

00-012468

To
Donald Davidson
(1926-1990)

Long-time executive of the Braves and Astros
without whose association my days in baseball
would not have been nearly as fulfilling

Small in stature but a Giant in the industry

Contents

Author's Note: Hall-of-Famers' numbers shown in parenthesis throughout.

Introduction

A Stitch in Time tracks baseball since its inception in 1845 when the game was played under the dimensions and rules that mirrored our game of today.

For the past 156 years in almost every category from hard statistics to the intense research to learn more of its many fascinations, to human interest pieces on the stars and the little-known players, and to the executives and umpires, no other sport has been documented as thoroughly as the history of baseball. Everything has been included from the minor leagues to the contributions made by women. All of the above share in making baseball America's National Pastime and all are found in *A Stitch in Time.*

All information in this chronology can be found somewhere in the archives of baseball and is available for public consumption -- but not in this form. This is not a statistical or record book. This is interesting baseball information, game highlights, and personal achievements, all rolled into a handy, easy-to-read short story form.

Where does baseball begin and end each season? This compilation of the game proves that hardly a day goes by without some happening in the game. It "begins" with spring training, then Opening Day and the World Series, then the unbroken circle continues through the fall and winter leagues. In reality it never ends.

Gene Elston is uniquely qualified to author this compendium of the games's history. As a long-time broadcaster for the Chicago Cubs, Houston Colt .45's, the Houston Astros, and Game of the Day, Gene brought the listeners an accurate and comprehensive account of the game he was covering each day and, in a broader sense, imparted an unparalleled knowledge and respect for the history of the Game.

Along the way, Gene became a tireless researcher of Baseball fact and Baseball lore. From personal experience, I can attest that many have come to rely on Gene when a question arises about events or people in baseball. There is no better or more willing a source. All of us that care about the Game are fortunate to have Gene share his love and knowledge of baseball with us in *A Stitch in Time.*

Tal Smith
President, Houston Astros

A Stitch in Time

a baseball Chronology, 1845-2000

Gene Elston

Chapter One

"90 feet between bases represents man's closest approach to absolute truth. The world's fastest man cannot run to first base ahead of a sharply hit ball that is cleanly handled by an infielder; he will get there only half a step too late. Let the fielder juggle the ball for one moment or delay his throw an instant and the runner will be safe. 90 feet demands perfection. It accurately measures the cunning, speed and finesse of the base stealer against the velocity of a thrown ball. It dictates the placement of infielders. That single dimension makes baseball a fine art."

--Red Smith

January 1

1924 — St. Louis Browns owner Phil Ball threatens to have the tenant St. Louis Cardinals evicted from Sportsman's Park because the Redbirds were 24 hours late on their rent payment. Cardinals owner Sam Breadon claimed the lack of payment was an oversight but Ball went through with a lawsuit that was eventually settled. The Browns would try it again on March 1, 1949 when they moved to evict the Redbirds in order to gain a rental increase. Both of these ploys were attempts to get the Cardinals out of Sportsman's Park and St. Louis. Ironically, the opposite happened, the Browns were sold and left town to become the Baltimore Orioles following the 1953 season.

1961 — Detroit's ballpark gets its fourth name since 1900 — Tiger Stadium. Originally called Bennett Park, it became Navin Field in 1912 and was renamed Briggs Stadium in 1938. Lights were installed in 1948. In 1989 the stadium was recognized by the Federal Government as a historic site and placed on the National Register of Historic Places. This means the property is of historical importance and worthy of preservation (however, the listing does not give the government any authority over the property, and would not save the stadium from the wrecking ball).

January 2

1912 — Brooklyn Dodgers president Charles H. Ebbets, after spending weeks scouring the borough of Brooklyn for the right location for a new ballpark to replace old Washington Park, settles on an area known as Pigtown. This is a neighborhood of broken-down shanties and endless stacks of garbage. On this spot he envisioned a beautiful new ballpark and immediately set upon acquiring the parcels of land needed through dummy deeds. During this period Ebbets would ease his pinched financial situation by selling half of the team to Ed and Steve McKeever. Although his sanity regarding the project was questioned by many of his friends, Ebbets completed the purchase of the parcel of land on which Ebbets Field would be built.

January 3

1916 — Peace between the outlaw Federal League and the majors is ratified. The clear sailing of the American and National leagues was interrupted in 1914 and 1915 by the Federal League. And although the league operated as a third "major league" it never was given that status by pro ball even though several major league players jumped to the new league. Most of the players leaving the majors were fringe players lured by expected big money. However, it did cost the established leagues over $2 million to hold the talent they already had. The Federal League spent as much time in court battles over the reserve clause as it did on the field. This was also costing the American and National leagues money and, in late 1915, some National League officials offered to buy out the outlaw league. There was some opposition to the plan, especially from president Ban Johnson of the American League, but he finally relented and on January 3, 1916 the majors and the Federal League ratified the peace agreement. It was the last threat of a third major league until the Continental League surfaced in the late 1950s and forced expansion in 1961 and 1962.

1920 — The Boston Red Sox sell Babe Ruth to the Yankees. Ruth, coming off his sixth season with the Red Sox in 1919, was beginning to complain that he was grossly underpaid at $10,000 per year. The movement of Ruth was also triggered by Boston's financial bind due to notes payable by owner Harry Frazee. The Yankees were very interested in Ruth and the deal took about a week to consummate — it was a straight cash deal of $100,000; however there were a few fringe benefits for the Red Sox. The Yankees gave Frazee $25,000 in cash and three promissory notes for $25,000 each with 6% interest, the last payable in late 1922. This brought the purchase price to $110,000. The crux of the deal was that Frazee wanted a loan of $300,000 and this was given to him by the Yankees in the form of a mortgage on Fenway Park. So Frazee acquired about $400,000 in the deal. The Red Sox owner had said "no-no" to Ruth's salary demands but Frazee, whose first love was being one of New York's leading theatrical figures, waited only until 1925 when he said "no-no" again by hitting a financial bonanza with Broadway's "No-No, Nanette".

1973 — It was 53 years to the day of Babe Ruth's purchase by New York that the Yankees made news again. George Steinbrenner forms a syndicate of 15 investors and buys the Yankees from CBS for $10 million. The general partners include James Nederlander, the head of a theatrical empire, Thomas W. Evans, managing partner of the law firm of which Richard Nixon is a partner, auto executive John DeLorean, baseball executive Gabe Paul, Nelson Bunker Hunt of Texas oil fame and Michael Burke who was a Yankee executive with CBS. Steinbrenner says, "I won't be active in the day-to-day operation of the club I've got enough headaches with my shipping company."

1974 — George Steinbrenner makes the first of a series of managerial changes when he replaces Ralph Houk with Bill Virdon one year to the day of his purchase of the Yankees. This move was necessary because Houk, who had managed the Yankees for 11 years had resigned following the 1973 season. Steinbrenner had first hired Dick Williams, at the time the manager of the Athletics, to replace Houk, but Oakland owner Charlie Finley fought and successfully had the signing nullified when American League president Joe Cronin upheld Finley's complaint. In June Finley would allow Williams to take the Angels job following the firing of Bobby Winkles because of his friendship with California owner Gene Autry. Thus Virdon was the first of the long line of skippers for Steinbrenner's Yankees. From 1974 to 1996, when Joe Torre took over for the Yankees, Steinbrenner made 20 managerial changes involving 13 men.

January 4

1932 — Brooklyn signs Casey Stengel to a coaching position. The Dodgers had just signed Max Carey as their new manager, and he and Stengel had been teammates at Pittsburgh in 1918 and 1919. This move led to Stengel's first major league managerial job with Brooklyn in 1934. 1925 would be his first managerial job as the Boston front office appointed him player-manager and president at Worcester in the Eastern League. When an opportunity arose at the end of the 1925 season for him to manage Toledo, the parent Boston club would not let him go, so he used his authority with the Worcester club to leave Boston. Stengel, as manager, released Stengel the player. As president he fired Stengel the manager and then resigned as president.

January 4-5

1943 — 37 year-old Yankees pitcher Red Ruffing is drafted into the army. This is a bit surprising since he lost four toes on his left foot in a mine accident when he was 15 years old. After missing two full seasons he returned to New York for two more years and finished his 22-year career in 1947 with the White Sox. He was 273-225 lifetime with an earned run average of 3.80 and had four straight 20-win seasons from 1936 through 1939. Ruffing (15) was 7-2 in World Series play and entered the Hall of Fame in 1967.

1977 — The Chicago White Sox announce the hiring of Mary Shane as an addition to their radio and television crew. Shane had a background of sports writing and play-by-play basketball in the Milwaukee area. During a game in Milwaukee late in the 1976 season, Sox broadcaster Harry Caray offered her the mic. This led to her hiring by WMAQ station manager Charlie Wagner. Shane would join the team of Caray, Lorn Brown and Jimmy Piersall for the 1977 season on WMAQ and WSNS-TV. A combination of Shane's inexperience and prejudice against her as a woman limited her to brief appearances on 35 games. She did limited play-by-play on radio and TV as well as game analysis. Shane returned to sports writing and in 1985 joined the staff of the *Worcester Telegram*. She died of a heart attack on November 3, 1987. Shane was not the first woman baseball broadcaster. Owner Charlie Finley had used Betty Caywood on the Kansas City Athletics broadcasts in the late 1960s. As far back as 1938, a female broadcaster hit the airwaves as a member of the General Mills baseball announcers crew. Although better known for her prowess as a golfer, Helen Dettweiller would cover all cities in which General Mills operated baseball broadcasts.

January 5

1920 — In a deal consummated two days earlier with the Boston Red Sox, the Yankees officially announce the purchase of Babe Ruth. The club delayed the announcement until they had Ruth under contract. When the Yankees bought Ruth he had two years remaining on his agreement with Boston. Ruth demanded the Yankees double his salary for those two years – from $10,000 to $20,000 – and that they give him a $1,000 up-front bonus. The Yankees gave in after the Bambino threatened not to report to New York. This probably classifies Ruth as the first player in history to request a contract renegotiation.

1931 — Mrs. Lucille Thomas becomes the first woman to purchase a professional baseball team when she buys the Topeka franchise in the Western League. The first woman to own a major league team was Mrs. Frank Dehass Robinson in 1911 when she became president of the St. Louis Cardinals.

1943 — The war has a profound effect on spring training. Commissioner Landis orders teams to train near their homes and lays out specific boundaries – above the Mason-Dixon line, north of the Potomac and Ohio rivers and east of the Mississippi. However, the two St. Louis teams could train in Missouri, with the Browns selecting Cape Girardeau and the Cardinals moving across the river to Cairo, Illinois. The Red Sox would train at Tufts College in Massachusetts and the Boston Braves at Choate Prep School in Wallingford, Connecticut. The Cubs and White Sox worked out together in French Lick, Indiana and many other Midwest teams also chose the Hoosier State — Cleveland at Purdue University in Lafayette, Detroit at Evansville, Pittsburgh at Muncie and Cincinnati at Indiana University at Bloomington. The New York and Philadelphia teams stayed close to home by setting up camps in New Jersey – the Yankees in Asbury Park, the Giants at Lakewood and the Phillies and Athletics at Atlantic City. The Dodgers worked out near West Point at Bear Mountain, New York, while the Washington Senators used the facilities at the University of Maryland in College Park.

January 6

1909 — Maximum price for World Series tickets set at $2.00.

1914 — The Players' Fraternity makes inroads with management when the National Commission grants free agency to players with 10 years in the majors, and it rules clubs must pay traveling expenses to spring training and supply uniforms. The Commission also ordered all parks place a blank green wall or "batter's eye" in center field.

1997 — Los Angeles Dodgers president Peter O'Malley stuns the baseball world with the announcement that his National League team is for sale. O'Malley says, "Family ownership is probably a dying breed — a high risk business – with groups and corporations the wave of the future." He said there is no rush to sell the team – no pressure – that they were talking and listening to no one at this time and they are not seeking a buyer. The O'Malley family had been in control of the Dodgers since 1950.

January 7

1924 — The Yankees make a shrewd move with the purchase of outfielder Earle

Combs from Louisville for $30,000. Combs played his entire 12 years in the majors with New York batting .325. In seven of those seasons he hit better than .300 while hitting .350 in four World Series appearances. Combs (1) was elected to the Hall of Fame in1970.

1933 — With the country in the throes of the depression, Commissioner Landis cuts his salary from $65,000 to $40,000 hoping others in the industry would follow his lead. Very few, if any, did.

January 8

1927 — Ty Cobb, who broke in with the Tigers in 1905, ends his 22-year career in Detroit and signs with the Philadelphia Athletics. Cobb won 12 batting titles and hit over .400 three times (.420 in 1911, .410 in 1912, .401 in 1922). He took over as manager of the Tigers in 1921, managing six seasons, finishing second once, third two times, fourth once and sixth twice. Cobb's relationship with owner Frank Navin and the Detroit fans had become almost hostile and Cobb had resigned his manager's post in November of 1926. Philadelphia owner Connie Mack needed an attraction for his A's, who had finished in the second division for ten of the last twelve years, and got it in Cobb. In 24 years Cobb accumulated 4,191 hits and batted .367, never hitting below .324 in any season in which he qualified for the batting title. He won nine straight batting championships (1907-1915) and three more (1917-1919), driving in 1,961 runs with 892 stolen bases during a career that began in 1905 and lasted through 1928. Cobb entered the Hall of Fame in 1936 as one of the five charter members.

1942 — Bill Terry, who spent his entire 20 major league years with the New York Giants, announces his retirement. Terry became a Giant in 1923, taking over as player-manager in 1932. He continued in that capacity through 1936, then retired as a player but remained as manager until turning over the reins to Mel Ott following the 1941 season. He finished his playing career with a batting average of .341 hitting .300 or better in 10 of his 14 seasons and in 6 of those years passed the 200 hit mark. After his retirement as a player he was moved upstairs in the Giants organization with the sole purpose of building a farm system. After only one year in the Giants front office he left baseball for the automobile business in Memphis. He was back in baseball for a short time in 1955 as president of the South Atlantic League for three years. Terry (3) hit .401 with 254 hits in 1930 to lead the league in both departments and entered the Hall of Fame in 1954.

1957 — Jackie Robinson announces his retirement from baseball. Robinson broke in with the Dodgers in 1947 and played his final game in the 1956 World Series against the Yankees. He was traded in December of 1956 to the New York Giants for pitcher Dick Littlefield and $35,000. Although Giants president Chub Feeney offered Robinson a most generous contract for 1957 Robinson decided his career was over. The way he went out was obviously the result of the tumultuous ten years he spent in the major leagues. Robinson withheld the announcement from the writers who had followed his career daily over the years. He scooped them all with a by-lined story in *Look* magazine and, once again, brought on much criticism. He shrugged this off by saying the writers would have done the same thing to pick up some extra money. Robinson played ten seasons in the National League after he became the first Negro to play in the majors since 1884 (Moses Fleetwood Walker played with Toledo in the American Association – then recognized as a major league). Robinson (42) hit .311 with Brooklyn, winning the National League batting title with a .342 mark and Most Valuable Player Award in 1949, and was elected to the Hall of Fame in 1962 in his first year of eligibility.

January 9

1892 — "Slide, Kelly, Slide," by George Gaskin, makes the pop music charts, the first baseball song to do so. Mike "King" Kelly was an intelligent, handsome Irishman who could pass any man going from bar to bar and on the baseball field going from base to base. He played sixteen years in the majors 1878 through 1893 seeing action at every position. In 1887 he was traded from the Chicago White Stockings to the Boston Beaneaters and was paid the unheard-of salary of $10,000. In the first five games with his new team he had more hits, scored more runs and stole more bases than the rest of the team. That was the beginning of the Boston fans' cries of "Slide, Kelly, Slide" throughout the South End Grounds. In 1894 Kelly contracted a cold that developed into pneumonia and while being carried into a Boston hospital, the litter bearers stumbled and Kelly slid to the floor and quipped, "That's my last slide." The fast-living Kelly died when he was only 37. In 1945 Mike "King" Kelly would join the other immortals in the Hall of Fame.

1903 — President Ban Johnson puts together a group to bring the American League to New York with the announcement of the purchase of the Baltimore team for $18,000. Johnson had organized the American League and became the circuit's first president in 1901 and served through 1927. He also was instrumental in bringing the National and American Leagues together in 1903. For his many contributions to the game Johnson was elected into the Hall of Fame. The new franchise for New York was called the Highlanders partly because the team would play their games at Broadway between 165th and 168th Streets – one of the highest points of land in Manhattan, and the current location of the Columbia-Presbyterian Medical Center. The name "Yankees" was used in reference to the team as early as 1904, and some writers began using the name in 1911, but it was not until 1913 that the name received common usage.

1918 & **1927** – The first two times Burleigh Grimes was traded happened on this date. In 1918 Grimes moved from Pittsburgh with shortstop Charles Ward and pitcher Al Mamaux to Brooklyn for Casey Stengel, second baseman George Cutshaw and $20,000. The same date nine years later he was traded to the New York Giants in a three-cornered deal that also involved the Philadelphia Phillies. In his 18-year major league career (1916-1934), Grimes would be traded, waived or sold a total of nine times and play with eight different teams. Grimes (21) won 270 games while losing 212 and was elected to the Hall of Fame in 1964.

1957 — The Cleveland Indians release Bob Feller, who had already announced his retirement. In 20 years with the Indians (1936-1956) Feller won 266 games despite missing almost four full seasons while serving in the Navy. He lost only 162 games giving him a winning percentage of .621. Feller posted six 20-win seasons with a high of 27 in 1940. He pitched in excess of 300 innings in 1940 (320), 1941 (343) and his first year back from service in 1946 he worked 371 innings with ten shut-outs. In 1939 he logged 297, and 299 innings in 1947. There were four other years he went over the 200 mark. Feller (19) led the league in strikeouts seven times, finishing with 2,581 and was voted into the Hall of Fame in 1962 during his first year of eligibility.

January 10

1918 — Connie Mack trades the final member of the Philadelphia Athletics' so-called $100,000 infield by dealing first baseman Stuffy McInnis to the Boston Red Sox for Larry Gardner, Tilly Walker and Hick Cady. Mack had sold second baseman Eddie Collins to the White Sox in 1914 for $50,000, shortstop Jack Berry to the Red Sox in 1915 for $8,000 and third baseman Frank (Home Run) Baker to the Yankees in 1916 for $37,500.

1963 — The Chicago Cubs continue their bizarre front office moves when they hire an "athletic director" – Air Force Colonel Robert V. Whitlow. During Whitlow's first spring training, he announced that the Cubs had "fine spirit". Henceforth, he was known among the media as the vice-president in charge of fine spirit.

January 11

1960 — The Phillies trade outfielder Richie Ashburn to the Cubs for pitcher John Buzhardt, shortstop Alvin Dark and third baseman Jim Woods. Ashburn, coming off a .266 season had spent 12 years in a Philadelphia uniform where he won two National League batting championships (.338-1955 and .350-1958). He would retire after one year with the Mets in 1962, with a 15-year career .308 batting average. Ashburn (1) was elected to the Hall of Fame in 1995.

1973 — The American League votes to adopt the Designated Hitter Rule on an experimental basis. This rule change is believed to be the first difference in playing rules between the two major leagues in 70 years. (In 1902, the American joined the National by penalizing hitters with strikes for foul balls up to two). Ironically, the National League first officially proposed the idea of a "10th regular" in 1929 but the American League, then the dominant circuit, wasn't interested.

January 12

1921 — Judge Kenesaw Mountain Landis signs an agreement to take over as the head man in baseball. Landis' contract calls for $50,000 a year for seven years. He not only was eligible to succeed himself, but had power over everyone in the game, including club owners and the presidents of both leagues. All the above waived recourse to the courts regardless of the severity of any discipline he might enact. It is generally accepted that Landis was appointed to the post because of the 1919 Black Sox scandal. However, as early as 1915 he was appointed the judge in the dispute between baseball and the outlaw Federal League.

The beginning of the end of the Commission happened during the World Series in 1918 when the Cubs and Red Sox threatened not to play when the National Commission attempted to trim the winners' and losers' share of the receipts. This threat probably was the result of the short season caused by a U.S. government edict calling for the end of the season on Labor Day as a result of the United States entry into World War I. The 1918 season was shortened by about 20 games per club and the series was played beginning on September 5. At this point the National League began a movement to break-up the three-man commission and began looking for a one-man commissioner. That person would be Judge Landis who would rule baseball for the next 24 years as no other commissioner has since and would be elected to the Hall of Fame in 1944.

January 12-14

1961 — Owner P.K. Wrigley announces that the Chicago Cubs would be managed by a group of coaches instead of a manager. These coaches were to be specialists in each phase of the game and each would alternate as head coach. The coaches named for the 1961 season were Vedie Himsl, Harry Craft, Lou Klein and Elvin Tappe. This system continued in use in some form or another until the 1966 season when Leo Durocher was named manager. Wrigley's list of coaches over that five-year period also consisted of Rip Collins, Charlie Grimm, Goldie Holt, Bobby Adams, Verlon Walker, Mel Harder, Mel Wright, Fred Martin, Charlie Metro, Alvin Dark, Buck O'Neill and Bob Kennedy. Overall, in the five seasons of this disastrous and lengthy experiment the Cubs' record was 353-449, a win percentage of .440 with finishes of two sevenths, two eighths and one 9th place finish. Ironically, in 1966, the year following the experiment, with Durocher as skipper, the Cubs finished in last place with a record of 59-103.

January 13

1972 — The New York Court of Appeals rules that Bernice Gera had been denied a minor league umpire's job because of her gender. She initiated the suit on March 15, 1971 after being denied a contract in 1969 by the National Association of Professional Baseball Leagues (minors) because she failed to meet the physical requirements of height (5'-10") and weight (170 lbs.). However, her tenure on the job was short lived as she resigned hours after umpiring her first game between Auburn and Geneva of the Class-A New York-Penn League in Auburn, New York on June 24, 1972. Gera said resentment from other umpires influenced her decision. "I quit after the game because I was physically, mentally and financially drained," she said. "I knew what I was going into, but it is hard to get used to having people spit at you and threaten your life. But I was determined to do it." In 1980 Gera made an unsuccessful attempt to establish a baseball school for kids in Pembroke Pines, Florida and later worked in the Mets public relations department.

January 14

1932 — Babe Ruth rejects the Yankees offer of $70,000. In 1930 Ruth signed a two-year contract for $80,000 a year, the highest salary he was to make. The comparison of that contract to what some of the other Yankees were paid in that period pales in comparison to today's payrolls. In 1927 Ruth drew $70,000 but the next-highest paid Yankees players were Herb Pennock ($17,500), Bob Meusel ($13,000), Waite Hoyt ($12,000) and Lou Gehrig ($8,000). Although it was never verified – Ruth supposedly said when asked if he thought it was right for a ball player to make more than the President of the United States (Herbert Hoover was making $75,000 in 1931), Ruth replied, "Why not? I had a better year than he did." The Yankees and Ruth settled their 1932 salary squabble with the Bambino accepting a cut of $5,000 to equal the $75,000 Hoover made in 1931.

1940 — Commissioner Landis declares 87 Detroit minor league players free agents and orders payments of $47,250 to 15 others with whom the Tigers had dealings. Only four players on the Big Club were affected, notably Benny McCoy and Roy Cullenbine. Tigers general manager Jack Zeller had traded McCoy to the Athletics for Wally Moses a month before, and Landis ordered Moses returned to Philadelphia and declared McCoy a free agent. For some time the commissioner had been suspicious of some of Zeller's player deals. His complaint was that Zeller was holding strings to players and beating the rule on the number of times a player could be sent out on option even though they never appeared as Detroit property. Landis charged that Zeller abused the working agreement privilege by making "secret arrangements". Contrary to baseball rules, Detroit controlled more than one club in a minor league – both Beaumont and Fort Worth in the Texas League and Alexandria and Lake Charles in the Evangeline League. One player originally on Landis' free agent list was Dizzy Trout. Landis restored Trout to the Detroit roster following further inspection of his releases and options to Toledo and Beaumont. Over the next twelve years Trout would win 152 games for the Tigers including two 20-win seasons. Also, among the minor leaguers given free agency was a young pitcher named Johnny Sain.

1963 — The White Sox trade Luis Aparicio, one of the greatest shortstops of all time, along with Al Smith to Baltimore for Hoyt Wilhelm, Ron Hansen, Pete Ward and Dave Nicholson. Both Wilhelm and Aparicio would be elected, in back-to-back years, to the Hall of Fame – Aparicio in 1984 and Wilhelm in 1985. Wilhelm (49) pitched in 1,070 games with nine different teams, starting only 52 games in his 21 years. He finished with 227 saves and an ERA of 2.52. Aparicio (11) split his 18 years between the White Sox, Baltimore and the Red Sox batting .262. He stole 506 bases and was awarded nine Gold Gloves.

January 15

1934 — Babe Ruth's salary is cut for the third straight year – his last with the Yankees – to $35,000. He had gone from his high of $80,000 in 1930 and 1931 to $75,000 in 1932 to $52,000 in 1933.

January 15

1936 — Unlike today, Internal Revenue Service figures show the highest paid person in baseball to be a club executive — Branch Rickey of the St. Louis Cardinals is making $49,470. Rickey took over the top spot when commissioner Landis cut his own salary from $65,000 to $40,000 because of the Depression.

1942 — President Roosevelt gives baseball the "Green Light" to continue during war years as a morale booster. Although Judge Landis and Roosevelt were not on the same wavelength politically – the commissioner, among other things, was against the president's third term – but in this case Landis thought it wise to pursue his guidance. The owner of the Washington Nationals (Senators), Clark Griffith, was a close friend of Roosevelt and was probably instrumental in persuading the president to give baseball the go-ahead during the war. Griffith was quoted during this trying period, "Landis wasn't much more welcome at the White House than the Japanese Ambassador." Be that as it may, Landis wrote the president, "What do you want it (baseball) to do?...If you feel we ought to continue, we would be delighted to do so. We await your order." Roosevelt responded on this day in 1942, "I honestly feel that it would be best for the country to keep baseball going. I hope that night games can be extended because it gives an opportunity to the day shift to see a game occasionally." Roosevelt continued in his "Green Light" letter to Landis, "As to the players themselves, I know you agree with me that individual players who are of active military and naval age should go, without question, into the service. Even if the actual quality of the teams is lowered by the greater use of older players, this will not dampen the popularity of the sport." —

Moe Berg, former Red Sox catcher is named Goodwill Ambassador to Latin America. Berg was baseball's most prominent scholar-athlete, a legendary linguist and . . . *spy*. He was a graduate of Princeton and broke into the majors as a shortstop with Brooklyn in 1923 and worked behind the bat for the White Sox, Senators, Indians and Red Sox. For sheer intellectual accomplishment baseball never has seen anyone even vaguely resembling Moe Berg. His thesis on Sanskrit (an ancient language of India) is a valuable reference work. He spoke Latin, French, German, Russian, Hebrew, Greek, Italian, Spanish, Japanese and English. He was a spy for the United States prior to World War II using a trip to Japan with an American All-Star team in 1934 to photograph armament plants, railroad lines, industrial complexes, oil refineries and warships in Tokyo Bay. Berg also parachuted into Yugoslavia and impersonated a Nazi officer. He worked with the Office of Strategic Services and the CIA, in disguise, to beat the Germans to Italy's top aeronautical expert and bring him to the United States. Armed with a pistol and a cyanide capsule (should he be captured), Berg sat in on a lecture full of Nazi agents in Switzerland – mission: to assassinate Germany's top nuclear scientist, Werner Heisenberg if it was determined the Nazis were getting close to developing the atomic bomb. Moe Berg was always a third-string catcher — a better spy than he was a hitter. However he did set an American League record during 1931 to 1936 when he caught 117 consecutive games without a error.

—

The Chicago Cubs abandon plans to install lights at Wrigley Field. They cancel their contract and the steel goes to the war effort.

1959 — Joe Cronin is named American League president, the first player to reach such heights in the game's management. Originally signed by Pittsburgh as a second baseman in 1926, Cronin went on to play 18 of his 20 years in the majors as a shortstop with the Red Sox and Washington, batting .301. He managed the Red Sox for 13 years and the Senators for two seasons, finishing with a win percentage of .540 and winning a World Championship with each team. In those two World Series his teams won 12 of 16 games. Prior to becoming American League president he served as general manager of the Red Sox. Cronin held the office of League President for 15 years and was voted into the Hall of Fame in 1956.

January 16

1905 — The St. Louis Browns trade outfielder Jesse Burkett to the Boston Red Sox for outfielder George Stone. Burkett played 16 years in the majors with the Giants, Cleveland, Red Sox, Browns and Cardinals. He hit .400 three times in the majors and had 200 or more hits in six of seven consecutive seasons (1895-1901) with 199 hits in the other. The Veterans Committee voted Burkett into the Hall of Fame in 1946. Incidentally, we have been led to believe that Reggie Jackson, another Hall-of-Famer, had initiated the practice of standing at home plate to admire balls hit into the seats and beyond, however, this appeared in the St. Louis *Globe-Democrat* concerning a game of September 5, 1901: "Burkett hit a high one, stood still and watched it clear the left field fence and then trotted around the bases behind Magee."

1970 — Curt Flood files a civil suit against the Reserve Clause. Flood's troubles with baseball had started on October 7, 1969 when the Cardinals traded him along with Tim McCarver, Byron Browne and Joe Hoerner to the Phillies for Dick Allen, Cookie Rojas and Jerry Johnson. Flood refused to report, was suspended, and sued to become a free agent. Flood, in the interim, sat out the 1970 season, and the Phillies traded him to Washington on November 3, 1970. He appeared in only 13 games with the Senators in 1971 and his 15-year major league career was over. His case eventually found its way to the Supreme Court which handed down a decision in June 1972, sustaining baseball's anti-trust exemption by upholding the reserve clause.

January 17

1934 — Following his National League Most Valuable Player season Carl Hubbell is given a new contract calling for $35,000. Hubbell won 23 and lost 12 with an ERA of 1.66 with the New York Giants in 1933. He would win 21 games in 1934 and continue his run of five consecutive 20-win seasons through 1937. Hubbell pitched his entire 16-year career with the Giants (1928-1943) and finished with a winning percentage of .622 (253-154) and an ERA of 2.97. The left-handed Hubbell is known as the father of the screwball but said he never claimed to have invented the pitch. The press and fans began calling the pitch the dipsy doodle. Quoted in 1937, "King Carl" said "It really isn't anything but an out-drop by another name. In Matty's (Christy Mathewson) day, I believe it was called a fadeaway. Old Smiling Mickey Welsh was right when he said there are only three ways to make a ball curve – in, out and down." Hubbell went on to say, "I haven't any trick delivery. I'm no different from any other pitcher. I just try to guess the batter's weaknesses, that's all." However, Hubbell's pitch remained in the eyes of many a screwball, but in the music world Hubbell's pitch was made more famous when The Larry Clinton Orchestra recorded *The Dipsey Doodle* to honor the pitch. Hubbell (11) was elected to the Hall of Fame in 1947.

January 18

1947 — Hank Greenberg, coming off a 44-homerun and 127-RBI season with Detroit, hears on the radio he has been waived by the Tigers out of the American League and is sold to the Pirates. Detroit owner Walter Briggs never offered an explanation for Greenberg's sudden disposal and his sale for $75,000. Greenberg never forgave Briggs for the way the transaction was handled and after failing to report to the Pirates for weeks, he was lured to Pittsburgh by the highest major league contract in history up to that time — $100,000 – with the agreement he would receive his unconditional release at the end of the season. Partially because of Greenberg's acquisition, the Pirates attendance increased by more than 500,000 in 1947. It was the 13th and last year of his playing career. Greenberg (5) finished with 331 homeruns and a batting average of .313. He was elected to the Hall of Fame in 1956.

1973 — The designated hitter rule, recently voted into the American League, makes its first impact on the future for veteran players when 35-year old Orlando Cepeda, nearing the end of his career, becomes the first player signed solely for that position. Cepeda is signed by the Boston Red Sox just one week after the new rule is voted in. Designated Hitting in all of his 142 games, he hit .289 with 20 home runs and 86 RBI. In 17 major league seasons from 1950 through 1974 he hit 379 home runs while driving in 1,365 runs and a batting average of .297. Cepeda (30) led the National League in homeruns with 46 in 1961, was the NL Most Valuable Player in 1967. He was voted into the Hall of Fame in 1999.

January 19

1931 — 23 year-old Ernie Lombardi is purchased from Oakland of the Pacific Coast League by Brooklyn. He will hit .297 with the Dodgers in only 73 games in 1931, and will be traded to Cincinnati with Babe Herman and Wally Gilbert for Tony Cuccinello, Joe Stripp and Clyde Sukeforth before the 1932 season. Lombardi went on to play 17 years with Brooklyn, the Reds, Boston Braves and New York Giants with a batting average of .306, winning two National League batting titles. "Schnoz" hit .342 in 1938 at the same time winning the Most Valuable Player Award. His other batting title came in 1942 with an average of .330. Lombardi (4) was elected to the Hall of Fame in 1986.

1934 — "Shoeless" Joe Jackson's appeal for reinstatement is denied by Judge Landis. Jackson was banned from baseball following the 1920 season along with seven other White Sox players for being part of an alleged conspiracy to throw the 1919 World Series against the Cincinnati Reds. At the end of their trial, which spanned June, July, and August of 1921, the players were acquitted. The morning after the verdict was in, on August 2, the front pages carried the following statement from Landis: "Regardless of the verdict of juries, no player who throws a ball game, no player that undertakes or promises to throw a ball game, no player that sits in conference with a bunch of crooked players and gamblers where the ways and means of throwing a ball game are discussed and does not promptly tell his club about it, will ever play professional baseball."

Jackson, after years of playing semi-pro ball, had hoped Landis would relent and let him play a year or so. There were frequent petitions to Landis, generally collected from friends and admirers and, even to this day, there is an occasional call for his reinstatement — but the judge would not forgive and forget and both men went to their graves with the decision etched in stone. Landis died while still in office on November 25, 1944 and Jackson died December 5, 1951, while running his store in Greenville, South Carolina. There is nothing on Jackson's tombstone other than names, birth, and death dates of he and his wife Katie. However, Jackson, a simple, unlettered man was quoted once as saying, "God knows I gave my best in baseball at all times and no man on earth can truthfully judge me otherwise."

January 20

1931 — Joe Sewell, released by Cleveland after the 1930 season, signs with the New York Yankees. Sewell's major league career began dramatically when Ray Chapman, Cleveland's shortstop, was killed by a ball pitched by Carl Mays of the Yankees in 1920. Sewell, then 21, was called up from New Orleans to replace Chapman at shortstop and he hit .329 for the remainder of the season as Cleveland went on to win the pennant and the World Championship. Sewell holds the record for the fewest strikeouts per-at-bat in major league history. He struck-out only 114 times in 7,132 at-bats during his 14-year career — or one strikeout for every 62.6 at-bats. From May 17 through September 19, 1929 he played 115 consecutive games (437 at-bats) without striking out. That year, he struck out only four times in 578 at-bats. Sewell would play three years with New York and retire following the 1933 season. He didn't lose his batting eye in those final years with the Yankees, striking out only 15 times in 1,511 at-bats - once every 100.7 at-bats. Sewell (21) hit .312 during his stay in the majors and was voted into the Hall of Fame in 1977.

1984 — The New York Mets lose Tom Seaver to the White Sox when he's left off the protected list and Chicago drafts him as compensation for the loss of Dennis Lamp to Toronto. This is the third year of the pool-arrangement created in the summer of 1981 with the settlement of the 50-day strike by players over the issue of compensation for premium free agents. Not much was said in the first such draft in 1982 when the White Sox selected Joel Skinner from the Pirates as compensation for the loss of Ed Farmer to Philadelphia. Hardly anyone noticed when the White Sox chose Steve Mura from St. Louis as compensation for the loss of Steve Kemp to the Yankees or Seattle's selection of Danny Tartabull from the Cincinnati organization for the loss of Floyd Bannister to the White Sox. But, when Seaver was left off the protected list and was plucked by the White Sox it set off an uproar. The Mets evidently assumed no one would dare touch the franchise's jewel, but Chicago shocked the New York front office by doing so, and left the Mets humiliated.

January 21

1936 — The Hollywood Stars of the Pacific Coast League become the San Diego Padres. In 1926 the Salt Lake City franchise moved to Los Angeles and became the Hollywood Stars, playing their home games in Wrigley Field owned by the Los Angeles Angels. The Stars were great favorites in Los Angeles but the Angels had consistently better attendance. The Stars fell to last place in 1935 and when unable to pay the $8,000 annual rent on Wrigley Field moved the franchise to San Diego. The Hollywood Stars would resurface in 1938 when the Mission club of San Francisco was moved to Los Angeles and became the reborn Hollywood Stars. With major league expansion in 1969 San Diego would continue the city's tradition of using Padres as the nickname for their new National League team.

January 22

1913 — The New York Giants consent to have the Yankees as tenants in the Polo Grounds. The Yankees-Highlanders had played their home games at Hilltop Park at 168th and Broadway since 1903 when the franchise was moved to New York from Baltimore. However, the lease expired at the end of the 1912 season. In April 1911, when fire ravaged the Polo Grounds, the Giants accepted an offer from the Yankees to use Hilltop Park until their stadium was rebuilt in June. It is interesting that on May 14, 1920 the Giants informed the Yankees that after the season their lease would not be renewed. No reason was given but the recent signing of Babe Ruth appears to be the main cause for their announcement. This may have caused a knee-jerk reaction by the Giants since they changed their mind and the Yankees remained at home in the Polo Grounds until Yankee Stadium opened in 1923.

1918 — In a blockbuster deal, 300-game winner Eddie Plank is traded by the St. Louis Browns with Del Pratt and $15,000 to the Yankees for Les Nunamaker, Fritz Maisel, Nick Cullop, Urban Shocker and Joe Gedeon. Instead of pitching for New York, Plank elects to retire, ending a 17-year career that included 327 wins and only 193 losses (a win percentage of .629). Regardless, the deal stood; the other players reported and played with their new teams. Plank had spent his first 14 seasons with the Philadelphia Athletics and was one of the few big-name players to jump to the outlaw Federal League in 1915. When that league folded he was sold back to the American League Browns. Plank was elected to the Hall of Fame in 1946.

January 22-23

1969 — The Houston Astros trade Rusty Staub to the Montreal Expos for Donn Clendenon and Jesus Alou. Flown to Houston for a press conference, Clendenon seemed pleased with the deal and he agreed to a one-year contract for $36,000. However, in February, he would announce his retirement to join Scripto, Inc. as a vice-president. The Astros asked the deal be nullified, but Bowie Kuhn, who was at this point an interim commissioner, ultimately ruled the deal would stand and the Astros are forced to accept pitchers Jack Billingham and Skip Guinn to complete the deal. On March 24th the Astros file a petition in U.S. District Court against Montreal, and on April 3rd Clendenon changes his mind and decides to sign with the Expos after agreeing to a two-year contract for $100,000. In the final settlement of this case, the Astros became the victim of pressure from the National League; not to push legal action with a new commissioner arriving on the scene and the fact that Montreal was an expansion team. Houston was forced to accept baseball's decision – Staub for Billingham and Guinn plus a cash settlement believed to be $100,000. Meanwhile, Clendenon opened the season in Montreal, was traded to the Mets in June and ended up with a winners' share in the World Series with New York.

January 23

1932 — One month after being traded by the Cubs to the Cardinals with Bud Teachout for Burleigh Grimes, Hack Wilson is moved again without putting on a St. Louis uniform. The Redbirds trade Wilson to Brooklyn for minor league pitcher Bob Parham and $45,000. Wilson broke into the majors with the New York Giants in 1923 but they lost him following the 1925 season due to an oversight in the Giants front office. Wilson had been optioned to Toledo during the 1925 season, and when New York failed to exercise their option they discovered the Mudhens had already sold Wilson to the Cubs. Wilson spent 12 years in the majors but had his most prolific seasons with the Cubs. He hit for a lifetime .307 average with 244 homeruns, 169 of those in six years (1926-1931) with Chicago. Wilson led the National League in homeruns four times, winning the title outright in 1926 (21), 1930 (56) and tying for the title in 1927 and 1928. In his first five years with the Cubs he had 109, 129, 120, 159 and 191 runs batted in. Wilson (4) was voted into the Hall of Fame in 1979.

1950 — The Associated Press selects the 1914 Boston Braves season as the biggest sports upset of the 20th Century. On July 19, 1914 the "Miracle Braves" were in last place in the National League and eleven games behind the leading New York Giants. Along with a fantastic job of motivation by their manager,

George Stallings, the Braves won nine of twelve on their next western swing. By Labor Day they had pulled into a dead-heat for first place with the Giants, then went on to win the pennant by 10 and one-half games. The team that featured only one .300 hitter, only three dependable pitchers and only two top name players – Johnny Evers and Rabbit Maranville – finished the season by winning the World Series from the Philadelphia Athletics. It was the first time in history a team had swept four games in the fall classic.

1967 — Four years after his retirement as a player, Stan Musial is named general manager of the St. Louis Cardinals. He replaces Bob Howsam who had resigned to accept a similar position with the Cincinnati Reds. Musial's reign would last only ten months despite the fact that he became the first GM in Major League history to win a pennant and World Series victory in his first year. Musial's resignation would come on December 5, 1967 saying he resigned because ". . . of the pressure of his other business interests." He was replaced by Bing Devine who returned to St. Louis from the Mets, a position he had accepted after being ousted by the Cardinals in 1964. Musial would stay on with St. Louis as a senior vice president and consultant.

January 25

1928 — After just one season with the Washington Senators, and 39 years old, Tris Speaker is given his release. Speaker had spent 21 seasons with the Red Sox and Cleveland before joining the Senators. Following his release he teamed up with Ty Cobb with the Athletics and both called it a career following the 1928 season. "The Gray Eagle" or "Spoke" hit a lifetime .344 (leading the American League with .386 in 1916) during which he accumulated 3,515 hits and drove in 1,559 runs. Speaker was elected to the Hall of Fame in 1937, the second year of the hall's existence.

1934 — Giants manager Bill Terry makes one of the most memorable quotes in baseball history. Coming off a World Series championship in 1933 Terry attended the annual major league winter meetings in New York. While surrounded by writers was asked by *New York Times* reporter Roscoe McGowen, who normally covered the Dodgers, "How about Brooklyn, Bill?" Terry turned to him and smiled, "Brooklyn? I haven't heard anything about them. Are they still in the league?"

1943 — Lefty Gomez spent 13 years with the Yankees, but following a 6-4 won-lost season and an ERA of 4.28 in 1942 is sold to the Boston Braves.

Gomez was released before getting into one game with Boston and subsequently signed in May with Washington. He would appear in only one game with the Senators, losing that one, and ending his 14-year major league career. Gomez (11) won 65% of his decisions (189-102) beginning in 1930, and in 1931 was the American League's Most Valuable Player. He was voted into the Hall of Fame in 1972.

1945 — Larry MacPhail purchases the New York Yankees for $2.8 million from three women who had been willed the ball club by the late Jake Ruppert, a bachelor. MacPhail's early attempt to buy the team had been held up by commissioner Landis because of MacPhail's involvement with an owner of racehorses. Also, some form of litigation over the estate would present problems. Almost a year later the bankers contacted MacPhail and he signed the deal. Now MacPhail had the Yankees but no financing. Enter Dan Topping who agreed to come in as a partner, but the two were still short of money. Topping suggested Bing Crosby but Landis said he would approve the deal only if Crosby sold the Del Mar racetrack. When Crosby suggested Del Webb, a Phoenix contractor, the deal was set. The partnership was not harmonious and in October of 1947 MacPhail sold out with a tidy profit for his minimal investment. Topping and Webb bought him out for $1,750,000. For his many accomplishments in the game, MacPhail was voted into the Hall of Fame in 1978.

1947 — Judge W.G. Bramham, the National Association president (minors) issues a withering indictment of the Evangeline League, a Class D circuit based in Louisiana and Mississippi. Bramham concluded that gamblers conspired with players to fix the playoff games after the 1946 season. I.N. Goldberg, president of the Abbeville club, first revealed the scandal on October 23, 1946. In addition it was said that gambling on games during the regular season had been investigated. Five players were banned, but three were reinstated; Lenny Pecou, Houma, Louisiana outfielder, Don Vettorel, Abbeville, Louisiana player (never played again) and Bill Thomas, Houma pitcher. Thomas is a special case worthy of recognition here if only for his tenure in the game. He pitched 24 years in the minors beginning in 1926, played for 24 different cities, and saw action in 13 leagues. Thomas never played in the majors but reached the Pacific Coast League in 1937 and pitched seven seasons in that circuit. Thomas was 21 when he started pitching professionally and 42 years of age in 1949 when he resumed his career (following his banishment in 1947). He pitched four more years and retired at age 47 in 1952. The year prior to his suspension, when he was 41, he won 35 games and lost only seven for Houma. Thomas set career minor league records in games pitched (1,015), innings (5,987), wins (383) and losses (346).

January 26

1879 — Indianapolis and Milwaukee withdraw from the National League, and Cleveland, Buffalo and Syracuse are admitted; the circuit is once again an eight-club organization with the addition of Troy, New York. The Troy Trojans were ready to play having already committed to salaries of $10,240 for 11 players and a manager. The league also made numerous changes in the schedule, umpire set-up and rule adjustments, but the most significant innovation of the year was the reserve clause, guaranteeing a club a player's services for as long as the club wished. This clause was introduced to stop player-stealing by more opulent clubs and player-jumping by more avaricious athletes. At first, clubs reserved only five men, the number later was increased to 11, then to 14 and eventually covered the entire team. Looking back on the reserve clause, it was often referred to as a chain, holding the baseball peon in bondage, but early players felt it was a decided honor to be placed on the reserve list. John B. Foster, an early Cleveland and New York baseball writer summed up the players' feeling on the rule: "The athlete eagerly scanned the winter reserve list to see whether his name was included. Only the stars and better players were reserved. If a player wasn't on the list, he was a baseball nobody."

1930 — Carl Mays ends his 15-year major league pitching career and signs with Portland of the Pacific Coast League. This is nine years after the right-handed submarine pitcher struck and killed Cleveland shortstop Ray Chapman in 1920 with a pitch to the head. Mays was pitching for the Yankees at the time and pitched with New York through the 1923 season before moving to Cincinnati and spending his final year with the Giants. Mays won 208 games and five times won 20 games or more. Unfortunately, he is not remembered for these achievements. Quoted just before his death in 1971 Mays said, "Of Course I regret Ray Chapman's death. He was a good friend of mine, but regret is not the word, I felt awful. But I've never regretted anything I did. I was pitching honestly."

January 27

1927 — Commissioner Landis exonerates Detroit's Ty Cobb and Cleveland's Tris Speaker of charges that they conspired to fix a game on September 25, 1919. The accusation, made by former Tiger pitcher "Dutch" Leonard, claimed that Indians pitcher Smokey Joe Wood was also involved in the scheme. Cobb and

Speaker were the player-managers in Detroit and Cleveland when the teams met in a season-ending series in 1919. The Tigers needed a victory to clinch third-place money, so Cobb, Speaker, Leonard and Wood agreed that the Indians, with nothing to lose, would roll over for Detroit. On the side, the players would also put up $1,200 each and Cobb placed the bet with a ballpark policeman. It could have been that Leonard, known to have put up his money, was short-changed in the transaction and blew the whistle on Cobb and Speaker. Leonard produced letters concerning the deal, one of which supposedly was from Cobb that explained how the money was split.

Landis was not commissioner in 1919 (he took over in 1921) but it was not until December 21, 1926 that Landis released the collection of documents of Leonard's charges. With Landis in charge, it probably was not co-incidental that Cobb resigned as manager of the Tigers in early November of 1926 and some three weeks later Speaker announced his resignation as manager of the Indians. Cobb fought the charges vigorously, threatening to reveal information about team accounting and turnstiles counting-practice as well as exposing other fixes and scandals that would implicate certain owners. These threats obviously had a great bearing on the outcome of the case and the complete exoneration of Cobb and Speaker. Before releasing his final statement, Landis cited accuser Leonard's refusal to appear at the January 5th hearings as a factor in his decision. In the Commissioner's final ruling, Landis released this statement: "These players have not been, nor are they now, found guilty of fixing a ball game. By no decent system of justice could such a finding be made."

By the time this decision came down, Wood and Leonard had both retired. Wood pitched in only one game in 1920 for Cleveland and Leonard continued with Detroit through the 1925 season. Cobb joined the Philadelphia Athletics in 1927, and Speaker joined Cobb with the A's in 1928. That was the last season for both players. ("Dutch" Leonard in this case was Hubert Leonard who pitched for the Red Sox and Tigers [1913-1925] and not Emil "Dutch" Leonard whose pitching career spanned 20 years with Brooklyn, Washington, the Phillies and Cubs [1933-1953]).

1982 — The Philadelphia Phillies trade Larry Bowa and an unknown infielder to the Chicago Cubs for Ivan DeJesus. That infielder was Ryne Sandberg.

January 28

1901 — The American League is formally organized with a player limit of 14 and a 140 game schedule. The teams represented are the Philadelphia Athletics,

Boston Somersets, Washington Nationals, Detroit Tigers, Chicago White Stockings, Milwaukee Brewers, Cleveland Blues, and Baltimore Orioles. Washington, Baltimore, Boston and Philadelphia were the new clubs replacing Indianapolis, Kansas City, Buffalo and Minneapolis.

1953 — Fred Saigh, owner of the St. Louis Cardinals is found guilty of income tax evasion and is sentenced to 15 months in Federal prison. The Cardinals had been sold twice in the preceding five years and as the result of Saigh's conviction underwent a third change of ownership. Anheuser-Busch, Inc. purchased the club for $3.750 million on the eve of opening day in 1953.

1958 — Roy Campanella is seriously injured in a one-car accident at Glen Cove, Long Island about one mile from his home. Driving on ice, his car skidded on a curve, crashed into a telephone pole and turned over. When help arrived it was found he was paralyzed from the chest down. His baseball playing days were over, ironically, at the same time the Dodgers era ended in Brooklyn. His career in the big leagues was short-circuited by the color-line at the beginning when he was 26-years old, and at the end when he was 36. Campanella (39) played 10 seasons with the Dodgers, hit .276 with 242 homeruns, was National League MVP in 1951, 1953, and 1955 and was elected to the Hall of Fame in 1969.

1974 — Outfielder Sam Thompson who played 15 seasons with the Tigers and Phillies 1885-1906 is voted a seat in the Hall of Fame. At 6-2 and 210 pounds he was the foremost slugger of his era hitting 128 homeruns while batting .331 with 221 stolen bases.

January 29

1936 — Ty Cobb, Babe Ruth, Honus Wagner, Christy Mathewson and Walter Johnson become the first five players elected to the Hall of Fame. There were 226 ballots cast in this initial election and Cobb received the highest percentage of votes — 98.23. He was left off four ballots while Ruth and Wagner received 215 votes, Mathewson 205 and Johnson 189 of the 226. Some of those receiving votes but less than the required 75% were Mickey Cochrane, Jimmie Foxx, Lou Gehrig and Rogers Hornsby. Also receiving votes in this initial election were Shoeless Joe Jackson and Hal Chase, both touched with gambling charges. Jackson, incidentally, is the only player with a .400 season average (Indians-1911 .408) not in the Hall of Fame.

January 29-30

1961 — Sliding Billy Hamilton, a 14-year veteran of the National League with the Phillies and Braves from 1891 through 1901, is voted into the Hall of Fame. In his career he stole 937 bases, hit .344 and scored 1,690 runs. Only three players in the history of the game scored more runs than games played and Hamilton is number one on the list – 1,591 games and 1,690 runs scored.

January 30

1923 — Herb Pennock is traded by the Boston Red Sox to the Yankees in a one-for-three-deal plus cash. Pennock was sent to New York and Boston received outfielder Camp Skinner, infielder Norm McMillan, pitcher George Murray and $50,000. Pennock had spent three-plus years with the Athletics when he began his major league career in 1916 and in 11 seasons with Boston and Philadelphia his record was 76-72. In 11 years with the Yankees he would win 162 and lose only 90 for a 22-year career mark of 240-162. He went back to the Red Sox to finish his career in 1934 pitching in only 30 games, most of them in relief. Pennock (16) was elected to the Hall of Fame in 1948.

1926 — The major league rules committee agrees that pitchers may have access to a resin bag. On February 8 the American League will refuse to permit its use but changes its policy in April.

1936 — The Boston Braves are renamed the Bees as a result of a fan poll handled by Boston newspapermen. Boston management changes the name in an effort to project a new image. In early years the Boston National League franchise was known as the Beantowners, Tenneys, Doves, Rustlers and Pilgrims. The club became known as the Braves in 1912 and returned to Braves in 1941 when the five-year Bees nickname "experiment" was never fully accepted by the fans.

1978 — Commissioner Bowie Kuhn voids Cincinnati's purchase of Vida Blue from Oakland. For the second time in two years Kuhn hits his principal antagonist, Charlie Finley, by killing the deal made in December 1977. In June of 1976 Kuhn had negated the sale of Blue, Rollie Fingers and Joe Rudi with Blue going to the Yankees for $1.5 million and Rudi and Fingers to Boston for $1.0 million each. Finley had filed suit against Kuhn over the 1976 deal and that case was still pending when the Commissioner voided Finley's deal with Cincinnati. On April 7, 1978 the U.S. Court of Appeals upheld the lower court decision and ruled that Kuhn had acted in good faith.

January 31

1950 — Pittsburgh signs the first $100,000 "bonus baby" — Paul Pettit — a 6-2, 195 pound left handed pitcher, from Lomita, California. Pettit, 19 years old, was already under contract with a Hollywood producer for his life story before he even threw a pitch in professional baseball. An elbow injury would cut short his career, pitching in only 13 games for the Pirates with a 1-2 mark and an ERA of 7.34 in parts of 1951 and 1953. Pettit went to the low minors and attempted to work his way back to the majors as a first baseman-outfielder, struggling as high as the Pacific Coast League before calling it quits in the early 1960s. He enrolled in college at California (Long Beach), earned a Master's Degree and became a high school teacher and coach.

1971 — Joe Kelley, who played for five different teams during his 17-year career from 1891 through 1908, is elected to the Hall of Fame. Playing all positions except pitcher and catcher, Kelley totaled 2,245 hits while batting .316 with 194 triples and 443 stolen bases. Aside from his outstanding talent as a player he was noted for pulling a mirror from his uniform pocket and preening himself in full view of the fans.

"My arm is sore"
Antony and Cleopatra, William Shakespeare

Carl Hubbell

Ernie Lombardi

Chapter Two

"More than anything, it's a game of innocence. Politicians come and go, but they always get booed at the ballpark. And now, each day, the words come over the radio, and the pictures fill the sports pages. The pitchers and catchers are in camp; the hitters are on their way; the kids are doing their best. The world is with us, the issues crowd in, disasters loom like thunderclouds. But still, its spring. I'm sure of that. And in a few more weeks, when the chill is gone, there'll be flags flapping in the wind around the ballparks, and someone will walk out of a dugout, spit tobacco on the ground, and hand the umpire the lineup. I'll see you there."

--Peter Hamill

February 1

1904 — Cincinnati sells Jake Beckley to the St. Louis Cardinals. One of the finest early-day players, Beckley came up to the big leagues in 1888 with Pittsburgh. The left-handed hitting and throwing first baseman spent 20 years in the majors and hit more than .300 in 13 of those seasons, batting .308 lifetime with 1,575 runs batted in. Beckley was just as well known for his scatter-arm as his batting. Anytime he needed to throw the ball, runners automatically headed for the extra base. On defense he developed a different type of hidden ball trick, placing the ball under the corner of the bag, extracting it and tagging out the runner. Beckley finished his career following the 1907 season and was elected to the Hall of Fame in 1971.

1913 — All-America football great Jim Thorpe signs with the New York Giants. The 1912 Olympic star will spend five seasons in the majors, most of them with the Giants but also will see action with Cincinnati and the Boston Braves. Thorpe had trouble hitting curve balls and ended his big league career with a batting average of .252, seven homers and 82 RBI.

1957 — Owners reject the players' request to raise the minimum pay from $6,000 to $7,500, but do approve a 5-year pension plan offering more liberal benefits for players, coaches and trainers.

1959 — Outfielder Zack Wheat is unanimously voted into the Hall of Fame by the 11-member veterans committee. A 19-year veteran, who spent 18 of those seasons with Brooklyn, broke in with the Dodgers in 1909 when he was 23 years old and finished with the Athletics in 1927. The 5-10, 170 pound Wheat rolled up 2,884 hits in batting .317 with 1,265 RBI.

February 2

1876 — The National League is organized in the Broadway Center Hotel in New York City. Franchises are awarded to the Boston Red Caps, Chicago White Stockings, Cincinnati Red Stockings, Hartford Dark Blue, Louisville Grays, New York Mutuals, Philadelphia Athletics and St. Louis Brown Stockings. The first president is Morgan Bulkeley, whose name is drawn out of a hat. He announced he would serve only one year and in 1877 turned over the chair to William A. Hulbert who, from the beginning, was the brains behind the league. Bulkeley would go on to be a banker, president of Aetna, mayor of Hartford, Connecticut, governor of that state and a U.S. Senator. Upon his death Bulkeley was voted into the Hall of Fame at the urging of Brooklyn's Charles Ebbets. Hulbert served as National League president (1877-1882) and would be elected to the Hall of Fame in 1995 joining Ford Frick and Warren Giles as former presidents now in the Hall. An interesting note – at the organizational meeting after Bulkeley's name was drawn, the name of Nicholas Young was also drawn and he was named secretary-treasurer. In 1903 Young became the fourth NL president.

1888 — Indianapolis, now a member of the National League, announces the roof of their new grandstand will hold 42 private boxes to be sold to season ticket subscribers only – baseball's first Sky Boxes. On January 22, 1889, one year later and facing over $30,000 in debts the team goes bankrupt and surrenders the franchise to the National League. Indianapolis would operate under new ownership in 1889, but it would be the city's last season in the league.

1895 — The first proposal to put numbers on uniforms is discussed but not instituted.

February 3

1910 — Miller Huggins is traded by Cincinnati to the St. Louis Cardinals. The little 5-7, 140 pound lead-off hitter and second baseman is traded with Rebel Oakes and Frank Corridon for Fred Beebe and Alan Storke. Huggins broke in with the Reds in 1904 and played 13 years with Cincinnati and the Cardinals, batting only .265 while leading the National League in walks for four years. He found his niche, however, as a manager. In 1913 he took over as player-manager of St. Louis and managed the Cardinals for five years before joining the New York Yankees as skipper in 1918. For 12 great and tumultuous years Huggins managed New York to six pennants and two World Championships, finishing in the second division only once. He was elected to the Hall of Fame in 1964.

1934 — Sam Breadon, president of the Cardinals and Louis B. von Weise, president of the Browns, announce an agreement between the two clubs that there would be no microphones in the press box during the coming season. The value of baseball broadcasts had long been in doubt. Some officials had been emphatic in their denunciation of air reporting. Others had been lukewarm, while a few had been strong in their support of the practice, claiming it made new fans who eventually pay their way into games. Breadon, in discussing the action, said he believed the move "was taken for the best interests of the clubs . . . there, no doubt, was a time when the microphones did us some good. But now we are at a point where we are willing to experiment a season without the 'mics'." Von Weise said, "I think the radio has its good features – then again, we have our paying clientele to look after. It might even have been that we were giving away the thing we were trying to sell."

St. Louis station KWK first started broadcasting games in 1926 and it was reported that one station paid as much as $10,000 for the privilege in 1931. While the two St. Louis teams were turning thumbs down on broadcasting, elaborate plans were going forward for air-reporting of the Chicago Cubs and White Sox games. Three, and possibly four, stations would be airing the games in Chicago, and three stations were scheduled to broadcast games of the Cincinnati Reds. By 1937 the Cardinals and Browns had returned to the air and all but the three New York teams had daily schedules, with some even feeding regional networks. The Giants, Dodgers and Yankees, afraid of keeping people from the parks, had entered a five-year anti-radio pact between 1934 and 1938. This changed when Larry MacPhail took over the Brooklyn franchise and put the Dodgers on the air in 1939 forcing the Yankees and Giants to follow suit.

—

Redland Field, home of the Reds in Cincinnati, gets a new name. Powell Crosley heads a syndicate to purchase more than half the stock in the ball club and renames the park Crosley Field.

1979 — After playing 12 years with the Minnesota Twins and winning seven batting titles, one MVP Award (1977) and the Rookie of the Year Award, Rod Carew is traded to the California Angels for outfielders Ken Landreaux, Dave Engle and pitchers Paul Hartzell and Brad Havens. The second baseman-turned first baseman half way through his career, would spend seven seasons with California to round out his 19 years in the majors with 3,053 hits and a batting average of .328. Carew's (29) career spanned 1967-1985 and he was elected to the Hall of Fame in his first year of eligibility in 1991.

February 4

1893 — The first recorded version of *Casey At The Bat* (recited by Russell Hunting) hits the charts. DeWolf Hopper's version would not be released until October 1906.

1956 — The Cy Young Award for pitchers is established. This is the brainchild of commissioner Ford Frick. He had become disturbed that voters generally tended to pay more attention to position players in the lineup every day, as opposed to pitchers who appeared only every fourth or fifth day. Frick concluded there should be a separate award for pitchers and inaugurated the Cy Young Award. He turned the project over to the Baseball Writers Association of America. Frick's choice to name the award after Cy Young was based on two important statistics — Young is baseball's biggest winner with 511 victories and the only pitcher to win 200 or more games in each league.

1969 — After easing General William Eckert out as baseball's Commissioner, major league owners select Bowie Kuhn, a lawyer for the National League, as Eckert's successor on an interim basis. Kuhn signs a one-year contract worth $100,000 annually, then will be given a seven-year contract extension in August. Eckert accepts a cash settlement from baseball after serving only three years of his contract.

1976 — U.S. District Judge John W. Oliver upholds an arbitrator ruling that declares Andy Messersmith and Dave McNally free agents. In 1975, both players, unable to agree to terms (Messersmith with Los Angeles and McNally with Montreal), played out the season without signing contracts. That didn't bother management which simply renewed their contracts. Baseball's 100-year-old reserve clause bound players to their teams for life. In December of 1975 the case had gone before arbitrator Peter Seitz who declared Messersmith and McNally free agents. They were free to sell their services to whomever they wished. In effect, Seitz said, no team owns rights to a player after his contract expires. Commissioner Bowie Kuhn fired Seitz and denounced the ruling as "destructive to baseball." Messersmith signed a five-year contract with Atlanta for $1.5 million or $300,000 a year (the average yearly major league salary in 1975 was $44,676) but, McNally, then 33, had decided to retire before the case was heard. He did not play after the 1975 season.

February 5

1886 — The patent dispute involving the invention of the catchers mask goes to court in Chicago. Jimmy Tyng, a catcher for Harvard in 1875, gave credit to the captain and pitcher of the team, Fred Thayer, for originating the mask. Thayer was impressed with Tyng's talent and wanted his services on the Harvard team. However, Tyng's parents objected, fearing he would be injured. Thayer, hoping to further his chances of retaining Tyng, fashioned a wire net contrivance to protect the catcher's face from foul balls. Thayer later filed for a patent which led to a dispute between his company and A.G. Spalding and Brothers. The case was settled by compromise; the Spalding Company would merchandise the masks and Thayer would receive royalties.

1935 — After spending 15 years in pinstripes and leading the Yankees to seven pennants and four World Series championships, New York releases Babe Ruth at age 39. During his years with the Yankees Ruth hit 659 homeruns (49 with the Red Sox and six with the Braves) and batted .349.

1956 — Owners reject players' request to up minimum salary from $6,000 to $7,000.

February 6

1958 — The Boston Red Sox agree to pay Ted Williams $135,000 making him the highest paid player in major league history up to that time.

February 7

1908 — The Philadelphia Athletics sell Rube Waddell to the St. Louis Browns for $5,000. This would be Waddell's final stop in his 13-year major league career; he retired following the 1910 season. Waddell broke into the majors in 1897 with Louisville (a National League franchise at the time that would be transferred to Pittsburgh in 1900). The complicated deal of dropping Louisville from the National League involved a total of 17 players, four of whom would end up in the Hall of

Fame (Waddell, Honus Wagner, Fred Clarke and Jack Chesbro). Waddell, after leaving the Pirates, also pitched for the Cubs as well as the A's and Browns. He compiled a record of 191-145 with an ERA of 2.16 and entered the Hall in 1946.

1958 — The Brooklyn Dodgers officially cease to exist. The Los Angeles Dodgers, Inc. are born.

February 8

1932 — Waite Hoyt is given his release by the Philadelphia Athletics. The right-hander had his glory days with the New York Yankees after breaking in and pitching only one inning with the Giants in 1918. He spent the next two seasons with the Red Sox. Hoyt joined the Yankees in 1921 and for the next nine seasons won 157 games while losing 98. After being traded to Detroit in 1930 he was more or less a journeyman pitcher. For the following nine years he pitched for six different teams and won only 80 games and the only outstanding season he had was a 15-6 record with Pittsburgh in 1934. Hoyt finished his 21-year career with Brooklyn in 1938 with a record of 237-182 and was voted into the Hall of Fame in 1969.

1941 — The Detroit Tigers release Earl Averill after acquiring him from Cleveland in 1939. This marked the virtual end of Averill's 13 years in the majors. After his release from Detroit he signed on with the Boston Braves but played in only eight games and then hung 'em up. Averill had a superb ten-plus years with the Indians following his purchase from the San Francisco Seals in 1929 for $50,000. He got his career started with a bang when he became the first American League player in history to hit a homerun in his first at-bat. Averill (3) hit 237 more homers, batted .318 and was voted into the Hall of Fame in 1975.

1982 — The Los Angeles Dodgers break up their starting infield, the longest-lasting infield unit in major league history (eight years), with the trade of second baseman Davey Lopes to Oakland for minor league second baseman Lance Hudson. Lopes had joined first baseman Steve Garvey, third baseman Ron Cey and shortstop Bill Russell in the Dodgers starting infield in 1974.

February 9

1920 — The "spitball" is banned by the Joint Rules Committee. This includes all foreign substances (saliva, emery ball, shine ball, resin, talcum powder and paraffin) or other alterations to the ball by pitchers. When the spitball was outlawed, there were 17 pitchers in the majors who were permitted to continue using the "wet one" until the end of their careers. No other pitcher was allowed to introduce the spitter if it wasn't already part of his mound repertoire. Of the 17 pitchers allowed to continue the pitch, three of them were eventually voted into the Hall of Fame: Burleigh Grimes, Stan Coveleski and Red Faber. Grimes, who finished his career in 1934 with the Yankees, would be the last to throw the spitter legally.

1927 — The Cincinnati Reds trade Edd Roush to the New York Giants for George "High Pockets" Kelly and cash. Both are future Hall-of-Famers. Roush had played briefly with the Giants in 1916 and he and manager John McGraw, to say the least, did not hit it off. Their breach was so wide that McGraw unloaded Roush to Cincinnati in July of 1916. McGraw later admitted he made a mistake and for the next nine years tried to get him back. When he did, Roush openly stated his dislike for McGraw and became a holdout asking for $30,000 a season. When McGraw offered a three-year contract-compromise for $70,000 Roush accepted the deal. In 1928 Roush suffered an abdominal injury that required surgery, and he played in only 46 games. In 1929 he came back to hit .324, but following that season he was sent a contract for $10,000 — a cut of $13,000. Roush told McGraw what he could do with his contract and stayed home the entire season. After being released by the Giants and signing with Cincinnati in 1931 Roush said, "I didn't hold out because I wanted to. But I never heard of any other method open to a ball player for getting more money."

In his 18-year career Roush hit .323 using a 48 or 50-ounce bat. Kelly, the other half of the 1927 trade for Roush, played first base, the outfield and some second base. He was a slow starter at the plate when he broke in with the Giants in 1915. At 6-4 190 Kelly was not too agile around first base, especially when compared to Hal Chase one of the most graceful at that position in all of baseball, whom he succeeded when be became a regular in 1920. Kelly played 16 years with the Giants, Pittsburgh, Cincinnati, the Cubs and Brooklyn and hit .297 lifetime. He hit with power and was a good RBI man, driving in 100 or more runs in six seasons and leading the league in homeruns with 23 in 1921. George "High Pockets" Kelly was not as colorful nor as good a ball player as Edd Roush but they both made it to the Hall of Fame — Roush in 1962 and Kelly (14) in 1973.

1951 — Out of baseball since pitching for Cleveland in 1949, Satchel Paige is signed by the St. Louis Browns. In July 1948, Paige, a legend in the Negro Leagues for 22 years, received the following telegram at his home in Kansas City: "DO YOU HAVE ENOUGH LEFT TO PITCH RELIEF IN THE MAJOR LEAGUES? CALL ME. BILL VEECK, CLEVELAND INDIANS." Paige, of course, accepted and became Major League Baseball's oldest rookie at age 42. In his first year he went 6-1 with an ERA of 2.48 for the pennant-winning Indians and 4-7 in 1949 with an ERA of 3.04. After being out of baseball for one year he was reunited with Veeck in St. Louis in 1951. He pitched three seasons with the Browns, went 3-4 in 1951, 12-10 in 1952 and 3-9 in 1953. Paige, at age 59, would make a one-game appearance in 1965 with the Kansas City A's, pitching three innings, giving up no runs and one hit.

Birth records were never verified for Paige but his accepted year of birth is 1906 — this probably due to his adding the letter "i" to his real name of Page, "to make it sound more high-tone." The "Satchel" came about when he was a 7-year old porter at the Mobile, Alabama, railroad station. Paige recalled: "I carried so many satchels that all you could see was satchels. You couldn't see Leroy Paige." Paige (26) pitched six seasons in the majors with a record of 28-31, an ERA of 3.29 and became the first black player to enter the Hall of Fame in 1971 by virtue of his accomplishments during 29 years in the Negro Leagues.

February 10

1916 — When the Federal League folded following the 1914-15 seasons there was heavy movement back to the established leagues by name players who had jumped to the outlaw circuit. Many of them were future Hall-of-Famers. On this date Chief Bender is sold to the Phillies by the Baltimore Terrapins; Eddie Plank is sold to the St. Louis Browns by the St. Louis Terriers with ten other players; Joe Tinker moves to the Chicago National League club from the Chi-Feds for cash and nine other players including Mordecai "Three Finger" Brown. Shortstop Tinker (of Tinker to Evers to Chance fame) would be inducted into the Hall of Fame in 1946, after playing 15 seasons hitting only .263. Thirteen of those years were spent with the Cubs, a team he ran in 1916 after managing Cincinnati (1913) and his two seasons in the Federal League. Bender would enter the hall in 1953 after pitching 12 of his 15 years with the Athletics, winning 210 and losing 127 for a win-percentage of .623 and an earned run average of 2.40. He was out of baseball following 1917 but returned when he was 41 years old to make a brief one-game appearance in 1925 with the White Sox. Brown did most of his work with the Cubs and finished his career with a winning percentage of .649 (239-129) and an ERA of 2.06. Brown was voted into the Hall of Fame in 1949. Three Finger had lost about one inch of his right index finger in a feed chopper accident when he was a youth in Indiana.

1924 — Bucky Harris, with three full seasons as a second baseman in the majors and only 27 years old, is named player-manager of the Washington Senators. Add to that a World Championship in his first season at the helm of the Senators and he became known as the "Boy Wonder." That was the spectacular beginning of a 29-year major league managerial career that saw him manage Washington three different times, Detroit twice, and one-time stints with the Red Sox, Phillies, and the Yankees. During his12-year playing career he hit .274. Harris (35) won 2,159 games as a manager and although he finished 40 games under .500 he was voted into the Hall of Fame in 1975.

February 11

1900 — The Baltimore Orioles of the National League sell teammates and fast friends, John McGraw and Wilbert Robinson, along with Bill Keister to the St. Louis Cardinals. McGraw would eventually join the New York Giants and manage that team for 31 years and Robinson would manage the Brooklyn Dodgers for 18 seasons. While with the Orioles, McGraw and Robinson were partners in a thriving cafe and bowling establishment, but it was dissolved in 1902 when McGraw took over as manager in New York. Robinson, a catcher and 10 years older than McGraw, left the game in 1904 after breaking a finger. He continued in the saloon and butcher shop businesses before joining the Giants as one of McGraw's coaches in 1911. Their friendship ended during the 1913 World Series in a difference of opinion over strategy.

The next season Robinson took over as skipper of the Dodgers while McGraw was already in his 13th season with the Giants. When McGraw was honored in spring training at the beginning of the 1927 season — his 25th year as the Giants manager – Robinson was persuaded to attend and the two healed their bitterness that had lasted 13 years. McGraw had the better managerial record of the two and a much better playing career. "Muggsy", as McGraw was known, had a lifetime .334 average and managed the Giants to 2,658 wins and won 182 games while managing Baltimore. He led New York to 10 pennants and three World Championships. With much less talent, Robinson's Dodgers won two National League Championships. Both, regardless of the love-hate relationship over the years, have plaques in the Hall of Fame – McGraw entering in 1937, the second year of the Hall's existence, and Robinson in 1945.

1937 — Baseball is made the medium for the first large-scale television demonstration of the Philco Radio and Television Corporation. In attendance are nearly 200 editors and publishers of national magazines and newspapers. Boake Carter, a well-known radio news commentator, interviews the veteran manager of the

Philadelphia Athletics, Connie Mack. The television demonstration is carried from the Philco factory to Philadelphia's Germantown Cricket Club, miles away, where the guests see and hear the pair almost as clearly as though they were in the same room.

1974 — 48 major league players file for the new arbitration procedure established to settle contract differences. The first is pitcher Dick Woodson of Minnesota who is asking for a $29,000 contract while the Twins are offering $23,000. Woodson is the winner.

February 12

1876 — The Spalding Sporting Goods Company has it beginning when Chicago National Association pitcher Albert Spalding joins with his brother, J. Walter, to form a company to sell all kinds of baseball goods. Although his was a short playing career, Spalding was a premier pitcher as well as a manager and club president. Spalding managed the Chicago White Stockings in 1876 and 1877 and, when he wasn't pitching, he was playing first, second, or third base, or in the outfield. In three seasons he hit .287. In 1876 he went 47-13 on the mound with an ERA of 1.75 and hit .312. Interestingly, he had a pitching decision in 60 of the team's 66 decisions, winning the pennant with a mark of 52-14. In 1901, a few years after he was out of baseball, he was instrumental in getting the warring American and National Leagues together. Albert Goodwill Spalding was elected to the Hall of Fame in 1939.

1922 — Grandstand seat prices for all major league parks are increased to $1.00 and bleachers to 50 cents.

1981 — Red Sox catcher Carlton Fisk is declared a free agent by arbitrator Raymond Goetz on the grounds that Boston mailed his contract two days after the December 20, 1980 deadline. He had been with the Red Sox since breaking into the majors in 1969 and signed with the White Sox following the ruling. Fisk (27) would go on the play 24 seasons and catch 2,229 games while batting .269 with 2,356 hits, 379 homeruns and be elected to the Hall of Fame in 2000.

February 13

1920 — The National Negro Baseball League (under the charter name National Association of Colored Professional Baseball Clubs) is organized in Kansas City.

February 13

This league is a dream come true for Andrew "Rube" Foster, owner of the Chicago American Giants, who convinced seven other owners to form the new league. Other teams in the new circuit include the Chicago Giants, Cuban Stars, Dayton Marcos, Detroit Stars, Indianapolis ABCs, Kansas City Monarchs and St. Louis Giants. The first team of paid Negro players was a group of waiters recruited by Frank Thompson in 1885 in the Argyle Hotel, Babylon, Long Island. They played ten games that summer against white teams on Long Island, and then went on tour billed as the Cuban Giants. Thompson hoped to ease the social barriers by passing the team off as Cubans, and a few players furthered the illusion by chattering in a rapid Spanish-sounding gibberish on the field. Thompson added the nickname Giants because it was a popular team in the majors at the time.

There would be other teams later from other cities playing baseball but none of these groups, even an attempt in 1887 to establish the National Colored League, would come up with anything stable until the 1920 organization. This new league operated through 1931 with clubs from various cities in-and-out of the eight-team circuit. But this league, along with others that sprang up during this period, would collapse during the Depression. The second Negro National League came on the scene in 1933 but folded after the 1949 season. However, the Negro American League which surfaced in 1937 would struggle to survive with fewer and fewer teams throughout the 1950s. In its final season it would field only four teams: the Kansas City Monarchs, Birmingham Black Barons, Detroit-New Orleans Stars and Raleigh Tigers.

Throughout its history, the league had teams in Toledo, Atlanta, St. Louis, Baltimore, Mobile, Philadelphia, Cleveland, Memphis, Newark, Indianapolis, Houston, Cincinnati, New York, Chicago, Jacksonville and Louisville. Other cities with Negro teams as early as 1885 were Akron, Columbus and Dayton, Ohio; Albany and Savannah, Georgia; Atlantic City and Palmyra, New Jersey; Asheville and Raleigh, North Carolina; Birmingham, Mobile and Montgomery, Alabama; Boston, Massachusetts; Brooklyn, New York; Charleston, South Carolina; Chattanooga, Knoxville and Nashville, Tennessee; Pittsburgh and Harrisburg, Pennsylvania; Little Rock, Arkansas; Milwaukee, Wisconsin; New Orleans and Monroe, Louisiana; Washington, D.C. and Wilmington, Delaware.

1953 — In honor of the Philadelphia Athletics great manager, Shibe Park becomes Connie Mack Stadium. Shibe Park was opened on April 12, 1909; the Athletics and Phillies played there through October 1, 1970. It wasn't a fitting end to the "old lady", as many called the venerable old playground. Fans became so rowdy the final game was almost forfeited and, by the time the last fan departed, the park wasn't good for much more than a junkyard.

February 14

1914 — Babe Ruth signs his first professional contract – at age 19 -- with Baltimore of the International League while attending St. Mary's Industrial School in Baltimore. Classified as "incorrigible," Ruth had entered the school in June 1902 at age seven. He was in and out of the school four different times before being released to play ball. The manager of the Orioles, Jack Dunn, signed Ruth. Dunn had signed other players off local ball clubs in the area, players who later played in the majors, including Frank "Home Run" Baker and Fritz Maisel. How Dunn found Ruth is not clear, but he either stumbled onto his talents on his own, or Ruth was recommended to him by Brother Gilbert, Director of Athletics at Mt. St. Joseph's. The most believable story relates that Dunn was interested in Ford Meadows, the only left-handed pitcher on the Mt. St. Joseph's College team. Brother Gilbert, afraid he might lose Meadows, diverted Dunn's attention to a player named Ruth down the road at St. Mary's. Because it was cold and snowy in Baltimore the day he was introduced to Ruth, Dunn never saw him play. Shortly thereafter, St. Mary's released George Herman Ruth to Jack Dunn and the Baltimore Orioles of the International League.

1934 — Following his release by the Washington Senators after the 1933 season, outfielder Sam Rice is signed by the Cleveland Indians. Rice had played with only the Senators in his first 19 years in the majors and the 1934 season would be his 20th and final year. He would play in only 97 games with Cleveland with 98 hits leaving him 13 hits shy of 3,000 for his career. Asked some years later why he never continued until that number was reached, Rice said, "There wasn't much emphasis of 3,000 hits when I quit. And to tell you the truth, I didn't know how many hits I had when I retired." That retirement came when he was 44 years old with a lifetime batting average of .322. Rice (3) was elected to the Hall of Fame in 1963.

February 15

1916 — Third baseman Frank "Home Run" Baker, who led the American League in homeruns from 1911 through 1914 for the Athletics (with 11, 10, 12 and 9), is sold to the Yankees for $37,500. Following the 1914 season, Baker, then only 28 years old, announced his retirement after a contract dispute with Athletics manager Connie Mack. He sat out the entire 1915 season but had a change of heart and joined the Yankees after his sale. Baker was the second player in Connie Mack's so-called $100,000 infield to be sold, following second baseman Eddie

Collins to the White Sox in 1914 for $50,000. Later, in 1915, shortstop Jack Barry would be sold to the Boston Red Sox for $8,000. This brought the total price received by Mack for three of his infielders to $95,500. In 1918 first baseman Snuffy McInnis would be traded to the Red Sox for players but no cash. Baker hit home runs on successive days in the 1911 World Series, and it touched the fancy of the fans enough to hang the nickname of "Home Run" on him. Although he hit .307 in the 13 years he played for the Athletics and Yankees, he hit only 96 home-runs – 42 of them from 1911 through 1914. Baker entered the Hall of Fame in 1955.

1990 — Major League owners, having announced on January 9 there would be a lockout of spring camps beginning February 15, unless there was a new basic agreement in place at that time, make good their threat and lock the gates. A 32-day lockout would ensue wiping out most of spring training, and delaying the start of the season for one week. All games missed were rescheduled. The new agreement between players and owners would be reached on March 18 — a four-year contract – calling for the top 17 percent of two-to-three year players eligible for salary arbitration.

1994 — Thomas Roberts, one of two arbitrators who found major league club owners guilty of collusion in 1986 and 1987 against free agents, issues an order awarding $59.5 million in claims. According to evidence uncovered at the first hearing before Roberts, the owners thought up the plan in a meeting in October 1985. The collusion era lasted from 1985 to 1988 freezing the free-agent market and arresting baseball's salary spiral. In the end it would cost the owners $280 million in damages. The awards were given on circumstances involving individual players, many of whom did not qualify and were denied payment. The two highest awards went to Jack Clark $2,112,555 and Lance Parrish $1,786,763. According to evidence, both Clark and Parrish had lucrative multi-year contracts on the table with St. Louis and Detroit, respectively, but both offers were withdrawn following the owners' meeting in October of 1985. Other players awarded more than $1 million were Andre Dawson, Carlton Fisk, Rich Gedman, Tim Raines and Tom Seaver. A total of 339 were awarded payments.

February 16

1921 — As quoted from *The Sporting News*: "Mrs. (Clarence L.) Keaton, then Allie May Schmidt, a member of the Presbyterian Church at Ferguson, St. Louis County, Missouri, was in charge of decorations for a meeting of the Men's

Fellowship Organization, at which Branch Rickey, vice president of the Cardinals, was to speak. At a loss for an idea, she happened to glance out the window, when out on the snow-covered landscape two red birds flew to a tree and perched on a branch. Immediately, it occurred to her to use red birds for decorations, especially since the Cardinal team was certain to be part of the discussion. Making cardboard cutouts of red birds, she used them in decorating the tables. On seeing them, Rickey complimented the young lady on the idea and adopted the emblem for the St. Louis national leaguers' uniform."

1934 — Two future Hall of Fame pitchers retire on back-to-back days. Eppa Rixey of the Reds announces his retirement on this date after 21 seasons with Cincinnati and the Phillies and a career 266-251 record. The following day, Urban "Red" Faber hangs 'em up with a 20-year mark of 254-212 with the Chicago White Sox. Both pitchers were workhorses; Rixey logged nine seasons of pitching 200 or more innings, and three in which he worked in excess of 300. Faber had seven-plus 200-inning seasons and three in which he worked more than 300 with a high of 353 in 1922. Both pitchers finished their careers with an ERA of 3.15. Ironically, both wore number (18) and were inducted into the Hall of Fame in back-to-back years — Rixey in 1963 and Faber in 1964.

February 17

1914 — The first announcement of the signing of Babe Ruth to a professional contract appears in the press. The article in the *Baltimore American* states: "George H. Ruth, southpaw, standing six feet one inch tall and weighing 180 pounds, is the latest Oriole. He pitched for St. Mary's Industrial School, and among his other feats he is credited with fanning 20 men in a game with Bill Byers' All-Stars. Hefty William [Byers] admits George made monkeys out of his boys, and while boasting him as a hurler took occasion to say that Dunn [Jack Dunn – manager of the Baltimore Orioles] will make a mistake if he doesn't play him at first base or in the outfield."

February 18

1909 — Cy Young is traded to Cleveland by the Red Sox for Charlie Chech, Jack Ryan and $12,500. Young began his 22-year major league career in 1890 with the Cleveland Spiders. In 1899, owners Frank and Stanley Robison, after unsuccessful efforts to sell the Cleveland franchise, purchased the St. Louis Perfectos. They changed the colors to red and white and, soon after, the team would be christened the Cardinals by a newspaper reporter. The new owners also brought Young and Jesse Burkett, among others, with them to St. Louis, leaving Cleveland in shambles in 1899 with a record of 20 wins and 134 losses, the poorest record in major league history. With the Cleveland and St. Louis franchises, Young would win 285 games before being traded to the Red Sox in 1901. With Boston he would win 193 games and would wind up his career in 1911 with 33 more victories with the Cleveland Indians and Boston Braves. His record was 511-313, a win percentage of .620 and an earned run average of 2.63. Young was elected to the Hall of Fame in 1937 — the second year of balloting. One other note on Young – he pitched in 125 games in 1890-92 when the pitching distance to home plate was only 50-feet, winning 72 games. When the distance was lengthened to 60'-6" in 1893 he won 32. In more than two seasons (1890-92) he was 72-41 at the shorter distance.

1922 — Richard LeMarquis is not a name known to baseball because a sports writer for unknown reasons changed that surname in the early 1900s – to Marquard. About the same time, Richard also became extinct and "Rube" took over because of his resemblance to Rube Waddell. Rube Marquard, after spending more than seven years with the New York Giants and the next six-plus years with Brooklyn and Cincinnati, is traded by the Reds to the Boston Braves with Larry Kopf for Jack Scott. Marquard would spend the next five seasons with the Braves and win 25 more games to bring his 18-year career totals to 201-177 before his retirement in 1925. In 1971 Marquard was elected to the Hall of Fame.

1944 — Joe Nuxhall, 15 years and six months old, accepts a $500 bonus and signs a contract to pitch for the Cincinnati Reds. He would make his major league debut on June 10, 1944. With the St. Louis Cardinals leading 10-0, Cincinnati manager Bill McKechnie sent Nuxhall in to pitch the ninth inning. Nuxhall walked his pitching rival Mort Cooper but retired the next two batters. He then walked four more batters, threw a wild pitch and gave up two singles – a total of five runs – before being taken out. The final score was 18-0. Nuxhall was sent down to Double-A Birmingham where he also pitched in 1945. He still had one-year eligibility remaining at Hamilton, Ohio High School. He appealed to the state high school athletic board and was allowed to play football and basketball his senior year. He would reappear in the majors in 1952, pitch 16 years and finish with a career record of 135-117.

February 19

1953 — Ted Williams begins his first full-fledged combat mission in the Korean War, piloting a Panther jet as part of a 200-plane sortie. After hitting the target area, his plane is hit by enemy flak and with his radio dead he manages to make it to the Suwan landing strip and crash-lands safely – belly-flopping his flaming jet some 2,000 feet along the runway. In June, with 18 missions to his credit, Williams is shipped home to join the Red Sox. Williams had been notified on January 9, 1952 to report for active duty on May 3rd. He would miss portions of both the 1952 and 1953 seasons and return to play seven more years to round out his 19 seasons in the majors. This would be Williams' second tour of duty as a Marine Corps pilot, having missed three seasons during World War II in 1943, 1944 and 1945. Williams' honors in baseball are almost endless. Two Triple Crowns, two Most Valuable Player Awards, six batting titles with a high of .406 in 1941, a career average of .344 with 2,654 hits, 1,839 RBI, 1,798 runs scored and 2,019 bases on balls. Williams (9) hit 521 home runs with a slugging percentage of .634, an-on base average of .483 and was voted into the Hall of Fame in his first year of eligibility in 1966.

This is John Upkyke's account of Ted Williams' last at bat, when he hit a homerun: "Like a feather caught in a vortex, Williams ran around the square of bases at the center of our beseeching screaming. He ran as he always ran out homeruns, hurriedly, unsmiling, head down, as if our praise were a storm of rain to get out of. He didn't tip his cap. Though we thumped, wept, and chanted 'We Want Ted' for minutes after he hid in the dugout, he did not come back. Our noise for some seconds passed beyond excitement into a kind of immense open anguish, a wailing, a cry to be saved. But immortality is non-transferable. The papers said that the other players, and even the umpires on the field, begged him to come out and acknowledge us in some way, but he refused. Gods do not answer letters."

1970 — After a five-hour meeting with two-time Cy Young Award winner Denny McLain, commissioner Bowie Kuhn announces McLain is being suspended for an indefinite period for 1967 bookmaking activities and association with gamblers. This story actually broke two days earlier when *Sports Illustrated* ran a copyrighted story stating McLain was " . . . a partner in a bookmaking operation during the 1967 season and had become inextricably involved with mobsters." Kuhn knew the story was going to break and had a February 13 meeting with McLain who allegedly incriminated himself with admissions related to his involvement. However, it was not until April 1 that Kuhn handed down his updated suspension when he announced: "It is my judgement that McLain's suspension should be continued to July 1. 1970."

Among other comments concerning bookmaking and association with gamblers, Kuhn said, "There is no evidence to indicate that McLain ever bet on a baseball game involving the Detroit Tigers or any other team." Reaction to the [less-than-severe] penalty handed down by the commissioner was not positive. Teammates were quoted with such words and phrases as: "puzzled - half a season?" Or, "If innocent, it should be nothing - if guilty than this is not enough" and "Most of the guys thought Denny would get one or two years or nothing at all."

The media was even more critical of the penalty with comments such as: "How do you spell travesty? Better yet, what's the definition of whitewash?" "Slap on the wrist penalty." and "Kuhn took the easy way out." McLain was activated on July 1 but his pitching was not his best and his extracurricular activities continued to go downhill. He was again suspended, this time for seven days, by the Tigers on August 28 for dousing two writers with buckets of ice water. The capper on the season came when McLain was called into Kuhn's office one day before that suspension ended and was suspended again for the remainder of the season for carrying a gun and breaking probation on an August 6-19 road trip. Still another twist to the 1970 season was announced on October 9 in Cincinnati. The day before the opening of the World Series between the Reds and Baltimore McLain was traded with Don Wert, Norm McRae and Elliot Maddox to Washington for Joe Coleman, Ed Brinkman, Aurelio Rodriguez and Jim Hannan. Interestingly, Bowie Kuhn made the announcement of that transaction.

February 20

1877 — The first minor league is organized and christened the International Association. The league was formed in Pittsburgh and comprised seven teams: the Pittsburgh, Pennsylvania, Alleghenys; the London, Ontario, Tecumsehs; the Columbus, Ohio, Buckeyes; the Guelph, Ontario, Maple Leafs; the Lynn, Massachusetts, Live Oaks; Rochester, New York and Manchester, New Hampshire also fielded teams. The first game was played at Lynn on April 26 with Candy Cummings (who was also the president of the new league) pitching and losing 14-3 to Manchester (this is the same Cummings who allegedly invented the curve ball). Cummings would finish the year pitching the final of his only two years in the National League with a 5-14 record.

1943 — P.K. Wrigley, owner of the Chicago Cubs, announces the formation of the All-American Girls Professional Baseball League. Wrigley thought World War II would decimate the major leagues' playing talent and saw a women's league as a way to keep the ballparks busy and the fans entertained. Players were paid $55-$80 a week, plus expenses and board. The league opened in 1943 (with four teams, eventually reaching a high of ten). The game was never identical to a softball league, but since the girls didn't start using the 9" major league baseball until mid-season of 1954 (the last year the league was in existence), the league's official name was a misnomer. Regardless, the girls had great skills and played hard-nosed ball. The league had tremendous success and reached its peak in 1948 when it attracted over one million spectators.

Beauty guru Helena Rubenstein was brought in to talk about makeup, how to walk and how to take off a coat, short hair was out but properly applied make-up was in. No slacks were allowed. Female chaperones lived with the girls around the clock, acting as disciplinarians, friends and surrogate parents. Former major leaguers such as Bill Wambsganss, Johnny Rawlings, Jimmy Foxx, Max Carey, Bert Niehoff and Leo Murphy taught the members of baseball history's most obscure pro league how to play the game. With the war over, the novelty wearing off, and televised baseball settling in, the league folded in 1954.

When the league opened in 1943 they played with a 12" softball and the pitching mound was 40' from home plate. In 1944 the ball was 11 and one-half inches and dropped to 11" in 1946. Also in 1946, the mound was moved back to 43' (as the distance between the mound and the plate was lengthened so was the distance between bases). Sidearm pitching was allowed beginning in 1947. In 1948 pitchers began throwing overhand with a ball 10 and three-eighth inches, but five and one-eighth ounces lighter than a baseball. Also in 1948 the pitchers threw from 50'. Getting closer to the game of baseball in 1951 the mound was moved back to 55' and half-way through the leagues' final season (1954) the official major league baseball was adopted. Clubs participating in the league were the Rockford Peaches, South Bend Blue Sox, Racine Belles, Kenosha Comets, Milwaukee Chicks, Minneapolis Millerettes, Grand Rapids Chicks, Fort Wayne Daisies, Chicago Colleens, Springfield, Illinois, Sallies, Kalamzoo Lassies, Battle Creek Belles, Muskegon Lassies and Peoria Redwings.

1957 — The Brooklyn Dodgers purchase Wrigley Field in Los Angeles along with the Angels franchise in the Pacific Coast League from the Chicago Cubs. Walter O'Malley, Dodgers owner, pays $3,250,200 in the deal that includes Brooklyn turning over the Fort Worth franchise in the Texas League to the Cubs organization. This purchase was O'Malley's last warning to the city of New York to build a new stadium in Brooklyn or lose the Dodgers.

February 21

1931 — Two major league teams play under lights for the first time against each other in an exhibition game at Buff Stadium in Houston. Houston, then a member of the Texas League, and always a great stop for major league teams during spring training, plays host to the Chicago White Sox and New York Giants. The two teams collect 22 hits in a 10-inning game. Night games were introduced into organized baseball in 1930 in the minor leagues, quite possibly as a novelty, but they proved such an immediate success that it saved dozens of minor leagues in the depression years. During the 1930 season, for example, Waco became the first team in the Texas League to install lights. Before that season ended, Houston, San Antonio and Shreveport were also playing night games.

1945 — The All-Star game is called off because of wartime travel restrictions. It marks the first time the game has been canceled since its inauguration in 1933.

February 23

1921 — Rabbit Maranville broke into the majors in 1912 with the Boston Braves and after spending ten years with that club is traded to Pittsburgh for Billy Southworth, Fred Nicholson, Walter Barbare and $15,000. James Walter Vincent was better known as "Rabbit", so nicknamed because of his large ears, accentuated even more on his 5-5, 155 pound frame. His career batting average was only .258 but he was an excellent shortstop and was the first to use the "vest pocket" catch, that later was popularized by Willie Mays but called the "basket" catch. Maranville was one of the few name-players on the 1914 "Miracle Braves", the team made famous for their fantastic run from last place, in mid-season, to win the pennant and sweep the Philadelphia A's in the World Series. He also played with the Cubs, Brooklyn and Cardinals, managing the Cubs in 1925 from July to September before being fired. Maranville (1) was voted into the Hall of Fame in 1954.

1960 — With Lucy Monroe singing the National Anthem, the demolition of Ebbets Field, the home of the Dodgers from April 9, 1913 to September 24, 1957, begins. The Ebbets Field housing development, along with Crown Heights Intermediate School, would be built on the site in 1963. The apartment complex was renamed the Jackie Robinson Apartments in 1972.

1968 — Major league minimum salary is increased from $7,000 to $10,000.

1976 — Club owners announce they are closing spring training camps until a player dispute is settled. This was the result of the arbitration panel's ruling that the owner's control over a player's contract was limited to the contract plus one year option. However, on March 17 commissioner Bowie Kuhn ordered the camps opened. The lockout lasted one month with the season starting on schedule. Players and owners reach a four-year agreement on July 12 that established procedure for free agency Players with at least six years of service may become free agents, but then must wait five years before becoming a free agent again. It also allows players to become eligible for salary arbitration after two years of service.

February 24

1943 — The Texas League announces suspension of play for the duration of World War II. President Alvin Gardner conducted a wire vote and six of the eight clubs were unwilling to start the 1943 season. During the war Baseball was faced with many difficulties, not the least of which was the manpower drain caused by the draft. In 1942 there were 31 minor leagues and the Texas League was the highest classification circuit to halt play. In 1943 and 1944 only 10 leagues would operate with only twelve playing in 1945. Following demobilization, the 1946 total increased to 43.

February 25

1933 — Tom Yawkey, a multi-millionaire sportsman and ex-player Eddie Collins, purchase the Boston Red Sox for $1.5 million from Bob Quinn. The Red Sox glory years were immediately before and during World War I. They won pennants in 1912, 1915, 1916 and 1918 defeating four different teams in the World Series. For the next fifteen years, until the advent of Tom Yawkey, the Sox never got out of the second division, finishing last nine times and never getting out of the American League cellar between 1925 and 1930.

Harry Frazee is the man generally blamed for the darkest hours for Red Sox fans. He sold baseball stars by the hat-full to keep his sinking theatrical productions afloat. Some of Boston's greatest heroes — Babe Ruth among them – were sold down the river to the Yankees. Bob Quinn headed a group that bought out Frazee in 1923, but Quinn's principal backer became too ill to assist financially and in 1933 Yawkey bought the sinking Sox. Yawkey spent millions in his effort to produce championships. In his 43 years as owner of the Red Sox his club won only three American League pennants and in each instance Boston lost the World

Series in seven games. Yawkey was voted into the Hall of Fame by a special Veterans Committee in 1980 becoming the first owner selected who never served as player, manager, or general manager.

1972 — Steve Carlton is traded by the St. Louis Cardinals to the Philadelphia Phillies for Rick Wise. While Wise would go 16-16 with the Cardinals in 1972, Carlton would win 27 and lose only 10 with an earned run average of 1.97. Carlton's performance for the last-place Phillies (59-97) ranks as one of the most remarkable in baseball history, as he won almost half of all games his team won. In fact, he lost 6 of his first 11 decisions and then, starting June 7 went 22-4 the remainder of the season. The Phillies, during that same period on days Carlton didn't pitch, won only 21 games and lost 64. He would go on to pitch 23-years in the major leagues, finish with a record of 329-244, with 4,136 strikeouts and winning four Cy Young Awards. He was guilty of being a hanger-on" as his career wound down and in his final three seasons he not only pitched for the Phillies but also San Francisco, the White Sox, Cleveland and Minnesota. In 1994 Carlton (32) became the 25th player elected to the Hall of Fame in his first year of eligibility receiving 436 votes of a possible 455.

1973 — Arbitration agreement for players' salaries is signed for the first time. The owners announced on February 8th that spring training would not begin without a collective-bargaining agreement and on the 25th of February the players and owners reached a three-year agreement establishing arbitration for players with two or more years of major league service. Other provisions in the agreement establish a minimum salary of $15,000 and the "10-5" trade rule goes into effect – allowing a player with 10 years service, five of which are with his current team, to veto any trade involving him. Spring camps open on March 1.

1988 — The Chicago City Council, signaling an end to a 72-year tradition of daytime-only baseball at Wrigley Field, votes 29-19 to lift the ban on night games at the only major league park without lights.

February 26

1935 — Babe Ruth signs a three-year contract with the Boston Braves. Ruth was released three weeks earlier by the Yankees. His New York salary had been cut sharply to $52,000 in 1933 and dropped to $35,000 in 1934. Ruth wanted to manage, but Yankees owner Jacob Rupert would have none of it, going as far at one point to turn down a request by Cincinnati to speak with Ruth concerning a managerial position with the Reds. Rupert then arranged a complicated deal; Ruth would leave New York and join the Braves as player, assistant manager and club vice-president. He would receive a salary of $20,000.

However, after playing in only 28 games, hitting only six homeruns, and driving in 12 runs with a batting average of .181, Ruth would end his 22-year major league career. The name Babe Ruth is probably the most recognized of any name in the history of baseball. One year after retiring, Ruth and four other immortals became charter members of the Hall of Fame in 1936. His statistics are staggering, not only as a position player but also as a pitcher. In ten years as a left-handed pitcher his record was 94-36, a win percentage of .671, with an earned run average of 2.28. He allowed only 974 hits in 1221 innings, and in World Series action Ruth was 3-0 with a 0.87 ERA. But his pitching prowess paled by what he accomplished as a hitter and fielder. The Bambino chalked up a .342 batting average with 2,873 hits, scored 2,174 runs, drove in 2,211 runs with 714 homeruns, an on-base percentage of .474, a slugging average of .690 while drawing 2,056 base on balls. Ruth led the American League in homeruns 12 times, in walks 11 years, runs 8 years and RBI 6 times. The other four to enter the Hall of Fame in the first election year with Ruth (3) were Honus Wagner, Christy Mathewson, Walter Johnson and Ty Cobb.

February 27

1909 — "Iron Man" Joe McGinnity is released by the New York Giants ending his short 10-year major league career. He was 28 years old in 1899 when he broke into the majors with Baltimore, then in the National League, and his big league career was over at age 37. His short stay was spectacular, winning 247 games with only 144 losses for a winning percentage of .632. His nickname originated in 1900 when he joined the Brooklyn Superbas and was asked by a writer what he did in the off-season. McGinnity replied, "I work in my father-in-law's iron foundry. I'm an iron man." His performance on the mound with the Giants proved to be no misnomer. On the first of August in 1903 he pitched and won both games of a doubleheader against Boston and one week later duplicated the feat against Brooklyn. Before the month was out, August 31, he pitched and won both ends of another twin bill, this time against Philadelphia. Two more times during his career he would pitch both games of doubleheaders, winning one and losing one. He proved to be that "Iron Man," rolling up 3,458 innings in his 10-year major league career.

Although his major league career ended with his release by the Giants, McGinnity would pitch and manage for 17 more years in the minors winning 200 more games before giving up the mound in 1925 at age 54. In 1926 he was back in the majors as a Brooklyn coach. McGinnity was probably best remembered for his 1904 season winning 35 games while losing only eight with an earned run average of 1.61. That season alone, he threw nine shutouts in the 408 innings he pitched. McGinnity was voted into the Hall of Fame in 1946.

1912 — The New York Yankees announce that players will wear the now-famous pinstriped uniforms. Although the Yankees did wear pinstripes on their home uniforms that season, they were not the first major league team to do so. The Boston Doves (later called the Braves) and the Brooklyn Dodgers wore pinstripes on their road uniforms as early as 1906. In 1910 the Pittsburgh Pirates became the first team to have pinstripes on their home uniforms.

February 28

1903 — In 1883 the Philadelphia Phillies – or Quakers – came into existence as a member of the National League when Alfred J. Reach purchased the Worchester, Massachusetts Brown Stockings and moved them to Philadelphia. Reach, who later became a wealthy sporting goods manufacturer, along with co-owner John Rodgers, would sell the Phillies on this date in 1903 to a syndicate headed by Barney Dreyfuss, owner of the Pittsburgh Pirates. At this time ownership in more than one team in the league was legal; it would not be outlawed until 1910.

1966 — Los Angeles pitchers Sandy Koufax and Don Drysdale create preseason excitement by staging a joint holdout. The pair informed the Dodgers that neither would sign until both were satisfied with terms of their contracts. On March 30th, after a 32-day holdout, they would accept general manager Buzzie Bavasi's offer calling for $130,000 for Koufax and $105,000 for Drysdale. Drysdale would go 13-16 in 1966 and Koufax would retire after winning 27 and losing nine while winning his second straight Cy Young Award. Both Koufax and Drysdale would enter the Hall of Fame; Koufax in 1972 and Drysdale in 1984. Drysdale (53) began his career with Brooklyn in 1956 and pitched 14 seasons with the Dodgers with a record if 209-166 and an ERA of 2.95.

February 29

2000 — Sparky Anderson, the only manager to win World Series titles in both leagues, is elected to the Hall of Fame by the Veterans Committee. Anderson led the Reds to back-to-back titles in 1975 and 1976 and won with Detroit in 1984. Only Connie Mack and John McGraw won more games than Anderson's career record of 2,194-1,834. The committee, as stipulated in the 1995 by-laws, also elected one 19th century player and one Negro League player. Bid McPhee, a 5'-8", 152-pound second baseman played 18 years with Cincinnati (1882-1899), hitting .275 playing most of his career barehanded when the pitching distance was 50 feet. Norman "Turkey" Stearnes was an outfielder with ten different teams in the Negro Leagues for 18 seasons (1920-1942). Many baseball people have been critical of the current by-laws and hope to change them following the 2001 election to allow such outstanding players as Bill Mazoroski, Gil Hodges, Joe Gordon, Mel Harder, and Tony Oliva to be elected.

"To sacrifice, or not to sacrifice, that is the question."
Soliloquy by a baseball Hamlet

Satchel Paige

The All-American Girls Professional Baseball League, 1947

Chapter Three

"The beauty of baseball is not that its rules, definitions, records, and heroes have endured, but that they have endured and are treasured. That's baseball's beauty – and its strength."

--Jim Hackleman

March 1

1891 — The Players League and the National League had been at each others throats throughout 1890, and at the end of the season they came to an agreement of sorts. However, controversy continued surrounding which league controlled which players. One of the sharpest disputes raged over Louis Bierbauer, a second baseman, who had been with the Philadelphia Athletics (American Association) in 1889 before jumping to Brooklyn of the Players League. Pittsburgh of the National League signed Bierbauer away from the Athletics for the 1891 season. Philadelphia and other clubs in the American Association were outraged by the "piratical" actions of Pittsburgh and the team began to be referred to as the Pirates from that point on.

1969 — Mickey Mantle announces his retirement at a press conference at the Yankees spring base in Fort Lauderdale. Following the 1968 season, Mantle indicated he might retire because of bad legs that caused him continuous pain but decided to give it one more try. He went to Florida early to convince himself he could no longer play, and it took only a little running before he decided not to put off his retirement. Baseball was over for Mantle after 18 seasons and with it his $100,000 a-year contract. He finished his career with a .297 average and 536 homeruns. In eleven of those 18 seasons, Mantle led all switch hitters in both leagues in homeruns and RBI. Mantle (7) won three MVP awards and entered the Hall of Fame in his first year of eligibility in 1974.

March 2

1893 — Buck Ewing is traded by the New York Giants to Cleveland for George Davis. Ewing was the catcher, captain and lead-off batter for the first Giants team when they started play in the National League in New York in 1883. The team was then known as the Gothams and had just been moved to New York City from Troy, New York. Ewing played all nine positions in his 18-year major league career and finished with a batting average of .303. To wind up his field activities he managed Cincinnati in 1899 and returned to the Giants as manager in 1900.

Ewing was voted into the Hall of Fame in 1939.

March 3

1953 — Lou Perini, owner of the Boston Braves, blocks the St. Louis Browns' attempt to shift their franchise to Milwaukee. The Braves, who owned the Milwaukee minor league franchise, invoke territorial privilege stating the Braves had not been offered enough. Eight days later (March 11) Perini proposes a ban on the move of any major league franchise into a minor league city until October 1. Two days later (March 13), the National League weighs the offer by the Braves to move the Boston franchise to Milwaukee. On March 18 (fifteen days after Perini's refusal to allow the Browns into Milwaukee) the Boston Braves move to Milwaukee and become the first franchise-shift in baseball since 1903 when New York purchased the Baltimore franchise and moved it to the American League.

1959 — The Giants' new stadium under construction in San Francisco is named Candlestick Park. The name was selected from 15,000 entries submitted by fans. Candlestick Park has been called a lot of other things since it opened April 12, 1960, among them the worst ballpark in baseball and an architectural laughing-stock. Built at Candlestick Point on land owned by construction magnate Charles Harney, the 67 acres have been the subject of derision by players and fans alike because of the wind and cold. Harney not only sold the land but also built the stadium for a total cost to the city of $10.5 million. The miserable conditions at the park were summed up in 1983 when Giants brass went so far as to accent the negative in a marketing campaign. Any fan braving an entire extra-inning night game would receive the "Croix de Candlestick" pin – "I came, I saw, I survived!"

1984 — Peter Ueberroth is elected to a five-year term as commissioner of baseball. He will take office on October 1 succeeding Bowie Kuhn, following his tenure as president of the U.S. Olympics that summer. Ueberroth, who will become the sixth commissioner, brings a successful business background in the travel industry to a game that has had only two men, Kuhn and Ford Frick, with any prior baseball experience. The line of former commissioners began with Kenesaw M. Landis (judge), "Happy" Chandler (politician), Frick (National League president), William D. Eckert (retired Air Force Lieutenant-General), and Kuhn (National League lawyer).

March 4

1871 — The first major league is founded — the National Association — and with it the National Association of Professional Baseball Players is organized. This was a player-controlled league with the structure set up to afford players freedom of bargaining, freedom to move where the pay was the highest, to organize and defend their collective interest, to improve playing conditions, and to secure pension rights. This was the first players' union as we know it today, but the association collapsed five years later in 1876. A group of owners plotted against the players and the organization folded as the league disbanded.

1914 — Ground is broken for Weeghman Park (Wrigley Field) in Chicago. The park would house the upstart Federal League, a circuit that started as a minor league in 1912 as the United States League. That league folded, but in 1913 franchises were established in Chicago, Cleveland, Pittsburgh, St. Louis, Kansas City and Covington, Kentucky. By 1914 the league had a new president, coal magnate James A. Gilmore. He was instrumental in enticing a number of prosperous businessmen around the country to become involved in baseball. As a result, the Federal League burst into full bloom as a so-called third major league. Gilmore's man in Chicago was Charles Weeghman who had made a fortune in various restaurant ventures.

During 1913 the Chicago entry in the Federal League was known as the ChiFeds. They played their home games at De Paul University's athletic field, but with the circuit going "major league" in 1914, Weeghman leased a vacant lot at Clark and Addison Streets in the midst of one of North Side Chicago's residential areas. He then enlisted the services of architect Zachary Taylor Davis who had drawn the blueprints for Comiskey Park which had opened in 1910. The ground breaking ceremony for the new North Side park attracted between two and four thousand spectators, and Weeghman saw to it that it was done up right. Aside from the usual speeches by public officials, a bottle of wine was broken over the spade amid the playing of patriotic music; Weeghman promised the park would be open the latter part of April — it was! The name Weeghman Park would cease to exist in 1916 when the Cubs and the National League took over the park. The name was changed to Cubs Park and later became Wrigley Field in 1926.

1921 — Outfielder Harry Hooper is traded by the Boston Red Sox to the Chicago White Sox for outfielders Shano Collins and Nemo Leibold. Hooper joined the Red Sox in 1909 and following his 12th season (1920) with the team, he held out for $15,000. This led to his trade, and he ended up with a $13,250 contract with

Chicago. He played with Boston during the "Golden Age of the Red Sox" when Boston played in the World Series in 1912, 1915-16, and 1918. Hooper was part of the great outfield with the Red Sox along with Tris Speaker and Duffy Lewis. Speaker preceded Hooper by two years and Lewis rounded out the trio in 1910. In 1919 Hooper suggested to Red Sox manager Ed Barrow that he convert Babe Ruth from a pitcher to an outfielder to take advantage of his hitting prowess. Hooper spent five seasons with the White Sox, retired after the 1925 season and was elected to the Hall of Fame in 1971.

1941 — Grace Comiskey takes over as president of the Chicago White Sox to become the first woman in the American League to hold that position. Mrs. Comiskey was the wife of White Sox owner J. Louis Comiskey who died in 1939. Before gaining operational control of the club the new president had to wade through a two-year battle of legal-sized red tape. In his will J. Louis left the club in the hands of the First National Bank of Chicago as trustee. The bank, believing the team to be an unsafe investment for a widow and three children, sought to sell the property. Mrs. Comiskey fought the sale and won on the premise that both her husband and former father-in-law, Charles (The Old Roman) Comiskey, desired the White Sox to eventually be owned by Grace's son Charles II. Women are, or have been, owners or presidents of major league clubs in six cities since 1911 when Mrs. Frank DeHass Robinson became president of the St. Louis Cardinals. Others were Jean Yawkey of the Red Sox, Joan Payson and Lorinda de Roulet of the New York Mets, Joan Kroc of San Diego and Marge Schott of Cincinnati.

1984 — The Special Veterans Committee votes Harold (Pee Wee) Reese into the Hall of Fame. He broke in as a Brooklyn Dodger in 1940 and finished his 16 major league seasons in 1958 as a Los Angeles Dodger. The 5'-9", 175-pound superb shortstop hit .269 with 2,170 hits, scored 1.338 runs, walked 1,210 times and stole 232 bases. Reese (1) played in 44 games in seven World Series and batted .272.

March 5

1914 — The first round-the-world barnstorming tour by two major league teams comes to a conclusion in New York City. In November of 1913, Charles Comiskey and John McGraw take the Chicago White Sox and New York Giants on a world tour. The teams were actually conglomerates. Only seven had been members of the White Sox and only five Giants made the trip. The balance of the two squads was bolstered by players from other teams. The term barnstorming arose from itinerant actors who usually performed on farms (the "silo circuit") and were first called "barnstormers" around 1884. Eventually, the term was used to describe any kind of traveling showmen and was applied to ballplayers on one-day stands with major league teams during spring training, or with traveling teams such as the bearded House of David, or the black Indianapolis Clowns.

1996 — Outfielder Ned Hanlon is voted into the Hall of Fame by the Veterans Committee. He made his niche in baseball as a manager with the feisty and belligerent old Baltimore Orioles in the National League winning three pennants and two second place finishes in seven seasons. He also managed Pittsburgh, Brooklyn and Cincinnati to an overall win percentage of .530 from 1892 through 1907.

March 6

1957 — The city of Los Angeles opens a drive to bring the Dodgers to the West Coast. This comes as the result of a meeting between Brooklyn's Walter O'Malley and Los Angeles Mayor Norris Poulson. However, efforts to obtain a major league franchise for L.A. really began more than fifteen years earlier. During the World Series in 1946, the *Sporting News* reported that *Los Angeles Examiner* sports columnist Vincent X. Flaherty was prepared to submit a bid by Louis B. Mayer, Hollywood film magnate, for the purchase of the St. Louis Cardinals with a view of moving that club to Los Angeles. In August of 1947 Flaherty reported the St. Louis Browns were for sale, and the possibility existed that a purchase would end up with the team in Los Angeles.

Even as O'Malley and Poulson were talking in 1957, Flaherty, who had left sports writing but was doing a general feature column, got members of the Los Angeles City Council to make an offer to Calvin Griffith to move the Washington Senators to the West Coast. It was at this time that Del Webb, owner of the New York Yankees, said, "Los Angeles isn't ready yet for big league baseball." Flaherty, the press-pusher who championed major league baseball for the city, saw it come in 1958 but by 1962 he was out of the newspaper business and bounced from various jobs and died penniless. This is not the only story of the *Examiner's* involvement in pushing for a big league club for L.A. In May 1935 Sports Editor Mark Kelly arrived in Chicago carrying with him airline schedules and Chamber of Commerce literature to launch a campaign to bring a franchise to Los Angeles. The idea had been bugging Kelly for a long time, but this was his first effort to get action beyond urging it in his column.

March 7

1893 — On this date National League clubs meet in New York to lengthen the pitching distance; pitchers were dominating the game. Baseball's original pitching distance was 45 feet from home plate. In 1881 the distance was increased to 50 feet, and it remained that way through the 1892 season. The season of 1892 had been one of the dreariest in National League history. Hitting seemed to be on the verge of disappearing and only a few reactionaries liked the game the way it was, but the general feeling was that something had to be done. Several radical suggestions were entertained, but the most interesting came from W.R. Lester, sports editor of the *Philadelphia Record*. The pitcher in 1892 did not work off a slab; since 1880, the rules had called for him to work from a box, five and one-half feet long by four feet wide, 50 feet distant from the center of home plate. Each corner of this space was marked by a flat, round rubber plate six inches in diameter, fixed in the ground flush with the surface. The extreme rear of this box was therefore 55 feet, six inches from home plate.

The Lester plan contained two planks involving pitching: (1) Make the base lines 93 feet in length, instead of 90. (2) Put the pitcher's point in the geometrical center of the diamond and abolish the pitcher's box. On March 7, 1893 National League club owners, exactly split over the Lester Plan, met at the old Fifth Avenue Hotel in New York. The Lester plan, calling as it did for 93 foot bases, meant the pitcher would stand 65 feet, nine inches from home plate and the distance from home plate to second base would be exactly twice that. After much haggling, the liberal clubs (Boston, Pittsburgh, Cleveland, Chicago, Louisville and St. Louis) agreed to compromise. The distance of 90 feet between bases was maintained but the pitcher was moved back five feet; the old pitcher's box was abolished and Lester's suggestion of a pitching rubber was adopted. The rubber was placed five feet behind the rear of the old box, or 60 feet, 6 inches from home plate. A final note concerning the new pitching distance – after two seasons with the new rule, baseball officials discussed the possibility of reinstating the old pitching distance. Several of the group were dismayed by the explosion of offense, which resulted in "long drawn-out and uninteresting contests."

1929 — Rick Ferrell is declared a free agent by Commissioner Landis. The Judge had been slapping around some major league clubs for covering up players and in this finding, the Detroit club lost one of its best catching prospects. Ferrell, a Detroit farmhand, had been with Kinston in the Virginia League and Columbus in the American Association in his first three years in professional baseball. When his name wasn't placed on the Columbus club's 1928 reserve list, Landis made the young catcher a free agent. Ferrell had accepted a $1,500 bonus in 1926 for signing with the Detroit organization, and with his free agency was available to the highest bidder. Owner Phil Ball gave Ferrell a $25,000 bonus for signing with the St. Louis Browns. Ferrell hit .281 in his 18 years in the majors, was one of the outstanding catchers during that period and retired following the 1947 season. In 1984 Ferrell (9) became the oldest living player, 78 years old, to be elected to the Hall of Fame.

1955 — Commissioner Ford Frick indicates he favors the legalization of the spitter, which he calls "a great pitch and one of the easiest to throw." When the spitball was outlawed in 1920, there were 17 pitchers in the majors who were permitted to continue throwing the "wet one" until the end of their careers. That's when it allegedly ended, but where did it all start? Here's one that sounds authentic and fits the period when it all began. Some years ago I received a hand-written note from a Homer Hildebrand that said, "I am 91 years young. I caught Elmer Stricklett who started the spitball in 1903, the first year he used it at Los Angeles." (Hildebrand never pitched in the majors, but Stricklett would spend four seasons with the White Sox and Brooklyn).

Research also reveals that Burleigh Grimes, when he was 87 years old, recalled when he was 11 years old (in 1904) he saw a pitcher in St. Paul named Hank Gehring go to his face with his hands. Grimes said, "I asked my uncle what he was doing, and he said he was throwing a spitball." Grimes went on to say, "so I went home and got some bark and started workin' on it." Twelve years later, in 1916, Grimes was throwing it for the Dodgers. Stricklett moved up to the White Sox in 1904 for one season and pitched the next three with Brooklyn. He was a right-hander who stood 5'-6", weighed 140 pounds and his record shows he could have been using the spitter. Although he won only 35 games while losing 51, he allowed fewer hits than innings pitched, walked almost as many as he struck out and had an ERA of 2.85. As for Gehring, if he threw the spitter it may not have been a good one. Gehring pitched in only 18 games in the majors with Washington in 1907-08 and finished his career with a 3-8 mark and a 3.91 ERA.

1979 — Warren Giles entered professional baseball after returning from overseas war service in 1920, as a result of attending a meeting of the Moline, Illinois, Three-I League team as a fan. The franchise was in trouble and Giles offered his ideas to put the team back on track; the stockholders were so impressed they made him president. His road to the top took him to St. Joseph in the Western Association in 1923 and he ended up as owner. Next stop was the International League with Syracuse and Rochester as general manager in the St. Louis

Cardinals organization. Giles took over as top man at Cincinnati in 1936, and in 1951 was a major contender for the open commissioner's post along with National League president Ford Frick. When a stalemate existed between the two, Giles stepped aside graciously and later succeeded Frick as NL president. After 18 years in that executive post Giles retired and on this day in 1979 was elected by a Special Veterans Committee to the Hall of Fame.

March 8

1900 — The 12-team National League votes to reduce the circuit to eight teams. Convinced the league was too unwieldy, and that top-to-bottom, competition was impossible, the committee recommended the league drop Louisville, Baltimore, Washington and Cleveland. The clubs that were expelled demanded indemnification of $150,000 and the National League agreed to set aside five percent of the gross receipts for the next two seasons and pay a total of $104,000: $10,000 to Louisville, $25,000 to Cleveland, $30,000 to Baltimore and $39,000 to Washington. As for the auction of the players, there were some big names involved. Honus Wagner and Fred Clarke moved from Louisville to Pittsburgh, John McGraw and Wilbert Robinson were sold by Baltimore to Brooklyn but refused to report. They eventually ended up in St. Louis with almost half of the season gone. The eight-team National League with Cincinnati, Chicago, Brooklyn, New York, Philadelphia, Pittsburgh, St. Louis, and Boston would remain intact until 1953 when the Braves moved from Boston to Milwaukee.

1930 — Becoming the highest paid player of all time (to date), Babe Ruth ends his holdout against Yankees management and signs a two-year contract for $80,000 a season. Yankees general manager Ed Barrow is quoted, "No one will ever be paid more than Ruth."

March 9

1897 — The Cleveland baseball club, as it is known today, could very well have been named on this date. A scout for the Cleveland Forest Citys in the National League signed Louis Sockalexis out of Notre Dame. He had transferred from Holy Cross where he had excelled in track as well as baseball. The 200-pound 6-footer was the grandson of a chief of the Penobscot Tribe, born on a Maine reservation in 1871. In his first year with Cleveland the outfielder hit .338 with three homeruns, 42 RBI, 16 stolen bases with 117 putouts and 10 assists. He did not strike out once in his 66 games. During his brief three seasons with Cleveland

March 9

Sockalexis would hit .313 in only 94 games and would die on Christmas Eve 1913 at age 41. The official cause of death was chronic alcoholism. In 1915 a Cleveland newspaper ran a contest and a fan suggested the nickname "Indians" in honor of an Indian player named Luis Francis Sockalexis, better known as The Chief.

1943 — Lloyd Waner, in the twilight of his career, is traded for the third time in less than two years. After spending 14 seasons with Pittsburgh, Waner moved to the Boston Braves, Cincinnati, and finally to the Philadelphia Phillies before this trade that sent him to Brooklyn with Al Glossop for Babe Dahlgren. Waner would not report to Brooklyn and spent the entire 1943 season on the voluntary retired list. He reported to Brooklyn in 1944 and played in only 15 games before being released. He was re-signed by the Pirates and would play only 42 more games through 1945 before retiring. The other half of the Hall of Fame brother combination, Paul, was never traded during his career but was released four times in his last seven years. After leaving Pittsburgh following 15 seasons Paul played with Brooklyn, the Boston Braves and New York Yankees. Like brother Lloyd his last year in the majors was 1945. Paul played 22 years and hit .333 with 3,157 hits. Lloyd hit .316 in his 18 seasons. Paul (11) entered the Hall of Fame in 1952 and Lloyd (10) was given that honor in 1967. Paul died on August 29, 1965; Lloyd lived until 1982. Mrs. Waner said that Paul had written the following poem just a few days before his death, apparently having the premonition he was going to die.

I sometimes pause for just a minute
To think of this world without me in it
I cannot think of a newborn day
Without me here somewhere, some way
I cannot think of a newborn day
Without me here, alert, aware,
I cannot think of another spring
Without my spikes and bat to swing
These precious years may come and go
With faster pace, but this I know
I have no fear or do I dread
Of what marked day that lies ahead
My flesh will turn to ash and clay
But I'll still be here, somewhere, some way.

1979 — In a ruling that is still opposed by some ball players, commissioner Bowie Kuhn allows women reporters access to clubhouses.

1995 — Major league club owners take enough time out from the 209-day-old strike to award expansion franchises to Phoenix and Tampa-St.Petersburg. Each new club will pay $130 million in actual cash as an expansion fee, with payments beginning July 1, 1995 and ending in November of 1997 — with actual play to begin in 1998. However, the total cost of each franchise will ultimately be $155 million because of exclusions from national broadcasting, All-Star and postseason money for five years.

March 10

1941 — The Brooklyn Dodgers announce their players will wear batting helmets. Larry MacPhail, reminiscing of his days at Brooklyn when Leo Durocher managed the Dodgers, relates "I had a manager with the reputation of throwing at people and naturally the other fellows threw at our players, and I had to act in self-defense. The thing started with a pad that could be inserted in the baseball cap. Many players rejected it and called it sissy. However, I know it saved the lives of Joe Medwick and Dolf Camilli and, for all I know, the development of the idea may have kept many more players alive through the years."

Some historians report that New York Giants catcher Roger Bresnahan may have been the first player to wear a protective covering in 1907. Bresnahan was beaned and shortly thereafter used a leather protector over his cap. 1937 was the beginning of serious thought in the direction of helmets. The *New York Daily News* printed an editorial in June of that year ". . . advising the use of helmets to minimize the danger of batters being hit by pitched balls." In April of 1937, the Des Moines Demons of the Western League experimented with polo helmets but found them too heavy along with the added task of adjusting the chinstraps and discarding them while running to first base.

In 1939 the "Safety Cap or Helmet" became official equipment in the International League. Designed by league president Frank Shaughnessey and Ed Rainey of Spalding, three caps were supplied to each team and their use by the players was optional. The helmet was first worn by Buster Mills of Newark. It weighed seven ounces and fit snugly over the regular uniform cap. Made of hard fiber and sponge-rubber knobs to protect the temples, it was held in place by a spring steel band. Frankie Frisch was managing at Pittsburgh in the early 1940s and expressed the hairshirt approach to the introduction of the batting helmet. "In my day, guys like [Burleigh] Grimes and [Dizzy] Dean would play tunes on those plastic thingamjigs, and make `em sound like Swiss bell-ringers." Frisch delighted in teasing modern players for wearing the protective helmets, which he called "inverted garbage cans."

Head protection was made mandatory in the National League in 1954 and in the American in 1958. The current ruling in the majors regarding helmets is: All players who entered the majors in 1983 or since must wear a single ear-flap helmet while at bat and can use double ear-flaps if they wish. Only those players who were in the majors in 1982 and who were recorded as objecting to wearing the batting helmet are excused from this mandatory protection.

1982 — Travis Jackson is elected to the Hall of Fame by the Special Veterans Committee. Jackson (5) was the New York Giants shortstop for 15 years from 1922 through 1936 hitting .291 and playing in four World Series. In 1928 manager John McGraw appointed Jackson his Captain, a position he held for the rest of his career. With his election he joined the three other members of the Giants 1927 starting infield already in the Hall of Fame – Bill Terry, Freddie Lindstrom, and Rogers Hornsby.

1986 — Bobby Doerr, a career Boston Red Sox for 14 years, is elected to the Hall of Fame by the Veterans Committee. Doerr (1) batted .288 with 223 homeruns and was equally outstanding at second base, racking up four fielding championships while representing Boston and the American League in nine All-Star games.

March 11

1901 — The *Cincinnati Enquirer* reports that Baltimore manager John McGraw has signed a Cherokee Indian named Tokohoma to play ball. The "Indian" turns out to be Charlie Grant, a black second baseman who played with the Chicago Columbia Giants in 1900. The contract is rejected.

1933 — Rogers Hornsby puts on a Cardinals uniform for the first time since 1926. Out of baseball since his August 1932 firing as manager of the Chicago Cubs, Hornsby reports to spring training with St. Louis. He would play in only 46 games with the Redbirds before moving to the Browns and taking over from Bill Killefer as manager. For all intents and purposes Hornsby's playing days ended when he appeared in only 100 games with the Cubs in 1931 and in the next six years, in which he was a player-manager, he participated in only 132 games. Hornsby played in the majors for 23 years and finished with a batting average of .358. As a batter he had few equals in the game. In 1925, he won his second Triple Crown with 39 homeruns, 143 RBI and a .403 average. It was one of three years he topped the .400 mark (401 in 1922, .424 in 1924 and .403 in 1925). He drove in 1,579 runs and missed the magic 3,000 hit mark by only 70. Most of his career was with the Cardinals, but he also saw action with the Giants, Braves, Cubs, and Browns. He managed all of those clubs at one time or another and also managed the Cincinnati Reds in his final two years in the majors. Hornsby wore three different numbers in his career (4,11, and 16) and was elected to the Hall of Fame in 1942.

March 12

1942 — Joe DiMaggio ends his holdout in accepting the second-highest salary a New York Yankee has ever received. Coming off his 1941 season, in which he hit safely in 56 consecutive games, batted .357 with 30 homeruns and 125 RBI, the Yankees had sent him a contract calling for the same $37,500 he made in that record-setting season. The offer from boss Ed Barrow more than upset DiMaggio. He was expecting a fat raise since he had become the game's greatest gate attraction since Babe Ruth. Barrow countered with an offer of $40,000 with a bonus, but DiMaggio turned it down stating it wasn't enough, plus he wanted his final settlement to be in cold cash — no bonuses! DiMaggio settled for $42,000 which was far from Ruth's $80,000 but moved him ahead of Lou Gehrig who had drawn $39,000 on one contract. Joltin' Joe's salary would be the highest in baseball for that year. In 1936, DiMaggio's first season with the Yankees, he made $8,000.

1951 — Happy Chandler fails in his attempt for re-election as commissioner. Baseball's first commissioner, Judge Kenesaw Mountain Landis had died in office on November 25, 1944. Chandler took office on April 24, 1945 and resented from the start his diminished authority following Landis' autocratic reign. It didn't take long for the new commissioner to get into hot water with the owners. At his first winter meeting in December of 1945, Chandler informed the press that the owners had passed legislation to reduce his power. Chandler's contract was for seven years, but in 1950 he was the victim of a secret revolt led by Fred Saigh of the St. Louis Cardinals. This coup was pulled off at the baseball meetings in St.Petersburg when Del Webb of the Yankees and Lou Perini of the Braves came out in support of Saigh. Two secret votes were taken and on the second ballot seven owners were opposed to Chandler's dismissal (the vote was 9-7); Chandler was fired. He would serve six of his seven years and would leave office on July

15, 1951. Ford Frick would succeed him in September to become the third commissioner. In 1982 Chandler would be elected to the Hall of Fame by the Special Veterans Committee.

March 13

1943 — Major league owners approve an official ball with the interior made from reclaimed cork and balata, materials not needed in the war effort. Balata is a hard substance extracted from the bully tree of the Caribbean and used as a rubber substitute in belting and golf balls.

1953 — Boston becomes a one-team major league city. In a meeting at the Viney Park Hotel in St.Petersburg, National League owners grant Lou Perini permission to transfer the Braves to Milwaukee. The Boston Braves attendance had dwindled from 1,081,795 in their 1948 championship season to 281,278 in 1952. Perini stated he would be happy to draw 750,000 fans in his first season in Milwaukee; 1.8 million moved through the turnstiles. By 1957 attendance would shoot up to over 2 million but in the lame duck year in Milwaukee (1965) just prior to the second move by the Braves (to Atlanta) the attendance would drop to 524,000.

1954 — Bobby Thomson, acquired by Milwaukee in a trade with the New York Giants a month earlier, suffers a broken right ankle sliding into third base in an exhibition game against the Yankees. On the first of February the Giants had moved Thomson and Sammy Calderone to the Braves in exchange for Johnny Antonelli, Don Liddle, Ebba St. Claire, Billy Klaus and $50,000. The injury to Thomson opened the door for a rookie infielder who had played shortstop for Eau Claire in the Northern League in 1952, second base at Jacksonville in the Sally League in 1953 to a starting outfield job for Milwaukee in 1954. That infielder, converted to the outfield to fill the void left by Thomson's injury, was Hank Aaron.

1960 — Bill Veeck announces the Chicago White Sox uniforms will have players' names on the back. The Yankees and Indians were the first teams to number the back of their uniforms in 1929 and that practice became standard. However, Veeck's latest innovation is still not followed by all teams in the majors. In the 1960s and '70s there was a trend to put first names and nicknames on uniforms such as "Vida" (Vida Blue) and "Wampum" (Dick Allen). In 1976 Ted Turner went radical and allowed his players to wear the following: "Nort" (Darrel Chaney), "Gallo" (Roger Moret), "Chopper" (Dave May), "Jay Bird" (Jerry Royster) and others. Turner's penchant for nicknames defeated the purpose of identification as most fans went crazy trying to figure out what they meant, if anything. If nothing else, Veeck's idea turned out to be a big boon for the fans watching televised games, especially the deaf.

March 14

1883 — The Peoria team, of the Northwestern (minor) League, calls a meeting to ban Negroes from playing in the circuit. The move targeted catcher Moses Fleetwood Walker who was playing for Toledo. Reports say the discussion got "hot and heavy" before the motion was withdrawn and Walker was allowed to continue playing. The next season, 1884, Toledo joined the newly-formed American Association, and even though it was not an established league, it was recognized as a major league. Walker was still playing with Toledo and thus became the first Black to play on a major league team. Walker was joined on that team by brother Welday Walker and although they both made history playing on that Toledo club, they quickly faded into oblivion. The Walkers were let go in September following a series of injuries to Moses and threats against his life. Moses Fleetwood Walker played in 41 games as a catcher and hit .251.

1961 — Former Yankees general manager George Weiss is lured out of retirement to become president of the expansion New York Mets. Weiss had been released by the Yankees following the 1960 season because of a new retirement policy at age 65. Weiss was associated with the Yankees for 29 years in which the team won 19 pennants. He was elected to the Hall of Fame in 1971.

1997 — Labor peace finally and officially returns to baseball, four years, three months and seven days after owners reopened the old labor agreement. The signing of the deal brought an end to the most destructive of baseball's eight work stoppages since 1972. A 232-day walkout wiped out the final seven and one-half weeks of the 1994 season, the first three weeks of 1995 and the World Series for the first time in 90 years.

March 15

1869 — The history of professional baseball begins in Cincinnati as the Red Stockings are organized by Harry Wright, Aaron B. Champion and Carl Ellard. Before the Red Stockings were put together, individual players had been paid for their services for about ten years. Among the most notable was Alfred Reach who was paid for his performances as early as 1860 and may have been the first professional baseball player. Now a team would be made up entirely of paid players and for the first time in history the organization admitted publicly they would be paid to play. Wright came up with the idea. He had come to America from England and went to Cincinnati from New York in 1865 as bowler for the Union Cricket Club for a salary of $1,200 a season. Baseball had been played in Cincinnati since 1860 and Wright soon discovered that baseball was more popular than cricket.

The Red Stockings were organized as an amateur team in 1866 and among the original members were Ellard and Champion. There was much opposition to paying players, and to some, professional ball players were under a social ban and amateurs were not supposed to associate with them. Wright had the backing of Champion, who had become the new president of the Red Stockings, and began constructing his team by bringing his brother, George, an engraver, from the Bronx to play shortstop for $1,400; a left fielder, Andy Leonard and a second baseman, Charles Sweasy, both hat makers from Newark; a right fielder, Calvin McVey, a piano maker from Indianapolis; Charles Gould a bookkeeper from Cincinnati to play first base and a marble cutter, Douglas Allison, to catch. Each of the five would receive $800 a season. Rounding out the team would be two insurance brokers, third baseman Fred Watermam, who would earn $1,000, and pitcher Asa Brainard hired for $1,100. Harry Wright, who incidentally was a jeweler by trade, would manage and play centerfield and receive $1,200. Also there was a 10th unnamed player to serve as a substitute for $600 and that rounded out the payroll for the season to $9,300.

Until this time baseball teams had worn long trousers, the same used by cricket players. Harry Wright wanted the team to wear knickerbockers to give them more freedom of movement and through Ellard, who owned the largest sporting goods company in the Midwest, this became a reality. Figures vary on how many games the Red Stockings would win in 1869 – some said 69, others say 65 but conservatively speaking the team would win at least 92 straight before losing in June of 1870.

We are a band of baseball players
From Cincinnati City.
We come to toss the ball around
And sing to you our ditty;
And if you listen to the song
We are about to sing,
We'll tell you all about baseball

And make the welkin ring.
The ladies want to know,
Who are those gallant men in
Stockings red, they'd like to know.

— from the original song of the old Red Stockings, written by a member.

Both Wrights were recognized for their contributions by the election of both to the Hall of Fame – George in 1937 and Harry in 1953.

1944 — These were the war years and like almost everything else, baseball was unpredictable. The Washington Senators open spring training with four knuckleball pitchers on their staff. One is left-handed – Mickey Haefner; the other three are Dutch Leonard, Roger Wolff and Johnny Niggling. This would be the first of two straight seasons the Senators would have four knuckleball starters. In the 1944 season this club would finish last and the 1945 club would finish second with the same four pitchers. The unpredictability of baseball during this period also spilled over to the knuckleballers whose individual records mirror the Senators' records in those two seasons. The won-lost record for Leonard, Haefner, Niggling and Wolff in 1944 was 40-52 .435. The next year with a second place finish they combined for 60-43 .583. Future Hall-of-Famer Rick Ferrell would handle the bulk of the catching and would lead the league in passed balls in both 1944 and 1945. Also on the 1944 team was another left-hander who threw the knuckleball out of the bullpen – his name was Bill Lefebvre.

March 16

1953 — Bill Veeck's request to move the St. Louis Browns to Baltimore is rejected. Veeck sold the Cleveland Indians and ended up with the Browns in 1951 and despite his many promotions his team was fighting a losing battle to the Cardinals. The use of midget Eddie Gaedel did not enamor the other moguls of the game and the addition of Satchel Paige didn't do enough to improve attendance. Veeck knew when he purchased the Browns that St. Louis was not a two-team city. It looked as though he was winning his battle against Fred Saigh, the Cardinals owner, to force the Red Birds out of St. Louis. It might have happened except Saigh had gotten himself into income-tax trouble and had to face the possibility of selling the club. Saigh came close to selling the Cardinals to Houston interests. However, the big blow that ended Veeck's tenure in St. Louis was when August Busch stepped in to buy the Cardinals; Veeck was forced to unload the Browns.

His attempt to move to Milwaukee was shot down when the National League approved the shift of the Boston Braves to that city. Then Veeck attempted to move to Baltimore. This was rejected by American League club owners with the condition the move could be made only if Veeck would first sell the Browns. Obviously, this was a move to get Veeck completely out of baseball. Out of options and being stonewalled by the American League, on September 29, 1953, the Browns left for Baltimore without Veeck, as he sells his St. Louis club for $2.475 million to a Baltimore group. Vowing vengeance on those he thought had blackballed him from Baltimore Veeck lived a sort of self-imposed banishment until late in 1958. After being ignored in several purchase attempts, he and Hank Greenberg in 1959 bought the White Sox and fell into a ready-made pennant winner built by Paul Richards and Chuck Comiskey.

Veeck was a promoter with a flair that bordered on genius and kept fans entertained with his sense of humor. He ended his career as owner of the Cleveland Indians, St. Louis Browns and Chicago White Sox. Despite his business acumen that provoked disapproval from other owners, Veeck was an independent who refused to go along with the group that attempted to put him down. The "Maverick" was still powerful enough to be voted into the Hall of Fame in 1991.

March 17

1886 — The first issue of *The Sporting News* rolls off the press in downtown St. Louis at 11 North Eighth Street. The young visionary was Alfred Henry Spink who had introduced to the sports-minded community a publication that has survived for over a century. Following are some comments about the newspaper: An anonymous sportswriter in the early 1900s said, "That isn't blood running in the veins of the St. Louis Spinks. They have baseballs for corpuscles and ink for the stuff that circulates through their arteries." In the *St. Louis Post-Dispatch*, 1977 — "*The Sporting News* is a unique publication. Its subscribers are sports nuts." An Iowa man who subscribed for 57 years requested that a copy of the paper be buried with him. It was! Carl Sandburg in his 1948 book *Always the Young Strangers*, "On many a Saturday I had sold *The Sporting News* at five cents a copy, and I had read about the `leather spheroid.'"

1984 — After 19 years of major league pitching, Ferguson Jenkins is given his release by the Chicago Cubs. He was in his second tour of duty with Chicago, after first appearing with the Cubs in 1966 following a trade with the Philadelphia Phillies. In 1967 Jenkins would begin a run of six consecutive seasons in which he won 20 or more games and winning the Cy Young Award in 1971. Besides his two stops with the Cubs, he had two different stints with Texas and also pitched for the Red Sox. Before his trade to the Cubs in 1966 with Adolfo Phillips and John Herrnstein for Larry Jackson and Bob Buhl, he had pitched in only eight games with Philadelphia in 1965 and 1966 with a 2-1 record. Jenkins won 284 games and lost 226 with an ERA of 3.34 while striking out 3,192 batters. He was voted into the Hall of Fame in 1991.

1992 — Detroit pitcher Hal Newhouser and American League umpire Bill McGowan are selected for the Hall of Fame. Newhouser spent all but two of his 17 seasons with the Tigers (1939-1953) and the final two with Cleveland. Newhouser (16) finished with a 207-150 record an ERA of 3.06. Four times he won 20 or more games with a high of 29 in 1944 while throwing 33 shutouts. McGowan was one of the American League's greatest umpires working 30 years (1925-1954), officiating in eight World Series and four All-Star games. He worked the first All-Star game in 1933 with Bill Klem, Bill Dinneen and Cy Rigler.

1998 — In one of the biggest transactions in sports history, Major League Baseball owners approve the sale of the Los Angeles Dodgers to Rupert Murdoch's Fox Group. The deal, reportedly worth between $311 million and $350 million, ends the Dodgers tradition of family ownership going back to 1950 when Walter O'Malley gained control of the Brooklyn Dodgers. President Peter O'Malley said on January 6, 1997 when he announced his club was for sale, "Family ownership is probably a dying breed — a high risk business — with groups and corporations the wave of the future."

March 18

1990 — The 32-day old lockout of spring camps is ended when owners and players reach a new four-year agreement. The owners attempt to create a "partnership" with the players that is looked upon by the union as a salary cap. In the final resolution the owners increase their pension contribution to $55 million a year. A player must have completed three years of service to be granted salary arbitration eligibility, but the top 17 percent of players with at least two years of service would also be eligible. Plus, a team that loses a free agent would be awarded draft-choice compensation only if the player is offered salary arbitration. The minimum major league salary is elevated to $100,000 (up from $68,000).

March 19

1966 — Baseball is played for the first time on an artificial surface. One year after the opening of the Astrodome in Houston the Astros and Los Angeles Dodgers fly from their spring exhibition bases in Florida to play two exhibition games on an artificially covered infield. The outfield was dirt sprayed green to give the illusion of grass. When the Astrodome was being built one of the owners, Judge Roy Hofheinz, stated that grass could be grown indoors. Originally, the stadium featured a translucent ceiling and fly balls were lost because of the glare of the sun on the roof. In order to solve this dilemma, the portion of the roof over the infield was painted; however, this hindered the growing of grass. Some 26,103 fans paid to watch the first game on an Astroturf infield with the Dodgers beating the Astros 8-3. Five errors were committed in the game – four of them in the infield. Two of the mishandled balls were by two of the best fielders in the game – Wes Parker and Joe Morgan. Morgan's eighth inning error eventually led to two unearned runs. The starting pitchers in this historic game were Larry Dierker and Johnny Podres.

March 20

1934 — Beaumont's all-around female athlete Mildred "Babe' Didrickson pitches the first inning for the Philadelphia Athletics in a spring exhibition game against Brooklyn. She walks one batter but allows no hits.

1946 — The outlaw Mexican League begins its schedule. The six wealthy Pascual brothers from Mexico City make a bold attempt to make inroads on major league baseball. Led by brother Jorge, they promised players more money, better living conditions and, in general, a baseball paradise. The Pasquals were offering some players $50,000 over a three-year period, others $15,000 a year, plus bonuses. They were offering this during a time the infant Player's Association was trying to get the minimum salary in the majors up to $7,500. The Pasquals were successful in luring few players to the promised land, among them Vern Stephens, Mickey Owen, Max Lanier, Sal Maglie, George Hausmann, Roy Zimmerman, Nap Reyes, Danny Gardella, Fred Martin, Louis Olmo, Bobby Estalella, Robert Ortiz, Alex Carrasquel and Lou Klein. The short-lived Mexican League bubble would burst in five months. By August it was all over and players began seeking reinstatement in the majors.

1963 — A former baseball player begins his role as Dr. Steve Hardy on ABC's

General Hospital. Former St. Louis Browns and Cleveland Indians infielder Johnny Berardino joins one of the most popular afternoon programs on television and during his stay is nominated for three Emmy Awards. Berardino's acting career started in the late 1920s with some minor roles in *Our Gang* comedies, and, after his baseball-playing days was seen regularly on *The New Breed* and *I Led Three Lives.* He also made guest appearances on *The Untouchables, Cheyenne* and *Laramie.*

Berardino made his major league debut with the St. Louis Browns in 1939 and played his last season in 1952, a total of eleven years with three years off for military service during World War II. When he was traded to Cleveland in 1947 his contract with the Indians specified that acting during the off-season was permissible. Owner Bill Veeck noted later that Berardino was the first player he ever dealt with through an agent. Incidentally, Berardino's major league average was .249 in 912 games while playing every position except pitcher and catcher.

There was another actor/ball player named Chuck Connors, but he was more thespian and less baseball. After his brief career with the Dodgers in 1949 (one pinch-hit appearance) and a short stay with the Cubs in 1951 (66 games), Connors went on to star in the *Rifleman* series on television for six years (1957-1962). Following that successful series, he would appear in numerous films as well as television movies.

1973 – The only time in baseball history the five-year-rule is waived for election to the Hall of Fame. The Baseball Writers of America conduct a special election and vote Roberto Clemente (21) into the Hall, not only for his baseball accomplishments but for his humanitarian efforts. Clemente and four others had been killed following the 1972 season when a cargo plane crashed in Puerto Rico while carrying food, clothing and medical supplies to earthquake-stricken Nicaragua.

It was just hours following Clemente's death that the BBWAA at the urging of people in Commissioner Bowie Kuhn's office, petitioned the Hall of Fame for a special election. The writers had already held one election in 1973 in which Warren Spahn was elected. Hall of Fame officials agreed to the special election but ruled they would never do it again. Six years later (1979) when Thurman Munson was killed in a plane crash there was another rush to have the rule waived – it was not. In succeeding years when Munson's name appeared on the ballot his vote total dropped. In the Clemente special balloting, 422 votes were cast; 31 votes were against his entrance into the Hall.

March 21

1936 — Sunny Jim Bottomley returns to the city where he made his mark in the major leagues. The Cincinnati Reds trade Bottomley back to St. Louis but this time he joins the Browns in exchange for Johnny Burnett. It was 1922 when Bottomley began his 16-year big league career with the Cardinals, Reds and Browns; a career that would lead to a lifetime .310 batting average and 1,422 RBI. Bottomley would play in four World Series with the Red Birds and help them win two World Championships before moving on to Cincinnati in 1933. His return to St. Louis with the Browns would herald the beginning of the end of his playing career. His last season was 1937, and he would finish that year as manager of the Browns following Rogers Hornsby's dismissal in July. Bottomley (3) was voted into the Hall of Fame in 1974.

March 22

1993 — Cleveland pitchers Steve Olin, Tim Crews, and Bob Ojeda are involved in a boating accident during spring training. The three, while riding in an 18-foot skiff in the evening on Lake Nellie near Claremont, Florida, hit an unlighted dock at a high rate of speed. Olin, 27, died at the scene and Crews, 31, suffered a damaged lung and massive head injuries. Crews died early the next morning after being admitted to the Orlando Regional Medical Center. The 35-year old Ojeda survived following surgery for severe head lacerations.

March 23

1938 — In what was to become known as the Cedar Rapids case, commissioner Landis comes down hard on the St. Louis Cardinals organization, especially their farm director, Branch Rickey, when he sets free 91 Cardinals farm hands. The most prominent are Pete Reiser who would win the National League batting championship in 1941 for Brooklyn, and Skeeter Webb who would log eleven years with four American League teams. The case was named after the Cedar Rapids, Iowa, club because that was the lead team the commissioner keyed on. Rickey was not fined by Landis but he did levy fines against Cardinals farm clubs in Cedar Rapids (Western), Sacramento (PCL) and Springfield in the Western Association. Other clubs affected by the Landis ruling were Fayetteville and Monett of the Arkansas-Missouri League, Newport in the Northwest Arkansas League, Crookston in the Northern League and Mitchell in the Nebraska State League. In Landis' findings he asserted working agreements were being perverted "into arrangements for complete control of the lower-classification clubs through secret understandings."

March 25

1914 — Babe Ruth, in his first professional season, is given his first starting assignment as a pitcher for Baltimore (International League) in a spring exhibition game. Although Ruth gave up 13 hits he was tough with men on base and defeated the world champion Philadelphia Athletics 6-2. Philadelphia's star second baseman, Eddie Collins, was quoted as saying: "Ruth is a sure comer. He has the speed and a sharp curve, and, believe me, he is steady in the pinches."

March 26

1976 — The American League votes to expand to Toronto, awarding the franchise to a group consisting of Imperial Trust, Ltd., LaBatt's Breweries, and the Canadian Imperial Bank of Commerce for $7 million.

1988 — Gene Mauch of the California Angels ends his 27-year managerial career with the announcement of his retirement. Only three others managed longer in the major leagues than Mauch – Connie Mack for 53 years, John McGraw for 33 years and Bucky Harris for 28 years. Mauch began his managerial career in 1960 with the Phillies and later managed Montreal, Minnesota, and California as well. He had the longest tenure as a major league manager without winning a pennant – his high points were divisional titles for the Angels in 1982 and 1986. Of those managers spending 25 years or more as skippers in the majors (Mack, McGraw, Harris, Casey Stengel and Sparky Anderson are the others), Mauch is the only one not in the Hall of Fame.

March 27

1902 — The nickname "Cubs" appears for the first time in a newspaper. Although the name Cubs had been applied to the Chicago National League baseball team as early as 1890, the outfit was variously called Orphans, Colts, and Babies as well as Cubs because of the many young players brought to the team when some of the original players jumped to the Players League. Legend has it that the newspaper writer first used "Cubs" while searching for a short name to fit a headline. The nickname would not be officially adopted until 1907.

March 28

1935 — Tracking the "slider," *The Sporting News* reports White Sox pitcher George Earnshaw uses a "new" baffling pitch — he refers to it as a slider. Using the pitch in an exhibition game on this date, Earnshaw held Pittsburgh to three hits in four innings. Earnshaw said the pitch was shown to him by Waite Hoyt of Pittsburgh who found the pitch a life-saver during the 1934 season when he won 15 games for the Pirates. Hoyt claimed that George Uhle taught him the pitch when both were pitching for Detroit in 1930. Some historians say the pitch was first named by hitters who faced George Blaeholder of the St. Louis Browns during this same period. When Uhle was in his first year with the Tigers (1929) and outfielder Harry Heilmann was in his final year with Detroit, Uhle said "I was the very first one to name it the slider." He said it was his innovation and that he developed it. Uhle went on to say, "It's a sailing fastball. Harry Heilmann and I were working out, throwing at each other one day, and I just hit on it. I turned it loose a certain way and it would sail. So I tried it a few more times. I said, `Look at that thing. It slides across'. So we nicknamed it the slider."

1977 — Prior to an exhibition game, Texas Rangers manager Frank Lucchesi is assaulted by Rangers infielder Lenny Randle. Randle was upset after being benched by Lucchesi and was further driven in his physical move when the manager called him a "punk". Lucchesi ended up in the hospital with a shattered cheekbone and one month later Randle was traded to the Mets. The Mets would be the first of four teams Randle would play for in the next five seasons. As for Lucchesi, he would be fired by the Rangers on June 22, becoming part of Texas Rangers history. Eddie Stanky would take over the Texas reins the same day, quit the next, and Connie Ryan would become interim manager for six games until Billy Hunter is hired on June 28. That's four managers for the Rangers in seven days.

March 29

1916 — The Baltimore Terrapins of the defunct Federal League sue organized baseball for $900,000. The outlaw league had operated for two years but folded in 1915 after agreeing to peace terms which amounted to a buy-out of the circuit by the American and National leagues. However, the Baltimore Feds were unhappy with the peace pact and brought an anti-trust suit against the majors. The Terrapins would win the suit in the Indiana State Supreme Court. That decision would later be overturned by the District of Columbia Court of Appeals and upheld by the U.S. Supreme Court in 1922. Justice Oliver Wendell Holmes wrote the majority opinion, finding "That the (owners) produce baseball games as a source of profit, large and small, cannot change the character of the games. They are sport, not trade."

1935 — Dazzy Vance is released by the St. Louis Cardinals five months after pitching in only one game of the only World Series in which he appeared. In 1935 he will sign with Brooklyn and pitch in 20 games in what will be his final season in the majors. Vance spent most of his 16 years with the Dodgers (1922 through 1932) and also played with the New York Giants and Yankees, as well as the Cardinals and Cincinnati. Vance (21) gained his nickname while pitching in the Nebraska State League by mimicking a cowboy's pronunciation of "Daisy". Falling just short of 200 wins, Vance struck out 2,045 batters in 2,967 innings, leading the National League in strikeouts for seven consecutive years. Vance finished his career with 197 wins and 140 losses and was elected to the Hall of Fame in 1955.

1954 — Phil Cavaretta, who took over the Cubs managerial reins from Frankie Frisch during the 1951 season, is fired during spring training in Mesa, Arizona and is replaced by Stan Hack. Owner Phil Wrigley is told by Cavaretta the Cubs had little chance of contending in the upcoming season and he was immediately canned for his defeatist attitude. The Cubs had won their last pennant in 1945 under Charlie Grimm, dropped to third in 1946 and started a long run in the second division in 1947. Cavaretta was only 18 years old when he joined the Cubs in 1934 as a first baseman. He spent 20 years in the organization, the final two and a-half as player-manager, and had a career batting average of .293. A few months after his firing he proved to be a better prophet than his ex-boss – the Cubs finished 64-90 under Hack and ended up in seventh place in 1954. In the meanwhile, Cavaretta went south and played his last two years with the White Sox.

1973 — At the urging of Oakland owner Charlie Finley, orange baseballs are used in an exhibition game with the Indians. Colored baseballs were first used in a regularly scheduled game at Ebbets Field on August 2, 1938 with the Dodgers beating the Cardinals. The balls used were yellow and they were also experimented with in three National League games in 1939. Getting back to orange, Ray Dumont, then-president of the National Baseball Congress (semi-pro) in Wichita used the orange ball in the late 1940s.

March 30

1935 — Bucky Walters broke into the majors with the Boston Braves in 1931 and spent his first four seasons playing third base. The Braves were not too impressed with his ability and sold him to the Phillies in June of 1934. Philadelphia liked his strong arm and began auditioning him as a pitcher. Walters liked the idea but had some of the ambition knocked out of him on this date by the Cincinnati Reds in an exhibition game in Tampa. The first six Reds to face him get on base, two on hits and four on walks. He also sandwiches in a wild pitch. Walters would officially begin his pitching career with Philadelphia a month later and finish the 1935 season with a 9-9 record and a 4.17 ERA. In the middle of the 1938 season the Phillies would trade Walters to Cincinnati for Spud Davis and Al Hollingsworth and $50,000. The Walters experiment was not too successful for the Phillies; Walters in four seasons with Philadelphia had a won-lost mark of 38-53 and an ERA of plus 4.00. However, the Reds liked him as a pitcher and in 1939 he won 27 games for Cincinnati and during the nine and a-half years he would spend with the team win 160 games with three 20-plus-win seasons and pitch in two World Series. Walters won 198 games in the big leagues following that disastrous spring outing in 1935.

March 31

1970 — After only one year in existence the Seattle Pilots move to Milwaukee. The Pilots finished last in the American League West in 1969. In early 1968 a Milwaukee group headed by Bud Selig, an automobile dealer, applied to the National League for an expansion team. San Diego and Montreal were the two teams admitted, but when the Pilots ran aground Selig thought Milwaukee might have a chance. Late in the evening of March 31, Selig received a phone call from the judge handling the bankruptcy case and Milwaukee was awarded the franchise. The reported sale price was $10 million. Suddenly, Milwaukee was back in the American League for the first time since 1901 and the new club immediately assumed the nickname Brewers that the team had carried in 1901.

1961 — The Professional Baseball Rules Committee vote down by 8-1 a proposal by the Pacific Coast League to use a designated batter for the pitcher. This comes 12 years before the American League begins using the DH.

1995 — Federal Judge Sonia Sotomayer agrees with a National Labor Relations Board request and issues an injunction against owners in their contract dispute with the striking players. The injunction restores salary arbitration, free agent bidding and anti-collusion rules. Sotomayer ruled that the owners were guilty of unfair labor practices in implementing new free agency and salary arbitration rules since the players began their strike on August 12, 1994.

"I have no joy in this contract"
— *Romeo and Juliet,* Shakespeare

Bucky Walters

Pee Wee Reese

Chapter Four

"...in the memory of almost every one of us, is there anything that can evoke spring - the first fine days of April - better than the sound of the ball smacking into the pocket of the big mitt, the sound of the bat as it hits the horse hide; for me, at any rate, and I am being liberal and not rhetorical – almost everything I know about spring is in it – the first leaf, jonquil, the maple tree, the smell of grass upon your hands and knees, the coming into flower of April. And is there anything that can tell more about an American summer than, say, the smell of the wooden bleachers in a small town baseball park, that resinous, sultry and exciting smell of old dry wood. I think I may have told you that one reason I have always loved baseball so much is that it has been not merely 'the great national game,' but really a part of the whole weather of our lives, of the thing that is our own, of the whole fabric, the million memories of America."

Thomas Wolfe, expressing his feelings for the game, in a letter to Arthur Mann, the noted baseball author.

April 1

1947 — Players score a victory when they secure the first all-out pension plan. The players first had attempted to form a union in 1885; the second try was in 1901 and with the Federal League on the horizon the third attempt came in 1912. The American Baseball Guild was organized in early 1946 with Robert Murphy at the head. Murphy was a lawyer and former examiner for the National Labor Relations Board. The American Baseball Guild sought to organize players by teams, but not all teams joined. Even though a strike threat by the Pirates was aborted, owners met with player representatives and gave in to a $5,500 minimum salary, expense money and severance pay. This was the end of the Baseball Guild but a company-union policy had been established.

The pension plan was led by shortstop Marty Marion of the St. Louis Cardinals. It was first accepted by four club owners, and they were successful in getting the others to go along. To join the plan, a player had to contribute $250. All players on the opening-day rosters in 1947 were eligible. Players active on the final day of the 1946 season would receive credit for past service if they had paid the $250. The plan enabled players with four or more years major league playing experience to draw a pension beginning at age 45. Although the Guild was slow in making gains, it was the foundation for the fifth and present unionization initially led by Judge Robert Cannon as chief counsel and negotiator. When it was obvious the association needed a stronger leader, pitcher Robin Roberts found him in Marvin Miller. Miller had been an assistant to the president of the United Steelworkers, and on March 5, 1966, he was appointed Executive Director of the Major League Players Association.

1950 — The Hollywood Stars of the Pacific Coast League open the season with a new look – shorts! They were advertised by the Rawlings Professional Baseball Department as "Hollywood styling at its best with hot-weather comfort and weighing only a third as much as regular uniforms." Officials of the Stars said the new look retained perspiration much less, permitted greater freedom of motion in fielding and throwing and gave the athletes more speed. Most of the Dodgers farm clubs would wear the new uniforms during the season whenever the weather permitted.

Baseball shorts were first introduced one year earlier in 1949. The Houston Buffalos of the Texas League, a Cardinal farm, pioneered the style but it didn't last long. The club's home park, Buff Stadium, was surrounded by marshland and there was an abundance of mosquitoes that feasted on the players. The look brought whistles and raspberries from the opposition but was not the first attempt to "style-up" uniforms. In 1937 National League President Ford Frick, answering criticism of the lack of color, type of material, the balloon-tire effect of the pants and the general streamlining of the uniforms, went into action. Frick consulted a fashion academy and asked the students to block out new uniforms on their designing boards. This is what ended up on the cutting-room floor: silk replacing cotton, undershirts disappear and trousers taking on the look of the riding habit. However, in 1945 the Montreal Royals of the International League did come out in silk uniforms of shiny blue and white with purple trimming. The Hollywood Stars wore the shorts sparingly throughout 1950, dropping them completely after the 1953 season. Later, in 1975, another member of the PCL, the Sacramento Solons, wore the shorts-look on opening day, but they were intended for use in mid-summer in Tucson and Phoenix.

1963 — Attention is focused for the first time on the special medical needs of athletes. Because he was a sports fan, Dr. Robert K. Kerlan started spending his free evenings with a friend, an internist named Bob Woods, at Los Angeles' old Wrigley Field, home of the Angels in the Pacific Coast League. They applied for the job of team physicians in return for free tickets to the ball games. When the Dodgers moved to Los Angeles in 1958 the two doctors wrote to general manager Buzzie Bavasi asking to continue in the same capacity with the National League team. The deal finally went through and Bavasi would say later that the signing of Kerlan was one of his most important signings in his eleven years with the Dodgers. Kerlan is quoted as saying, "I remember it was an April Fool's day and they [the Dodgers] were in Florida and I was in Los Angeles and Bavasi called and said, `Koufax's elbow is as big as a cantaloupe.' I said `Yeah, April Fool' and hung up. He called back right away and said `Look, this isn't a joke.' They sent Sandy back here and we made the diagnosis of his arthritic elbow and treated it for several years while he continued to play." Kerlan considers Koufax to have focused attention to the special needs of athletes, explaining: "He had enough stature so that attention was brought to his care." Through the early years, baseball medicine was almost non-existent save the use of ice for charley horses.

April 2

1907 — The Mills Commission, formed in 1904, declares baseball was invented by Abner Doubleday in Cooperstown, New York in 1839. In the 1880s evidence was strong that baseball evolved from the British game of rounders, but it became fashionable and patriotic to proclaim the game was of purely American origin. A.G. Spalding, a former player who later became president of the Chicago National League team and then went on to head the Spalding Sporting Goods empire, was one of the leaders showing his distaste for the rounders theory. With Spalding's guidance, a close friend, Abraham G. Mills, who had been the third president of the National League, formed the Mills Commission to determine the origin of baseball. The report incorporated uncorroborated testimony based solely on the foggy memory of Abner Graves whose only claim to baseball fame was that he at one time lived in Cooperstown. In any case, whatever historical material that had been assembled by the Mills Commission was destroyed in a fire, and when Mills issued the report he was the only person to sign it.

The report concluded that baseball was a purely American sport, not derived from rounders, and had been devised by General Abner Doubleday at Cooperstown in 1839. The Committee declared Doubleday the "George Washington of Baseball." At the time he allegedly invented the game, Doubleday was a "yearling" at West Point; the rules of the academy at that time stated cadets of that category were not allowed off the base. During Double-day's retirement he published his memoirs, *Reminiscences of Forts Sumter and Moultrie in 1860-61*, published in 1876, and six years later he also published *Chancellorsville and Gettysburg*. Nowhere in these memoirs does Doubleday allude to even a casual interest in baseball.

1931 — Virne Beatrice "Jackie" Mitchell strikes out Babe Ruth and Lou Gehrig in succession. Enterprising owner Joe Engel of the Chattanooga Lookouts (Southern Association), with an eye on the gate, signed the 17-year old woman to pitch in an exhibition game against the Yankees. Clyde Barfoot, once a Cardinal and Tiger, started the game for Chattanooga and allowed hits to Earle Combs and Lyn Lary. At this point Mitchell entered the game and promptly produced her two strikeouts, then walked Tony Lazzeri and left the game. Much to Engel's dismay the attraction drew only 3,200 fans. Mitchell would pop up again in 1933 pitching for a local team against the House of David.

1995 — 28 major league owners or their representatives, meet in Chicago and reluctantly agree to let the season begin following the player strike on August 12, 1994. The games would begin under the player-salary rules the owners tried so hard to destroy for almost eight months. Still there is no negotiated peace, only a temporary truce forced by a court injunction.

April 3

1888 — One of the greatest pitchers of his time, John Clarkson, is sold by the Chicago White Stockings to Boston for $10,000. Along with his pitching prowess, Clarkson played outfield, third base and first base when not pitching. He played from 1882 through 1894 winning 326 games and losing only 177 – a win percentage of .648 with a 12-year earned run average of 2.81. Clarkson was inducted into the Hall of Fame in 1963.

1966 — University of Southern California pitching star Tom Seaver, who was selected in a special drawing, signs his first pro contract with the New York Mets (Triple-A Jacksonville) for a bonus of $51,000. Seaver was selected by Atlanta in the January 1966 draft, the 20th pick in the secondary phase. He was signed by the Braves in February for $40,000. However, because USC had already begun its intercollegiate schedule, his signing constituted a violation of the college rule. The contract was nullified by Commissioner William Eckert. Atlanta was fined $500 and Eckert ruled the organization couldn't sign Seaver for a period of three years.

Although Seaver did not receive any payments from the Braves, he was declared ineligible by the NCAA for signing a professional contract. Because of this situation, a special draft was set up for Seaver. Only organizations willing to match the terms of the original Atlanta contract were eligible to participate. Cleveland, Philadelphia and the Mets were the only clubs involved in the special drawing. Seaver would be elected to the Hall of Fame in 1992. Needing 323 votes to qualify, Seaver received 425 of the 430 votes for 98.84% of the votes cast – making him the all-time leader in Hall of Fame history in percentage of votes received. He pitched for 20 years with the Mets, the Reds, White Sox and Red Sox and won 311 games while losing 205 for a win percentage of .603. He won three Cy Young Awards, all with the New York Mets. Seaver (41) wound up his career with Boston in 1986 with 3,640 strikeouts, an ERA of 2.86 and was elected to the Hall in his first year of eligibility.

April 4

1911 — The Most Valuable Player Award is introduced by automobile manufacturer Hugh Chalmers. The winners will be determined by a vote of one baseball writer from each league city. Ty Cobb of Detroit and Frank Schulte of the Cubs would be the first winners. Their prize was a new Chalmers auto. This award would last through the 1914 season. Beginning in 1922 in the American League and 1924 in the National, the league awards were administered by each league and were determined by a vote of one writer from each city. These awards were discontinued after the 1928 season in the American League and 1929 in the National. The MVP Award, as we know it today, traces its origin to 1931, when the Baseball Writers' Association of America began polling its membership annually. Lefty Grove of the Athletics and Frankie Frisch of the Cardinals were the recipients in 1931.

1918 — World War I causes problems in the minor leagues. The International League, along with severe cuts in funding, undergoes a change in franchises to keep the circuit in operation. The International would be the only minor league to play a full schedule in 1918. The reduction in spending helps cause the resignation of league president Ed Barrow, leading to his appointment as manager of the Red Sox and a world championship in the first of his three seasons with Boston. It was during the 1919 season that he informed Babe Ruth he would be an outfielder. This was not the first managing position for Barrow; he managed Detroit in 1903-04. Barrow would join the Yankees as business manager in late 1920. Until he retired as president in 1945 he would direct New York to 14 pennants and ten World Series. During his tenure with the Yankees, and with the country in a depression, he created a countrywide sensation by signing Ruth to an $80,000 a year contract. Later he would quip, "and to think I signed him for $7,500 in 1918 with the Red Sox." His extraordinary career led to his election to the Hall of Fame by the Committee of Veterans in 1953.

1937 — Outfielder Al Simmons is sold by Detroit to Washington for $15,000. Simmons was coming off a 1936 season in which he hit .327 and batted in 112 runs. A few days prior to his sale, the outfielder and manager Mickey Cochrane allegedly had words in front of their spring training hotel. Cochrane later told a friend that Simmons would not be with the club for long. Two days later Simmons was on his way to Washington. With the Senators in 1937 he would hit .279, only the second time in his 14 seasons he batted under .300. He would bounce back with .303 in 1938 and finish his career (20 years) with a .334 average. Simmons (7) entered the Hall of Fame in 1953.

April 5

1925 — Babe Ruth collapses in a railroad station in Asheville, North Carolina. Following his traditional pre-spring stay in Hot Springs, Ruth reported to camp in St.Petersburg with what was said to be a cold, flu or pneumonia and running a temperature. Through all of this, Ruth had a great spring on the field. Despite being ill, he could not give up his overeating, late hours, booze, and women as the Yankees moved through the south playing their exhibition schedule. Because of his lifestyle his collapse was not unexpected. When a writer labeled the Babe's illness "the bellyache heard round the world," the public mostly forgot his sickness and earlier groin injury. Ruth was rushed to St. Vincent Hospital in New York, and on April 17 he was operated on for an intestinal abscess. On June 1 he made his first start of the season.

1974 — Former New York Giants outfielder Fred Snodgrass dies. Snodgrass was by no means a well-known player. While not a Hall-of-Famer, Snodgrass played in the big leagues from 1908 through 1916, playing in three World Series with the Giants in 1911, 1912 and 1913. This leads to his recognition here. On October 16, 1912, the Giants and Red Sox were tied at three wins each in the World Series going into game eight (game two had ended in a 6-6 tie called because of darkness at the end of eleven innings). New York had taken a 2-1 lead in the top of the tenth, but Boston pinch hitter Clyde Engel led off the bottom of the tenth by lofting a high fly to centerfield. Snodgrass settled under the ball and, amazingly, dropped it. This was the beginning of the two runs the Red Sox would score to win the series. Snodgrass' misplay was dubbed by the press as the "$30,000 muff." That figure having been arrived at because it was the total dollar value that the Giants lost by losing the series; player shares that season were $4,025 for Boston and $2,566 for New York.

When Snodgrass died on this date in 1974 *The New York Times* printed his obituary. The headline on the obituary read: "Fred Snodgrass, 86, Dead, Ballplayer Muffed 1912 Fly." The account began: "Fred Snodgrass, who muffed an easy fly that helped cost the New York Giants the 1912 World Series, died Friday at the age of eighty-six." Note that the deed took place 62 years before his death and the obituary doesn't let Snodgrass off with a simple, unmodified "fly", it had to be an "easy" fly. Just for the record, after retiring from baseball, Snodgrass became the mayor of Oxnard, California and was a successful banker and rancher.

April 6

1929 — The Cleveland Indians appear with numbers on the back of their uniforms to become the first major league team to do so. Numbers would be assigned to correspond roughly to the players' positions in the batting order. The New York Yankees were the first to announce the plan on January 22, and a few weeks later the Indians followed suit (Thirteen years earlier, in 1916, Cleveland began numbering uniform sleeves; the practice never caught on because the numerals were not easily visible from the stands). Incidentally, had the St. Louis Cardinals held to their plan announced in 1923, they would have beaten both Cleveland and the Yankees by six years. For some unknown reason they abandoned their numbering plan. Both New York and the Indians were scheduled to open the 1929 season on April 6, but the Yankees were rained out of their first two games while Cleveland opened on schedule. On May 13,1929 the Indians and Yankees play in League Park in Cleveland in the first game ever with both teams wearing numbered uniforms. In 1931 the American League made numbers mandatory and the National League fell in line in 1933.

1973 — The Designated Hitter rule is put into play for the first time in the majors when Ron Blomberg of the New York Yankees is walked with the bases loaded in the first inning. Blomberg, walked by pitcher Luis Tiant of the Red Sox, finishes the game with one hit in three at-bats; Boston wins the game 15-5. The American League had voted to use the DH on an experimental basis on January 11th. It had been used previously in the minor leagues in 1969. The International League had used the same version adopted by the American League but the New York-Penn League, also in 1969, adopted a rule that allowed a "hitting specialist" to be used twice during a game, but never twice in the same inning. The hitting specialist could bat for any player and that player was allowed to remain in the game.

One of the most interesting aspects of the American League's adoption, and the National League's insistence on shying away from the rule, is that the National first proposed it back in 1929. At that time it was called the "tenth regular" and was suggested by then President John Heydler. At that time the American League was the dominant circuit and was not interested in the rule change. Before Commissioner Landis could break the tie along league lines Heydler withdrew his plan.

1977 — Seattle, back in the American League after a seven-year absence, opens the Kingdome losing 7-0 to the California Angels. The Seattle Pilots played only one season at Sicks Stadium, a minor league park, before the franchise filed for bankruptcy and was purchased by Milwaukee interests. The Kingdome would be the new home of the expansion Seattle Mariners until July 15, 1999 when the Mariners moved into their new park. The Kingdome would meet its doom on April 2, 2000 when it was demolished by implosion in 16.8 seconds to make room for the Seahawks open-air football stadium.

April 7

1931 — Seals Stadium is opened in San Francisco. Headed by Charles H. Graham, it was built by a triumvirate that owned the Seals of the Pacific Coast League. The park was located at 16th and Bryant streets on the site of an old mine. The original deed listed the name of the land as Home Plate Mine. Later the Seals would share the stadium briefly with the San Francisco Missions (PCL) before the Missions moved to Recreation Park. The San Francisco Giants would open their National League play against Los Angeles in Seals Stadium on April 15, 1958 before 21,192 — a rather sparse crowd for a major league game. Nonetheless, it was the debut of San Francisco in the majors, and a continuation of the Brooklyn-New York rivalry that had existed for years in the East. After only two seasons playing in Seals Stadium, the Giants would open Candlestick Park before a crowd of 42,269 on April 12, 1960 as Sam Jones pitches a 3-hitter to knock off St. Louis 3-1. Forty years later – following the 1999 season – the end would gratefully come for Candlestick, the windiest, coldest and most hated baseball stadium in the history of the game. The new downtown San Francisco home would open in 2000.

1970 — Major league baseball returns to Milwaukee following an absence of four years. The franchise is acquired only one week earlier for $10.3 million, on April 1, as the result of the 1969 Pilots going bankrupt following their only season in Seattle. Milwaukee becomes a member of the American League and the team is known as the Brewers – their historic minor league nickname.

1975 — The Astros break out their new uniforms on opening day and instantly become the talk of the National League. Deciding a new image was needed, following a disastrous 1974 season, management commissioned an advertising firm to come up with a new design. The new Houston concept was a bright burst of colors – burnt orange, yellow and red – that would come to be known as the "rainbow uniforms" to be worn both at home and on the road. The "rainbows" were dropped following the 1986 season.

1977 — The expansion Blue Jays begin their American League history with a 9-5 victory over the White Sox in Toronto's Exposition Stadium. The game was played with light-continuous snow falling, and the field was cleared of snow occasionally by a Zamboni machine borrowed from Maple Leaf Gardens. Exposition Park was built in 1959 as a football stadium and was modified to accommodate baseball. After 12 seasons playing in Exposition Stadium, the Blue Jays moved into the SkyDome on June 5, 1989 – an elegant new ballpark with a retractable roof, a hotel and other amenities.

1988 — Workers begin installing lights at venerable Wrigley Field. A helicopter arrived at 8 a.m., and began the first of two-dozen short trips alongside the left field wall, pulling white steel girders to a crew of workmen on the upper-deck roof. Cars stopped, pedestrians gawked, and more than one neighbor ran back to grab a camera. The Chicago City Council voted in March to pave the way for the first lights in the stadium; Wrigley Field first opened in 1914.

April 8

1876 — After four years in the National Association with the Athletics, Adrian Constantine Anson joins the Chicago White Stockings of the National League. Three years later (1879) he would become manager and begin a string of 19 years as skipper of the club, leading the team to five pennants and a record of 1,297 wins and 957 defeats – a win percentage of .575. The first baseman's playing career from 1871-1897 saw him compile a career batting average of .334, .329 or .339 with a total of 3,278, 3,415 or 3,518 hits depending upon which record book you believe. In his final year in baseball he played little, and briefly managed the New York Giants. Cap (he was also known as "Pop") was voted into the Hall of Fame in 1939.

1942 — A pitching summary is added to a box score for the first time when *The Los Angeles Times* adds: IP H R ER BB SO. This comes 97 years after the first box score was published in 1845 in the *New York Herald.* The retired sports editor of the *Times*, Paul B. Zimmerman, said, in reflecting back on the move, "It just seemed to us that the box score didn't take care of the most important guy on the team." *The Sporting News* almost immediately adopted the *Times'* brainchild but the wire services didn't add the pitching box until 1958. Since that time it also includes won-lost records, save totals and, to most average fans, too many items.

1974 — Hank Aaron breaks Babe Ruth's career homerun record at Atlanta Stadium by hitting number 715 in the fourth inning off lefthander Al Downing of the Dodgers. Atlanta relief pitcher Tom House catches the ball in the Braves bullpen in left field. Aaron would finish his career with 755 homeruns, the final 22 of which were hit in the American League with the Milwaukee Brewers.

April 9

1907 — A patent is issued to Wellington Stockton Titus for a portable baseball back stop. Titus was a well-to-do civil engineer, house builder, house and building mover, and a handyman who had dabbled in inventions of various types. He also had more than passing interest in baseball. Obviously tired of chasing errant baseballs while playing catch and during batting practice, Titus sent a series of drawings to the United States Patent Office on December 20, 1906 and was granted the patent on this date. From Little League parks to the major leagues you can see the modern version of the portable batting cage invented some ninety years ago.

1913 — Ebbets Field is officially opened in Brooklyn, during the most well known era in Dodgers history. Baseball in Brooklyn goes back to 1871; the team played in ballparks called Union Grounds, Capitoline Grounds, Ridgewood Park and Washington Park through 1913. In 1890 the team moved from the American Association, where they had just won the 1889 championship, to the National League. The team had so many newlyweds on the roster they were known as the Bridegrooms. However, the club became known as the Trolley Dodgers because of the maze of streetcar tracks and railroad lines in the borough. The name was later shortened to Dodgers.

During the managerial tenure of Ned Hanlon (1899-1905) it was changed to Superbas, and in Wilbert Robinson's reign as manager (1914-1931) the team was often referred to as the Robins. Prior to the move to Ebbets Field the Brooklyn club had made their home for 22 years at Washington Park in the East New York section near Jamaica Bay. Ebbets Field was officially opened on April 9, 1913 before a crowd of 10,000 in the 18,000-capacity stadium that cost $750,000 to construct. The Dodgers lose to the Phillies 1-0 as Philadelphia's Tom Seaton posts the first of his 27 wins in out-dueling Brooklyn's Nap Rucker. It was 419 feet to left field and only 301 to right. Dodger officials were somewhat embarrassed when they discovered — missing or forgotten at the stadium – a flag, a press box, and the keys to the bleachers.

1993 — The expansion Colorado Rockies play their first game at Mile High Stadium in Denver, defeating Montreal 11-4 before a National League regular season record crowd of 80,227. Mile High was built in 1948 as the original home of the Denver Bears of the Class-A Western League. The city remained in the high minors until finally granted an expansion franchise in 1993, after being passed over for years while San Diego, Montreal, Seattle and Kansas City entered the major leagues. Denver proved how wrong the baseball heads had been with record setting attendance in the minor league park in 1993 and 1994. All of that continued beginning April 26, 1995 when the Rockies moved into their new and smaller home, Coors Field. Following the removal of five inches of snow from the playing surface, 47,228 fans settled in to watch what turned out to be the first of many sellouts.

April 10

1947 — The Brooklyn Dodgers quietly announce the purchase of Jackie Robinson from Montreal of the International League. When first signed by the Brooklyn organization prior to the 1946 season, Robinson was given a $3,500 bonus and a salary of $600 a month with the Royals. Robinson hit .349 in his only season in the minors, hitting three homeruns with 66 RBI. He tied for the league lead in runs scored with 113 and led the International League in fielding percentage playing second base.

1961 — For the first time in 60 years two cities are given new major league franchises. The new Washington Senators replace the old Washington Senators who moved to Minneapolis-St. Paul to become the Minnesota Twins. The new Senators open their season in what would be the final year for Griffith Stadium –

opened in 1911 and demolished in 1965. On April 9, 1962 the new Senators move into D.C. Stadium and play before 42,143 fans. The name of the stadium would be changed to RFK Stadium (Robert F. Kennedy Memorial Stadium) in 1968. Washington, D.C. would lose its second major league franchise in the last eleven years when the team is moved to Texas in 1972.

1962 — The expansion Houston Colt .45s play their first game in Colt Stadium, an auxiliary facility built in only nine months. Houston opens National League play with an 11-2 win over the Cubs before 25,271 fans in the roofless sunshine-splashed park. The Colt .45s would play only three seasons in this stadium and move into the Astrodome in 1965 with a new name – Astros. The Astrodome opened on the weekend of April 9 with a series of five exhibition games featuring the New York Yankees and Baltimore. The gala opening is attended by president Lyndon Johnson along with press representatives from around the world. The Astros officially begin the 1965 National League season on April 12, before a total crowd of 48,846, with a 2-0 loss to Philadelphia. Chris Short pitches a 4-hitter and Richie Allen hits a two-run homer off Bob Bruce.

1973 — With the temperature in the high 30s, Kansas City opens its new park, Royals Stadium, with a 12 to 1 walloping of the Texas Rangers before 39,464 fans. The expansion Royals had opened play on April 8, 1969 in old Municipal Stadium, also the old home of the Kansas City Athletics for 13 years, and a well-known baseball landmark at 22nd Street and Euclid Avenue since 1923. The old park had also housed the Negro Kansas City Monarchs and the Kansas City Blues, the top minor league team of the New York Yankees.

April 11

1907 — Roger Bresnahan of the New York Giants becomes the first player to wear shin guards. Bresnahan, who had become a bit annoyed over spikings by home-coming runners and also wearied by suffering occasional bumps on his knees from foul balls, designed the guards for his shins which were almost identical to those used today. Wearing the guards would become common practice by 1910. It is interesting to note that one year earlier, in 1906, Red Dooin of the Phillies wore leg guards made of papier-mâché under his stockings while catching. As a result of Bresnahan's use of the guards, Pittsburgh manager Fred Clarke filed a protest with the National League over their use, but on May 21 league president Henry Pulliam dismissed the protest.

Bresnahan made his major league debut with Washington in 1897 as a pitcher but pitched in only four games in his 17-year major league career before taking up catching almost exclusively. Before he retired he would become one of the few players in major league history to play all nine positions. He had his best years with the New York Giants (1902-1908) under John McGraw while serving as batterymate for Christy Mathewson during Mathewson's greatest seasons on the mound. In December 1908, when the Cardinals were looking for a manager, McGraw traded Bresnahan to St. Louis for Bugs Raymond, Red Murray and Admiral Schlei so Bresnahan could assume the managerial position the following year. He would manage the Cardinals for four years and finish his final three seasons in the big leagues with the Cubs – becoming Chicago's player-manager his last year in 1915. Bresnahan was elected to the Hall of Fame in 1945.

1912 — Cincinnati opens its new ballpark, Redland Field, as the Reds beat the Cubs 10-6 before 26,336 fans. The Cincinnati baseball club had played its games on this site at Findlay and Western since 1884 and the new park was the fourth at this location. The previous stadium had burned down in the fall of 1911. That park had opened in 1902 and was referred to by sports writers as "The Palace of the Fans" because of its ornate pillars and columns, a style borrowed from the World's Fair of 1892. Waiters roamed "rooters row", along the first and third base lines, selling beers, 12 for $1.

Redland Field would be renamed Crosley Field in 1934 when Powell Crosley, Jr. bought control of the club. Six days after the final game at Crosley Field (June 30, 1970), 51,050 fans are on hand to help dedicate Cincinnati's new Riverfront Stadium located downtown near the Ohio River. Home plate had been removed from the old park and was in place when Reds pitcher Lynn McGlothlin served up the first pitch to Atlanta. The Braves would win 8-2.

—

In a Class-AA American Association game between Columbus and Kansas City there were a total of 28 hits and 15 runs, yet only one baseball was used in the entire game.

1932 — Outfielder Chick Hafey is traded by the St. Louis Cardinals to Cincinnati for Harvey Hendrick, Benny Fry and cash. Hafey had spent his first eight years in St. Louis and participated in four World Series with the Cardinals. Even though his play with St. Louis was outstanding, he was dispatched to the Reds because of his displeasure with his contracts over the past few seasons. Hafey made $9,000 in 1930 and asked for $15,000 in 1931. After all, he had hit .337 with 27 homeruns, 111 RBI in 1928; hit .338 with 29 homers, 125 RBI in 1929 and .336 with 26 homeruns and 107 RBI in 1930.

After considerable haggling, he signed for the 1931 season for $12,500 with the understanding that because he had missed much of spring training, the contract would not take effect until he was in shape to play. St. Louis then docked him $2,100 of the $12,500 and Hafey played the 1931 season for $10,400. Despite this disappointment, Hafey won the batting championship with a .3489 mark, edging out Bill Terry who hit .3486 and Jim Bottomley who finished with .3482. For the 1932 season Hafey asked the Cardinals for $17,000. This included the $2,100 the team had deducted the spring before, but Branch Rickey offered Hafey a raise of $500 to $13,000. The now-bespectacled Hafey (he began wearing glasses in 1931) bolted the team and went home to California. On opening day he was notified he had been traded to Cincinnati, a last place club that paid him $15,000. He would play his final five years with the Reds and retire following the 1937 season with a career batting average of .317. Hafey (4) was voted into the Hall of Fame in 1971.

1954 — Just before opening day in a trade that brought down the wrath of St. Louis fans, 38-year old Enos Slaughter is traded by the Cardinals to the New York Yankees. Slaughter is moved to make room for 24-year old Wally Moon. In return, St. Louis receives Bill Virdon, Mel Wright and Emil Tellinger. Slaughter played with the Yankees and Kansas City until he was 43. He saw action in two World Series with St. Louis and three with New York; he retired in 1959 with a career .300 average over 20 seasons. Slaughter (9) was elected to the Hall of Fame in 1985.

1969 — Sicks Stadium, originally opened in 1938 as the home of the Seattle Rainers of the Pacific Coast League, becomes a major league park as the Seattle Pilots play their first game in the American League. Gary Bell shuts out the White Sox 7 to 0 before a small crowd of only 14,993. Seattle's first stay in the majors would last only one year as the Pilots draw 678,000 for the season.

1994 — The Texas Rangers unveil their new home, The Ball Park in Arlington, with a 4-3 loss to the Milwaukee Brewers before a crowd of 46,056. The new park combined a blend of old-fashioned design with modern luxury — a short right field and tight foul lines. The new facility stands next to the site of old Turnpike Stadium where the Rangers made their first appearance. The name of that ballpark was changed to Arlington Stadium when the Rangers moved in to begin their major league tenure on April 21, 1972. The park was originally opened in 1965 to house the Dallas-Ft. Worth minor league teams.

April 12

1909 — The Philadelphia Athletics open their new home, Shibe Park, at 21st Street and Lehigh Avenue before a crowd of 31,160. The stadium was named for Ben Shibe, the largest A's stockholder and baseball manufacturer, and was opened exactly one year and one day after the ground breaking ceremony in 1908. Shibe Park cost some $500,000 to build. Eddie Plank threw the first pitch and led Philadelphia to an 8-1 win over losing pitcher Frank Arellanes and the Boston Red Sox. The playing field was gigantic: 360 to left, 515 to center and 360 to right. Later in the season the right field fence was shortened to 340 and the left field distance was lengthened to 378. Shibe Park replaced old Columbia Park which was located in the Brewerytown section of Philadelphia. The Shibe Park Ball Grounds, as it was originally called, resembled a church at the home plate entrance and, ironically, is now the site of the Deliverance Evangelistic Church.

1912 — The Chicago Cubs infield combination of Joe Tinker, Johnny Evers, and Frank Chance ends after a run of eleven years. This combination began in 1902 but for all intents and purposes ended following the 1908 season. It was after that year that Chance, the Cubs manager, reduced his playing time at first base and never again played in more than 92 games in a season. On this date Chance turned over the starting job at first base to Vic Saier. However, the stellar play of SS Tinker and 2B Evers would continue together through 1912. "Tinker to Evers to Chance" was immortalized in a poem published in the *New York Daily Mail* in July 1910 written by a diehard New York Giants fan, newspaperman and poet Franklin P. Adams:

> These are the saddest of possible words,
> *Tinker to Evers to Chance.*
> Trio of Bear Cubs fleeter than birds,
> *Tinker to Evers to Chance.*
> Ruthlessly pricking our gonfalon bubble,
> *Making a Giant hit into a double,*
> Words that are weighty with
> *Nothing but trouble,*
> Tinker to Evers to Chance.

This poem exaggerates the double play. By today's standards this trio did not complete an impressive number of double plays, even though their dexterity around second base was exceptional. Only in 1912 did the SS-2B duo complete the most twin killings in the major leagues – Evers (71) and Tinker (73). At the plate, their career averages were Chance .297, Evers .270 and Tinker .263. All three would manage in the majors. Chance for eleven years (Cubs-8, Yankees-2, Red Sox-1), Tinker for two years (Cincinnati-1, Cubs-1, plus two years for Chicago in the Federal League), and Evers for three years (Cubs-2, White Sox-1). Fittingly, the three entered the Hall of Fame together in 1946.

1922 — The National League season opens without a playing manager for the first time since 1900. It won't be until 1930 that the American League has all bench managers. Player-managers would surface again in the NL in 1924, 1928 and 1929. For the next five years (1931-1935) 30 teams in the majors used player-managers. The number gradually declined and by 1941 only Joe Cronin with the Red Sox and Leo Durocher with Brooklyn served in that capacity. Prior to Pete Rose's return to play and manage Cincinnati in 1984, the majors had not had a manager who played regularly since Cleveland's Lou Boudreau in 1950. Going back to the mid-50's before Rose re-joined the Reds, here are the only player-managers and the number of games they played – 1955 — Harry Walker, Cardinals (11), 1959 – Solly Hemus, Cardinals (24), 1961 — Hank Bauer, Kansas City (43), 1975-76 – Frank Robinson, Cleveland (49-36), 1977 — Joe Torre, Mets (26) and Don Kessinger, White Sox (56).

1955 — Chuck Tanner hits the first pitch served to him in the major leagues, an 8th inning pinch-homer, for Milwaukee to give the Braves a 4-3 win over Cincinnati. Tanner becomes the sixth major leaguer in history to homer on the first pitch. It was the first of six he would hit in his rookie year and the first of 21 home runs in eight big league seasons. Tanner is best remembered as a major league manager for 18 years with the White Sox, Oakland, Pittsburgh and Atlanta. —

In their first game as the Kansas City Athletics, the transferred Philadelphia club of the American League defeats the Detroit Tigers at Kansas City's Municipal Stadium 6-2. The first homerun is hit by the Tigers' Bob Wilson off Alex Kellner. Opened in 1923, this ballpark was an expanded minor league stadium at Euclid Avenue and 22nd Street. It was originally named Muehlebach Field, then Ruppert Stadium (1938), Blues Stadium (1943) and finally Municipal Stadium (1955). It would be the home of the Athletics until the franchise was moved to Oakland in 1968 and also served as the first park of the expansion Kansas City Royals from 1969 through 1972.

1966 — 50,671 fans welcome the transferred Braves to Atlanta and watch a 13-

inning Pittsburgh 3-2 victory. Willie Stargell's 2-run homerun would clinch the win. The first homerun hit in the National League park – Atlanta Fulton County Stadium — was hit earlier in the game by the Braves' Joe Torre off Bob Veale. This would be the Braves' third home since the turn of the century; first in Boston, then 13 years in Milwaukee before moving to Atlanta.

April 13

1962 — Baseball returns to the Polo Grounds for the first time since 1957 as the expansion New York Mets reopen the ballpark, spruced up to the tune of $350,000, for the return of the National League to New York. Only 12,447 show up as the Pirates whip the Mets 4-3. On April 17, 1964, after abandoning the Polo Grounds, the Mets opened in new Shea Stadium with another loss.

1972 — The first players' strike in baseball history ends with the season set to start in two days. 86 scheduled games were canceled and players' paychecks would be lightened for games missed. Only a one-year contract is signed.

April 14

1905 — The Boston Beaneaters open the season at the Polo Grounds before 40,000 and lose to the Giants 10-1. The losing pitcher is Irvin (Kaiser) Wilhelm who would go on to a season record of 3-23. When the season ended he had company with three teammates also losing 20 or more games – Irv Young (20-21), Vic Fraser (14-21) and Vic Willis (12-29). This amounted to a 51-103 seventh place finish for Boston two games ahead of last place Brooklyn with 48-104. The biggest loser for the Beaneaters was Vic Willis who would go on to pitch 13 years with Boston, Pittsburgh and St. Louis finishing with a career mark of 247-206 and a 2.63 ERA. Willis completed 388 of his 471 starts, winning 20 or more games eight times with 50 shutouts. In 1995 Willis would be voted into the Hall of Fame by the Veterans committee.

1910 — William Howard Taft becomes the first president to throw out the first ball on opening day, establishing what was to become one of baseball's most hallowed traditions. This was not a promotional coup. Taft was a true baseball aficionado who kept up with standings and statistics and often attended games unnoticed. On this day, in his second year in office, he decided to attend opening day and when someone suggested he throw out the first ball, the tradition was started. The president was almost upstaged as Washington's Walter Johnson was deprived of a no-hitter on a fluke hit by Philadelphia's Frank "Home Run" Baker that dropped into the overflow crowd for a ground rule double.

1936 — Rookie outfielder-first baseman Eddie Morgan is used as a pinch-hitter for the St. Louis Cardinals and hits the first pitch thrown to him in the major leagues for a homerun. This is only the second time in the history of the game that a player homered on his first pitch – Brooklyn pitcher Clise Dudley was the first on April 27, 1929. Morgan would have only 17 more at-bats with St. Louis and play in only 31 games with Brooklyn in 1937. In those two seasons he would never again hit a homerun.

1953 — County Stadium is opened for major league play as Milwaukee returns to the big leagues for the first time since 1901 – this time in the National League. The Braves move to Milwaukee from Boston in the first franchise shift in baseball since 1903 when Baltimore moved to New York to eventually become the Yankees. Milwaukee was a charter member of the American League in 1901, but in 1902 the franchise was moved to St. Louis and became the Browns.

1964 — Duke Snider is sold for the second time in just over a year as the New York Mets complete his sale to San Francisco. The Mets had purchased his contract in April of 1963 from the Dodgers with whom he had spent the first 16 years of his 18-year major league career. In 1964 he would appear in only 91 games with the Giants, hit the final four of his 407 career homeruns and hit only .210. Snider (4) finished with a batting average of .295 and was voted into the Hall of Fame in 1980.

1967 — Billy Rohr, making his major league debut for the Red Sox in Yankee Stadium, holds New York hitless until two out in the ninth inning. After working the count full, Elston Howard lines a single to right-center, but the rookie holds on for a 3-0 win over Whitey Ford. The victory for Rohr would be the first of only three games he would win in his major league career.

1969 — Major league baseball comes to Canada for the first time as the expansion Montreal Expos defeat the St. Louis Cardinals 8-7. Montreal's first major league home is Jarry Park located on city park land with the ball field renovated from an amateur recreational facility. The temporary stadium holds 28,000. After eight seasons in the roofless temporary park the Expos move into their new home, Olympic Stadium, on April 15, 1977. 57,592 fans see the Phillies win the opener 7-2. It also marks the beginning of a multitude of stadium and attendance problems for years to come.

April 15

1915 — New York Giant pitcher and future Hall-of-Famer, Rube Marquard, throws a no-hitter against the Brooklyn Dodgers in the Polo Grounds for a 2-0 victory. Marquard was coming off a 22-loss year in 1914 and during the off-season had accepted $15,000 from the Brooklyn Tip Tops to jump to the Federal League. Following a change of mind and the return of the money, he faced the Dodgers in his first start of the season knowing full well his tenure with the Giants hung in the balance. Marquard allowed only three base runners but went on to a mediocre season with the Giants and was sold to the Dodgers on August 31.

1947 — Jackie Robinson makes his major league debut with Brooklyn playing first base. In his first game he goes 0 for 3 at the plate but scores the deciding run in a 5-3 win over the Boston Braves. Although this was one of the most significant events in baseball history, it was not treated as such. Only two major columnists of the eight New York papers, plus Brooklyn and Long Island dailies, attended the game and wrote of the historic event. One just mentioned Robinson's name and the other did not make too much of the event. In game coverage in the *New York Herald-Tribune* Robinson's name did not appear until the fifth paragraph. *The Sporting News*, summing up the 1947 year-in-review, gave the story only one line on page five. Attendance was only 25,000 in a park that seated 34,000.

1954 — Before 46,354 fans, the Baltimore Orioles play their opening game at Memorial Stadium following their move from St. Louis. On April 6, 1992 Baltimore would beat the Cleveland Indians in the opening game at Oriole Park in Camden Yards. The new stadium came up with a glimpse of yesteryear with the asymmetrical field, natural grass, the old archways, with the historic Baltimore and Ohio warehouse rising behind right field. The Orioles would squeeze out a 2-0 win over Cleveland in their dream park that would begin a frenzy to build new stadiums in the majors.

1994 — Lefthander Kelly Wunsch strikes out five batters in one inning while pitching for Class-A Beloit in the Midwest League against Springfield. Wunsch, a Milwaukee farm hand, becomes the first starting pitcher in professional baseball history to turn the trick. Helped by his inability to control his curve ball, Wunsch had two third-strike wild pitches to keep the inning alive. This incident earned the 22-year-old pitcher a temporary exhibit in the Hall of Fame museum. Officials requested his cap, an autographed baseball and his photo that would be on display for the next three years. However, lack of control on Wunsch's curve ball eventually led to his demotion to Rookie level Helena of the Pioneer League. He would spend the next three seasons in the lower minors and the next two in AA and AAA. His big break came in March of 2000 when he signed as a six year free agent with the White Sox Triple-A team in Charlotte. Wunsch was moved up the Sox at the start of the major league season and became a force in the bullpen during Chicago's surprising season.

2000 — Cal Ripken adds another big number to his Hall of Fame resume with the 3,000th hit of his major league career. He had already singled twice to set up the big one for the seventh inning when he became the 24th hitter to reach the 3,000 mark with a single up the middle off Hector Carrasco. The Metrodome in Minneapolis has been the site of the most 3,000 hits in baseball – Dave Winfield in 1993 and Eddie Murray in 1995.

April 16

1895 – The nickname "Tigers" first appears in a headline in a Detroit newspaper. First credited to Phillip J. Reid, city editor of the *Detroit Evening News* in 1896, research later revealed it was used first on this date by an unknown headline writer over the game story and a notes column in the *Free Press*. In early Detroit baseball history the team was simply called "Detroit", "the Detroits," and sometimes the "Wolverines" or "Creams".

1938 — Dizzy Dean is traded to the Chicago Cubs by the St. Louis Cardinals for Curt Davis, Clyde Shoun, Tuck Stainback, and $185,000. In 1938, Dean would win seven and lose only one with an ERA of 1.87, helping the Cubs win the pennant. In the next two seasons he was 9-7 and appeared in only one game in 1941. Aside from a token appearance in 1947 with the St. Louis Browns his career was over. Dean played 12 years in the majors with a winning percentage of .644 (150-83) and an earned run average of 3.03. His 150 wins are the fewest of any starting pitcher in the Hall of Fame. Dean (17) entered the hall in 1953.

1940 — In 46-degree weather Bob Feller pitches the first opening day no-hitter in history. Feller knocks off the Chicago White Sox 1-0 at Comiskey Park. Rollie Hemsley drives in the only run with a triple in the fourth inning and Edgar Smith is the losing pitcher. Feller had to face Luke Appling in the ninth inning, and he was concerned that Appling might go into his "foul ball" routine which Feller knew would not be conducive to helping a tiring hard thrower. After working the count to 2-2, Appling does go into his act and continually fouls off pitches until he draws a walk. Feller would later state the walk he gave to Appling was intentional although no one knew it at the time. Taft Wright would ground out and Feller had his no-hitter. In 1909 Red Ames of the New York Giants almost beat Feller to the "first" when he held Brooklyn hitless for nine innings on opening day, but he gave up a hit in the 10th and lost the game in the 13th.

1946 — The Boston Braves open the season but find that freshly applied paint in some sections of the grandstand had not dried and at least 5,000 fans left the ballpark with soiled clothing. The next day this ad appeared in the Boston papers:

> **AN APOLOGY TO BRAVES FANS**
>
> The Braves management regrets the inconvenience to its patrons who sustained damage to their clothing at Tuesday's opening game due to recently applied paint in certain sections of the grandstand.
>
> The management will reimburse any of its patrons for any expense to which they may be put for necessary cleaning of clothing as a result of paint damage.
>
> For today's game the management assures its patrons that no section of the grandstand will be open for public sale where there is the slightest possibility of any similar damage occurring.
>
> **BOSTON BRAVES**
>
> JOHN QUINN, *General Manager*

Some 330 fans had appeared at the club's offices following the game, exhibiting paint-smeared clothing, but following the publication of the ads, more than 13,000 claims were filed. The Braves not only received local claims but some from California, Florida and Nebraska, necessitating the opening of a "Paint Account" at a Boston bank. Eventually, some 5,000 claims were honored ranging from $1.50 to $50, costing the club $6,000; it was money well spent because of the goodwill and free advertising it generated.

1978 — St. Louis fans see their first no-hitter since 1953 as Bob Forsch no-hits the Philadelphia Phillies 5-0. There were no difficult chances for Cardinals fielders behind Forsch, although an error call on Ken Reitz in the eighth inning on a ground ball hit by Garry Maddox aroused the ire of the Phillies. The last no-hitter in St. Louis was pitched in 1953 by the Browns' Bobo Holloman, and the last

Cardinal pitcher to throw one in St. Louis was Jesse Haines in 1924.

April 17

1968 — Owner Charlie Finley finally completes his move from Kansas City and opens with his Athletics in their new home in the Oakland-Alameda County Coliseum. Boog Powell leads Baltimore to a 4-1 Orioles victory with the first homerun hit in the new stadium off Lew Krausse.

1969 — The Montreal Expos, less than two weeks old as an expansion team in the National League, produce their first no-hitter. Bill Stoneman throws only the second complete game of his career and pitches his first win as a starter, baffling the Phillies 7-0 before a sparse crowd of 6,494 fans at Connie Mack Stadium. This would be the final no-hitter of nine pitched in the stadium that opened as Shibe Park in 1909.

1976 — Entering the game batting only .167, Mike Schmidt of the Phillies hits four consecutive homeruns and a single in a 10-inning 18-16 win over the Cubs at Wrigley Field. Schmidt hit two of his homers off Rick Reuschel, one off Rick's brother, Paul, and the other off Darold Knowles to become the 10th major leaguer to hit four homers in a game. Mike Schmidt broke in with the Phillies in 1972 and spent his entire 18 years through 1989 as one of the most productive third basemen in baseball history. The glove and power went hand-in-hand with Schmidt. His record includes 548 homeruns (leading the National League in that category eight times), 1,595 runs batted in, tops in the league four times, 2,234 hits and a batting average of .267. He was the league's Most Valuable Player twice (1980-1981) and won 10 gold gloves. In 1995 (20) Schmidt became only the eighth third baseman to be elected to the Hall of Fame.

1979 — The announced attendance for the Athletics game with Seattle at the Oakland Coliseum is 653. Because it was a chilly night not everyone who bought a ticket for the game was in attendance. The front office estimated about 550 fans were actually in the park. Although this set a record low for the franchise in the Bay Area, it fell short of equaling the lowest attendance for a professional baseball game in Oakland – by 652. On November 8, 1905 only one man watched the Pacific Coast League Oaks play Portland. Note: in 1905 the PCL schedule was the longest in baseball history, 230 games from March 30 to December 3.

April 18

1923 — Yankee Stadium is opened as New York beats Boston 4-1. For the past 10 seasons the Yankees had been tenants of the Giants in the Polo Grounds, but by 1920 new ownership began pumping new dollars into the franchise. Babe Ruth was purchased from the Red Sox and he immediately turned the team into the game's top attraction. Appropriately, reporter Fred Lieb of the *New York World Telegram* referred to the new facility as "The House That Ruth Built." It was estimated that over 25,000 were turned away, but 74,217 watched as the opening day festivities featured John Phillip Sousa's band and Governor Al Smith throwing out the first ball. Ruth highlighted the game with the first homerun off Howard Ehmke, and winning pitcher Bob Shawkey also homered for the Yankees. The Yankees (Highlanders) played their first game on April 30, 1903 with a 6-2 win over Washington. The club was originally the Baltimore Orioles, but moved to New York after the club's purchase for $18,000. The team that would become the most recognized franchise in baseball opened at Hilltop Park at 165th-168th and Broadway, playing there for ten seasons.

1945 — Pete Gray, who lost his right arm just below the shoulder as a child, makes his major league debut with the St. Louis Browns. Gray had been playing in the minors since 1942 and following a .333 season with Memphis of the Southern Association in 1944 he was purchased by St. Louis for $20,000. Although he was one of the most exciting players in baseball in 1945, it would be his only season in the big leagues. In 77 games he hit only .218 with no homers and stole only five bases. Gray played four more seasons in the minors, finishing with Dallas of the Texas League in 1949. Although his skills were not up to major league standards, he played almost 500 games in the minors and hit a career .308 with 98 stolen bases.

1946 — One year away from his major league debut, Jackie Robinson appears in his first minor league game with Montreal in the International League. At Roosevelt Stadium in Jersey City he picks up three singles and a 3-run homerun as the Royals beat the Jersey's 14-1 on opening day. Robinson would win the IL batting title with a .349 average and Montreal would win the Junior World Series that year.

1958 — Playing their first home game since their move from Brooklyn, the Dodgers debut in Los Angeles with a 6-5 win over San Francisco. 78,682 are on hand in the Coliseum (a football stadium) as Hank Sauer hits two homeruns for the Giants. The distance from home plate to the left field screen, which was 40 feet high, was 251 feet, the power alley in left center was 320, center field 425, the right field power alley 440 and the right field line 301 feet from home. The Dodgers would play their first four seasons in the Coliseum before moving to Dodger Stadium on April 10, 1962. Dodger Stadium is the first privately financed baseball park to open since Yankee Stadium was completed in 1923. The Dodgers lose to Cincinnati 6-3 in their opener before 52,564. Shortly after the season opened it was discovered the foul poles were in foul territory, however the National League gave its approval to play the full 1962 season with the poles as-is, allowing any balls hitting the poles ruled homeruns. The Dodgers are still playing at Dodger Stadium – a ballpark that refuses to grow old.

1962 — Milt Pappas, making his first start for Baltimore since undergoing an appendectomy in spring training, beats the Yankees 1-0. He had held New York to only two hits through five innings and with two outs in the bottom of the fifth, Pappas hits a homerun into the Memorial Stadium stands off Bill Stafford for the only run of the game. He was lifted after six innings and Hoyt Wilhelm finished with three scoreless innings for the save. Stafford also pitched well – allowing only one other hit beside Pappas the game winner.

1964 — Sandy Koufax becomes the only the second pitcher in major league history to strike out the side on nine pitches twice in his career. He does it In the third inning against the Cincinnati Reds in a Dodgers loss 3-0. The New York Mets were the first to be wiped out on nine pitches by Koufax on June 30, 1962. Lefty Grove of the Philadelphia A's was the first to do it twice – both times in the 1928 season.

1981 — On a cold and windy night at Pawtucket's McCoy Stadium the Red Sox and Rochester Red Wings begin their International League game that will be suspended at 4:07 a.m. the following morning. After eight hours and seven minutes, 32 innings of play and the score tied at 2-2 umpires call a halt to play. An estimated 17 to 20 fans were still in the stands huddled in the 28-degree chill. Ironically, the last 16 of the 32 innings never should have been played. International League by-laws stated that no inning shall begin after 12:50 a.m. on Saturday night. However, there was nothing in the umpire's handbook that called for a curfew and that fact was not discovered until close to the 30th inning. In the middle of inning 32 league president Harold Cooper called and instructed officials to: "Call the damn game after this inning." The game would not be resumed until Rochester's next visit to Pawtucket on June 23 and the Red Sox would win it 3-2 in just 18 more minutes after a total of 33 innings.

April 19

1938 — Two players, on different teams, hit homeruns in the first inning in their first at-bats in the major leagues. It was opening day at Baker Bowl in Philadelphia; Brooklyn was the visiting team. In the top of the first inning Dodgers left fielder Ernie Koy hits a homerun off Wayne LeMaster and in the bottom of the first Brooklyn pitcher Van Lingo Mungo serves up a homerun to rookie Emmett Mueller in his first plate appearance.

1949 — In opening-day ceremonies, matching granite monuments to Babe Ruth and Lou Gehrig are unveiled in deep center field at Yankee Stadium joining their manager, Miller Huggins, whose monument was dedicated in 1932. Originally, this shrine was on the playing surface, but was later moved behind the outfield fences when the stadium distances were changed.

April 20

1908 — Known widely in the game as the "Father of Baseball," Harry Chadwick dies in Brooklyn at age 85. The British ex-cricket player compiled the game's first printed rule book, edited the first weekly publication devoted entirely to baseball, edited and published the first baseball guide in 1872, and created the modern box score. The first box score appeared in the *New York Herald* on October 25, 1845 but consisted of very little information. It was a short form showing outs made and runs scored by each player. By the 1860s box scores began to appear on a regular basis, especially in the *New York Clipper*. In one such box score, appearing in that weekly paper on August 22, 1863, were items such as: the line score, players' positions, homeruns, strikeouts by pitchers, catches missed (errors), fair and foul balls caught, and the number of putouts made at first base and home plate were recorded. It also listed the time of game.

During this period Chadwick introduced his concept of the scorecard and box score and by 1876, the same year the National League was born, Chadwick's box score was in wide use with only one major change since. Chadwick's box score included individual at-bats, individual defensive statistics such as putouts, assists, errors and passed balls, as well as umpire and time of game. Team totals included left on base, double plays and earned runs. The only major change since came on April 8, 1942 when retired *Los Angeles Times* sports editor Paul Zimmerman suggested the addition of the individual pitching box –

innings pitched, hits, runs, earned runs, bases on balls and strikeouts. These stats first appeared in games played by the Los Angeles Pacific Coast League Angels.

Today more elaborate box scores include pitchers' won-lost records, save totals, holds, blown saves and other more detailed information suited to the hard-core statisticians and those involved in rotisserie leagues. These high-tech box scores are published by *USA Today*, *Baseball Weekly* and *AP*, but most dailies continue to use the less sophisticated form. Henry Chadwick was elected to the Hall of Fame in 1935 for his meritorious service.

1910 — Cleveland's Addie Joss pitches the second no-hitter in his brief major league career. His first was thrown in 1908 and that one was a perfect game. Both of his no-hitters were won by 1-0 scores and both were against the Chicago White Sox. In this no-hitter only three batters reached first. 1910 would be Joss' final season. During spring training in 1911 he fainted while on the bench. The illness appeared to be pleurisy and Joss was sent home to Toledo. He was unable to rejoin the Indians for the opening of the season and died on April 14, 1911 at age 31. The cause of death was a rare form of tubercular meningitis. Joss, whose first name was Adrian, played his entire nine year career (1902-1910) with Cleveland. He won 160 games and lost only 97 — a win percentage of .623 with a 1.88 career ERA and 46 shutouts. In 1978 the Veterans Committee waived the ten-year stipulation for service and voted Joss into the Hall of Fame because his career was tragically cut short.

1912 — New ballparks open in Boston and Detroit. The Red Sox whip the New York Highlanders (Yankees) 7-6 in 11 innings with 27,000 in attendance at Fenway Park. The Huntington Avenue Baseball Grounds had been the home of the Boston team since 1901; today Tufts Medical Center is located near where third base used to be, and a plaque commemorates the location of the old right field foul pole. The owner of the Red Sox, John Taylor, chose to name the new facility Fenway Park because, ". . . It's in the Fenway section [of Boston], isn't it? Then call it Fenway Park." It was also Taylor who changed the club's name from Pilgrims to Red Sox in 1907. In the opener at Detroit, the Tigers beat Cleveland 6-5 in 11-innings before 24,384 fans. The new Detroit park was named Navin Field after Tigers owner Frank Navin, and was built on the same site as old Bennett Park that served the Tigers beginning in 1901. The park's name was changed to Briggs Stadium in 1938 and to Tiger Stadium in 1960.

1916 — The Chicago Cubs play their first game in their present home. With the

April 20
Federal League out of business, the National League takes over Weeghman Park (the park built for, and used by, the Federal League Whales in 1914-1915). The Cubs win their opener from the Cincinnati Reds 7-6 in 11-innings. The National League Cubs (first the White Stockings and then the Colts beginning in 1876) played in five different locations in the Windy City before locating on the near North Side. They had played the last 22 years at West Side Grounds located at Polk and Lincoln (now Wolcott Street and the current site of the Illinois State Hospital and Medical Center). With a new team, the name of the stadium was changed to Cubs Park; it would remain that until 1926 when it was officially named Wrigley Field in honor of William Wrigley, Jr. who had acquired majority ownership in 1921. The first game played in Weeghman Park took place on April 13, 1914 when the Federal League Chicago Whales beat the Kansas City Packers 9-1.

1939 — Rookie Ted Williams makes his major league debut for the Red Sox in Yankee Stadium and picks up his first hit – a double off Red Ruffing as Boston loses to New York 2-0. This game is also notable because it would be the only time Williams and Lou Gehrig would appear in the same game. On this day, Gehrig was playing in his 2,123rd straight game and would appear in only seven more before the streak would end. Showing little of his old power, and with his physical problems quite obvious to all in attendance, Gehrig would go hitless in four at-bats. His spring training statistics also mirrored his continuing downhill trend. Appearing in all but one of 31 games, Gehrig hit only .218 with a slugging percentage of .281, and at first base he made eight errors. The box score of this game was loaded with future Hall-of-Famers – besides Williams, Gehrig, and Ruffing, it included: Joe DiMaggio, Bill Dickey, Jimmie Foxx, Joe Cronin, Bobby Doerr and Lefty Grove. Others in the Hall who attended the game were the retired Babe Ruth and former Red Sox Manager and the then-current President of the Yankees, Ed Barrow. Probably no other game ever played pointed out so dramatically the leaving and entering of two legends of baseball.

1944 — Outfielder Elmer Gedeon of the Washington Senators is the first major league player to be killed in action in World War II. Gedeon was a bomber pilot who was shot down on April 20, 1944 over German-occupied France. Gedeon played in only five games for the Senators in 1939. Only one other major leaguer was killed in action during the war. His name was Harry O'Neil who caught in only one game in 1939 with the Philadelphia Athletics. O'Neill, filling in defensively for regular catcher Frankie Hayes, never came to bat. O'Neill was killed on Iwo Jima on March 6, 1945.

1948 — On opening day, rookie first baseman George Vico of the Detroit Tigers homers on the first pitch thrown to him in the majors. The pitch is served up by Joe Haynes of the White Sox and would be the first of only eight homeruns Vico would hit in 1948. His major league career lasted only 211 games over the 1948 and 1949 seasons and in that time he would hit a total of 12 homers. Vico is the fifth player to homer on his first pitch in the majors.

April 21

1898 — Bill Duggleby becomes the first player to hit a bases-loaded homerun in his first major league at-bat. Interestingly, Duggleby was a pitcher for the Philadelphia Phillies who, in his seven seasons, hit five more homers. However, the really strange twist in this story concerns the pitcher who served up the homerun ball to Duggleby. He was Cy Seymour of the New York Giants who would win the National League batting championship (.377) in 1905 while playing the outfield for the Cincinnati Reds. When Seymour first broke into the majors, he played the outfield when he was not pitching but gave up the mound in 1902 and devoted his career to the bat.

1905 — When a storm washed out the game between the Washington Senators and the Yankees at Hilltop Park, the New York club discovered it had failed to issue rain checks. The next day the Yankees opened the gates to the public to rectify the gaff — 30,000 fans accepted the invitation. Rain checks were not common in baseball in the majors at this time, but teams issued tickets to fans leaving the park when the game was postponed. It was soon found to be unprofitable since tickets were being handed out to everyone leaving the park — even those who had snuck in.

1910 — 19,876 watch as the Cleveland Indians play and lose 5-0 to Detroit their first game at rebuilt League Park, located at 66th Street and Linwood Avenue. The original park, a wooden structure, had been the Indians' home since 1901. The park was the original home of the National League Cleveland Spiders and opened in 1891. New owner James Dunn would change the name to Dunn Field in 1916 but it reverted back to League Park in 1927. It remained the home base of the Tribe until the middle of the 1932 season — through 1933 – when the club moved to the new lakefront Cleveland Stadium. From 1934 through 1946 the Indians would play a split schedule at both sites until the complete move downtown in 1947. An interesting note – during League Park's final season 1946, the Indians erected tepees inside the park to become the first to place the Indian homes on a baseball reservation beating the Atlanta Braves to the idea by some 20 years.

1961 — After a road opening at Yankee Stadium, the new Minnesota Twins play their inaugural game at Metropolitan Stadium in Bloomington, Minnesota, a suburb of the Twin Cities. The franchise shift from Washington had been approved by the American League in October 1960. Ironically, the Twins' first home game was against the new Washington Senators, an expansion franchise, added along with the California Angels. Dale Long homers off Minnesota pitcher Camilo Pascual to give the Senators a 5-3 victory. This would be home for the Twins until moving into the Metrodome, in downtown Minneapolis, on April 6, 1982. Seattle would spoil the opener before 52,279 fans with an 11-7 victory.

April 22

1876 — The National League begins operation for the first time with eight teams – Chicago, St. Louis, Hartford, Boston, Louisville, New York, Philadelphia and Cincinnati. The Philadelphia Athletics play host to Boston in the league's first game and lose to the Redcaps 6-5. This game was an atrocious defensive contest in which 20 errors were committed as Boston scores two runs in the ninth to win. Joe Borden is the winning pitcher for Boston and Lon Knight is the loser, with Boston's Jim O'Rourke picking up the first hit, a single, in the first inning. 3,000 fans attended this historic game at 75 cents a ticket, but the cost of admission was lowered to a dime after the third inning had been completed. The game was played at the Jefferson Street Grounds in Philadelphia (25th and Jefferson Street). This would be the only season for the Athletics in the National League as the club was expelled from the circuit before the season ended because the owners refused to make the final western swing. The Phillies would not become part of the National League until 1883.

1898 — The National League is highlighted by two no-hit games. Theodore Breitenstein pitches one for Cincinnati in an 11-0 win over Pittsburgh at League Park in Cincinnati, and Baltimore's Jim Hughes no-hits the Boston Beantowners 8-0, at Union Park in Baltimore, in his second major league start.

April 23

1952 — Pitcher Hoyt Wilhelm, working in relief for the New York Giants, homers in his first major league at-bat at the Polo Grounds against the Boston Braves. He will never hit another homerun in his career that spanned 21 years and 1,070 games. Wilhelm's homer was hit off Braves pitcher Dick Hoover and strangely, it would be the only homerun Hoover would allow since this would be his only major league game – giving up eight hits and three walks in his four and two-third innings.

1964 — A no-hitter and a loss are combined for the first time in a 9-inning game in the majors when pitcher Ken Johnson of the Houston Colt .45s turns out to be the victim. Houston and Cincinnati battled through eight scoreless innings at Colt Stadium before the Reds came up with an unearned run in the ninth for the 1-0 win. With one out, Pete Rose reached second on a two-base throwing error by Johnson and moved to third on a fielder's choice. .45s' second baseman Nellie Fox then bobbled a hopper hit by Vada Pinson and Rose scored. Johnson still had his no-hitter – but lost the game – when Houston failed to tie or win in the bottom of the ninth. Only 5,426 paid to see this game that falls into the trivia category – Ken Johnson lost it, but who won it? – Joe Nuxhall.

April 24

1901 — The American League opens play in its first season of operation with eight teams: Chicago, Boston, Detroit, Philadelphia, Baltimore, Washington, Cleveland and Milwaukee. Three of the four scheduled games are rained out leaving only the Cleveland Blues at Chicago the honor of playing the first game. With a crowd of around 14,000, Chicago wins 8-2 at White Stockings Park located at Princeton and Wentworth Avenues at 39th Street (now Pershing Road). The game was played in one hour and 30 minutes with rookie pitcher Roy Patterson the winner and Bill Hoffer the loser for Cleveland. No homeruns were hit, but the next day the first American League homerun was hit by the Blues' Erv Beck.

1934 — An announcement appears in *The Sporting News* with a listing of upcoming games for both the Cardinals and Browns at Sportsman's Park. Ticket prices are included — the same for both teams – 55c 80c $1.10 $1.35 $1.65 $1.80 $1.90.

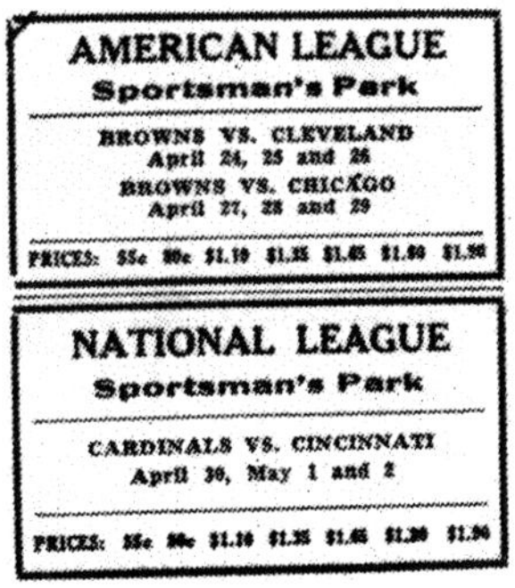
AMERICAN LEAGUE
Sportsman's Park
BROWNS VS. CLEVELAND
April 24, 25 and 26
BROWNS VS. CHICAGO
April 27, 28 and 29
PRICES: 55c 80c $1.10 $1.35 $1.65 $1.80 $1.90

NATIONAL LEAGUE
Sportsman's Park
CARDINALS VS. CINCINNATI
April 30, May 1 and 2
PRICES: 55c 80c $1.10 $1.35 $1.65 $1.80 $1.90

1945 — Following the death of Judge Landis in November 1944, major league owners gather in Cleveland and elect Albert "Happy" Chandler the new commissioner of baseball. The list of possible successors for Landis had been cut to six: Ford Frick, president of the National League, and five politicians - Jim Farley, Carl Vinson, Robert Patterson, Bob Hannegan and Frank Lausche. After Larry MacPhail brings up the name of Chandler (a Senator from Kentucky), the list is narrowed to Chandler and Hannegan. The first ballot gives Chandler an 11-5 lead, but short of the three-fourths vote required for election. After a one-vote switch, Chandler is elected unanimously to a seven-year term as the game's second commissioner. He would not last the full tenure and would be ousted by the owners; Frick would become his successor in 1951.

1946 – Boston sported two outstanding outfielders on the Beaneaters National League teams of 1892-94; the twosome was so talented, so Irish and so popular they were dubbed the "Heavenly Twins." The "twins" were Tommy McCarthy and Hugh Duffy both 5'-7", 170 pounds and both outstanding enough to be voted into the Hall of Fame. The two were among the first practitioners of the hit and run play, and McCarthy pioneered the trap play that led to his 53 assists. Umpire Bill Klem later stated that this play by McCarthy led to the adoption of the infield fly rule. Tommy is also credited with being one of the first to steal catchers' signs. Hugh Duffy was not as innovative as McCarthy but was a much better hitter. With Boston in 1894, he hit an all time high .438 with 236 hits in 539 at bats going hitless in only 17 games and finishing his career with 2,314 hits and an average of .328 over 17 years from 1888 to 1906. McCarthy hit .292 in 13 years from 1884 to 1869 entering the Hall of Fame on this date with the other "Heavenly Twin" preceding him on April 25, 1945.

1956 — American League umpire Frank Umont becomes the first arbiter to wear glasses in a regular season game between Detroit and Kansas City.

April 25

1904 — 37-year old Cy Young, pitching for the Boston Red Sox, gives up six hits in a 2-0 loss to Rube Waddell of the Athletics. The hit allowed by Young was a double by Harry Davis leading off the sixth inning, giving Young three hitless innings the remainder of the game. This was the start of a string of 25 and one-third consecutive innings that Young would hold the opposition hitless. Here is Young's line for the next three outings: April 30 – 7 innings in relief in a 4-1 win at Washington; May 5 – 9 innings in his perfect game against Philadel-phia and May 11 — no hits allowed until one out in the 7th inning when Detroit's Sam Crawford singled. This game ended with Young besting Ed Killian 1-0 in 15 innings. Putting it another way, Young had retired 76 batters without giving up a hit.

1928 — This could be the most lop-sided game ever played – it was a regularly-scheduled game between two Iowa high schools, with the final score Atlantic 109 and Griswold 0. Before the game was called after eight innings, 145 Atlantic batters had stepped to the plate and had 92 hits (26 doubles, seven triples, 16 homeruns, 113 stolen bases, and Griswold fielders made 22 errors). Surprisingly, Griswold coach, Phil Morrison, used only one pitcher. The Atlantic pitcher, Don King, pitched a no-hitter striking out 13 with no walks and three hit batsmen. As the leadoff batter, King went 15-for-17, two homeruns, scored 14 runs and stole 19 bases. Atlantic scored in double figures in four of the eight innings — 30 in the second, 12 in the third, 27 in the seventh and 18 in the eighth. Incidentally, King was a 5'8" lefthander who went on to a 12-year professional career, all in the minors, pitching briefly in Triple-A.

1945 — Dan Brouthers, who started his career as a pitcher then switched to first base is voted into the Hall of Fame. He played 19 years in the majors from 1879 to 1896 returning in 1904 for a few appearances with the Giants. He is often referred to as the Babe Ruth of his day because of his power at the plate. He hit 103 homeruns while winning four batting titles and a final average of .342 as well as 263 stolen bases while playing with ten different teams.

1995 — More than eight months after players walked out on August 12, 1994 to begin the longest strike in professional sports history, baseball resumes with a shortened schedule of 144 games. The season begins without a new collective bargaining agreement and starts under the same basic rules that existed when the strike began. Following a favorable court ruling, the players agreed to return. The start of the season is delayed by 23 days with the bulk of regular spring training taken up with the use of replacement players. However, the situation is not entirely back to normal since the games begin with replacement umpires. The regular umps had been locked out by the owners since their contract expired at the end of December. This is not the first time the game has been without regular umpires. In 1991 the two sides agreed to settle their differences just hours before the first pitch of the season; some of the regular umpires missed seven or eight games. In 1985 the umpires struck for the first seven games of the playoffs and in 1979 they struck for the first seven weeks of the season.

1999 — On a sun-splashed afternoon at Yankee Stadium a sellout crowd gathers for the unveiling of the granite and bronze monument in memory of Joe DiMaggio who died on March 8 of that year. Former teammates Whitey Ford, Yogi Berra, Jerry Coleman, Phil Rizzuto, Gil McDougald and Hank Bauer are on hand as the

April 25-27
DiMaggio monument joins those of Babe Ruth, Lou Gehrig, Mickey Mantle and Miller Huggins.

April 27

1912 — 23 year-old right-hander Hanson Horsey appears in his only major league game in relief for Cincinnati against Pittsburgh. Horsey worked four innings, gave up 14 hits, ten runs and three walks. He also went hitless in two at-bats.

1929 — At Baker Bowl in Philadelphia, Clise Dudley, a pitcher for Brooklyn, becomes the first player to hit a homerun on the first pitch thrown to him in the major leagues. The pitch was served up by right-hander Claude Willoughby and would be the first of two Dudley would hit in his rookie season. During his next four years with the Dodgers, the Phillies, and Pittsburgh he would hit only one more.

1947 — Babe Ruth returns to Yankee Stadium for "his day" and 59,339 attend to honor him. There was the usual plethora of speeches, and Ruth, thin, his color bad, and with a croaking voice, moved close to the microphone and delivered a touching speech:

> *"Thank you very much, ladies and gentlemen, you know how bad my voice sounds. Well, it feels just as bad. You know, this baseball game of ours comes up from the youth. That means the boys. And after you've been a boy, and grow up to know how to play ball, then you come to the boys you see representing themselves today in our national pastime. The only real game in the world, I think, is baseball. As a rule, some people think if you give them a football or a baseball or something like that, naturally, they're athletes right away. But you can't do that in baseball. You've got to start from way down, at the bottom, when you're six or seven years old. You can't wait until you're 15 or 16. You've got to let it grow up with you, and if you're successful and try hard enough, you're bound to come out on top, just like these boys have come to the top now. There's been so many lovely things said about me, I'm glad I had the opportunity to thank everybody. Thank you."*

Ruth would make one more trip to "The House That Ruth Built" in June of 1948. Two months later, he was dead.

1961 — The expansion Los Angeles Angels play their first home game at Wrigley Field. The park had been the home of the Pacific Coast League team by the same name since 1925. Named after William Wrigley, owner of the Chicago Cubs, it was designed to resemble Wrigley Field in Chicago. Located in south-central Los Angeles at 42nd and Avalon with a 1961 seating capacity of 20,457, Wrigley Field was a "homer haven" with power alleys of 345 feet, only some 5 to 7 feet more than the foul poles. In the lone season the new Angels would spend in the minor league park it would yield 248 homeruns. In 1966 Wrigley Field would be felled by the wrecking ball. Also in 1966, the Los Angeles Angels (later the California Angels) left Dodger Stadium where they had co-habitated with the National League Dodgers for four years. The Angels moved to Anaheim Stadium on April 19, 1966 and before a crowd of 31,824 lost to the White Sox 3-2. The team's sale to the Disney Company called for another name change in 1997 when the team became the Anaheim Angels.

1971 — Curt Flood, who had been coaxed out of premature retirement by the Washington Senators, jumps the club after 13 games and a .200 average and takes a plane to Spain. This will end his 15-year major league career with his antitrust suit against baseball still pending before the Supreme Court. Flood had spent the 1970 season in Denmark after his refusal to report to Philadelphia following his trade from St. Louis. He had challenged the reserve clause with a $4.1 million damage suit that he would eventually lose.

1973 — The temperature is cold but Steve Busby of the Kansas City Royals is hot; he pitches a 3-0 no-hitter against Detroit at Tiger Stadium. With a chilly wind blowing, Busby gives up six walks but is helped by two double plays and homeruns by teammates Ed Kirkpatrick and Amos Otis. 16,435 watch the first no-hitter by a Royals pitcher and the first in Tiger Stadium since 1952 when Virgil Trucks handcuffed Washington.

April 28

1896 — Bennett Park is opened for the first time as the Detroit Wolverines defeat the Columbus Senators in a Western League game 17-2. Situated at Michigan and Trumbull Avenues, the same address as Tiger Stadium, this site saw continuous major league baseball for 104 years. The park was erected on the site of Detroit's old Haymarket where farmers brought their hay to be weighed and sold. The new park was named after Charley Bennett, a standout catcher with the Detroit club of the National League between 1881 and 1888, who lost both legs when he fell beneath the wheels of a train. One name stands out as a participant in this first game played in Bennett Park – the player-manager of the Wolverines George Stallings who not only hit the first homerun but would later gain fame as the manager of the 1914 Miracle Braves World Champions.

1930 — Although night games date back to 1880, either amateur or exhibitions, they did not surface in organized baseball until 1930. In the winter of 1929 at the National Association (minors) meeting, E. Lee Keyser of the Des Moines club, in the Class-A Western League, boldly announced his Demons would play the first night game ever to open the 1930 season. However, Keyser, who spent $19,000 to install lights in his park, was robbed of the distinction when Independence, Kansas, in the Class-C Western Association, erected temporary lighting and played Muskogee, Oklahoma four days before Des Moines could open its home season. That game was played at Riverside Park with Muskogee winning 13-3 on a soggy field with about 1,000 in attendance. However, to Des Moines goes the distinction of hosting the first night game in organized baseball under permanent light standards on May 2, 1930.

1961 — Warren Spahn, fresh off his first no-hitter in September of 1960, throws another in the refrigerator of County Stadium (44 degrees at game time) before 8,518 fans in a 1-0 victory over San Francisco. The only run was scored in the first inning off losing pitcher Sam Jones on a single, a passed ball and another hit. Spahn, just five days past his 40th birthday, faced only 27 batters, walking Chuck Hiller and Willie McCovey, both of whom were rubbed out on double plays. Spahn pitched until he was 46 years old and spent all but one of his 21 years in the majors with the Braves (Boston and Milwaukee). His last season was 1965 when he pitched in 20 games with the Mets and 16 with San Francisco. Spahn (21) finished with 363 wins, 245 losses and had 13 20-win seasons. He pitched briefly in 1966 (Mexico City Tigers) and 1967 (Tulsa-Pacific Coast League) and was elected to the Hall of Fame in his first year of eligibility in 1973.

1986 — With the Yankees in last place, manager Yogi Berra is fired after losing ten of the team's first 16 games. This would be the end of Berra's career as a manager (1964 and 1984 Yanks and 1972-1975 Mets). Lawrence Peter Berra was best known as an 18-year catcher with the Yankees from 1946 through 1963. Three times the Most Valuable Player in the American League, Berra had 358 homeruns, 1,430 runs batted in and an average of .285. He played in 14 World Series (75 games) with 71 hits and an average of .274. Another outstanding item he did for America's Pastime – he proved you don't have to look like a ball player to be a great one! Berra (8) entered the Hall of Fame in 1972.

April 29

1887 – Ladies' Day as a regular feature is inaugurated when the New Orleans Pelicans of the Southern Association open their gates "free to women." The first professional team to play in Buffalo (1877) had offered reduced prices to ladies, and the New York Gothams held the first Ladies' Day in the majors in 1883 at the Polo Grounds. However, neither became an established ritual as it came to be in New Orleans. Charles Abner Powell, owner, manager, and player for the Pelicans, started it and stayed with it. His initial promotion on this day attracted only nine women, but Powell saw a substantial increase in attendance for each following game. Not giving up on his idea, crowds continued to grow not only on the weekly day for ladies, but overall attendance kept rising, sometimes hitting 5,000 on weekdays and 10,000 on weekends.

Powell had been a player in the majors for two seasons as a pitcher-outfielder (1884 with Washington in the Union Association and 1886 with Baltimore and Cincinnati in the American Association). Throughout his innovative years in the game as an owner he gave baseball the first rain check, the field tarpaulin and the knothole gang. In the early 1900s, the St. Louis Browns were the first team to push Ladies' Days in the majors but that eventually was reduced to a free ticket when accompanied by a male. In 1917 St. Louis made it a regular event. William Wrigley, owner of the Chicago Cubs, garnered the most success from his free Ladies' Day inaugurated in the 1930s. Interestingly, to this day, the Cubs' record for a single game total attendance is 51,556 set on Ladies' Day June 27, 1930 against Brooklyn.

1901 — The first American League game is played in Washington as the Nationals open the season at American League Park, located at Florida Avenue Northeast between 12th and 13-1/2 Streets. This stadium is credited with one of the first baseball public address announcers, E. Lawrence Phillips. Phillips, megaphone in hand, strolled the left and right field lines to announce the batteries and later the entire home and visiting team lineups. He would handle the megaphone for 28 seasons before retiring in 1928. There were three other "megaphone announcers" during this era: George Levy, who handled the Yankees and Giants games, Boston's Wolfie Jacobs, and Pat Pieper at Wrigley Field in Chicago. Phillips has gone down in baseball history as one of the most prominent pioneering voices of the game.

April 29-30

1922 — Four inside-the-park homeruns are hit by the New York Giants in one game at Braves Field in Boston. James E. Gaffney purchased the Braves in 1912 and orchestrated the building of Braves Field, which opened in August of 1915. Prior to ground breaking, Gaffney stated he wanted the playing field to be large enough so it would be possible to hit an inside-the-park homerun in any of the outfield directions. When opened, the park's left field foul line was 405 feet, right field 402 and 550 feet to deepest centerfield. Before the park opened, Ty Cobb visited the new stadium, and standing at the plate said a ball would never be hit out of the park. He didn't miss it by much. For example, in 1921, of the 38 homeruns hit, only four were hit out of the park. In 1927, bleachers were erected in left and center and an eight-foot barrier was installed to cut most distances by 70 feet. By 1944 Braves Field was 340 to left and right and 370 to center.

1936 — Cecil (Dynamite) Dunn hits five homeruns plus a single for Alexandria at Lake Charles in an Evangeline League game. For the season Dunn hit 47 homeruns, drove in 185 runs and hit .378. Dunn never made it to the big leagues but played eleven seasons in the minors and hit 208 homers. In 1942 he would play for six different teams in five leagues.

April 30

1922 — Amid continued complaints by Tigers hitters that he was practicing illegal tricks, Charles Robertson of the Chicago White Sox pitches the 3rd perfect game in history with a 2-0 win over Detroit. Other than the pitching of Robertson, with his impeccable control, and nothing but ordinary fielding plays – this was not a spectacular game. The Detroit crowd of 25,000 at Navin Field began the game howling and booing Robertson, but the fans entered into the game-ending excitement by carrying him off the field. The game stories neglected to mention that Ray Schalk was Robertson's catcher and that this was the third no-hit game he had caught (Joe Benz in 1914 and Ed Cicotte in 1917). He also was behind the plate in 1914 when Jim Scott pitched nine innings of no-hit ball but gave up two hits in the tenth and lost 1-0 to Washington. Schalk played 18 years, all but one with the White Sox, and retired after a few games with the Giants in 1929. He had a lifetime average of .253 and was behind the plate in 1,726 games, catching in over 100 games for eleven consecutive seasons. Schalk had a brief fling as manager of the White Sox in 1927-28 and was elected to the Hall of fame in 1955.

1939 — Lou Gehrig plays the last game of his 2,130 consecutive game streak, and the end of his career. At Yankee Stadium against Washington, Gehrig fails to hit in four at bats, has two assists and makes seven putouts. He had stumbled through spring training, weak and uncoordinated and it continued through the first eight games of the regular season. Gehrig made up his mind that the end had come, he stated later, when he struggled to make what his intellect told him was a routine play in this game against the Senators. Returning to the dugout his teammates congratulated him – he knew then he was through.

1946 — Dispelling any rumors he had lost his fastball following four years in the Navy, Bob Feller lowers the boom on New York at Yankee Stadium with his second no-hitter before a crowd of 34,144. This one wasn't easy for Feller as he hooked up with Floyd Bevens in a tremendous pitching dual that wasn't decided until Frankie Hayes homered in the ninth for the 1-0 Indians win. Feller did walk three batters, but he was in his usual strikeout mode with eleven New York victims.

1961 — Willie Mays hits four homeruns and eight RBI, and his San Francisco teammates chip in with four more homers; the Giants wallop the Braves at County Stadium 14-4. Mays hits two of his homers off Lew Burdette and one each off Don McMahon and Seth Morehead. Mays becomes the 9th player in major league history to do this.

1969 — Jim Maloney humbles Houston 10-0, pitching the second no-hitter of his career. Maloney's teammates made a "laugher" out of the game with a seven-run fourth inning that gave the Reds an 8-0 lead. Not many fans watched the lopsided game at Crosley Field – the paid crowd was only 3,898. Maloney was near his best in the strikeout department; even though he walked five he countered with 13 strikeouts giving him 25 Ks in his two no-hitters. As a footnote – Maloney pitched 10 hitless innings in 1965 but lost to the Mets in the 11th – in that game he struck out 18.

"*Strike*" — Richard III
William Shakespeare

Chapter Five

"Baseball means what those of us who hold it in our hearts need it to mean. It can be a game, a pastime, or it can be something by which we measure the seasons of our lives, or it can be something that serves metaphorically for the battles, the wars, the triumphs and the tragedies of any kind of human conflict. And I think more than anything else, it tells me that there is something else, it tells me that there is something in the world that I can count on and that is never going to let me down."

Daniel Okrent, editor of *Life* magazine

May 1

1926 — 19 year-old Satchel Paige makes his debut with the Chattanooga Black Lookouts in the Negro Southern League, pitching a 5-4 win over Birmingham.

1880 — Catcher Moses Fleetwood Walker becomes the first black to play in the major leagues, joining the Toledo Blue Stockings in the American Association. His first game is against the Louisville Eclipse, the same team that had denied him the right to play three years earlier when he was with a semi-pro team. In Walker's first game he failed to hit safely in three at-bats, committed four errors and two passed balls as Louisville beat Toledo 5-1. His brother Welday was also on the Toledo team. Walker played in 41 games and hit .251. Between the Walkers' brief tenure at Toledo and Jackie Robinson's epochal entrance into Brooklyn in 1947, there were several Negro players in organized ball – all of them in the 19th Century minor leagues. They included such standouts as Clarence Matthews, Frank (U.S.) Grant, Charles Kelly and J.W. (Bud) Fowler.

1920 — Boston Braves Joe Oeschger and Brooklyn's Leon Cadore, each pitch all 26 innings of a 1-1 tie, which was finally called because of darkness. The game took place at Braves Field and lasted 3 hours and 50 minutes with Oeschger shutting out the Dodgers for the final 21 innings. In Brooklyn's next two games the Dodgers would lose to Philadelphia in 13 innings and to Boston in 19 innings — playing a total of 58 innings in three days. Oddly, Oeschger and Cadore would not speak to each other for the next 37 years, until 1957 when they met at an old-timers game. At that time Cadore was quoted to have said, "We had a strict fraternization rule in the National League back then."

1959 — 39-year old Early Wynn pitches and bats the Chicago White Sox to a 1-0 win over Boston at Fenway Park. Wynn allows only one hit, a first inning single to Pete Runnels, strikes out 14 and preserves his shutout even though he allowed seven walks. Wynn completes his day with an eighth inning homerun off Tom Brewer with a drive that tips the glove of the leaping Bill Renna, sending the ball into the stands for the only run of the game.

1969 — Don Wilson throws a 4-0 no-hitter against the Reds, one night after Cincinnati pitcher Jim Maloney's no-hit game against the Astros. Not too many fans can say they saw both games, as a total of only 7,940 watched on the two nights at Crosley Field. It was Wilson's second career no-hitter as he walked six batters and struck out 13. His first no-hit game came against Atlanta on June 18, 1967.

1991 — Nolan Ryan pitches his seventh and final no-hitter at Arlington Stadium before 33,439 with a 3-0 win over Toronto. The Rangers' right-hander strikes out 16 Blue Jays and walks two while retiring 27 of 29 batters. This is only the second no-hitter pitched at Arlington Stadium; the other was a perfect game by California's Mike Witt on the last day of the season in 1984. Ryan will be best remembered by his phenomenal seven no-hitters and his 5,714 strikeouts. He pitched in the majors for 27 years and was 46 years old when he retired.

Ryan's longevity had much to do with some of his accomplishments. His won-lost record was 324-292 yet he posted a 3.19 ERA. Very important in his career was the number of innings he rolled up – 12 seasons pitching over 200 innings and two other years working 326 and 333. In six seasons he recorded over 300 strikeouts and led the league in that department in eleven of his 27 years. The "Ryan Express" (34) was inducted into the Hall of Fame in 1999 in his first year of eligibility.

1995 — The lockout of umpires ends with Major League Baseball and the Umpires Association agreeing on a new five-year contract. Under the new agreement, rookie umpires will receive a minimum of $75,000 with the veteran umps increasing to $225,000. Each umpire, whether or not he works in the post-season, will receive a $20,000 bonus at season's end. Umpires will be reimbursed an additional $5,000 for All-Star service, $12,500 for the Division Series, $15,000 for the League Championship Series and $17,500 for the World Series. Per Diem will be $220 with cost of living in subsequent years.

May 2

1917 — Only 1,000 spectators can lay claim to watching this classic game at Cubs Park. Pitchers Fred Toney of the Reds and James "Hippo" Vaughn of the Cubs each pitch through the first nine innings without giving up a hit. With one out in the tenth, Larry Kopf of the Reds singles to right field, Greasy Neale makes the second out on a fly ball to right, but Cy Williams drops Hal Chase's line drive moving Kopf to third. Jim Thorpe then hits a bouncer in front of the plate and Vaughn's throw home is too late, and Kopf scores the only run of the game. This is the first run scored by the Reds in 34 innings. Toney then finishes his 10-inning no-hitter and Vaughn is hung with a 10-inning two-hit loss. On May 11, 1909 Toney pitched a 17-inning no-hitter for Winchester in the Class-D Blue Grass League also winning 1-0 with only one walk and 19 strikeouts.

1939 — After going almost 14 years and 2,130 games, Lou Gehrig benches himself at Briggs Stadium in Detroit. Gehrig had a morning meeting with his manager, Joe McCarthy, and told him he was taking himself out of the lineup because he couldn't help the team any longer. McCarthy told him to think it over, but Gehrig said his time had come and he would stick to his decision. He is replaced at first base by Babe Dahlgren and would not play another game. Gehrig started his consecutive game streak on June 1, 1925 when he appeared as a pinch-hitter. The story of Wally Pipp's "headache" is not true since manager Miller Huggins had informed the Iron Horse before the next game that Gehrig from that point on would be the Yankees first baseman.

Gehrig played 17 seasons with the Yankees and finished his career with a batting average of .340, 493 homeruns and 1,990 runs batted in. Throughout his career Gehrig would record 100 or more RBI seasons 13 times. Gehrig (4) was elected to the Hall of Fame December 8, 1939 by acclamation by the Baseball Writers Association of America without a formal ballot. During this period there were no specific guidelines – such as being retired from the game for five years -- to be eligible for consideration.

May 3

1936 — 21 year-old Joe DiMaggio makes his major league debut in left field at Yankee Stadium. In his first at-bat he grounds out to third base off Jack Knott of the St. Louis Browns. Before the day is over, DiMaggio will have two singles and a triple as New York knocks off St. Louis 14-5. Hitting .340 and driving in 169 runs (a league high) with the San Francisco Seals, major league teams began courting DiMaggio after his first full season in the Pacific Coast League. However in June of 1934, while in the midst of another outstanding season, he tore ligaments in his left knee and some clubs (the Red Sox and Pirates) began to back off. Riding the fact that DiMaggio was listed under the category of "damaged goods" Yankees scouts Joe Devine and Bill Essick stayed with it and convinced their bosses, general manager Ed Barrow and owner Jacob Ruppert that the youngster was more than worth the risk. New York and the Seals settled on $25,000 for DiMaggio, plus five players from the Yankees farm system. Then Barrow sweetened the deal by allowing DiMaggio to remain with the Seals in 1935 to receive regular knee treatments in San Francisco.

This transaction ranks as one of the greatest deals in baseball history. Of the five players sent to the Seals only first baseman Les Powers made it to the majors (two years – 1938 with the Giants and 1939 with the Phillies). Pitcher Floyd Newkirk had pitched in one game for the Yankees in 1934. Incidentally, DiMaggio replaced the regular 1935 Yankees left fielder, Jesse Hill, who was traded to Washington before spring training of 1936. A year later Hill would be out of baseball and surface as a football coach, track coach and athletic director at the University of Southern California.

May 4

1960 — The Chicago Cubs make a switch in managers after a 6-11 .353 start under Charlie Grimm. His replacement is Lou Boudreau. The logistics of this move are simple – Grimm, the manager becomes Grimm the Cubs broadcaster, and Boudreau, the Cubs broadcaster becomes Boudreau the manager. Boudreau would finish with a 54-83 .394 record; it would be the final season for both as managers.

1989 — Junior Felix of the Toronto Blue Jays hits a homerun off California's Kirk McCaskill on the first pitch thrown to him in the major leagues. Felix had made his major league debut the day before against Oakland as a defensive replacement in the ninth inning. He becomes the eleventh player in history to turn around the first pitch thrown to him and send it out of the park.

May 5

1904 — Before 10,000 wildly excited fans at Boston's Huntington Baseball Grounds, Cy Young pitches the first perfect game in major league history since the pitching distance was extended to 60'6" in 1893. Young pitched the Pilgrims to a 3-0 victory over the formidable Philadelphia Athletics and the great Rube Waddell. This would be the second no-hitter for Young, pitching his first September 18, 1897 for Cleveland against Cincinnati. This game was played in one hour and 30 minutes, and was called by Frank Dwyer, the only umpire.

1922 — On May 14, 1920, the New York Giants had informed the Yankees that following the 1920 season their lease sharing the Polo Grounds would not be renewed. This lease had been in force since 1913. Speculation surfaced that the Giants' reason centered on the Yankees' signing of Babe Ruth. As it turned out, the Giants reneged and the Yankees stayed as tenants through 1922. Meanwhile, Yankees owners had already taken an option on land directly across the Harlem River from the Polo Grounds for a park of their own. Ground was broken on this day on a 10-acre site, formerly a lumberyard, purchased for $600,000 from William Waldorf Astor in February of 1921. The new stadium would be built in only 284 days at a cost of $2.5 million; opening day ceremonies were held on April 18, 1923.

1949 — One of the premier second basemen of all time, Charlie Gehringer (2) is elected to the Hall of Fame. Known as the "Mechanical Man," he spent his entire 19 playing years with Detroit and after serving in the Navy was appointed general manager of the Tigers for two years. He continued with the organization as a vice president through 1959. Gehringer hit .320 during his career with 2,830 hits and was especially adept at hitting doubles (574). In 1937 Gehringer led the American League in batting with .371 and was named the league's Most Valuable Player.

1965 — Some great pitching match ups never really develop – this one did. Warren Spahn of the Mets and Jim Bunning with the Phillies hook up in a dual of talented veterans with Bunning coming out the winner 1-0. Despite a shaky start he settled down, pitching and fielding brilliantly the rest of the way – picking up six assists, among them a pick off at second base. Meanwhile, Spahn matched him until the sixth inning when Bunning swung at a high fastball from Spahn and sent it into the right field seats at Shea Stadium for the only run of the game. Both Spahn and Bunning would end up in the Hall of Fame.

1978 — 37 year-old Pete Rose, in his 16th season with Cincinnati, singles off Montreal's Steve Rogers and picks up his 3,000th career hit. Rose becomes the thirteenth player in history to record the magic number and goes on to eclipse the 4,000 mark and finish his career with 4,256. Rose had 200 or more hits in ten seasons, more than any other player to reach the 3,000 mark.

1999 — Colorado becomes the first team in 35 years to score in every inning, whipping the Chicago Cubs 13-6 on an 18-hit attack. Only Vinny Castilla fails to hit safely for the Rockies as the line score reads: 111-121-222. This is only the third time in the twentieth century a team has scored in all nine innings; it was the second time it happened at Wrigley Field. The Cubs also lost to St. Louis on September 13, 1964 and the New York Giants pulled the nine-inning trick at Baker Bowl in Philadelphia June 1, 1923. There were two other occasions teams scored in every inning in the American Association, then a major league: June 13, 1883 when the Columbus Buckeyes did it with a 25-10 win in Pittsburgh over the Alleghenys and May 20, 1889 when the Kansas City Cowboys elected to bat first in their home ballpark and lost 18-12 to the Brooklyn Bridegrooms.

May 6

1892 — The Reds and Boston, playing at League Park in Cincinnati, play 14 innings without a run being scored. Beantowners pitcher John Clarkson had given up four hits and walked five, and the Reds Elton Chamberlain had walked one and allowed only three hits. The significance of this game surfaced when the game's lone umpire, Jack Sheridan, decided the sun was too strong in the eyes of the batters. He then called everything off; apparently, neither team was offended. In fact, the *Cincinnati Enquirer* reported the next day that "his decision, while it may appear ridiculous on the face of it, was . . . a just and sensible one." This game took place in the original League Park. Two years later (1894) when Cincinnati opened League Park II at the same site, home plate was positioned in the Southwest corner of the square, instead of its former location in the Northeast corner, putting the afternoon sun in the right fielders' eyes. From then on most new parks followed this procedure until the 1970s when some new stadiums where positioned without regard to the position of the afternoon sun.

1917 — In the second game of a doubleheader at Sportsman's Park, Browns pitcher Bob Groom throws a 3-0 no-hitter at the Chicago White Sox. Only an 8-4 victory by the Browns in the first game separated back-to-back no-hitters. The day before, St. Louis pitcher Ernie Koob tossed a 1-0 no-hit win over Chicago. Unlike the small crowd of 3,000 that witnessed the first no-hitter, an overflow crowd of some 20,000 was on hand for the twin bill. The fans saw Groom in action in both games – he relieved Eddie Plank at the start of the eighth in the opener and pitched his masterpiece in the nightcap for a total of 11 innings for the day. Groom would finish the season 8-19.

1953 — If a pitcher ever made a career out of one day it was Bobo Holloman of the St. Louis Browns. The 27-year old rookie right-hander, making his first start, pitches a 6-0 no-hitter against the Philadelphia Athletics at Sportsman's Park before a sparse gathering of 2,473. If it weren't for the no-hit game, the highlight of the afternoon would have been the many sparkling defensive plays made behind Holloman. Three of them were of the startling variety by Jim Dyke, Bobby Young and Billy Hunter. Holloman also helped himself in the field by stabbing Allie Clark's liner headed for centerfield. Three months following this game Holloman was no longer with the Browns. This would be his only major league season, his only start, his only complete game and a career record of 3-7 in 22 games with a 5.23 ERA. One other note to corroborate that this was Holloman's career-day -- he had two hits and three runs batted in – the only two hits he would get in the majors.

1982 — Seattle's Gaylord Perry rings up the 300th victory of his career with a 7-3 win over the New York Yankees. He becomes the 15th pitcher in history to achieve the mark, and it comes at age 43 in his next-to-last active season. Perry broke in with the San Francisco Giants in 1962, and it was the beginning of a parade of eight clubs with whom he would pitch during his 22 seasons in the majors (Giants, Cleveland, Texas-twice, San Diego, Yankees, Atlanta, Seattle and Kansas City). He was a workhorse, rolling up 11 seasons in which he pitched in excess of 200 innings, plus exceeding 300 innings in six other years. With San Francisco in 1970 and 1971 he worked back-to-back 325 and 328 innings. Perry finished with 314 wins and 265 losses, winning 20 or more games five times with a high of 24 with Cleveland in 1972. Perry (36) was voted into the Hall of Fame in 1991.

May 7

1906 — In a game with Washington at New York, American League umpire Ted Hurst is suspended for five days by president Ban Johnson for striking New York Highlanders manager Clark Griffith in the mouth during an altercation. Griffith, besides getting hit in the mouth, did almost everything in the game of baseball during his career. He played all positions except catcher for 22 years from 1891 through 1914. He was used as a position player when not pitching; he did very little hitting (.233). While pitching he won 240 games while losing only 144 for a win-percentage of .625. He managed in 20 of his 22 seasons with the White Sox,

Cincinnati and Washington as well as the Highlanders (Yankees). Despite winning only one pennant his winning percentage was .522 over 2,918 games.

Probably his biggest contribution to the game was his influence during the formation of the American League. With the prodding of president Ban Johnson the White Sox released Griffith – knowing Griffith would be vital in overseeing the New York operation at a time when the new American League needed that city in its competition with the National League's New York Giants. Griffith's talent and popularity proved to be invaluable. In 1912 an opportunity arose for him to buy into the Washington franchise. He mortgaged his Montana ranch and eventually he and his family would own controlling interest in the club into the 1960s. Griffith was voted into the Hall of Fame in 1946.

1925 — Pittsburgh shortstop Glenn Wright makes an unassisted triple play in the ninth inning against the Cardinals. Wright catches Jim Bottomley's line drive, steps on second to double Jimmy Cooney and tags Rogers Hornsby coming from first. Wright's is the fifth unassisted triple play in history.

1957 — Coming off a 20-9 season in 1956, Cleveland pitcher Herb Score is hit in the right eye by a line drive off the bat of the Yankees' Gil McDougald. Score suffers three broken bones in his face and eye damage and never recovers enough to sustain the talent level he had reached in his first two seasons with the Indians when he won 36 games. In his next six years with Cleveland and the White Sox he would win only 19 more games and retires following the 1962 season.

May 8

1929 – 25 year-old Carl Hubbell, purchased at the beginning of the 1928 season by the New York Giants from Beaumont of the Texas League, throws an 11-0 one-walk no-hitter against Pittsburgh. The first two batters to face Hubbell reached on errors, but a strikeout and double play got him out of the first inning jam. The small crowd of some 8,000 witness the first no-hit game in the majors by a left-hander since the Red Sox Hub Leonard no-hit Detroit on June 3, 1918. Despite the 11-0 score Hubbell and three Pirates pitchers reel off the game in one hour and 35 minutes.

1966 — The St. Louis Cardinals and San Francisco put the final wrap on Busch Stadium (Sportsman's Park) as the Giants win the final game 10-5. The original Sportsman's Park was opened on May 6, 1875 when the St. Louis Brown Stockings were a member of the American Association, and in 1876 became a charter member of the National League. Actually, there were four different stadiums named Sportsman's Park, but all were at the same site at Grand Boulevard, Dodier and Spring Streets and Sullivan Avenue. Aside from improving the seating, the major changes involved the placement of home plate. That location was moved back and forth and around, between the Southeast, Northeast and Southwest corners of the block, where it eventually ended up in 1909 with the completion of Sportsman's Park IV. The American League Browns began play in the park in 1902 and remained until the club was moved to Baltimore following the 1953 season. The Cardinals began play at Sportsman's Park in 1920 and stayed for the remainder of the stadium's existence, although the name was changed to Busch Stadium in 1954. St. Louis opened its downtown park on May 12, 1966.

1968 — 22 year-old Jim "Catfish" Hunter pitches Oakland to the seventh perfect game in major league history as the Athletics beat Minnesota 4-0. Only 6,298 fans watch at Oakland Coliseum as Hunter becomes the first American League pitcher in 46 years to hurl a perfect game (Charlie Robertson for the White Sox in 1922). There were no tough fielding plays behind Hunter as he strikes out 11 while having a great day at the plate with three hits – two singles and a double and drives in three runs. Hunter began his 15-year major league career in 1965 with the Athletics (Kansas City-Oakland), and in 1974 was made a free agent by an arbitrator in a dispute with A's owner Charlie Finley. Hunter signed with the Yankees for his final five seasons. He went on to a career record of 224-166 and an ERA of 3.26 winning 20 or more games five years in a row, leading the league with 25 victories in 1974 when he won the Cy Young Award and 23 wins in 1975 his first with New York. He worked ten consecutive seasons of 200-plus innings – reaching highs of 318 and 328. Hunter (27) appeared in six World Series and was voted into the Hall of Fame in 1987.

1994 — The Colorado Silver Bullets become the first all-woman baseball team to play against a professional men's team. They are beaten 19-0 by an All-Star team from the Independent Northern League. In pre-game ceremonies, Jean Eastman, 69, throws the first pitch. Eastman had played in the All-American Women's Baseball league in the 1940s. Women have played the game since the sport's early days, but struggled to gain a foothold in organized ball. In 1953, baseball commissioner Ford Frick banned women from the pros when he voided the contract of minor league prospect Eleanor Engle. After four years the Silver Bullets were out of business when their sponsor, Coors Brewing Co., which had invested more than $8 million, ended its affiliation with the team. 1994 would be their final season, and their first with a winning record (23-22) after switching to aluminum bats. In the Silver Bullets' first three seasons they were 6-22, 11-33 and 18-34. Hall-of-Famer Phil Niekro managed the team for the first three seasons and was general manager for their swan song year. He closed it out by saying, "I can't describe how proud I am of this team. There were a lot of skeptics when we started this program. They said there was no way women could play baseball."

May 9

1888 — Elton Chamberlain pitches both right and left-handed for the Louisville Colonels against the Kansas City Cowboys in an American Association game. With the Colonels enjoying a big lead, Chamberlain pitches the last two innings with his left arm in an 18-6 rout. He is the third pitcher to pitch both left and right handed in the same game. Tony Mullane (Louisville AA) was the first on July 18, 1882 and Larry Corcoran (Chicago NL) followed on June 16, 1884.

May 10

1909 – Right-hander Fred Toney pitches a 17-inning no-hitter for the Winchester, Kentucky Hustlers in the Class D Blue Grass League against the Lexington, Kentucky Colts. The 20-year old was in his first full season in professional baseball. This no-hitter would lead him to the major leagues with the Chicago Cubs in 1911. It was a cold and rainy day at Garner's Park when only 300 were on hand to see Toney strike out 19, walk only one and hit one batter. His pitching opponent was also a youngster, named Baker, and he too pitched the entire game giving up only seven hits and six bases on balls.

From the eighth through the sixteenth inning neither Toney nor Baker allowed a hit. It was a throwing error on a sacrifice bunt by Baker that led to the only run of the game in the bottom of the seventeenth that scored on a squeeze bunt. Time of game was 2:45. Toney's stay with the Cubs lasted three seasons, pitching in only 34 games (mostly in relief). He was sold to Cincinnati in 1915 and two years later, on May 2, 1917, he and Hippo Vaughn of the Cubs had no-hitters through nine innings and Toney and the Reds picked up two hits and a run in the 10th for Toney's major league no-hit game.

May 11

1923 — In a Pacific Coast League game, Pete Schneider of the Vernon club hits five homeruns (including two grand slams) and a double with 14 RBI and goes

6-for-8 for the day in a 35-11 win over Salt Lake City. Schneider, a lame-arm ex-pitcher for Cincinnati and the Yankees, left the majors in 1919 to become a position player in the minors. He hit only .221 with five homeruns in the big leagues in six years and only 19 (five in this game) in 1923 with Vernon. Schneider's won-lost record in the majors was 58-86.

1963 — A Dodger Stadium crowd of 55,530 watch as Sandy Koufax pitches the second no-hit game of his career, an 8-0 victory over the San Francisco Giants. It was just under a year before when he tossed his first no-hitter on June 30, 1962 against the Mets, the same season a circulatory ailment in his left index finger first flared up. Despite the problem Koufax would go 25-3 in 1963, pitch his third no-hit game in 1964 and top it off with his fourth – a perfect game in 1965.

Following 1966 he was forced to retire because of finger and arm problems. He finished his 12-year career with probably the finest final four years in baseball – 1963 (25-3 1.99), 1964 (19-5, 1.74), 1965 (26-8, 2.04) and 1966 (27-9, 1.73). His four-year totals were 78-20 with a win percentage of .790. Koufax captured the National League Cy Young Awards in 1965 and 1966 and was the Most Valuable player in 1963. During his career he averaged 9.27 strikeouts per game and allowed only 6.79 hits per nine innings finishing with an ERA of 2.76. Koufax won 165 games while losing 87 for a win percentage of .655. His low win count is due to his arm problems and his slow start in the majors because of his lack of control. Splitting his 12 years in half he won 36 games the first half and allowed 5.27 walks per nine innings. In his final six seasons he allowed only two bases on balls per nine innings and won 129. Koufax (32) was elected to the Hall of Fame in his first year of eligibility in 1972.

1972 — Willie Mays is traded by the San Francisco Giants to the New York Mets for pitcher Charlie Williams and $50,000. Mays, close to the end of his 22 years with the New York Mets and San Francisco Giants, would play through the 1973 season and then retire. He broke in with New York in 1951 and finished his career with 660 homeruns, 3,283 hits, 1,903 RBI, a .302 batting average and was the winner of 12 Gold Gloves. He was the leagues' Most Valuable Player in 1954 and 1965, was National League batting champ with .345 in 1954 and led the league in stolen bases four straight years (1956-59). Mays (24) was voted into the Hall of Fame in his first year of eligibility in 1979.

1977 — With Atlanta mired in a 16-game losing streak, owner Ted Turner gives his manager Dave Bristol a 10-day leave of absence. Turner in the meanwhile signs himself to a coaching contract and enters in the dugout to manage the

Braves. His managerial tenure lasted only long enough to lose to Pittsburgh 2-1 and then be fired by National League president Chub Feeney who advised Turner he was in violation of a major league rule which states: "No manager or player on a club shall directly or indirectly own stock or have any financial interest in the club by which he is employed except under an agreement approved by the commissioner." Incidentally, the millionaire owner-manager didn't buy his own shoes for the game – he borrowed a pair from Cito Gaston whose managerial career would be much more successful.

May 12

1910 — It took Chief Bender only one hour and 36 minutes to mesmerize the Cleveland Naps 4-0 on a one-walk no-hitter for Philadelphia at Shibe Park. Cleveland's Terry Turner was the only Naps player to reach base and he was promptly thrown out trying to steal by catcher Ira Thomas. Bender's no-hit game is the first at the new Philadelphia Stadium opened the year before. The Athletics would go on to win the American League pennant by 14 and a half games over the Yankees with 102 victories.

1955 — Pre-game rain on Chicago's North Side held the Cubs-Pittsburgh attendance to only 2,918 but what they saw was one of the most bizarre finishes in big league history. Chicago right-hander Sam Jones entered the top of the ninth inning with a no-hitter and the Cubs in front 4-0. Jones had walked four Pirates and struck out three and he began the ninth by walking Gene Freese. While Preston Ward was batting with a 2-2 count, Jones' wild-pitched Freese to second and on the next pitch Ward drew a base on balls. With Roman Mejias running for Ward, Jones worked the count on Tom Saffell to 3-1 then missed the plate with the next pitch to fill the bases. Dick Groat was at the plate representing the tying run and, with the bullpen working at full speed, Cubs manager Stan Hack went to the mound to talk to Jones and was greeted by a cheer from the crowd when he left him in. At the top of the ninth with nobody out Jones, not having given up a hit, had loaded the bases with the second, third and fourth place hitters for the Pirates waiting to bat. The first, Groat, looks at three curve balls and strikes out. Rookie Roberto Clemente is next. He swings and misses the first two pitches, fouls off two and on the next pitch goes down swinging. With one out to get Jones started Frank Thomas off with a 1-1 count. Thomas swung and missed for the second strike – then looked at strike three – Jones had his no-hitter.

1956 — Brooklyn's Carl Erskine pitches the second no-hit game of his major league career beating the Giants 3-0 before a paid crowd of 17,395 at Ebbets Field. Only two men reached base, Willie Mays walked in the first inning and Alvin Dark drew a pass in the fourth. This is the first no-hitter at Ebbets Field since Erskine pitched his first no-hit game, a 5-0 win over the Cubs on June 19, 1952. Erskine is the only Brooklyn pitcher to throw two no-hitters at Ebbets Field, which opened in 1913 and closed in 1957.

1966 — After opening the season at old Busch Stadium (Sportsman's Park) the Cardinals settle into their new home, Busch Memorial Stadium, in downtown St. Louis. The old park had been their home beginning in 1920 and through 1953 they had shared the stadium with the Browns. With the same home plate used at the old park, dug up and transplanted to the new digs, the Redbirds win the opening game from the Braves in 12-innings 4-3. Lou Brock drives in the winning run, and the honor of hitting the first homerun goes to Atlanta's Felipe Alou off Ray Washburn.

May 13

1952 — 21 year-old Ron Neccai of the Bristol Twins strikes out 27 batters on his way to a 7-0 no-hitter against the Welch Miners in an Appalachian League game. Neccai would later give up only two hits and strike out 24 in another game. He would pitch in six games for Bristol and strike out 109 in 42 and two-third innings before making the quantum leap from Class D to Pittsburgh. 1952 would be Neccai's only season in the majors, pitching in 12 games with a record of 1-6 and an earned run average of 7.08. He would allow 63 hits in 54 and two-third innings, 31 strikeouts and 32 walks. A teammate pitcher of Neccai's at Bristol had been overlooked in this saga of minor league pitching expertise. He was Bill (Ding Dong) Bell who threw three no-hit games for Bristol while Neccai was on his strikeout roll. Bell made the trip to Pittsburgh with Neccai but worked in only four games in 1952 with an 0-1 record. He did accomplish something Neccai did not — Bell was back with the Pirates in 1955 — but lasted only one inning. His downfall was his failure to get the ball over the plate.

1958 — 37-year old Stan Musial, still five years from retirement, racks up his 3000th career hit at Wrigley Field and becomes the eighth player in major league history to accomplish the feat. Manager Freddie Hutchinson had held Musial out of the game at his own request so, "I could save the big one for the fans back home." The trouble was, Hutch needed him, and in the sixth inning with the Cards trailing the Cubs 3-1, Musial was sent up to bat for Sam Jones. He lined a 2-2 curve off Moe Drabowsky into the left field corner for a run-scoring double to help St. Louis win 5-3. Following the 1963 season Stan-the-Man would retire with 3,630 hits.

May 14

1920 — Walter Johnson, an eventual 400-plus game winner, registers number 300 as Washington knocks off the Detroit Tigers 9-8. The 32 year-old Johnson is the tenth pitcher to reach the 300 mark. He would wrap up his career in 1927 and finish with a won-loss record of 416-279, 3,506 strikeouts and a 2.17 earned run average. His entire 21-year career was spent with the Senators, appearing in 802 games with an average of 281 innings per season. In nine consecutive seasons, 1910-1918, he pitched 300 or more innings. Johnson's two winningest years were 1912 (33-12) and 1913 (36-7) when he pitched a total of 18 shutouts. In his career he registered 110 shutouts, winning 38 of those by a 1-0 score and also losing 26 by 1-0 scores. It's interesting to note that Johnson pitched in only two World Series (1924-1925) and pitched his only no-hitter July 1, 1920, against Boston, the only year in which he ever had a sore arm. After retiring as a pitcher Johnson managed Washington for four seasons beginning in 1929 then took over as Cleveland skipper for three years in 1933. Johnson would join Ty Cobb, Christy Mathewson, Babe Ruth and Honus Wagner as one of the first five inductees into the Hall of Fame.

1941 — Dizzy Dean asks the Cubs for his release, but the request is refused. He signs a coaching contract with Chicago but doesn't fit in. After being suspended for five days with a $50 fine following an argument with umpire Beans Reardon, Dean retires on July 3. His retirement came with the announcement he had signed a contract with the Falstaff Brewery Co. to broadcast St. Louis Cardinals games. In 1940 Dean's arm was so bad he had asked the Cubs to demote him hoping a stay in the minors would help resurrect his career. In early June Chicago placed him on waivers, and when they got no takers he was sent to Tulsa. Dean pitched in 21 games for the Texas League team and was 8-8 but it was obvious his arm was gone. Before the year was out he would make promotional appearances with Sioux Falls and Denver in the Western League and Fargo-Morehead in the Northern League. In 1947 he would sign on with the St. Louis Browns and pitch in his final game. It was merely as a gate attraction – starting and pitching four innings.

1993 — Called up the day before from Colorado Springs, Jay Gainer hits the first pitch thrown to him in the majors into the right field seats at Riverfront Stadium for a homerun. The homer comes off Cincinnati's Jim Pugh and is the 13th time a player has hit a homerun on the first pitch in major league history.

May 15

1894 — With many wooden baseball parks in existence in the later part of the century, it was not unusual that they were subject to fires great and small. The fire that occurred in Boston at South End Grounds was a conflagration. During the third inning of a National League game between the Beaneaters and Baltimore a fierce fight broke out on the field between the Orioles' John McGraw and Boston's Tommy Tucker. This resulted in a gang of fans starting a fire in the right-field stands; the fire spread, completely destroying the park as well $70,000 worth of equipment. In three hours it would wipe out 12 acres of the South End of Boston, including some 70 homes, schools, stores, and warehouses with at least 100 other structures damaged. There were no fatalities. The park would be rebuilt in two months with Boston playing at the Congress Street Grounds in the interim.

1912 — Ty Cobb, on the receiving end of a verbal attack from a fan, asks Claude Lueker to discontinue his tirade. When he becomes more abusive, Cobb charges into the stands and slugs his tormentor. The incident takes place at Hilltop Park in New York and when the Tigers reach Philadelphia for their next series, Cobb is notified of his suspension by American League president Ban Johnson. Cobb's teammates rally behind him and demand the suspension be lifted, but when that is rejected the Detroit players refuse to play and go on strike. Detroit owner Frank Navin faces a fine of $5,000 should he fail to field a team; he orders manager Hughie Jennings to come up with a team of local amateurs for the May 18 game in Philadelphia.

This results in one of the weirdest games in history. Jennings quickly makes the rounds in Philadelphia hiring sandlot and high school players for his game with the Athletics. Jennings puts two of his coaches in the lineup, 48 year-old Deacon McGuire catches and 42 year-old Joe Sugden, also a catcher during his active years, plays first base. The Tigers use Aloysius Travers, a seminary student, as their only pitcher. He throws a 26-hitter and Detroit loses 24-2. One other player, third baseman Ed Irvin hits two triples in three at-bats for a one-game major league slugging percentage of 2.000.

Others who play for the Tigers were Bill Leinhauser, Dan McGarvey, Bill Maharg (whose real name was Bill Graham, "Maharg" spelled backwards), Jim

McGarr, Pat Meany, Jack Coffey and Hap Ward. Only one of these unknowns ever plays in another major league game: Maharg will bat once for the Phillies in 1916. He will also be involved as a conspirator in the Black Sox scandal of 1919. The strike by the Tigers would last only this one game and Cobb would return to the lineup after sitting out ten days and paying a $50 fine. When Jennings put this club together for the historic game, he was in the first year of what would be 14 seasons as Detroit manager from 1907 through 1920. His Tigers played in three World Series and his managing record was 1131-972, .532. Jennings had taken over the team in the twilight of his 17 seasons as a shortstop and first baseman with Louisville, Baltimore, Brooklyn, Philadelphia and Detroit. Jennings hit .312 during his playing days and entered the Hall of Fame in 1945.

1941 — The New York Yankees, playing only .500 ball in mid-May, are in fourth place and five one-half games behind Cleveland. At the same time, Joe DiMaggio is in a severe batting slump. The Yankees lose again but DiMaggio hits a run-scoring single off White Sox lefthander Edgar Smith marking the beginning of his 56-game hitting streak.

1952 — Quite a few Detroit fans miss a good one at Briggs Stadium – only 2,215 diehards attend. Virgil Trucks pitches a no-hitter against Washington and Vic Wertz hits a homerun with two outs in the ninth for the 1-0 win. Trucks strikes out seven, walks one and hits two batters while the Tigers defense keeps the game interesting by committing three errors behind Trucks – all by second baseman Jerry Priddy.

1973 — California's Nolan Ryan pitches the first no-hitter of his career setting down the Royals 3-0. He strikes out 12 and walks one before a crowd of 12,205 in the first no-hit game pitched in Kansas City's major league history. For Ryan's catcher, Jeff Torborg, it is the third no-hit game he has caught. He was behind the plate during Sandy Koufax's perfect game in 1965 and Bill Singer's gem in 1970. Torborg would be one of four players in Ryan's no-hitter to go on to manage in the majors along with Bobby Valentine, Frank Robinson and Lou Piniella.

1981 — Pitching in misty 48-degree weather at Cleveland's Municipal Stadium, the Indians Len Barker throws the eighth perfect game in major league history. He and his teammates rack up a 3-0 win over the Toronto Blue Jays before a crowd of 7,290 fans. Barker, who led the American League in strikeouts in 1980, strikes out 11 Blue Jays – all of them in the final six innings.

May 15-16

1996 — The long-awaited takeover of the California Angels by the Walt Disney Company becomes complete when Disney purchases 25 percent of the American League club and assumes control of day-to-day operations. Disney held the option to buy the remaining 75 percent of the club after the death of 88-year old owner Gene Autry (that option was exercised upon Autry's death on October 2, 1998). The deal calls for a 33-year lease on the stadium with Disney retaining a 20-year bailout option.

May 16

1902 — Outfielder Elmer Flick, after playing in only 11 games with the Philadelphia Athletics, is sold to Cleveland. Flick began his career with the Phillies in 1898 and following his brief stint with the A's would finish his career with the Indians. He was only 5'-9" and 170 lbs. but played 13 seasons in the majors and hit .313. He was the American League batting champ in 1905 after having been edged out of the National League title in 1900 by Honus Wagner's .381 to his .378. In the spring of 1908 he was stricken with a mysterious stomach ailment that for all and intents and purposes finished his career, although he played through the 1910 season. His speed was gone after stealing in double figures in his first eleven years. Flick was 87 years old when he was voted into the Hall of Fame in 1963, and with help of friends was able to attend his induction where he told the audience: "This is a bigger day than I've ever had before. And to think that this plaque will hang here until the end of time." He would live to be 95.

1953 — The White Sox load the bases in the ninth inning against the Yankees with Vern Stephens due to bat. Stephens, who had hit 10 grand slams in his career, is lifted by Sox manager Paul Richards for a pinch hitter. Stephens' replacement is pitcher Tommy Byrne, a former Yankee who has hit six homeruns in his eight-year career. Byrne sends a Ewell Blackwell pitch into the seats for a bases loaded homerun for his only round-tripper of the 1953 season.

1984 — The Baltimore Orioles release Jim Palmer and ask him to retire and accept a position within the organization. Palmer declines in hopes of finding a roster spot elsewhere but this marks the end of his major league pitching career. Seven years later in 1991 he still believed he could pitch; Palmer joined the Orioles as a non-roster player and in two innings allowed five hits and two runs and retired for the second and last time. He spent all 19 years with Baltimore and finished with a winning percentage of .638 (268-152) with an ERA of 2.86. Among his many pitching achievements were eight 20-win seasons and three Cy Young

Awards. Palmer (22) was voted into the Hall of Fame in 1990 in his first year of eligibility.

May 17

1925 — Cleveland's Tris Speaker becomes the fifth player in history to record 3,000 hits when he singles off Tom Zachary in a 2-1 loss to Washington. The 37 year-old Speaker will retire after the 1928 season with 3,514 hits.

1929 — Joe Sewell, who struck out only 114 times in 14 seasons with Cleveland and the Yankees (7,132 times at-bat) is fanned by George Blaeholder of the St. Louis Browns in the third inning. He would not strike out again until the Red Sox Danny MacFayden set him down in the sixth inning on September 20. During this streak Sewell would play in 115 games and go to bat 442 times.

1939 — Baseball goes on television for the first time when station W2XBS in New York City covers the game between Princeton and Columbia at Baker Field, Columbia's home park. Only a handful of viewers see Princeton win 2-1 in 10 innings with Bill Stern announcing. The *New York Times* in reviewing the game said, "It is difficult to see how this sort of thing can catch the public fancy."

1970 — Hank Aaron cracks the 3,000 hit barrier, scratching out an infield single off Cincinnati's rookie right-hander Wayne Simpson. The hit comes in the night-cap of a doubleheader between Atlanta and the Reds at Crosley Field, the historic park that will be closed within a month to make way for the opening of Riverfront Stadium. The 36 year-old Aaron becomes the ninth player to reach the coveted mark, and the first to have 500 homeruns. He finished his career with 3,771 hits.

1998 — The Yankees' David Wells pitches the first perfect game in Yankee Stadium since Don Larsen threw his in 1956. In the clubhouse, following the field salute from the crowd, Larsen was on the phone to confirm that he had graduated from the same high school as Wells – Point Loma High in San Diego. Wells had just thrown the 13th perfect game in the major leagues 4-0 over Minnesota, striking out eleven Twins before the 49,620 roaring fans.

May 18

1872 — The regular catcher for the Brooklyn Eckfords in the National Association is hit in the eye by a foul ball and knocked unconscious. When no other member of the team would catch, a fan in the stands volunteers and catches the remainder of the game against the New York Mutuals. The substitute catcher hits a double in three at-bats, scores a run, has three putouts and three errors. New York newspapers covering the game indicate that no one bothered to ask his name so he went into the record books as John Doe.

1946 — The Detroit Tigers knew something when they traded outfielder Barney McCosky to the Philadelphia Athletics for 23-year old third baseman George Kell. They, of course, did not know they were getting a future Hall-of-Famer. In four seasons with Detroit McCosky had hit .311, .340, .324, and .293, while Kell's batting figures were considerably lower with the A's. It would turn out to be one of those trades that "helps both clubs". Kell would hit .300 or better for the next three seasons, to say nothing of his great defensive play at third, and McCosky would be no slouch during his stay in Philadelphia. However, Kell would hit .306 in the 15 seasons he spent in the majors and lead the American League in batting in 1949 with .343. Kell (21) would enter the Hall of Fame in 1973.

1962 — Once upon a time there were seven minor league classifications - AAA, AA, A, B, C, D. and E. This is the day of reorganization - Class B, C and D become extinct following the 1962 season and all will be grouped into to Class A. Class AA and A combine to become AA and Class AAA remains the same. Also, in 1963 the Rookie Leagues would begin operating and in 1965 another new classification would surface – Short Season Class A.

Some long-time fans may ask what happened to Class E. The classification was established at the National Association meeting in December 1937. Class E leagues would be restricted to players with no experience in Class D or higher. The classification was created in order to compete with the successful Semi-Pro National Baseball Congress operating out of Wichita, Kansas. There was only one such league ever in existence. It was the Twin Ports League and consisted of only four teams, and if it was an experiment it was not a success. Three of the clubs represented Duluth, Minnesota (Marine Iron, Dukes and Heralds) with the fourth team based in Superior, Wisconsin. The league disbanded on July 13, 1943 with each team having only played between 15 and 19 games each.

There also was an Open Classification that was established in 1952 exclusively for the Pacific Coast League. It was rated one-notch above the Triple-A class and was established for the purpose of aiding the PCL build itself into a third major league. Those hopes died, of course, when the Giants and Dodgers moved to San Francisco and Los Angeles in 1958, thus reverting the coast league back to AAA. One other note – classification 1A was established in 1936, which was one notch above Class A and one below AA. Only two leagues used 1A, the Texas and the Southern Association. Both leagues were 1A beginning in 1936 and the Southern Association would continue in that classification through 1945. With the end of the war in 1946 the Texas League would resume operating and both the Texas and Southern circuits would be elevated to AA.

May 19

1987 — Of the 710 games played in the California League this season Fresno hosts the only one postponed because of weather. Put another way, 99.86% of the league's games were played as scheduled.

May 20

1880 — Chicago White Stockings manager Cap Anson begins using hurlers Larry Corcoran and Fred Goldsmith in alternating games, establishing the first "pitching rotation".

May 21

1938 — New York Yankees pitcher Spud Chandler hits a homerun to win his own game 1-0 at Comiskey Park in Chicago. The scoreless duel is broken up in the eighth inning when Chandler drives a ball off Thornton Lee 400 feet into the left field stands. It would be Chandler's first of nine major league homeruns in his eleven years with New York.

May 22

1907 — Taylorville and Charleston face each other in the Class-D Eastern Illinois League and Taylorville wins 1-0 without getting a hit. Two Charleston pitchers share the no-hitter. The starter is lifted in the eighth inning because of a sore arm and is replaced by the first baseman. The only run of the game comes in the third as Taylorville combines a walk, two sacrifices and an error for the ultimate victory. The game has another odd twist. In the fifth inning Charleston has runners on second and third with no one out and two strikes on the batter. With the suicide squeeze on – the batter jabs at the ball and misses; a triple play results on throws to third and second without the ball being hit.

May 23

1901 — An intentional walk with the bases loaded is one of the rarest happenings in baseball. The first in history is given by pitcher-manager Clark Griffith of the Chicago White Stockings in the ninth inning to the Athletics' Nap Lajoie. Chicago had a two-run lead and Griffith elected not to pitch to Lajoie who had become one of the most feared hitters in baseball. He would finish the 1901 season with 229 hits and average .422. Lajoie, a second baseman, spent 21 years in the majors hitting .349 with the Phillies in his first five seasons before jumping to the Athletics in 1901 for more money. The Phillies sued and the State Supreme Court ruled that Lajoie could play only with the Phillies (not A's) in Pennsylvania. As a consequence, the A's traded him to Cleveland in the middle of the 1902 season. Lajoie was a .338 lifetime hitter, winning three batting championships and three RBI titles. In 1905 he was appointed player-manager of the Cleveland Blues, and in his honor, the team's nickname was changed to Naps. It would remain the Cleveland Naps until 1915 when the team became known as the Indians. Lajoie entered the Hall of Fame in 1937.

1935 — The first night game in major league history, scheduled for Cincinnati, is postponed because of rain.

May 24

1912 — Although the Boston Rustlers of the National League wanted Cy Young to remain with the team, he decides to retire. Young had been released by Cleveland in August 1911, then signed with the Rustlers. After going south with Boston in 1912 and pitching well in spring games, he did not appear in any regular season games for the first six weeks. In his retirement statement to the papers Young said, "My arm will no longer do the work that was so easy."

1935 — Delayed one day by rain, the Reds and Phillies play the first night game in major league history. With a crowd of 25,000 on hand at Crosley Field, it is only fitting this historic game should take place in Cincinnati where professional baseball began in 1869. It was a cool, damp evening that failed to dampen the enthusiasm of the spectators. With celebrities from all over the country present, the lighting system was activated from the White House by President Roosevelt. In the absence of Commissioner Landis, because of illness, National League President Ford Frick threw out the first ball. The evening under the lighting plant installed by General Electric for approximately $50,000 was a success . Reds general manager Larry MacPhail reported the cost of lighting each game would amount to about $250. Cincinnati beat Philadelphia 2-1.

1936 — Tony Lazzeri has one of his greatest days as a Yankee with two grand slams, a third homerun, and a triple for 15 total bases as the Bronx Bombers slaughter the Athletics 25-2. Many fans had wondered for years why he had never received his call to join the others already in the Hall of Fame – he got it 45 years after his death. "Poosh 'Em Up" Tony Lazzeri joined the Yankees in 1926 and served on six World Series teams in his 12 years in the Bronx, playing a steller second base and batting .292. He hit in the third spot in the batting order on the 1927 "Murderers' Row" (a nickname hung on the team by a sports writer). Lazzeri played under the handicap of epilepsy but never had an attack that was seen by a fan although he left many a game suddenly. The sportswriters covering the team knew it – but never wrote about it.

1946 — 45 year-old Ted Lyons, back with the White Sox after three years in the Marine Corps, ends his pitching career and is named the club's manager the next day. He takes over the job held by Jimmy Dykes who had managed the team for the past 13 seasons. Lyons pitched in only five games in his first year back from service and ended his active career after 21 major league seasons – all with Chicago. He joined the White Sox in 1923 and won 260 games while losing 230. He was the consummate complete-game pitcher, completing 60% of the 594 games he started, leading the league in 1927 with 30 and in 1930 with 29. The final 28 games he pitched, dating back to 1941, were complete games. Lyons (16) was voted into the Hall of Fame in 1955.

1972 — Pitcher Don Rose packages up most of his major league career in one game when he pitches the California Angels to a 6-5 win over Oakland. The victory will be the first and only win he will achieve against four losses in three seasons. At the same time he also hits his only homerun in the big leagues off Vida Blue; it comes on the first pitch thrown to him in the majors, making him the ninth player in history to accomplish the feat. His career would last only 19 games, 16 with the Angels, one with the Mets and two with San Francisco.

May 25

1935 — Babe Ruth, winding up his career with the Boston Braves, hits three homeruns and a single at Pittsburgh. Just the day before, Ruth had told a writer that he was just about through playing, stating his legs did not have it anymore and that he was fearful of being beaned because his eyesight wasn't what it used to be. At Forbes Field on this day, in his first at-bat, he drove a line drive into the lower right field stands off pitcher Red Lucas. By the third inning, Guy Bush had relieved Lucas and Ruth pulled a pitch down the right field line that just made the seats. Bush was quoted later as telling his catcher, "The next time he comes to bat, I'm going to find out how good he is. I don't think he can hit the fastball off me. I believe I can throw it right by this guy." Ruth hit Bush's second fastball into right center, over the upper deck and over the roof at Forbes Field. Now, The Bambino, believing he had a few more games left in his 40-year old aching body, went on to play his last game on May 30 in Philadel-phia. He struck out in the first inning and in the bottom of the first hurt his knee going after a fly ball and never played again.

Ruth's career ended on the downside in Philadelphia. Ruth and Judge Emil Fuchs, the owner of the Braves, spent the next few days in contention over Ruth's next appearance. In the Braves clubhouse on June 2 Ruth told reporters he was quitting and would go on the voluntary retired list. But, while he was talking to the writers, Fuchs sent a message to the clubhouse stating that Ruth had been released as a player and assistant manager and had been fired as a vice-president.

1937 — Detroit manager-catcher Mickey Cochrane suffers a career ending beaning that fractures his skull in two places. Cochrane was struck in the head by a pitch thrown by the Yankees Bump Hadley. The beaning, which kept Cochrane unconscious for 10 days, came only 27 games into Cochrane's 13th major league season with the Tigers and Philadelphia Athletics. Hadley would pitch through 1940 with New York and finish his 16-year career in 1941 pitching for both the Giants and Athletics. Cochrane managed Detroit beginning in 1934 and up until his beaning was player-manager for the first four seasons before being fired during the 1938 season. He took the Tigers to two World Series and in his five years as skipper won 413 games and lost 297 for a win percentage of .582. Cochrane (3) played in five World Series with a career .320 batting average and was elected to the Hall of Fame in 1947.

May 26

1959 — Pittsburgh's Harvey Haddix, after pitching 12 innings without allowing a hit to Milwaukee, loses to the Braves in the 13th. After retiring 36 men in a row, Felix Mantilla is safe on a throwing error by Don Hoak, then is bunted to second by Eddie Mathews. Hank Aaron draws an intentional walk. Then in a bizarre ending, Joe Adcock homers over the right center field fence which presumably gives

Milwaukee a 3-0 victory. However, Aaron leaves the field after touching second base and Adcock, not realizing Aaron's mistake, obviously passes him on the base line and automatically becomes the second out. The Braves win, but the final score is not decided until the next morning by league president Warren Giles. His ruling states that Adcock is credited with a double, not a homerun, and only the run that wins the game counts – that being Mantilla's run. The final score is Milwaukee 1, Pittsburgh 0 with Haddix losing a one-hitter and Lew Burdette, who also pitched the distance for the Braves (12 hits allowed), the winning pitcher.

May 27

1928 — After playing only 20 games with Washington following his sale by the St. Louis Browns for $25,000, George Sisler is sold again. The Nationals sell his contract to the Boston Braves for $7,500. Sisler had hit only .245 with Washington, but went on to hit .340 the rest of the season for Boston. Sisler's first year in the majors with St. Louis was 1915, and he would retire in 1930 after playing more than two seasons with the Braves. His career batting average was .340 with two .400 seasons (.407 in 1920 and .420 in 1922). In only one season, 1926, did Sisler fail to hit .300 or better, falling only 188 hits shy of 3,000 for his 15-year career. He also managed the Browns in 1924, 1925 and 1926. Sisler was elected to the Hall of Fame in 1939.

1931 — Will Harridge becomes the American League's third president. He began his baseball career as secretary to the circuit's first president, Ban Johnson, shortly after the American League began operating in the early 1900s. Following the death of the second president Ernest Bernard in March, Harridge was offered the job but demurred at first and said he would serve as acting president until a successor could be named. Charles "Old Roman" Comiskey, owner of the White Sox, proposed he be elected immediately. Harridge retired following the 1959 season and was elected to the Hall of Fame in 1972.

1960 — Baltimore Orioles catcher Clint Courtney uses the big mitt ("Big Bertha"} for the first time to catch knuckleball pitcher Hoyt Wilhelm. The mitt designed by manager Paul Richards, a Wilson model #1050 CL with a griptight pocket, weighed 38 ounces, 11 more than the normal catchers' mitt and was 44 inches in circumference. Overall it was one-third larger than the mitts generally being used. In 1964, when Richards was general manager of Houston, the rules committee banned any mitt more than 38 inches around.

May 27-28

1968 — In another wave of expansion, Major League baseball crosses the international frontier and awards a franchise to Montreal, and to San Diego as well. Both will join the National League, balancing each circuit with 12 teams each. The move will create two six-team divisions in each league in 1969, leading to the necessity of playoffs to determine league champions. Baseball suffers another blow to tradition as the 162 game schedule is kept intact, creating an imbalance in the schedule – teams in the same division will play each other 18 games, but only 12 games against the six other teams. Montreal is a surprise choice because it did not have a ballpark of major league specifications, yet it beat out Dallas-Fort Worth, Buffalo, Denver, and the recently-abandoned Milwaukee. The new team's entrance fee is $120 million.

2000 — Tony Perez is paid homage as one of Cincinnati's most popular players as his number is retired before 38,744 Reds fans. This coming prior to his induction into the Hall of Fame in July. He was known as "Doggie" by his teammates, joining Cincinnati in 1964 playing 20 of his 23 seasons with the Reds at first and third base while hitting in the heart of the Big Red Machine batting order. Perez (24) hit .279 in picking up 2,732 hits, 379 homeruns and 1,652 runs batted in.

May 28

1989 — The curtain falls for the final time at Exhibition Stadium as the Toronto Blue Jays play their last game in their original major league park opened on April 7, 1977. On June 5 the Blue Jays would move into their new palace, the $350 million SkyDome. 46,120 Toronto fans turn out for the old stadium's wake to mark the end of the beginning of Blue Jays baseball in the American League.

1993 — Baseball owners approve a six-year, joint TV package with ABC and NBC. In opting for a divide-and-conquer game plan, the owners attempt to re-establish the sport by regionalizing network coverage. For 12 consecutive weeks, beginning after the 1994 All-Star game, the two networks will divide the country into as many as 14 separate viewing areas. Instead of up-front rights fees, as had been the rule, Major League Baseball will form an in-house TV department and receive a percentage of ad sales revenue. Not all clubs think it will be good deal even though the plan is approved by a vote of 25-2 (The Mets and Red Sox voted 'No' and the Yankees abstained).

Yankees owner George Steinbrenner wanted to postpone the balloting because the deal was agreed to "without sufficient study." The Mets and Red Sox veto votes and Steinbrenner's abstention proved those three clubs insight were right — it turned out to be a disaster! Acting commissioner Bud Selig commenting on the winning vote, came up with this classic remark, "We're seizing control of our destiny."

1998 — Arizona manager Buck Showalter becomes the third skipper in baseball history to issue an intentional base on balls with the bases loaded. With the Diamondbacks leading 8-6 over San Francisco, Barry Bonds is intentionally passed to cut the lead to one run. Arizona would go to win. Chicago White Stockings pitcher-manager Clark Griffith was the first on May 23, 1901 when he walked Philadelphia's Nap Lajoie. On July 23, 1944 Giants manager Mel Ott, in the same situation, would purposely pass the Cubs' Bill Nicholson.

2000 — Oakland second baseman Randy Velarde turns in the eleventh unassisted triple play in the history of the game. With the Yankees' Tino Martinez on second base and Jorge Posada on first, Velarde catches Shane Spencer's line drive, tags Posada between first and second, and tags Martinez before he can return to the bag.

May 30

1894 — Bobby Lowe, a second baseman for the Boston Beaneaters, becomes the first major leaguer to hit four homeruns in a game; he does it in consecutive at-bats. The game was played at South End Grounds in Boston and was the afternoon attraction of a double header. Lowe had failed to get a hit in six at-bats in the morning game and also was retired in his first plate appearance in the second game. All four of his homers were hit off Cincinnati pitcher Elton (Icebox) Chamberlain, two of them in the third inning, one in the 5th and one in the 6th. Following his fourth round-tripper fans showered the home plate area with $160 in silver, then Lowe wrapped up the afternoon with an eighth inning single. Chamberlain pitched a complete game for Cincinnati despite Boston's 20-11 win. Lowe went on to an 18-year major league career, hitting a one-season high of 17 homeruns in 1894 and finishing with only 70 lifetime.

1927 — In the fourth inning of a morning game against Pittsburgh, Cubs shortstop Jimmy Cooney pulls off an unassisted triple play. With runners on first and second, Cooney takes Paul Waner's liner, steps on second to double rookie Lloyd Waner and tags Clyde Barnhart coming down from first. Cooney completes the sixth unassisted triple play in history.

May 30-31

1932 — The first plaque to be placed in centerfield in Yankee Stadium is unveiled in honor of Miller Huggins the Hall of Fame manager of the Yankees. Huggins managed 17 years in the majors, 12 of them with New York from 1918 through 1929 and took his team to six World Series.

1934 — William (Lou) Frierson hits five successive homeruns for Paris of the Class C West Dixie League in a 17-12 win at Paris, Texas. Frierson would lead the league in homers this season with 40.

1967 — Just seven games into the season, New York Yankees left-hander Whitey Ford announces his retirement. At 40, Ford had pitched 16 years with the Bronx Bombers and had accumulated a fantastic winning percentage of .690 with 236 wins and only 106 defeats. He finished his career with an ERA of 2.75 and had a 2.71 earned run average in 22 World Series games with the Yankees, winning 10 and losing eight. Ford (16) was voted into the Hall of Fame in 1974.

May 31

1909 — Decatur and Bloomington play a 26-inning game in the Class B Three-I League. Otto Burns of Decatur pitches 25 consecutive scoreless innings after giving up a run in the first inning to win the pitching dual with Ed Clarke, who also went the distance. In the 2-1 Decatur win, Decatur had 11 hits and three errors, Bloomington 13 hits and two errors.

1927 — Just one day after shortstop Jimmy Cooney of the Cubs executed an unassisted triple play, Detroit first baseman Johnny Neun duplicates the feat against Cleveland. This is the second pulled off by a first baseman in history and the seventh overall. With runners on first and second, in the ninth inning, Neun catches Homer Summa's liner, tags Charlie Jamieson between first and second and touches second base before Glenn Myatt can return to end the game. The Tigers win 1-0. Keeping in mind that the unassisted triple plays by Cooney and Neun came on back-to-back days, one writer covering the game failed to make mention of the play in his game story and when questioned by his editor why he neglected to do so said, "I thought it was common place since only yesterday one was made in a game at Pittsburgh." There would not be another for the next 41 years.

1934 — The lead paragraph of *The Sporting News* editorial states, "In the little town of Cooperstown, New York, there is a plot of ground that should represent to baseball what Plymouth Rock means to the United States, Bunker Hill to New England, and the Alamo to Texas." Although the legend of Abner Doubleday inventing baseball in 1839 in a Cooperstown cow pasture had been disproved, the Chamber of Commerce in 1920 raised $5,000, bought the cow pasture, named it Doubleday Field, and designated it a municipal playground. At the time of the editorial only an obscure marker, put up by the New York State Historical Society, existed on the site. Although "Hall of Fame" was never mentioned in this article, it did state, "Receipts might well be set aside as to such a cause as the restoration of Doubleday Field so that it will become a suitable shrine for the game." Later a one-room baseball exhibit was established with questionable artifacts. With the persuasive power of the president of the National League, Ford Frick, the Hall of Fame was born and officially christened in 1939, the centennial of Doubleday's alleged invention.

1942 — Clyde Vollmer of the Cincinnati Reds homers on the first pitch thrown to him in the majors. He becomes the fourth player in history to succeed in this. The homerun comes in the second game of a doubleheader against Pittsburgh and results in a 3-0 Cincinnati win. Vollmer would play in only 12 games in 1942 and his initial homerun would be his only one of the season. His one season high of 22 would come with the Red Sox in 1951 with a total of 69 in his 10-year career.

"A hit, a very palpable hit"
– *Hamlet*, Shakespeare

Bob Feller

John Vander Meer

Chapter Six

"There is always an insistence, year after year, from the general sporting public that the word "greatest" should be brought in. There is no such word in sport. There has never been a "greatest baseball player." There has never been a "greatest pitcher." There have always been too many too evenly matched – Cobb, Ruth and Wagner among every-day players; Cy Young, Mathewson, Johnson, Alexander among the pitchers. Once again I would like to repeat: There is no such animal."

From Grantland Rice's November 13, 1944 column
Setting the Pace.

June 1

1923 — The New York Giants score in all nine innings to beat the Phillies at Baker Bowl 22-8. Heinie Groh, Ross Youngs and Jimmy O'Connell each collect five hits with O'Connell hitting the game's only homerun. In this, one of the rarest team feats in baseball, the Giants scored their final run after the first two batters were retired in the ninth – Youngs tripled and George Kelly doubled to left-center. Here is the sequence of New York's scoring: 4 2 1 1 5 5 1 2 1.

1925 — Lou Gehrig is used as a pinch hitter for infielder Pee Wee Wanninger in the eighth inning of the Yankees' 5-3 loss to Washington. This is the beginning of Gehrig's 2,130 consecutive games-played streak. History has recorded that Gehrig's streak began when Wally Pipp complained of a headache on June 2 and was replaced by Gehrig. In 1937 Gehrig was asked about the Pipp incident and he replied, "Nearly every story I have read about my start on the Yankees say that Wally Pipp was hit in the head by a ball pitched by Charley Caldwell and then I got Pipp's job. That is not so (actually Pipp was not hit until a month later). On June 1 Hug sent me in as a pinch hitter. The next day he called me into his office and said, 'Well, here's that chance you've been hollering for. You're the new first baseman of the Yankees.'"

1942 — Jimmie Foxx, waived by the Red Sox and claimed by the Cubs, begins his final three seasons in the majors. "Double X" winds down his 20 seasons that began in 1925 with eleven years with the Philadelphia Athletics and six with Boston. He would play his final season with the Phillies in 1945 in a career that saw him mostly as a first baseman; but he also caught, played third base, and had limited appearances at shortstop, in the outfield, and on the mound. Foxx was the Most Valuable Player in the American League in 1932, 1933 and 1938, hitting 58, 48 and 50 homeruns respectively. Foxx (3) hit .325 during his career with 534 homeruns and 1,921 RBI; he was voted into the Hall of Fame in 1951.

1947 — In the Class-C Sunset League at Reno in the first game of a double header against the Ontario Orioles, Reno's Vince Pascale and Phil Alotta each hit four homeruns in the same game. The Reno Silver Sox hit a total of 12 homeruns in the 22-19 win over the California team. Neither Pascale nor Alotta would reach the majors. Alotta would hit 43 homeruns in 1947 and total 62 in his career. Pascale hit 23 in 1947 and only 22 more in his final two years in pro ball.

1975 — 18,492 spectators at Anaheim Stadium watch as Nolan Ryan pitches the fourth no-hit game of his career, a 1-0 win over the Baltimore Orioles. It is a typical Ryan game, nine strikeouts and four walks with the Angels scoring the only run in the third inning on consecutive singles by Mickey Rivers, Tommy Harper and Dave Chalk. Ryan ends the tension in the ninth inning by throwing a change-up that Bobby Grich takes for strike three.

June 2

1891 — Old Hoss Radbourn stood 5'-9", weighed 170 pounds and pitched his entire career before the pitching distance was lengthened to sixty-feet, six-inches in 1893. Yet, he would have to be classified as a legitimate workhorse. On this day he would win his 300th game in the eleventh and final year of his career, as Cincinnati beats the Boston Beaneaters 10-8. He is the fourth pitcher in baseball's early years to win 300 games. Radbourn, while pitching in the National League with the Providence Grays, the Boston Beaneaters, Cincinnati, and one season in the Players League for the Boston Reds, worked 4,535 innings (an average of 412 per season). In 1884 he won 60 games and pitched 679 innings, and in four consecutive years (1885-1888) he completed all 181 games he started. In his career, he completed 503 of his 528 starts for a completion percentage of 95.3. Radbourn won a total of 308 games and lost only 195 with an ERA of 2.68 and was elected to the Hall of Fame in 1939.

June 3

1888 — Ernest L. Thayer's famous poem "Casey At The Bat" appears in print for the first time in the *San Francisco Examiner* on page 4, column 4. The little known poem was made popular, long before it was published, by a young actor-comedian named William DeWolf Hopper who's on-stage renditions delighted his audiences. Thayer was a prize specimen of the "one-poem poet", he wrote nothing else of merit. Several players claimed to be the inspiration for the baseball ballad, but Thayer emphatically denied he had any player in mind when he wrote:

> Oh, somewhere in this favored land the
> *sun is shining bright;*
> The band is playing somewhere,
> *and somewhere hearts are light;*
> And somewhere men are laughing, and
> *somewhere children shout;*
> But there is no joy in Mudville — Mighty
> *Casey has struck out!*

1895 — Roger Connor becomes the all-time homerun leader hitting number 122 of his career, driving in the only two runs in a St. Louis 5-2 loss to Brooklyn. This homerun would come in Connor's 16th major league season, an era (1880-1897) when homeruns were a rarity. He would play two more seasons and finish with 138. The first baseman played 12 of his 18 seasons with the Giants and the homerun was not his only claim to fame. Connor hit .317 with 233 triples, 244 stolen bases and was voted into the Hall of Fame in 1976.

1918 — Hub "Dutch" Leonard pitches his second career no-hitter facing only 28 batters as the Red Sox whip the Tigers at Detroit's Navin Field 5-0. His other no-hit game was pitched in Boston against St. Louis on August 30, 1916. The only base runner off Leonard on this day was a walk with two outs in the first inning. The only run he needed to win was supplied by center fielder Babe Ruth with a homerun in the first inning.

1921 — Lou Gehrig makes his professional debut with Hartford in the Class A Eastern League under the name of Lou Lewis. In the spring of 1921 Gehrig had enrolled in a special extension course at Columbia University with the intention of becoming a full-time student in the fall. Although only full-time regular students could participate in intercollegiate athletics, the Columbia baseball coach invited Gehrig to work out and play in practice games. In one of the games, against a professional team, Gehrig so impressed the opposing manager that he was asked to play professionally that summer. When Gehrig signed with Hartford, at age 17, be began using the name Lou Lewis. After June 15 his name ceased to appear in Hartford's box scores without explanation. Later it was learned that Columbia athletic officials had discovered that Gehrig was playing under an assumed name and ended his brief stay in pro ball.

Gehrig went 0-for-3 in his debut with Hartford on June 3 against Pittsfield and would triple against Waterbury the next day for his first hit. He would play only 12 games for the Senators at first base and hit .261. Gehrig had to wait until the fall of 1922 to play for Columbia but by 1923 he shared time with Hartford and the New York Yankees.

1925 — White Sox second baseman Eddie Collins becomes the sixth player in history to collect his 3000th hit. At age 38 he singles off Detroit pitcher Harry Collins and would go on to a total of 3,310 in his 25-year major league career. Eddie Collins began and finished with the Philadelphia Athletics, totaling 13 seasons with that club and playing 12 years with the Chicago White Sox, serving as player-manager in 1925-26. His teams won 160 games and lost 147 in this period but never finished higher than fifth place. Collins hit .333 in his career and appeared in six World Series in which he hit .328 in 36 games. Collins was elected to the Hall of Fame in 1939.

1930 — Grover Cleveland Alexander is released by the Phillies and retires after 20 years of pitching excellence. He had been traded by the Cardinals to Philadelphia during the winter, but an 0-3 start in nine games with an earned run average of 9.14 forced the move by the Phillies. His major league career over, he signed with Dallas in the Texas League but was released on July 21 with a 1-2 record and ERA of 8.25. As late as 1937, when he was 50, he pitched one inning of semi-pro ball with the Springfield Empires against the Spencer Coals of Chicago. Alexander had split most of his career (which began in 1911) between the Cubs and Phillies and finished with a winning percentage of .642 – 373 wins, 208 losses and an ERA of 2.56. He recorded 90 shutouts, won 20 or more games in nine of his seasons and won more than 30 games in three successive years in 1915-16-17.

Alexander spent most of 1918 in the service as an artillery sergeant, and spent the rest of his life suffering from fits of epilepsy (possibly as a result of being exposed to poison gas). Despite this, and his excessive drinking habit, he managed to win 126 games with the Cubs in just over seven seasons before being sent to St. Louis in 1926. Alexander completed 438 of the 696 games he started, appeared in three World Series and was voted into the Hall of Fame in 1938.

1932 — Lou Gehrig hits four consecutive homeruns against the Athletics and narrowly missed a fifth, as the Yankees and Philadelphia slug it out at Shibe Park in a 20-13 New York win. Gehrig hits his first three homers off George Earnshaw in the first, fourth and fifth innings and his fourth off Roy Mahaffey in the seventh. He is retired in his last two plate appearances. Gehrig is the first player to hit four homeruns in a game since 1896 and is only the third player to do so.

However, Gehrig's accomplishment would take second billing on the sports pages late that afternoon. On his way to the Giants clubhouse following the rain-out of a doubleheader with Philadelphia, reporter Tom Meany of the *World Telegram* is tipped by a hot dog vendor that Giants manager John McGraw had stepped down and Bill Terry had taken over. Meany's inadvertent discovery developed into the biggest sports exclusive in years.

1964 — The following memo was circulated on this date in 1964:

THE NATIONAL LEAGUE OF
PROFESSIONAL BASEBALL CLUBS
CAREW TOWER
CINCINNATI 2, OHIO

June 3, 1964

To National League General Managers
and Public Relations Directors

Gentlemen:

Our office has had complaints over the years, and recently, about gestures players have made on the field; gestures which could be properly termed "obscene". I have also seen players at bat "adjusting" themselves, which is not very attractive.

These gestures are more prominent when seen on television and players should be reminded they are on television much of the time and the necessary "adjusting" should be done when possible on the bench or as inconspicuously as possible.

Obscene gestures are repulsive and harmful to the game and the use of any <u>obscene</u> gestures which come to our attention will be penalized.

General managers and P.R. men are hereby requested to see that this message gets to the manager, players and coaches.

Warren C. Giles
President

WCG/akm

1971 — Ken Holtzman racks up the second no-hitter as the Chicago Cubs defeat the Reds 1-0 in the first no-hit game pitched in Cincinnati's new Riverfront Stadium. Holtzman's first no-hit game was pitched at Wrigley Field August 19, 1969 against Atlanta. Holtzman walked four Reds but finished with a flourish by striking out both Tommy Helms and Lee May. The only run of the game was scored in the third inning, by Holtzman, when he reached on an error, moved to second on a ground ball and came home on a single by Glenn Beckert.

June 4

1890 — Tim Keefe, on his way to 342 pitching victories, wins number 300 for the New York Giants in a 9-4 complete game against the Boston Reds. The 33-year old Keefe becomes the second pitcher to win 300 games, reaching the magic number while pitching in the Players League, a circuit operated by the players, but a league that lasted only one year. The other clubs were the Brooklyn Wonders, Buffalo Bisons, Chicago Pirates, Cleveland Infants, Philadelphia Quakers and Pittsburgh Burghers. Although Keefe pitched most of his career at the shorter pitching distance in a three-year period (1886-1888), he won 112 games and finished his career with 225 losses to go with his 342 victories. Keefe would pitch through the 1893 season (the first year of the sixty-feet, six-inch pitching mound) and was elected to the Hall of Fame in 1964.

1953 — Ralph Kiner, who had hit 294 homeruns in his first seven seasons with the Pirates (an average of 42), is traded by Pittsburgh to the Chicago Cubs. The Pirates also give Chicago Joe Garagiola, Howie Pollet and George Metkovich and the Bucs receive Toby Atwell, Bob Schultz, Preston Ward, George Freese, Bob Addis and Gene Hermanski, as well as $150,000 in cash. He would play only ten seasons in the majors because of back problems and at 33 years old, with a drop in production, would retire after spending one year with Cleveland in 1955. In his final two years his homeruns dropped from 35 in 1935 to 22 and then to 18. However, his final figures were 369 homeruns, 1,015 runs batted in and an average of .279. Kiner led or tied for the National League homerun title seven straight years and entered the Hall of Fame in 1974.

1964 — Sandy Koufax of the Los Angeles Dodgers pitches his third no-hitter in three seasons with a 3-0 win over the Phillies at Connie Mack Stadium before 29,709 fans. His previous no-hit games were against the Mets June 30, 1962 and May 11, 1963 over San Francisco. The only batter to reach base was Richie Allen in the fourth inning when Koufax lost him on a 3-2 count walk. The Dodgers lefty faced only 27 batters as Allen was thrown out by catcher Doug Camilli in an attempt to steal second base. Koufax struck out 12.

2000 — Esteban Yan not only was the winning pitcher for Tampa Bay over the Mets but he hit the first pitch thrown to him as a professional batter for a homerun. Yan's homer came with one man on base in the second inning off Mets pitcher Bobby J. Jones. He becomes the 14th player to join this elite group and the fifth pitcher to pull off the surprise.

June 5

1882 — There are many theories as to the origin of the seventh inning stretch, but the most plausible beginning of this tradition occurred on this date at a Manhattan College baseball game in New York City. Or, you may choose from the following – it is reported by some historians that Cincinnati Red Stockings fans in 1869 stood in the seventh to stretch and relax from the hard benches; a Providence, Rhode Island newspaper referred to the seventh inning as "lucky seventh;" in 1890 the *New York Times* stated "the beginning of this baseball ritual has been stranded in the reefs of antiquity, but it probably came from the idea of the lucky seven in craps;" or that president William Howard Taft, at the 1910 season opener in Washington, stood to stretch and the fans followed suit out of respect of the chief executive; however, it is also reported that the "Taft stretching" had taken place at a game in Pittsburgh.

The Manhattan College game against a semipro club known as the Metropolitans was held at a park near 107th Street between Sixth and Seventh Avenues. The college baseball team was coached by Brother Jasper (the origin of the team nickname – the Jaspers), who also was the athletic director and Prefect of Discipline. He also supervised the student fans at games, requiring them to sit reverently and quietly while the teams played. During this game, Brother Jasper noticed that when the Manhattan College team came to bat in the seventh the students were becoming restless and fidgety. To relieve the tension, Brother Jasper told the students to stand up and stretch for a couple of minutes before the game resumed. This exercise "to give it the old seventh inning stretch" was repeated at other Manhattan College games, and when the Jaspers played annually at the Polo Grounds against the New York Giants in the 1890s the practice spread to major league fans.

June 6

1892 — 20-year old Willie Keeler makes his professional debut as a left-handed shortstop for Binghamton in the Eastern League. He had one hit in three at-bats and had one error. He would finish the season with a league-leading batting average of .373. He usually played third base and committed 48 errors. At season's end he was purchased by the New York Giants, played in 13 games and hit .306. He later was traded to Baltimore, also in the National League, where he became a regular outfielder for the rest of his career. "Wee Willie" Keeler was only 5-4, weighed 140 pounds and made the phrase "hit 'em where they ain't" famous. In 1897 he hit in 44 consecutive games, a record that he held until 1941 when Joe DiMaggio broke it. Wee Willie played 19 seasons in the majors and hit .343 and batted .300 or better in 15 of them. In 1897 he led the league with a .424 average. Keeler played his final season as a pinch hitter for the Giants – going 3-for-10 and finishing his career with 2,932 hits. He was voted into the Hall of Fame in 1939.

—

The first president of the United States to attend a major league game, Benjamin Harrison, watches the Cincinnati Reds defeat the Washington Senators 7-4 in 11 innings. Washington was a member of the National League at this time and the game was played at Boundary Field located at the site where Griffith Stadium would later be built.

1937 — Ebbets Field in Brooklyn was loaded with advertising signs – Phillip Morris, Gem Razor Blades, Botany Ties, and Coca-Cola. The Dodgers use Lifebuoy and Burma Shave; but none received the notoriety as "Hit Sign Win Suit." This sign was placed by Abe Stark, a Brooklyn clothier who served for a time as president of the New York City Council, and as Brooklyn Borough president. The sign was almost impossible to hit, being only four or five feet high and located at the bottom of the scoreboard in right field. Most of the outfielders played directly in front of the sign and the only way the sign could be hit was for a ground ball to go through the legs of the right fielder. On this date it is reported that the Dodgers' Woody English accomplished the feat but no record is found of how he did it. One other player turned the trick according to former Brooklyn writer Bill Roeder who said an unidentified Pittsburgh player did it when a bad hop got by Carl Furillo and hit the sign on one bounce. Stark acknowledged the "hit", but decided it deserved only a pair of slacks.

June 7

1907 — Jimmy Collins, the first manager of the Boston American League club, is traded to the Philadelphia Athletics for infielder Jack Knight. Player-manager Collins had been relieved as skipper, and replaced by Chick Stahl during the 1906 season, even though Collins had won pennants for Boston in 1903 and 1904. Collins, a third baseman, played his first season in the majors in 1895 with the Boston Beaneaters and Louisville Colonels, both in the National League, and went on to play 14 years, finishing with the Athletics in 1908. Collins hit .294 during his career, was best known for his brilliant defensive play at third base, and was elected to the Hall of Fame in 1945.

June 8

1909 — Clarence T. "Cack" Henley pitches Organized Baseball's longest shutout, a 24-inning 1-0 win for San Francisco over Jimmy Wiggs of Oakland in a Pacific Coast League game. Henley gives up nine hits and one walk in a game lasting three hours and 35 minutes. Henley never made it to the majors but spent eleven of his 12 seasons in the coast league with brief stops in the California and Western Leagues. He was a big winner, chalking up 223 wins while losing 178 and twice won more than 30 games in a season. In the last years of his career, 1911-1915, when innings pitched records were kept, Henley averaged 289 innings per season.

1955 — Two future Hall-of-Famers are involved in a nondescript transaction by Brooklyn and their top farm club in Montreal — both are left-handers. One is Sandy Koufax, a 19 year-old wild rookie whose contract stipulated he remain on the major league roster for two years, and the other is Tom Lasorda, who was moved to the International League Royals to make room for Koufax. Lasorda is sent to Montreal with a 0-0 record and an ERA of 13.50. In 17 years (1972) Koufax would enter the Hall of Fame. After 42 years (1997), Lasorda would also be inducted. Lasorda didn't make it as major league pitcher – three years with the Dodgers and Kansas City A's with a 0-4 record and an ERA of 6.48. His playing days over after 1960, he started his long run as a staff-member in the Dodgers organization, first as a scout (four years), then minor league manager (12 years), and topped it off as skipper for Los Angeles for 20 years. While at the helm Lasorda (2) guided the Dodgers to four National League pennants and two World Championships, winning 1,599 games while losing 1,430 – a win percentage of .528.

1965 — Baseball's first amateur draft kicks off and the Kansas City Athletics, by virtue of finishing last in the American League, pick 19-year old outfielder Rick Monday from Arizona State. The game had been hoping for years a miracle would pop up to curtail the "excessive" bonuses being paid to untested youngsters out of college and high school. This became evident in 1964 when the Los Angeles Angels awarded a bonus of $205,000 to Rick Reichart, who never played baseball in high school, but had two explosive seasons at bat at the University of Wisconsin. Aside from attempting to limit the spiral of bonuses, major league owners thought the draft would more evenly distribute the talent among all clubs. Monday, the first player drafted under the new system was paid a bonus of $104,000. By 1999 three of the 30 first round selections would be paid in excess of $3 million each, seven in excess of $2 million each, 19 in excess of $1 million and one received $845,000. In 1991 the New York Yankees were the first team to pay an amateur draftee over a million dollars when they signed pitcher Brian Taylor out of high school for a bonus of $1.5 million.

1970 — Players receive a $2,000 raise in minimum salary from $10,000 to $12,000 per year. Since 1947 the minimum had increased from $5,500 to $12,000.

1992 — Commissioner Fay Vincent suspends New York Yankees pitcher Steve Howe after the 34-year old left-hander enters a guilty plea in federal district court in Missoula, Montana to a cocaine charge. This is the seventh time Howe has been involved in drug or alcohol related incidents, having been hospitalized six times for treatment between 1982 and 1988. Vincent would hand down a lifetime suspension for Howe on June 24 and in his decision said, "Howe has the longest disciplinary record of drug offenses in the history of baseball." The Major League Players Association then filed a grievance on Howe's behalf and on November 12 arbitrator George Nicolau ordered the lifetime ban revoked. Nicolau's 54-page opinion said, "We know now Howe has an underlying psychiatric disorder that was never diagnosed or treated; that this disorder has been a contributing factor to his use of drugs; and that, absent treatment for the condition, he remains vulnerable to such use. The office of the commissioner cannot escape its measure of responsibility for what took place in 1991. Based on medical advice the commissioner had solicited, the need for continuous testing was obvious. To give Howe 'yet another chance' of returning to the game without implementing those conditions was not, in my judgement, a fair shot at success." Howe continued his pitching career through 1996.

—

Chicago Cubs right-handed pitcher Jim Bullinger, who made his major league debut two weeks earlier, finally gets to face big league pitching himself, and hits the first pitch thrown to him for a homerun. The pitch is served up by the Cardinals' Rheal Cormier in the first game of a doubleheader in St. Louis before 38,572 fans. Bullinger was drafted by the Cubs in 1986 as an infielder and hit 19 homeruns in four minor league seasons before being switched to the mound in 1990. Bullinger becomes the twelfth player, and fourth pitcher, to homer on the first pitch thrown to him in the majors.

June 9

1914 — 40 year-old Honus Wagner becomes the second player in history to collect 3,000 hits. Cap Anson was the first to record 3,000 hits reaching that mark in either 1894 or early in the 1895 season. Wagner, the Pittsburgh shortstop, doubles off the Phillies' Erskine Mayer in the first inning. On March 16, 1908 Wagner, at age 34, had announced his retirement but continued on to play 151 games, more than he had played in any of his previous nine seasons and leads the league in hitting for the sixth time. He also led the league that season in hits, total bases, doubles, triples; runs batted in and stolen bases. He would miss the Triple Crown by hitting two fewer homeruns (10) than the Dodgers Tim Jordan.

Wagner, rated as one of the top shortstops in history, began his career with Louisville (then a member of the National League) in 1897. He moved with the club in 1900 when owner Barney Dreyfuss moved the franchise to Pittsburgh. In his rookie season Wagner hit .344 and for 17 straight years would not hit under .300, compiling a career average of .329, with 3,430 hits and 1,732 runs batted in while winning eight batting titles. He was 43 when he retired for good in 1917 and sixteen years later would return to the Pirates as a coach and goodwill ambassador. Wagner (33) was one of the original five inducted into the Hall of Fame in 1936.

1950 — The St. Louis Cardinals' scheduled Sunday night game with Brooklyn at Sportsman's Park is ordered postponed by commissioner Happy Chandler. Since no night games had ever been played on Sunday in the majors, National League President Ford Frick advises the Cardinals to reschedule the game. They comply. Thirteen years later to the day the first Sunday night game would be played.

1963 — The first Sunday night game in major league history is played at Colt Stadium in Houston and results in a 3-0 victory for the Colt .45s over the San

Francisco Giants. Following a Sunday afternoon doubleheader against the Los Angeles Dodgers on June 10, 1962 special permission had been sought by Houston to play at night on Sundays. Houston, infamous for its high humidity and excessive heat, had an estimated 75 to 80 of its 33,145 fans overcome by the heat on this sunny day. The temperature was 90 degrees and the humidity registered 75%, with only a light breeze, in a stadium without a roof. In 1963 permission is granted by the National League and the first Sunday night game is played on a delightful (for Houston) evening with a soft breeze and a temperature of 83 before a crowd of 19,389. Houston pitcher Skinny Brown picks up the win in relief of Dick Farrell who is knocked out in the third inning. Brown finishes the game and allows only one hit the rest of the way. Jack Sanford is the losing pitcher for the Giants. This marks the beginning of what would become a fairly commonplace occurrence in the majors — Sunday night baseball.

June 10

1938 — Rookie pitcher Bill Lefebvre makes his major league debut with the Boston Red Sox working four innings and allowing eight hits in relief. However, in his first at-bat he tags White Sox Monte Statton's first pitch for a homerun becoming the third player in history, and the second pitcher, to accomplish the feat. This would be Lefebvre's only big league appearance in 1938 and the only homerun he would hit in his four-year career. Lefebvre pitched for the Red Sox and Washington and also played some first base with a batting average of .276 (24-87).

1959 — Cleveland's Rocky Colavito hits four consecutive homeruns at Baltimore's Memorial Stadium to lead the Indians to an 11-8 win. Only Bobby Lowe and Lou Gehrig had hit four in a row prior to Colavito's outstanding accomplishment. He becomes the eighth player in history to hit four homers in a game. Colavito entered the game in a 3-for-28 (.107) slump and drew a base-on-balls his first time up. His first homerun was hit off Jerry Walker, the next two off Arnold Portocarrero and his last off Ernie Johnson.

June 11

1938 — Cincinnati lefthander Johnny Vander Meer fashions a no-hitter chalking up a 3-0 victory over the Boston Bees at Crosley Field before a sparse crowd of 10,311. He strikes out four and walks three batters – two of the three are doubled off base on strong throws by catcher Ernie Lombardi. The Reds, leading 1-0 going into the sixth inning, are treated to the clincher when Lombardi homers following a walk to Wally Berger.

1990 — Nolan Ryan, four months past his 43rd birthday, registers the sixth no-hitter of his career, a stunning 5-0 win for the Texas Rangers over Oakland. Practically every play made behind Ryan was routine except for a sinking liner caught by centerfielder Gary Pettis in the sixth inning. Ryan also was at the top of his game in the strikeout category – whipping 14.

June 12

1939 — Baseball's Centennial Celebration is held at the Hall of Fame in Cooperstown, New York, with the dedication of the museum and an exhibition game at Doubleday Field. The field was opened in 1920 but for this event had been brought up to major league standards, albeit cozier than modern big league parks (296 to left, 390 to center, 312 to right). Attending the gala and participating in the six-inning exhibition game were those first elected to the Hall in 1936 – Ty Cobb, Walter Johnson, Christy Mathewson, Babe Ruth and Honus Wagner. From the 1937 class came Nap Lajoie, Tris Speaker, Cy Young and Connie Mack. Grover Cleveland Alexander, a 1938 inductee, and Eddie Collins and George Sisler from 1939 were also in attendance.

1970 — The Padres, just a year old in the National League, succumb to the first no-hitter thrown in San Diego Stadium. Pittsburgh's Dock Ellis succeeds in the second game of a doubleheader played before only 9,903 spectators on a rainy Southern California night. In the true sense of the word this was not a "gem" – a no-hitter, yes, but not a gem. Ellis struggled throughout the game giving up several hard-hit balls, his erratic control contributing to eight walks, with three of the recipients stealing second base. Ellis later would reveal he pitched the game while under the influence of LSD. The Pirates picked up only five hits off losing pitcher Dave Roberts but two of them were homeruns by Willie Stargell accounting for the 2-0 Pittsburgh victory.

1981 — At half-past midnight, union chief Marvin Miller announces the players' strike is on. Relations between the two sides had begun to sour over the free agency compensation issue on February 19 when management, in keeping with the 1980 accord, invoked its right to implement its compensation proposal and demands for a salary cap. Also, according to the accord, the Players Association could serve notice by March 1 that it planned to strike if still dissatisfied. Less than two weeks later, on February 25, the Executive Board of the union approves a May 29 strike date. On May 7, still without a settlement, the union files charges of unfair labor practices with the National Labor Relations Board. Because of this action the original strike deadline is delayed by two weeks, but on June 12 the players stage their first midseason strike in history. On July 31 the players and owners would reach an agreement, ending the strike after 50 days resulting in 712 canceled games. Owners would not get their salary cap but would receive some compensation by receiving either a minor-league or major-league player in a pool culled from rosters of all clubs. The agreement would extend the contract through December 31,1984. The season will resume on August 10 – one day after the All-Star game in Cleveland.

1996 — Owner Marge Schott of the Cincinnati Reds is suspended by baseball's 10-man Executive Council and loses daily control of the club through the 1998 season. The crux of her suspension was an interview in which she said that Adolph Hitler was "good at the beginning" but "went too far." This is the second time in three years the only female controlling owner in baseball has been suspended. In February 1993 she was given a one-year suspension, which was later shortened to eight months, for bringing "disrepute and embarrassment" to baseball. Schott would sell the Cincinnati club in 1999 and leave baseball.

Of the six owners subjected to suspension in the history of the game only Schott and New York Yankees' owner George Steinbrenner have been hit twice. Three lost their ownerships; two of them owned the Phillies. In 1912, owner Horace Fogel made several accusations that the pennant race was being fixed by some managers, players, and umpires to favor the New York Giants. He was found guilty on five of seven of his charges and drummed out of baseball. William D. Cox, president of the Phillies was shown the exit from the game for betting on his own club in 1943 and St. Louis Cardinals owner Fred Saigh was sent to prison for income tax evasion in 1953 and forced to sell his team. Steinbrenner's two confrontations with baseball came as the result of his conviction by a federal court for making illegal contributions to Richard Nixon's 1972 presidential campaign and in 1990 for dealings with an admitted gambler. Atlanta Braves owner Ted Turner was suspended in 1976 for "tampering" in an attempt to obtain San Francisco player Gary Matthews.

1997 — Baseball's 96-year tradition of keeping the National and American Leagues separate comes to an end as the San Francisco Giants beat the Texas Rangers 4-3 in Arlington before 46,507 fans. The game introduces the controversial interleague play as its latest innovation in an effort to boost attendance figures while continuing to change the face of the game. This would be the first of 214 NL-AL confrontations in interleague play's inaugural season.

June 13

1905 — After pitching a no-hitter on July 15, 1901 against St. Louis, Christy Mathewson of the New York Giants repeats the performance at West Side Park in Chicago beating the Cubs 1-0. Errors by shortstop Bill Dahlen and second baseman Billy Gilbert prevent Mathewson from going into the books with a perfect game. Although Chicago pitcher "Three Finger" Brown was being hit hard, he held the Giants scoreless going into the top of the ninth inning. Dahlen (who had committed one of the two errors behind Mathewson) singles in the only run of the game to the dismay of the 8,000 Chicago spectators watching the one-hour and twenty-five minute encounter.

1912 — New York Giants right-hander Christy Mathewson, in his 13th season in the National League and only 32 years old, defeats the Chicago Cubs 3-2 for his 300th victory. He becomes the eighth pitcher to reach the coveted mark and would go on to win a total of 373 games.

1930 — Two future Hall-of-Famers, Goose Goslin, in his tenth season with the Washington Senators, and Heinie Manush, who had spent his first six seasons with Detroit and the St. Louis Browns, are involved in a trade for each other – Goslin to the Browns and Manush to Washington. Goslin had won the American League batting championship while with Detroit in 1926 with an average of .378 and Goslin had beaten Manush out of the batting championship in 1928 on the last day of the season (.379 to .378). Goslin played in the majors 18 years with Washington, the Browns and Detroit batting .316 with 1,609 runs batted in with 248 homeruns, appearing in five World Series. Manush was a better average hitter (.330) in his 19 years with six different teams. Manush entered the Hall of Fame in 1964 and Goslin followed in 1968. Manush died on May 12, 1971 followed by Goslin three days later on May 15, 1971

1940 — The National and American Leagues, having arranged to schedule annual exhibition games at Doubleday Field in Cooperstown, inaugurate the program with a meeting between the Chicago Cubs and Boston Red Sox. Lefty Grove starts on the mound for Boston, joining five future Hall-of-Famers: Ted Williams, Jimmie Foxx, Joe Cronin, Bobby Doerr and Billy Herman. The Cubs' Bill Nicholson hits the first homerun and Williams tags the second. There was one casualty, Dom DiMaggio runs into the outfield fence while making a spectacular catch; he's hospitalized with facial cuts. The game is called after seven innings with the Cubs leading 10-9.

1948 — Yankees legend Babe Ruth, battling throat cancer, is honored by 49,641 fans on the 25th anniversary of Yankee Stadium (The House That Ruth Built) with Ruth wearing his old uniform. Fourteen years following his release by New York his number 3 is finally retired (Ruth's uniform number was worn by George Selkirk, Allie Clark, and Bud Metheny before it was retired). The uniform would ultimately be sent to the Hall of Fame Museum. Ruth lost his fight with cancer and died two months later on August 16 at age 53.

1973 — The Los Angeles Dodgers play Steve Garvey at first, Davey Lopes at second, Bill Russell at shortstop and Ron Cey at third together for the first time. The Dodgers suffer a 16-3 loss to Philadelphia, but this is the beginning of the quartet's playing as a unit for the next eight and a half years.

June 14

1919 — Joe Wilhoit with Wichita in the Class-A Western League begins his 69 game hitting streak that would last through August 19. He would lead the league with a batting average of .422, 222 hits and score 126 runs in 128 games. Wilhoit's baseball career lasted 11 years with eight minor league teams in five different leagues in which he hit .336. The outfielder got to the majors in 1916 with the Braves, and also played with the Giants and Pirates in three seasons (1917, 1918,1919) before returning to the minors to set his 69 game hitting record. He finished his major league career at the end of the 1919 season with the Boston Red Sox with a career major league average of .257 and played through the 1923 season in Triple A with Toledo and Salt Lake City. Wilhoit accomplished something that many seasoned major leaguers never have – he played in two World Series games with one official hitless at-bat and a walk with the New York Giants in 1917.

1940 — The Boston Braves and Pittsburgh swap catchers; Boston trades Al Lopez to the Bucs for Ray Berres and $40,000. Lopez broke into the majors with Brooklyn in 1928, was traded to Boston in 1936 and finished his 19 seasons as a player with Cleveland in 1947. He was a consummate stud behind the plate registering 1,918 games caught, with a career .261 batting average. However, it was in the managing department he left his mark in baseball. That phase began with the Indians in 1951 and continued with the White Sox in 1957, winning one pennant with each team. In his 17 years as a skipper Lopez (10) finished in the second division only twice with a record of 1,422-1,026 .578 and entered the Hall of Fame in 1977.

June 15

1902 — Jay Justin "Nig" Clarke hits eight homeruns in one game for the Corsicana Oilers against Texarkana in a Class-D Texas League game. Sunday ball was banned in Corsicana and this game was moved to a small park in Ennis, Texas, which resulted in a 51-3 win for the Oilers. It's difficult to piece together the exact happenings of this game because there were several printed box scores, none of which were identical. Also, in 1947 *The Sporting News* interviewed Clarke on the subject and his remembrances did little to clarify some of the batting statistics. However, one thing is certain – Clarke did hit eight homeruns! He was quoted as saying he did it in eight at-bats but it is more likely he made at least 10 trips to the plate. Besides the eight homers hit by Clarke, his teammates contributed 13 others, with Corsicana scoring in every inning collecting 53 hits to go with five Texarkana errors. Clarke said the game lasted 3 hours and 45 minutes but two box scores agree on 2:10. Clarke went on to catch nine seasons in the majors with Cleveland, Detroit and the St. Louis Browns from 1905 to 1911, the Philadelphia Phillies in 1919 and Pittsburgh in 1920 hitting .254. One more note of interest – the eight homers Clarke hit on June 15, 1902 would be two more than he would hit in 506 games in the major leagues.

1938 — 38,748 fans really get their money's worth as they attend the first night game at Ebbets Field in Brooklyn. All expected a great show with a circus atmosphere put on by Dodgers vice-president Larry MacPhail – a band, a fife and drum corps, an exhibition by Olympic hero Jesse Owens and baseball celebrity Babe Ruth in attendance. What the fans did not expect is what happened in the game itself between Brooklyn and Cincinnati. Reds lefthander Johnny Vander Meer, fresh off a no-hit game just four days earlier against the Boston Bees at Crosley Field, repeats with a 6-0 no-hitter against the Dodgers. An incredible night! Some 15,000 hoping to see the first night spectacle in Brooklyn were turned away when the fire department ordered the gates closed long before game time.

The second consecutive no-hitter by Vander Meer is far from being a classic. He strikes out seven but walks eight batters — three of them in the ninth inning. After getting one out, Vander Meer walks Babe Phelps, Cookie Lavagetto and Dolph Camilli, calling for a mound conference of the entire infield and manager Bill McKechnie. The meeting ends with Vander Meer still on the mound. Ernie Koy grounds to third baseman Lew Riggs whose throw to catcher Ernie Lombardi forces pinch runner Goody Rosen for the second out. The crowd, now frantic, waits not only to see baseball history made, but baseball history two-times over – back-to-back no-hitters by one pitcher. Leo Durocher is in the batter's box and after working the count to 2-2 lofts a fly to short center where the ball is immediately surrounded by second baseman Lonnie Frey, shortstop Billy Meyers and center fielder Harry Craft. Craft takes charge, calling off the others, making the historic catch for the final out.

1949 — Philadelphia Phillies first baseman Eddie Waitkus is shot by an obsessed female fan in her room in Chicago's Edgewater Beach Hotel just before midnight. Waitkus, who had been with the Cubs before being traded to Philadelphia following the 1948 season, had been adored from afar by Ruth Ann Steinhagen during her high school days in Chicago. With the Phillies in town to play the Cubs she had taken a room in the hotel intent on shooting him and then killing herself. Steinhagen had seen at least two psychiatrists before the encounter with Waitkus and at times had talked about committing suicide. After shooting Waitkus with a rifle in the abdomen she panicked and called the front desk to report what she had done. This move saved his life. Waitkus underwent lung surgery and missed the rest of the 1949 season but returned in 1950 and played six more years in the majors. Steinhagen would spend three years in an Illinois mental hospital before being released.

1957 — After spending his first eleven years with the St. Louis Cardinals and a short stay with the New York Giants, Red Schoendienst is traded to Milwaukee for Danny O'Connell, Ray Crone and Bobby Thomson. In 1961 he would return to St. Louis for his final three playing seasons. In 1965 he began a run of 13 years as Cardinals manager, taking St. Louis to the World Series in 1967 and 1968. Schoendienst (2) played 19 years batting .289 with 2,449 hits and was elected to the Hall of Fame in 1989.

1963 — Juan Marichal of the San Francisco Giants, who pitched a one-hitter in his first major league start in 1960 and duplicated that feat in 1961, gets the total job done this time and throws a no-hitter against the Houston Colt .45s. This one is a magnificent pitchers dual as Houston's Dick Drott has given up only one hit going into the bottom of the eighth in a scoreless tie. Jim Davenport's double and a run-scoring two-base hit by Chuck Hiller gives Marichal all the room he needs going into the top of the ninth. He quickly retires Johnny Temple on a foul pop up and proceeds to strike out Pete Runnels and rookie Brock Davis. 18,869 witness the first major league no-hit game in San Francisco history, as well as the first no-hitter by a Giants pitcher since Carl Hubbell subdued the Pittsburgh Pirates in 1929. Marichal spent 14 of his 16 seasons with the Giants beginning in 1960 and his final two with the Red Sox; he retired after two ineffective appearances with the Dodgers in 1975. He had six 20-win seasons and four times pitched over 300 innings. Marichal (27) finished with a career 243-141 .633 record with an ERA of 2.89 and was elected to the Hall of Fame in 1983.

1964 — Three days before his 25th birthday, Cubs outfielder Lou Brock is included in a six-player deal with the St. Louis Cardinals. Brock is packaged with pitchers Jack Spring and Paul Toth in exchange for pitchers Bobby Shantz and Ernie Broglio as well as outfielder Doug Clemens. Hitting .257 through his three seasons with Chicago, Brock would spend his next 16 years in a St. Louis uniform and wind up his 19-year major league career in 1979 with a batting average of .293. He not only reached base 35% of the time but once he got there he made things happen. He led the National League in stolen bases eight years and was the league leader in runs scored twice. Brock finished his career with 938 steals, with a success ratio of 75%, and scored 1,610 runs – seven seasons in which he tallied more than 100. Brock (20) was voted into the Hall of Fame in 1985 in his first year of eligibility.

1977 — Sending shock waves through the baseball world, The New York Mets trade Tom Seaver to the Cincinnati Reds for pitcher Pat Zachry, infielder Doug Flynn and two minor league outfielders – Steve Henderson and Dan Norman. The shock is especially felt in New York as Seaver is 7-3 at the time of the trade and had finished 22-9 and 14-11 in 1975 and 1976, respectively. He leaves the Mets with a total of 189 major league victories in ten years.

The trade was a matter of money. Seaver had signed a three-year agreement with the Mets following the 1976 season for $675,000 or $225,000 a year plus incentive bonuses making him, at the time, the highest-paid pitcher in baseball (In 1977 the total Mets payroll was $1,469,800, or an average of $58,792 per player). This contract was signed just prior to the first re-entry draft for free agents when some owners would begin handing out more money to much less talented players than Seaver. It had been reported that Seaver had asked to renegotiate, but Seaver stated this was incorrect and instead he requested his existing contract be lengthened an additional three years. In early June, with negotiations going nowhere, Seaver asks to be traded but agrees to stay if he receives an additional amount of money in the first and second years of his extension. The

Mets agree, but Seaver on the day of his trade is upset concerning personal statements made in the press about his family, and he again says he wants out.

Seaver would win 75 and lose 46 in the next six seasons with the Reds. Following a 5-13 year in 1982 he is traded back to the Mets. In 1983 Seaver has an 9-14 season with New York and is left off the protected list. This error enabled the White Sox to draft him on January 20, 1984 as a compensation pick in the third year of the pool arrangement created in the 1981 strike settlement. After Seaver is traded in 1977 by New York, he continued on his Hall of Fame course winning 122 more games with Cincinnati, the Mets, White Sox and Red Sox and finished with 311 victories.

June 16

1884 — Larry Corcoran pitches with both hands in a National League game for the Chicago White Stockings against the Buffalo Bisons. Corcoran had a sore right index finger and managed to pitch four innings using both arms alternately. He was lifted by manager Cap Anson following two homeruns, five singles and three walks. The diminutive Corcoran (he weighed only 120 pounds) finished the game at shortstop and went 3-for-4, including two triples. He would be the losing pitcher 20-9 to Buffalo. His injured finger was quick to heal – eleven days later he pitched a no-hitter against the Providence Grays. Corcoran is the second pitcher in the majors to pitch both right and left in the same game. In 1882 Tony Mullane of the Louisville Eclipse (American Association) was the first in a game at Baltimore.

1945 — Joe Medwick is traded for the last time in his career. The New York Giants send him to the Boston Braves for left-hander Ewald Pyle who would pitch four games for Boston and retire. Medwick would play through the 1948 season finishing his career with the Cardinals (where he started in 1932), and became an instantaneous success as the left fielder of the Gas House Gang. In 17 years Medwick hit .324, winning the Triple Crown (.374-31-154) and Most Valuable Player Award in 1937. Playing in two World Series with the Cardinals in 1934 and Brooklyn in 1941 he hit .326 (15-46) in 12 games. He picked up his nickname "Ducky" while walking on the beach at Galveston during his days in the Texas League with Houston – because a fan thought his walk resembled a waterfowl. Medwick was elected to the Hall of Fame in 1968.

1978 — After three Cy Young Awards, four times a 20-game winner, and in his 12th season in the majors, Tom Seaver pitches a 4-0 no-hitter for Cincinnati against the St. Louis Cardinals. He had come close on five other occasions, twice taking a potential gem into the ninth inning. Seaver is not overpowering in this game, striking out only three batters, walking three, and three fine defensive plays behind him by Dave Concepcion, Joe Morgan and Ray Knight. The Reds give Seaver a 3-0 lead in the fifth and score again in the sixth inning as Seaver takes over the rest of the way in front of 38,216 fans at Riverfront Stadium.

1981 — The Wrigley family's involvement with the Chicago Cubs ends with the sale of the club's assets for $20.5 million in cash to Tribune Company, a major media company located in Chicago. The Wrigley connection with the Cubs started following the 1915 season when William Wrigley Jr. and a group of Chicago businessmen purchased the team from the Taft family of Cincinnati. In 1921 Wrigley became majority stockholder. Following his death in 1932 his interest passed to son Philip K. Wrigley and when Philip died in 1977 principal interest in the club was left to William Wrigley. The sale ends the longest continuous operation of a franchise by the same family in the same city in major league history. Of the eight original charter members of the National League, only the Cubs have operated continuously in the same city in which they were franchised.

June 17

1983 — Los Angeles pitcher Bob Welch, batting .111, gets hold of a Mario Soto fastball and hits the first homerun of his major league career. It comes before a crowd of 42,870 at Dodger Stadium in the sixth inning of a 0-0 game against Cincinnati. Welch's homer would be the only run of the game as he holds the Reds to six hits and completes a 1-0 shutout.

June 18

1904 — President Barney Dreyfuss of the Pittsburgh Pirates charters a special train at a cost of $2,000 to transport his players and those of the Cardinals to St. Louis for a game the following day. The trip was made in record time of 23 hours and 15 minutes.

1947 — Cincinnati's Ewell Blackwell, the side-arming right-hander with a 6-foot, 6-inch 185 pound frame, buggy-whips the Boston Braves into no-hit submission 6-0 at Crosley Field. The rain had stopped just before game time and bad weather had canceled batting practice, but the Reds didn't need the extra hitting on this night and scored three runs in the opening inning on the wings of Babe Young's three-run homer. The first baseman duplicates the feat in the eighth to account for all of Cincinnati's runs. In Blackwell's next start he would set the Brooklyn Dodgers down without a hit for eight and one-third innings before Eddie Stanky smashed a single through the pitcher's legs, spoiling Blackwell's dream of matching Johnny Vander Meer's two consecutive no-hit games in 1938.

1967 — If ever a better no-hit game was pitched than the one rookie Don Wilson fired up on this day it would have to be a perfect game. The Astros win 2-0 over Atlanta with Wilson sending 15 Braves back to the dugout on strikes – 14 of them go down swinging. Wilson gives up three bases on balls, the first after he retires 14 batters. Denis Menke draws the pass with two outs in the fifth. Hank Aaron gets to look at another pitch in the seventh after catcher Dave Adlesh drops a third-strike foul and then walks. Menke walks again to open the eighth but Wilson strikes out the next three batters. Except for the three walks and a brilliant defensive play by Bob Aspromonte on a ball hit by Felipe Alou with two outs in the sixth, Wilson had little trouble. The third baseman dives to his left to spear the ball while on his stomach, then getting to his knees throws a strike to Eddie Mathews at first.

Houston fans had already witnessed two no-hitters in the first five years of the club's existence, both in old Colt Stadium, but this would be the first in the Astrodome. Now, as the ninth inning dawns, 22,173 tense and wide-eyed fans await the outcome on this Father's Day. Wilson has 13 strikeouts and his blazing fastball has yet to show any sign of slowing down with Alou, Tito Francona and Aaron waiting at the plate. Alou pops foul to Aspromonte on a 1-1 pitch and Francona waves at three consecutive pitches for strikeout number 14. Now the magic moment – with Aaron at the plate Wilson needs one out for the no-hitter. He has already struck out Aaron in the first and fourth innings and almost had him a third time except for the dropped third-strike foul in the seventh. This is Wilson's day – Aaron strikes out swinging on a 3-2 pitch! The 6-foot-3, 205 pound Wilson strikes out five of the last six batters and runs his game total to 15.

1986 — After spending 21 years in the majors with five different teams, 41-year old Don Sutton pitches the California Angels to a 5-1 victory over the Texas Rangers and picks up win number 300. Sutton began his career with the Los Angeles Dodgers in 1966 and also pitched for Houston, Milwaukee and Oakland on his way to becoming the 19th pitcher to eclipse the 300 barrier. He won his first 230 games for Los Angeles and would win the final three of his 324 victories back with the Dodgers in 1988. In his first 15 seasons, all with the Dodgers, he pitched in excess of 200 innings in each, and went on to do the same in 20 of his 23 years in the majors. Sutton (20) finished with a record of 324-256 and was voted into the Hall of Fame in 1998.

June 19

1846 — The New York Club defeats the Knickerbockers 23-1 in the first officially recorded game played under Cartwright's rules at Elysian Fields in New York. Organized as a gentleman's social and fraternal group, the Knickerbocker Baseball Club is commonly recognized as being the first organized baseball team, with origins in 1842. 25-year old civil engineer Alexander Cartwright, founder of the club, set down standard dimensions, positions, conduct and etiquette for the early game of baseball. Most of them still stand today, 90 feet between bases and standard positions on the field. The pitching distance was originally 45 feet, changed to 50 feet in 1881 and lengthened to 60 feet, 6 inches in 1893. The shortstop in Cartwright's arrangement was stationed in front of the baseline and the catcher stood far back behind the plate. Although it has been recorded that there were earlier town ball clubs, it was Cartwright and the Knickerbocker Club that drew up the rules that have since been certified as those which designed the present-day sport. Cartwright was voted into the Hall of Fame in 1938.

1927 — Phillies right-hander Jack Scott pitches two complete games of a doubleheader against the Cincinnati Reds, winning the first game 3-1 and losing the nightcap 3-0. Scott, 35 years old, and in his only season with Philadelphia would finish the year with a 9-21 record and would be the last pitcher in major league history to pitch two complete games in a doubleheader. In six of his 12 years in the majors he would pitch 200 or more innings, hitting a high of 291 innings in 1920.

1938 — The Reds' Johnny Vander Meer makes his first appearance since pitching back-to-back no-hitters against Boston (June 11) and Brooklyn (June 15). He now is facing the Braves again, and has not given up a hit through one out in the fourth inning when Deb Garms hits a 3 and 2 pitch through the box into center field. The hitless streak ends at 21 and two-third innings. Garms, a left-handed batter, did not play against the left-handed Vander Meer in his first no-hitter. Vander Meer allows only three more hits to Boston in posting his eighth victory and seventh in a row against two defeats. 34,511 fans watch Vander Meer attempt his third straight no-hitter; one of those spectators is 71-year old Cy Young, who had set the major league record of 24 and one-third consecutive hitless innings in 1904.

1942 — 39-year old Paul Waner delivers the 3,000th hit of his career with a hot single up the middle off Pittsburgh's Rip Sewell at Braves Field in Boston. It was ironic Waner would pick up his milestone hit against the Pirates, with whom he had played for 15 years before moving to Brooklyn and then to Boston in 1941. In becoming the seventh player in history to reach 3,000 hits, Waner's popularity surfaced when umpire Tom Dunn called for the ball and presented it to Waner at first base. At the same moment, Pittsburgh manager Frankie Frisch charged out of the dugout, and at the same time Braves manager Casey Stengel headed for Waner. Even pitcher Rip Sewell walked to first with hand extended to offer his congratulations. The game was further delayed while the personalities posed for a group photograph. Waner would finish his major league career with 3,152 hits.

1952 — Brooklyn right-hander Carl Erskine pitches a no-hitter in a 5-0 victory over the Chicago Cubs at Ebbets Field. Despite a rainy day (the game is delayed for 45 minutes in the fourth inning), 5,000 "Knot hole day" fans and a paid crowd of 7,732 see Erskine's gem. In the third inning Erskine walks relief pitcher Willie Ramsdell on four pitches and he is the only Cubs base runner of the day. Roy Campanella, Andy Pafko and Carl Furillo get Erskine a 4-0 lead in the first two innings, each connecting for a homerun off Cubs starter Warren Hacker.

1974 — Kansas City's Steve Busby pitches his second no-hitter in 14 months as the Royals right-hander shuts down Milwaukee 2-0. On April 27, 1973 the 23-year old rookie pitched a no-hit game against the Detroit Tigers. In his first gem, Busby walked six batters, but against the Brewers only one man reached base. After getting ahead of George Scott with a two-strike count in the second inning, the big first baseman waited Busby out and drew a walk. Busby did have some great defensive support behind him with second baseman Cookie Rojas especially brilliant with several outstanding plays. Busby becomes the first in history to pitch no-hitters in each of his first two seasons. He would finish the 1974 season with a record of 22-14 then go 18-12 in 1975 before arm problems began to end his career. With a 3-3 mark in 1976 Busby would become the first major league pitcher to undergo rotator cuff surgery. He pitched in 40 games following his return in 1978 with an 8-9 record and retired after the 1980 season.

June 20

1901 — This is the beginning of a record streak that will last forever. Right-hander Jack Taylor pitches a complete game for the Chicago (National League) Colts and the string of complete games would not end until August 13, 1906. During this "iron man" stint, Taylor would complete all of his 187 starts and make an additional 15 appearances out of the bullpen. During the post-season Chicago City Series in 1903 Taylor was accused by Colts president James Hart of having thrown games to the White Stockings. After winning the first game Taylor lost his other three starts and, because of the accusations by Hart he refused to pitch the final game of the series and insisted on being traded. Hart obliged in December and traded Taylor to the Cardinals in a deal that sent Mordecai Brown to Chicago. While pitching for St. Louis in 1904, charges were made that Taylor had bet against the Cardinals in a game with Pittsburgh but were dropped because of insufficient evidence. In July 1906 he would be traded back to Chicago (now the Cubs) and on August 13, 1906 his complete game streak would end. Taylor was knocked out in the second inning by Brooklyn. Even so, he pitched well for the Cubs and helped Chicago clinch the pennant with 116 wins. Taylor, however, was not used in the World Series, possibly because of his tarnished image. In Taylor's streak (1901-1906) he put together four 20-win seasons and pitched 300 or more innings four straight years, topping off with 352 in 1904. Taylor averaged 262 innings pitched in his ten seasons in the majors.

June 21

1952 — The Harrisburg, Pennsylvania club of the Class-B Interstate League signs Mrs. Eleanor Engle, 24 years old, as a player. The 132-pound stenographer works out at shortstop the next day prior to a game with Lancaster. Harrisburg manager Buck Etchison was not notified by club officials nor was umpire Bill Angstadt, both of whom are in opposition to her playing. Engle would not play when President George Trautman of the National Association (minors) immediately voided the contract with the backing of commissioner Ford Frick. At the same time Trautman barred any club from signing women players. Earlier in history, efforts were made for female players to enter pro ball but most of those efforts were for publicity (i.e. Babe Didrikson and Jackie Mitchell in the 1930s). However, the Fayetteville, Arkansas *Daily Democrat* reported in the September 8, 1936 edition that Frances (Sonny) Dunlap, All-America girls A.A.U. basketball player of the Tulsa Stenos worked out a third base prior to a game between Fayetteville and Cassville in the Class-D Arkansas-Missouri League and then played the entire game in right field. There was no advance publicity nor were league officials notified that Dunlap would play in this next-to-last day of the season.

1964 — Jim Bunning, in his first National League season, spins a perfect game for the Philadelphia Phillies in a 6-0 victory over the New York Mets. It is Bunning's second career no-hitter and the fifth perfect game pitched in major league history. He threw his first no-hit game while pitching for Detroit against Boston July 20, 1958 and becomes the first pitcher to win no-hitters in both leagues. The 32-year old Bunning had little trouble with the Mets lineup, getting a three-ball count on only two batters and striking out 10 while battling through a humid, 90-degree day before 32,026 fans at Shea Stadium on Father's Day. The 32 year old Bunning would spend 17 years in the majors, winning 224 games and losing 184 while striking out 2,855 batters and logging more than 200 innings in 13 of those seasons, reaching the plus 300 mark twice. Bunning (14) was voted into the Hall of Fame in 1996.

One other note on his perfect game – his catcher, Gus Triandos, offers another highlight when he becomes the first receiver in history to catch no-hitters in both the National and American Leagues. Triandos was behind the plate in 1958 for Baltimore when Hoyt Wilhelm pitched a 1-0 no-hit game against the Yankees. Jeff Torborg would later duplicate the feat after catching two no-hitters for the Dodgers (Sandy Koufax' perfect game in 1965 and Bill Singer's no-hitter in 1970). Torborg caught his American League no-hitter for Nolan Ryan as the "Express" pitched his first no-hit game in 1973 for the California Angels.

June 22

1947 — Cincinnati's side-arming right-hander Ewell Blackwell comes close to duplicating Johnny Vander Meer's two consecutive no-hitters. The Reds' Vander Meer threw back-to-back no-hit games in June of 1938 against the Braves and Dodgers. Blackwell was coming off a June 18 no-hitter against Boston and in his next start against Brooklyn he had not allowed a hit through the first eight innings. Blackwell made it eight and one-third innings by retiring the first batter in the ninth before Dodgers second baseman Eddie Stanky grounded a single through the box that grazed Blackwell's right knee before going into center field. After the next batter, Al Gionfriddo is retired, Jackie Robinson sends a single to right before Blackwell finishes with a two-hitter and a 4-0 win. His hitless streak is stopped at 19 innings. It would be the 6'-6" pitcher's ninth win in a row, and he would go on to the most productive season of his 10-year career. He finished with a league leading 22 wins, 23 complete games and 193 strikeouts. Blackwell lost only eight games and finished the year with an earned run average of 2.47.

1984 — The longest family ownership reign in baseball comes to a close with the sale of the Minnesota Twins to Minneapolis banker Carl Pohlad. The letter of intent to sell is signed in an emotional pre-game home plate ceremony by Calvin Griffith and his sister Thelma Haynes. The Griffiths had headed the franchise for 65 years since Clark Griffith was named president of the Washington Senators in 1920. Upon Clark's death in 1955 Calvin, Clark's adopted son, took control of the club and moved the franchise to the Twin Cities in 1961. This sale, for $32 million, represented 52% of the club's stock. Pohlad would later purchase the remaining shares from a Tampa group, running the total sale price to just over $44 million.

June 23

1917 — Red Sox starting pitcher Babe Ruth is ejected after walking Washington leadoff batter Ray Morgan in the first inning. Ruth and umpire Brick Owens had a heated dispute going from the start, with Ruth questioning each called ball. When Owens called ball four Ruth rushed the umpire and planted a right to his jaw. Ruth did not get fined for his actions but did receive a 10-day suspension. Ernie Shore relieves for Boston, and after Morgan is caught stealing, Shore retires the next 26 batters in order for a 4-0 Red Sox victory.

1988 — New York Yankees owner George Steinbrenner fires manager Billy Martin for the fifth and last time. Martin was originally hired as Yankees manager on August 2, 1975 and his resignation was accepted on July 24, 1978 following his problems with Reggie Jackson. Martin, referring to Jackson and Steinbrenner said, "The two of them deserve each other. One's a born liar; the other's convicted." The conviction comment about Steinbrenner stemmed from the owner's illegal contributions to president Nixon's 1972 campaign. Five days later during Old Timers Day at Yankee Stadium the club announces over the public address system that Martin would return as manager in 1980. He was back at the helm as early as June 19, 1979 but would be fired at the end of the season. After two years as skipper at Oakland, Martin was hired by the Yankees for the third time at the beginning of the 1983 season but would lose his job again in December. In April of 1985 he would be back for his fourth term only to be canned after another one-year term. Following the 1987 season Steinbrenner stuck his neck out for the fifth and last time for Martin, but this time the troubled skipper would last only three months into the 1988 season. Following closely behind Steinbrenner and his penchant for hiring and firing managers (20 in the first 22 years as owner of the Yankees) is Charley Finley of the Kansas City/Oakland Athletics, who made the change 17 times in 20 seasons from 1961-1980.

June 24

1946 — Nine members of the Spokane Class B Western International League team lose their lives, and the driver and six other players are injured when their bus careens off a narrow road at the 3,400-foot level of the Cascade Mountains in Washington State. The driver swerved to avoid an oncoming car on a rainy night, and the bus plunged through the guardrail and caught fire as it fell down the steep mountainside. The average age of the nine players who died was 24; only three of the six survivors would ever play again. They were outfielder Levi McCormack and pitchers Gus Hallbourg and Pete Barisoff. Two other pitchers, Milt Cadinha and Joe Faria, scheduled to work the first two games of the series in Bremerton, had gone ahead of the team by automobile the day before. Prior to the accident the team had stopped for fuel and food at Ellenburg, Washington, and a message was waiting for second baseman Jack Lohrke notifying him he had been called up to San Diego's Pacific Coast League team with orders to report at once. Ever since the incident he was known as "Lucky" Lohrke. He went on to play seven seasons in the National League with the Giants and Phillies and appeared in the 1951 World Series with New York.

1970 — The final game is played at Crosley Field in Cincinnati as Johnny Bench and Lee May hit back-to-back eighth inning homeruns off San Francisco's Juan Marichal to give the Reds a 5-4 victory. Opened as Redland Field in 1912 and changed to Crosley Field in 1934 when Powell Crosley purchased the team, the Red Stockings had begun play on the site at Findlay and Western in 1884 when the name of the stadium was League Park. Probably the best-known feature of Crosley Field was its outfield "terrace;" playing the outfield was an adventure. The "terrace" was an area that began 15 feet in front of the left field wall that rose four feet by the time it reached the fence. The park also had many other memorable features: The Superior Towel and Linen Service building (referred to as the laundry) behind the left field wall; a five-story high, 65 foot long scoreboard in left center topped by a huge clock – all of this area was "in play." Also memorable was the Young and Bertke sign that featured an animated "tin man" with moving legs located behind the bleachers in right center field.

Crosley Field closes after 58 years and the location is abandoned following 86 seasons of use by the Red Stockings and Reds. Crosley field hosted the major leagues' first night game, survived the 1937 Mill Creek flood, and was the only park to have a ground rule posted on the outfield fence — a vertical white line painted on the wall in right center reading: "Batted ball hitting concrete wall on fly to right of white line – homerun." Six days after the closing of this historic park the Reds would open their new home, Riverfront Stadium, on June 30, 1970 in downtown Cincinnati.

June 25

1879 — The home of the Cincinnati Reds, Avenue Park, becomes the first ball field where seat cushions are rented to grandstand customers. This facility was used by the Cincinnati club from 1876 through 1879 and was located near the Baltimore and Ohio railroad tracks in Chester Park. Seat cushions started out as a luxury but over the years developed into a baseball staple because of the hard seats. At Dodger Stadium in Los Angeles during the 1960s and 1970s most of them sailed onto the field following games.

June 26

1883 — The first regular umpiring staff is appointed by the National League. The four are Stewart Decker, Frank H. Lane, William Furlong and Albert Odlin. Their positions were by no means secure, all it took to remove an umpire was for four of the eight clubs to register an objection at any time after the start of the season. Within three weeks the first objection was raised and Odlin, a law student who had never umpired a professional game, was removed.

1916 — Identifying numbers first appear on player's uniforms in the major leagues at League Park in Cleveland. With the Indians playing the Chicago White Sox, the first batter to wear a number to the plate is Cleveland's left fielder Jack Graney. The numbers were only worn on the left sleeve of the Indians uniforms and were hardly discernible from the grandstand thus defeating the purpose of selling scorecards. The innovation did not survive the season. It would not be until 1929 that numbering would take hold in the majors. That season both Cleveland and the New York Yankees began numbering the back of uniform shirts.

Baseball's first use of numbers occurred in the Pacific Coast League in 1912 when the entire league adopted the practice of using identifying numbers on the left sleeves. The idea was to sell scorecards, and with smaller parks the four or five-inch patches could be seen by fans closer to the action. It seems that this is when and where the vendors coined the phrase, "You can't tell the player's without a scorecard", originated. The practice died at season's end when league directors abolished the system. Team membership changed so much it was nearly impossible to keep the players' numbers conformed to the scorecards. Also the problem of switching the numbers on uniforms to fit the new players became a sewing nightmare.

1920 — The Inter-City High School baseball championship game being played in Chicago at Cubs Park (Wrigley Field), between Chicago's Lane Tech and the High School of Commerce of New York, is tied 8-8 going into the top of the ninth inning. With the bases loaded, a wide-shouldered, thick-limbed kid hits the first pitch over the right field fence for a 12-8 New York win. That night the name of 17-year old Lou Gehrig would be carried over the nation's sports wires for the first time. In three years he would be playing the first of his 17 seasons with the Yankees.

1944 — Over 50,000 fans jam the Polo Grounds to watch baseball's first and only "triple header" played between three teams — the Giants, Yankees and Dodgers. With World War II in full swing, the event is billed as a War Bond fund-raising game that would fill the coffers to the tune of over $6,500,000. The evening opened with field events – fungo hitting, throwing for accuracy and sprint contests. Milton Berle is the MC with Al Schacht and Joe Lauri, Jr. providing the pre-game comedy. The rare game was in reality a round-robin with each team playing six innings – two consecutive innings in the field and at bat and then sitting one inning out. The Dodgers won with five runs to one for the Yankees, and the Giants were shut out with only two hits. Leo Durocher was the winning manager, Mel Ott the loser and Joe McCarthy skippered the Yankees.

The Line Score:

	1-2-3	4-5-6	7-8-9	- F
DODGERS	1 2 X	0 0 X	0 2 X	- 5
YANKEES	0 X 0	0 X 0	0 X 1	- 1
GIANTS	X 0 0	X 0 0	X 0 0	- 0

The war had taken its toll on major league talent with many well-known players in service. However, many who participated in this game were well known to the intense Baseball fan. Four future Hall-of-Famers, all of whom were within three years of retirement, saw action. The oldest was Paul Waner, 41, who played right field for Brooklyn and three Giants: Ernie Lombardi, 36, Ott, 35 and Joe Medwick, 33. Also, baseball immortals Herb Pennock, Zack Wheat, and Roger Bresnahan (each of whom would eventually be elected to the Hall of Fame), were introduced by New York mayor Jimmy Walker.

June 27

1936 — Ted Williams makes his organized baseball debut with San Diego of the Pacific Coast League. In the second inning Williams is called upon to pinch-hit for pitcher Jack Hill, and he takes three called strikes from Sacramento pitcher Henry C. Pippen. The 17 year-old Williams would play in 42 games in 1936 and hit .271 but did not hit a single homerun. With the Padres in 1937 he hit 23 homers with an average of .291, and with Minneapolis in 1938 Williams would lead the American Association in homeruns with 43, 142 runs batted in and a .366 average. At age 20 in 1939 he was wearing the uniform of the Boston Red Sox.

June 28

1970 — Almost 61 years to the day after the Cubs' Ed Reulbach beat the Pirates 3-2 in the opening game of Forbes Field on June 30, 1909, Bucs second baseman Bill Mazeroski starts a double play that closes the venerable stadium forever with a doubleheader victory 3-2 and 4-1 over Chicago. Rookie pitcher Jim Nelson was the Pirates winning pitcher in the finale with Dave Giusti picking up the save. It would be one of only six wins Nelson would have for Pittsburgh in his short two-year stay in the majors. The Cubs' Milt Pappas served up the final homerun to Al Oliver as 40,918 fans came out to watch the swan song of the park that had sported many future Hall-of-Famers in the uniform of the Pirates as well as playing host to many visitors who also ended up in the shrine.

There was some sanity by the fans when the game ended as drawings were held for prizes, such as Mazeroski's and Roberto Clemente's clubhouse chairs, three sets of bases, home plate and bricks from the outfield wall. However, when that ended some rowdy fans dismantled the scoreboard, taking every number. Even the bronze plaque on the statue of Barney Dreyfuss, the owner whose vision and money built the new park, was stolen but later returned. The University of Pittsburgh's expansion now occupies the hallowed land, but a remnant of the 12' vine-covered brick wall, with the 457' marker, still stands.

June 29

1905 — Archibald Wright (Moonlight) Graham, who achieved belated fame in the movie *Field of Dreams*, plays in his only major league game. Graham entered in the late innings for the New York Giants as a replacement for George Browne in right field. For the record, the Giants beat the Dodgers 11-1 at Washington Park in Brooklyn; Graham had no at-bats and no chances in the field. Graham was no country bumpkin. He grew up in North Carolina in a family of substance and accomplishments but not wealth. A 1901 graduate of the University of North Carolina with a bachelor of arts and pre-med courses, Graham put himself through the University of Maryland medical school by playing baseball. In 1904 he played pro ball moonlighting with Scranton in the Class-B New York State League, thus his famous nickname. Moonlight Graham enjoyed baseball but used it as a means to an end for a medical career.

1913 — Before the beginning of the game at Redland Field in Cincinnati, Reds manager Joe Tinker handed umpire Hank O'Day three new baseballs for use in the Reds game with the Chicago Cubs. O'Day tossed one of them to Cincinnati starting pitcher Leon Ames and the game was underway. When the game ended, Reds catcher Johnny Kling carried the same ball off the field and umpire O'Day still had two shiny unused balls in his coat pocket. It wasn't that this was a no-action game, as the Reds won 9-6 banging out 12 hits. The Cubs chipped in with eight to make it a 20-hit affair.

1990 — Baseball is highlighted with two no-hitters by the Dodgers Fernando Valenzuela and Oakland's Dave Stewart. Stewart starts the day at SkyDome in Toronto by walking the first two batters then retires the next 25 Bluejays before giving up a two-out base on balls in the ninth inning. Stewart and the Athletics win 5-0 as 49,817 fans look on. Valenzuela's gem is a 6-0 victory over St. Louis. Valenzuela struck out seven Cardinals and walked three as ex-Dodger Pedro Guerrero hits into a game-ending double play to the delight of the 38,583 fans at Dodger Stadium,

June 30

1908 — At 41 years and three months, Cy Young spins the third no-hit game of his career, this one an 8-0 win for the Boston Red Sox over the New York Highlanders at New York's Hilltop Park. The veteran pitcher almost duplicated his perfect game against Philadelphia on May 5, 1904 but he walked Harry Niles, the first batter to face him. Attempting to steal second Niles was thrown out by Boston catcher Lou Criger and Young ended up facing only 27 batters. Young didn't let his age bother him either at the plate picking up three singles in five trips with four RBI and scoring one run. Young pitched his first no-hit game for Cleveland against Cincinnati on September 18, 1897.

1909 — Only four months following the ground breaking, Forbes Field in

June 30

Pittsburgh opens with 30,338 fans crammed into the new 24,000-seat capacity concrete and steel structure. Chicago's Johnny Evers is the first to bat off Bucs' right-hander Vic Willis and the Cubs second baseman singles to left field. It is interesting to note that a no-hitter was broken up by the first batter in the new stadium and for the next 61 years of Forbes Field's existence there would never be a no-hit game pitched in this park. Located in the northwest corner of Schenley Park in the heart of the Civic Center, Forbes Field is named in honor of General Forbes who furnished Pittsburgh the nucleus for its name by wresting Fort Duquesne from the French and calling it Fort Pitt. Pittsburgh's organized baseball history began as the Alleghenies in 1882 when the city joined the new American Association, then entered the National League in 1887. They became known as the Pirates in 1891 when they began playing their games at new Exposition Park. Following 61 years at Forbes Field, Three Rivers Stadium would open on July 16, 1970.

1938 — The final game is played in Baker Bowl in Philadelphia as the New York Giants beat the last place Phillies 14-1. It was only appropriate that these two teams should close down the old park. They had opened on this site in 1887 when the park was called the Philadelphia Baseball Grounds and had also opened this stadium against each other in 1895 when it was renamed Baker Bowl. For years there had been talk of the Phillies moving to Shibe Park as tenants of the Athletics. It became a reality when A's owner Connie Mack stated he was willing to have the Phillies share his stadium. When Baker Bowl opened it was the most ostentatious in baseball, but fell victim to disaster. There was the big fire in August of 1894; the collapse of a wall from third base to left field killed 12 people and injured some 200, many of whom were crippled for life. And in May of 1927 one fan was killed and 50 hurt with the collapse of the right field stands. Baker Bowl had become known as the graveyard of the majors and the fans of Philadelphia thoroughly endorsed the move.

1948 — 49,628 Detroit fans watch as Cleveland pitcher Bob Lemon no-hits the Tigers 2-0. It's the first no-hitter pitched in Detroit in 26 years – since White Sox Charley Robertson threw a perfect game at the Tigers in 1922. The 27-year old Lemon started his pitching career with Cleveland in 1946 but also played the outfield and third base after breaking into the majors in 1941. Indians manager Lou Boudreau switched Lemon solely to the mound on July 31, 1947, and he finished with 11 wins and five losses. Lemon would go on to a 20-14 record in 1948, pitching 10 shutouts and was on his way following his switch to the mound. He spent three years in the Pacific theater during the war with the Navy baseball team at which time he honed his pitching skills. In 13 seasons with Cleveland he won 207 while losing 128, winning 20 or more games in seven of those years while leading the American League in complete games for five seasons. He could also handle the bat, hitting .232 with 37 homeruns and 147 runs batted in. Lemon (21) was voted into the Hall of Fame in 1976.

1962 — Dodgers pitcher Sandy Koufax, who had struggled through the early years of his career with wildness and inexperience, thrills the 32,769 fans looking on at Dodger Stadium with a 5-0 no-hit victory over the New York Mets. The 26-year old left-hander was coming off an 18-13-269 strikeout season in 1961 and was finally showing the patient Los Angeles brass what they expected of him when he signed for a reported $20,000 bonus in 1955. It wasn't an easy evening for Koufax as he walked five batters, had a super play behind him by shortstop Maury Wills and was helped by two double plays. Koufax helped himself by striking out 13, getting an early start by whiffing all three Mets in the first inning on nine pitches.

1995 — Eddie Murray, after breaking in with the Baltimore Orioles in 1977, runs his hit total to 3,000 while playing with the Cleveland Indians in the Metrodome. Murray becomes the 20th player, and just the second switch-hitter to reach the coveted plateau, driving a single through the right side of the infield off Minnesota's Mike Trombley. The 39-year old Murray joins Pete Rose as the only switch-hitters to get 3,000 hits. 2,045 of those hits came batting left-handed while playing with Baltimore, the Mets, Los Angeles and Cleveland. He would finish his career with 3,255 hits.

"Fair is foul and foul is fair"
Shakespeare, *MacBeth*

Chapter Seven

"Fans, for the past two weeks you have been reading about a bad break I got. Yet, today I consider myself the luckiest man on the face of the earth."

Lou Gehrig, July 4, 1939 at Yankee Stadium

July 1

1859 — The country's first intercollegiate baseball game is played between Amherst and Williams in Pittsfield, Massachusetts. The confrontation was fairly close until the fourth inning when Amherst broke the game open and won 73-32. The playing field had the pitcher only 25 feet from the batter and the bases were only sixty feet apart. Each player (be they lucky or unlucky) was chosen by lottery from the schools' enrollment in order to be a member of the two teams.

1899 — The St. Louis National League franchise, having fallen on hard times because of large debts as well as personnel and family problems was purchased by Frank Robison owner of the Cleveland Spiders. It was not illegal at this time for one owner to have an interest in two clubs in the same league. Until 1899 the Spiders had fielded good teams, but Robison had become disenchanted with his Cleveland club and the lack of Cleveland fans, and he turned his full attention to his new team in St. Louis. He shifted many of his star players, including Cy Young, Jesse Burkett, Jack Powell and Bobby Wallace to St. Louis, completely decimating the Spiders. By the end of June, his Cleveland club was off to an 11-48 start and fans were staying away in droves. With these dismal facts to face, Robison decided to close the Cleveland home stand with a doubleheader on July 1 and to send the team on the road for the rest of the season. The Spiders did return to Cleveland for a six-game stand in August but only some 100 fans showed up for the first game. After splitting the first two games with New York the season record stood at 19-94. With only 41 games remaining on August 24, the Spiders would begin a 24-game losing streak with the team winning only one of those 41 games. At season's end the Cleveland Spiders record was 20-134. During the winter of 1899 the National League decided to cut back to eight teams and the Spiders were one of the casualties. In 1901 the Cleveland Blues (Indians) would surface in the new American League.

1902 — Athletics lefthander Rube Waddell becomes the first pitcher in history to strike out three batters on nine pitches in one inning. He was in the fifth season of his 13-year career in which he struck out 2,316 batters.

1910 — White Sox Park (Comiskey) opens for play just five months after Charles A. Comiskey announced the $100,000 purchase of a lot from the estate of Chicago's first mayor, John Wentworth. What an opening day it was for Comiskey! A motorcade from the Loop preceded the festivities attended by Chicago's Mayor Fred Busse, C.C. Johnson Spink, publisher of *The Sporting News*, famous football coach Amos Alonzo Stagg and other dignitaries. It was a banner day for "The Old Roman" despite a 2-0 loss to the St. Louis Browns before an estimated crowd of 28,000. Ground was broken on February 15th, and on St. Patrick's Day a green brick was laid near the main entrance symbolizing the team's attachment in its early years to the South Side Irish population. That brick stayed green until 1960 when Bill Veeck painted the park white. The new Comisky Park replaced the venerable stadium on April 18, 1991.

1920 — Washington's Walter Johnson pitches the only no-hitter of his career with a 1-0 win at Fenway Park in Boston. The Senators took the lead in the top of the seventh inning when second baseman Bucky Harris singled in Braggo Roth to break up the scoreless tie. Harris' error in the last of the seventh on Harry Hooper's ground ball allowed the only Red Sox runner to reach base. Johnson was suffering through the 1920 season with the only sore arm in his 21-year career pitching in only 21 games with an 8-10 record. However, he bounced back in 1921 winning 112 games in his final seven years.

1943 — The American Girls Professional Baseball League plays a night All-Star game for the benefit of the Women's Army Air Corps at Wrigley Field in Chicago. Following a day-long WAAC recruiting drive the game was played with players selected from the four teams that made up the league in its first year of operation. Those four teams were Racine and Kenosha, Wisconsin, Rockford, Illinois and South Bend, Indiana. The All-Star game was played before a crowd of some 7,000 with Wisconsin beating Illinois-Indiana 16-0. Three banks of temporary lights on poles were set up behind home plate, first and third bases. One year later, July 18, 1944 the league did it again with an admission-free double header that drew more than 16,000. The crowd included Red Cross workers, members of the Armed Forces and blood donors who were awarded box seats. This time the lights were better – rigged up in the lower part of the upper deck – with the Milwaukee Chicks and Minneapolis Orphans winning over the South Bend Blue Sox 20-11. The nightcap between the Kenosha Comets and Racine Belles was called after four innings with a 6-6 tie to allow players to make train connections.

1951 — Bob Feller was 17 years old when he made his major league debut for the Cleveland Indians in 1936 and 15 years later, despite spending four years in the Navy, pitches the third no-hit game of his career. Feller now, 32, beats Detroit 2-1 at Cleveland Stadium before 42,891 fans in the opener of a double header. To top off the afternoon, 23-year old rookie pitcher Bob Chakales blanks the Tigers in the nightcap 2-0. Unlike his no-hitters against the White Sox on April 16, 1940 and the Yankees on April 30, 1946, Feller was the consummate veteran against Detroit, using his fastball only sparingly and relying on his cunning, control, curve, slider, and change up. He struck out only five batters while walking three and had excellent support on three tough defensive plays by shortstop Ray Boone, second baseman Bobby Avila and third baseman Al Rosen. Feller would finish the 1951 season with 22 wins and only eight losses. Winning a total of 36 games in his next four seasons, he would retire in 1956.

July 2

1903 — Ed Delahanty dies under mysterious circumstances when he staggers, jumps, falls, or is pushed off a bridge at Niagara Falls, New York. Only 36, Delahanty had spent 13 seasons with the Phillies but was induced by a larger pay check to jump to the American League Washington Nationals in 1902. This moved proved to be a decision he later regretted making, and probably was a factor in his demise. Following a suspension by Washington manager Tom Loftus for Delahanty's failure to show up for a game, he decided to return to his home. He boarded a Michigan Central train the night of July 2 bound for Buffalo from Detroit. At this point he disappeared and his body was not found until July 9 about 20 miles from the bridge. His money and jewelry, reportedly worth $2,000, were not found. All reports substantiate Delahanty was put off the train for causing some sort of row – either for being drunk and/or brandishing a razor in the dining car. What happened to him after he was put off the train just before the International Bridge at Fort Erie, Ontario, will never be known. What is certain is that Ed Delahanty was one of the most prolific hitters of all time. One of five brothers to play in the majors (Jim, Frank, Joe and Tom) he finished his 16-year career with a .346 average, 2,597 hits and 1,464 runs batted in. Delahanty hit over .400 in three seasons (.407 - 1894, .404 - 1895, .410 - 1899) and played all defensive positions except pitcher and catcher. He became a member of the Hall of Fame in 1945.

July 3

1948 — Dick Lane hits five homeruns for Muskegon at Fort Wayne in the Class-

A Central League. He would finish the season with only 12 homers but would lead the league with 121 runs scored. Lane would be called up to the parent Chicago White Sox in 1949 but his major league career would last only 12 games with no homeruns and an average of only .119.

July 4

1928 — Future Hall of Fame manager Ray Schalk resigns as manager of the Chicago White Sox and is replaced by Lena Blackburne, a six-year infielder with the White Sox, Boston Braves, Cincinnati and the Phillies. Blackburne batted only .214 in the majors and managed only through the 1929 season. In the early '30s, while serving as third base coach for Connie Mack, Blackburne discovered the mud that was destined to become the umpire's and pitcher's best friend. He found the "base-substance" somewhere in Pennsauken Creek – a tributary of the Delaware River in Pennsauken, New Jersey. The discovery of the secret elixir led to its usage by umpires to rub the shine off baseballs. The magic mud was first used in the American League in 1938 but the National League did not adopt it until 1955. Blackburne died in 1968 without heirs and left the recipe to the father of Catherine Bintliff who along with husband, Burns, continued to produce the product for baseball at a reported cost of anywhere from $20 and $75 per can.

1932 — The usually quiet and courteous catcher for the New York Yankees, Bill Dickey, loses his cool in a game against Washington when he misreads the purpose of Senators outfielder Carl Reynolds return to the plate after he and Dickey collided. Reynolds, making certain he had touched the plate, returns only to be greeted by a Dickey punch that fractured Reynolds' jaw. Dickey was fined $1,000 (his salary that season was $14,000) and was suspended for 30 days. He didn't miss many games after that – beginning in 1929 through 1941 he caught more than 100 games each season and finished his 17-year career with 1,712 games behind the plate. He caught 38 games in eight World Series hitting .255 with 24 RBI. Overall he hit .313 in his career with 202 homeruns and 1,207 runs batted in. After two seasons in the Navy (1944-1945) Dickey returned to the Yankees and became a player-manager when owner Larry MacPhail let Joe McCarthy go 35 games into the 1946 season. With a record of 57-48, the club in third place with only 14 games remaining, MacPhail relieved Dickey of his duties and appointed Johnny Neun as his third manager of the season. Dickey (8) was elected to the Hall of Fame in 1954.

1939 — 61,808 fans, most of them tearful, listen as Lou Gehrig utters a handful of sentences that will always be remembered in baseball history. The scene is Yankee Stadium as the 36 year-old ex-Yankees first baseman, dying of amyotrophic lateral sclerosis and deeply moved by other speeches, approaches the microphone at home plate:

> *"Fans, for the past two weeks you have been reading about a bad break I got. Yet, today I consider myself the luckiest man on the face of the earth. I have been in ballparks for 16 years and have never received anything but kindness and encouragement from you fans.*
>
> *"Wouldn't you consider it an honor to be with such great men even for one day? Sure I'm lucky! Who wouldn't consider an honor to have known Jake Ruppert, builder of baseball's greatest empire; to have spent six years with such a grand little fellow as Miller Huggins; to have spent nine years with that smart student of psychology – the best manager in baseball today – Joe McCarthy. Who wouldn't feel honored to room with such a grand guy as Bill Dickey? When the New York Giants, a team you have given your right arm to beat, and vice versa, sent a gift —that's something. When the grounds keepers and office staff and writers and old-timers and players and concessionaires all remember you with trophies – that's something.*
>
> *"When you have a wonderful mother-in-law, who takes sides with you in squabbles against her own daughter – that's something; when you have a father and mother who work all their lives so you can have an education and build your body — it's a blessing.*
>
> *"When you have a wife who has been a tower of strength, and shown more courage you know existed – that's the finest I know.*
>
> *"So I close in saying that I have had a tough break; but I have an awful lot to live for."*

On the field with Gehrig were several of his teammates including Everett Scott, the player Gehrig passed in 1934 wiping out the old record of 1,307 consecutive games. Also by his side were Waite Hoyt, Tony Lazzeri, Herb Pennock, Bob Meusel and Wally Pipp. As applause and tears filled the stadium, Babe Ruth threw his arms around his old teammate, ending years of hard feelings between the two great sluggers. Within two years Gehrig would be dead.

July 5

1898 — Long before Ed Barrow managed the Boston Red Sox, was president of the New York Yankees and was eventually voted into the Hall of Fame, he was president of the Atlantic League, a minor league in Pennsylvania. It was during his tour of duty in that capacity that he was instrumental in bringing the first woman player into professional baseball. Although her name was Elizabeth Stroud, she played under the name of Lizzie Arlington and appeared in only one game for Reading against Allentown. With Reading leading 5-0 in the ninth inning she entered the game as a pitcher and retired the first two batters on a foul pop up and a ground ball back to the mound. After loading the bases with two hits and a walk she forced the final out on another foul pop up. That one inning would be her only appearance in pro ball. This would be the first of only two instances a girl would appear in a minor league game. On September 7, 1936 Frances (Sonny) Dunlap would play the entire game in right field for Fayetteville against Cassville in the Arkansas-Missouri League.

1904 — Even though the National and American Leagues began operating in harmony in 1903, leading to the first World Series, New York Giants owner John T. Brush was still angry over the inter-league peace treaty, and Giants manager John McGraw still despised American League president Ban Johnson. With the National League race all but over by mid-season, following the Giants 18-game winning streak and posting a record of 53-18 at the time, Brush and McGraw announce they have no intention of playing a post-season series with the American League champions. Explaining his decision to reject the World Series challenge, Brush said, "There is nothing in the constitution or playing rules of the National League which requires its victorious club to submit its championship honors to a contest with a victorious club in a minor league." At season's end the Giants held true to their promise and went on a two-week barnstorming trip. However, at their annual meeting in December, National League directors re-elected Harry Pulliam president, and the league endorsed a World Series for future seasons.

July 6

1933 — Following a suggestion and persistent persuasion by Arch Ward, sports editor of the *Chicago Tribune*, the first Major League All-Star game is played between the American and National Leagues at Comiskey Park. The reluctant owners finally gave in to Ward's proposal and the game would be played in conjunction with Chicago's Century of Progress Exposition. The *Tribune* conducted fan voting and baseball's brightest stars were selected to participate; the game was a tremendous success resulting in a 4-2 victory for the American League. Baseball's two grand old managers Connie Mack and John McGraw, who came out of retirement to manage the National League, were chosen to lead the two squads.

Lefty Gomez and Wild Bill Hallahan were the starting pitchers, and Babe Ruth put the American League in front in the third inning with a two-run homer. The first National League homerun was hit in the sixth inning by Frankie Frisch. Gomez was the winning pitcher and was followed to the mound by Alvin Crowder and Lefty Grove. Hallahan was the loser and he was backed up by Lon Warneke and Carl Hubbell. Even though the game was to be only a one-time affair, and turned out to be a tremendous success with an attendance of 49,200, many owners were reluctant to continue the extravaganza, but it did become an annual event. Along with Mack and McGraw 17 of the 30 players who participated would eventually be inducted into the Hall of Fame: Chuck Klein, Frisch, Paul Waner, Chick Hafey, Bill Terry, Pie Traynor, Hubbell, Gabby Hartnett, Charlie Gehringer, Ruth, Lou Gehrig, Al Simmons, Joe Cronin, Rick Ferrell, Gomez, Earl Averill and Grove.

1956 — At the suggestion of Commissioner Ford Frick the Cy Young Award is inaugurated to honor the outstanding major league pitcher each year. The Dodgers' Don Newcombe was the first to be honored in 1956. Through 1966 only one pitcher received the award, but each league selected a winner beginning in 1967.

1986 — Atlanta's Bob Horner hits four homeruns against the Montreal Expos but the Braves lose the game 11-8. It is the second time in history that a team loses when a four-homer game is accomplished. In 1896 Ed Delahanty homered four times for the Philadelphia Phillies in a losing cause to the Chicago Colts 9-8. Horner becomes the eleventh player to hit four homeruns in a game, connecting three times (2nd, 4th and 5th innings) off Andy McGaffigan and in the 9th inning off Jeff Reardon.

July 7

1942 — In what has been billed as "A Forgotten All-Star Game", 62,094 paid fans and 2,000 servicemen attend a military wartime All-Star game at Cleveland's Municipal Stadium with the American League All-Stars playing against the

Service All-Stars from various Army and Navy bases across the country. Baseball writer Frederick G. Lieb writing in *The Sporting News* captured the feelings of the evening, "It was a fine exhibition of wartime team play, with the services co-operating with the National Game in putting over a spectacle such as one sees only once in a lifetime. Rumbling tanks, jumping jeeps, drilling Marines, music from the famous Great Lakes Naval Station's band, parading the colors of the Army, Navy and Coast Guard, and 65,000 awed persons filling one of the nation's great stadiums, made an unforgettable spectacle. As though it were a contagion, one could feel the patriotic fervor of the entire 65,000; it sent needles shooting down one's spine, started honest tears trickling down the cheeks, and made one murmur to one's self: "Thank God, I am an American!"

The service squad was organized, trained and managed by Lieutenant Mickey Cochrane USN and he was assisted by Lieutenant George Earnshaw of the Naval Air Station in Jacksonville, Florida. Cochrane's team had Pat Mullin of Detroit in center, Benny McCoy of the A's at second, Don Padgett of the Dodgers in left, Washington's Cecil Travis at short, Joe Grace of the Browns in right, the Yankees John Sturm at first, Ernie Andres of Louisville at third, Vinnie Smith of Pittsburgh catching and the Indians Bob Feller pitching. The American League All-Stars had Lou Boudreau ss, Tommy Henrich rf, Ted Williams lf, Joe DiMaggio cf, Rudy York 1b, Bobby Doerr 2b, Ken Keltner 3b, Buddy Rosar c and Jim Bagby pitching. Phil Rizzuto, Stan Spence, George McQuinn, Sid Hudson and Tex Hughson also saw action for the American League while Sam Chapman, Emmett Mueller, Chet Hajduk and Frankie Pytlak also played for the service team. The American League won 5-0.

July 8

1994 — Boston Red Sox infielder John Valentin becomes the tenth player in major league history to complete an unassisted triple play. It happens in the sixth inning at Fenway Park against the Seattle Mariners in a 4-3 Boston win. Valentin caught a sinking liner off the bat of Marc Newfield, stepped on second to double off Mike Blowers and trotted a few steps to tag Keith Mitchell. It is the sixth unassisted triple play executed by a shortstop and the second by a Red Sox player — first baseman George Burns had the other in 1923.

July 9

1939 — The National Association of Professional Baseball Clubs (minors) celebrates the game's 100th anniversary with a minor league All-Star game at

Cooperstown. In addition to the game the program consisted of the dedication of a research library. However, the only other mark left behind at the Hall of Fame to record the day was a bronze marker dedicated to the seven founders of the National Association.

The game was at best recognition of the minor leagues, and at worst a failure. Bad timing (two days before the major league All-Star game in New York City), the economic factor (expense involved in sending player representatives from each league to Cooperstown) and a lack of proper planning, coordination, and publicity all contributed to its lack of success. Although not the most memorable day in baseball history, the game was played at Doubleday Field with the Doubledays defeating the Cartwrights 9-6. Only 17 of the 41 minor leagues operating in 1939 participated but at least it was an attempt to recognize the value of the minors to professional baseball.

1972 — Nolan Ryan of the California Angels becomes the third pitcher in major league history to strike out the side on nine pitches for the second time in his career. Ryan first did so on April 19, 1968 while pitching for the New York Mets. This time he struck out all three Boston batters with the minimum number of pitches in the second inning. Sandy Koufax (1962 and 1964) and Lefty Grove (twice in 1928) are the only other pitchers to accomplish the feat two times.

1998 — Bud Selig, acting baseball commissioner for nearly six years, is given the job on a permanent basis in a special executive session of major league owners in Chicago. He becomes the ninth full-time commissioner and the first since Fay Vincent resigned on September 7, 1992. Selig, owner of the Milwaukee club, will step down as Trustee, Director, President and Chief Executive Officer of the Brewers while serving as commissioner.

July 10

1932 — With Philadelphia leading 3-2 A's manager Connie Mack removes starting pitcher Lew Krausse in the first inning against the Cleveland Indians. Mack calls Ed Rommel in from the bullpen to start the second inning and Rommel pitches the next 17 innings and picks up his only win of the season 18-17. It was a fantastic performance. In 17 innings he allowed 14 runs, 29 hits, walked nine and threw two wild pitches. The Indians scored six runs off Rommel in the seventh inning to give Cleveland a 14-13 lead, but for the next 11 innings he allowed only three runs while the A's scored five. Why was Rommel subjected to such punishment by Mack? Prior to this game, Philadelphia had played three successive doubleheaders on July 7, 8, and 9 and Mack was faced with another twin bill against Cleveland following this game. 1932 would be Rommel's last season, ending a 13-year career with the Athletics during which he would post a 171-119 record. Six years later, in 1938, Rommel would return to the majors to begin 22 years as an American League umpire.

1936 — The Phillies' Chuck Klein hits his fourth homerun of the game in the 10th inning giving Philadelphia a 9-6 victory over the Pirates in spacious Forbes Field. He narrowly misses another homerun in the second inning when he backed Paul Waner against the stands with a long fly. Klein hit his first two homers off Jim Weaver in the first and fifth innings and his third in the 7th off Mace Brown. With the game tied after nine innings rain threatened to wipe out Klein's bid for another, but he connected off Bill Swift and the game was completed making Klein the fourth player in history to hit four homeruns in one game.

July 11

1900 — Only 30 years old, right-hander Kid Nichols becomes the youngest man in major league history to record his 300th win. He is the sixth to reach the plateau and he does so in his 11th season in the big leagues. The win for Nichols was a 3-0 shutout in which the Boston Braves beat the St. Louis Cardinals. Nichols broke in with the Braves in 1890 and his first three seasons were pitched from the 50-foot distance. During those years he won a total of 92 games. Nichols had a career winning percentage of .634 in posting 361 wins while losing 208 with an ERA of 2.95. He spent most of his years with the Braves and Cardinals, winning 30 or more games seven times in his 15-year career. In 12 of those seasons he pitched 300 or more innings and in five of those he topped the 400 mark. He was also handy with the bat – as a switch-hitter he batted .226. He served as player-manager for St. Louis in 1904 and 1905. Kid (Charles) Nichols retired following the 1908 season while playing for the Phillies and was inducted into the Hall of Fame in 1949.

1914 — The Boston Braves finished in fifth place in 1913, 31 and a half games behind the pennant-winning New York Giants. On this date in 1914 the Braves were in last place and trailed the leading Giants by 11 and one-half with 75 games to play. Boston proceeded to win 59 of those games and went on to capture the National League pennant by 10 and one-half games. The last-to-first march was climaxed by a brilliant World Series victory over the Philadelphia Athletics in a four-game sweep (7-1, 1-0, 5-4, 3-1) to forever label that Boston team of 1914 "The Miracle Braves."

July 12

1825 — The legend of Abner Doubleday takes another hit as the earliest-known printed reference to organized baseball is turned up in the July 13, 1825 edition of the *Delhi* (New York) *Gazette* — 14 years before Doubleday allegedly devised the game at Cooperstown. The newspaper notice from Hamden, New York, dated July 12, 1825, contains the names challenging any group in Delaware County to a game of baseball at the home of Edward B. Chase for $1 each per game.

1901 — Denton "Cy" Young, pitching for the American League Boston Somersets, defeats the Philadelphia Athletics 5-3 and racks up the 300th victory of his career. The 34-year old Young becomes the seventh pitcher to win his 300th game on his way to a career record of 511-316. 72 of his victories came while pitching from the old 50-foot distance (1890-1892).

1951 – Right-hander Allie Reynolds, traded by Cleveland to the Yankees for Joe Gordon in 1946, spins a 1-0 no-hitter against the Indians at Cleveland Stadium before 36,195 fans. It is his third shutout of the season against his former team. His pitching opponent was Bob Feller who 11 days earlier had thrown his third career no-hit game against the Tigers. Feller allowed only four hits but one of them was a seventh inning 365 foot homerun by Gene Woodling to account for the only run of the game. Left fielder Hank Bauer saved Reynolds no-hitter in the seventh inning when he raced to the fence to haul down Sam Chapman's would-be extra base hit. It was one of seven putouts for Bauer in left. Only four batters reached base off Reynolds – three on walks and an error by shortstop Phil Rizzuto.

1979 — The Chicago White Sox stage one of the most bizarre and controversial promotions in baseball history with "Disco Demolition Night" at Comiskey Park. Michael Veeck, son of club owner Bill Veeck, served as promotions director of the White Sox and he had a particularly bitter attitude towards the increasingly popular disco craze. Chicago's WLUP-FM disc jockey, Steve Dahl, had been pushing the disco-record bashing antics for some time with his "Disco Sucks" motif and had legions of fans as his followers. The promotion was staged between games of a White Sox-Detroit doubleheader and Dahl would put a quarter stick of dynamite in a crate of disco records and blow them up. 49,000 fans, swelled by a 98-

cent ticket to anyone bringing disco records to be blown up (98 was the radio station's frequency), eagerly awaited the between game intermission. Dahl, dressed in army fatigues and riding in a jeep, drove out to centerfield and detonated the dynamite, destroying several thousand disco records. Moments later fans began entering the playing field and began some demolition of their own. An estimated 8,000 out-of-control anti-disco supporters were on the field when the second game was canceled and the game forfeited to Detroit.

July 13

1877 — When 17 year-old John Montgomery Ward decided to give up his education at Penn State to try his hand in professional baseball his hometown newspaper, the Bellefonte, Pennsylvania *Democratic Watchman* commented negatively that he had violated the sacred memory of his forebears. The newspaper stated they expected Ward to become a scholar and statesman and not a hired baseball pitcher. As it turned out he became one of the game's best pitchers, as well as a reliable hitter, a manager, a union organizer and club owner. Ward played 17 seasons in the majors, 12 of them with Brooklyn and the Giants and hit .278 with 326 stolen bases. In seven seasons as a pitcher he was 161-101. Later in his career the *Watchman* softened it attitude: "There is nothing *wrong* with pitching ball anymore than there is in making shoes or picking type." At 5'-9", 153 pounds he played every position except catcher and first base and was voted into the Hall of Fame in 1964.

1896 — The Phillies Ed Delahanty clubs four homeruns in a losing cause to the Chicago Colts 9-8. Delahanty homered in the first inning, singled in the third and hit his second round-tripper in the fifth inning. Number three was an inside-the-park homerun in the seventh and number four came in the ninth inning. Chicago pitcher William "Adonis" Terry pitched the complete game for the Colts at Chicago's West Side Park before only 1,100 fans. Delahanty, who eventually would enter the Hall of Fame, hit 13 homeruns in 1896 and only 101 during his entire career. Delahanty becomes the second player to hit four homers in one game, following Bobby Lowe's four home runs for Boston in 1894 against Cincinnati.

1963 — After a 10-month wait following number 299, Early Wynn finally hits the 300 win mark in his 23rd major league season. Wynn had registered his 299th victory with the White Sox in 1962 and before reaching the magic number would make seven more starts and one relief appearance. Wynn, 43 years old, ended his career following the victory in which he struggled through five innings, allowing four runs and six hits before giving way to Jerry Walker. Walker pitched shutout ball for the final four innings to pick up the save in a 7-4 Cleveland win over Kansas City. Only one pitcher in history prior to Wynn had failed to pitch a complete game in his 300th victory. Washington's Walter Johnson failed in this feat in 1920 when he beat Detroit 9-8. Wynn is the 14th pitcher to register 300 victories. Beginning in 1939 with Washington, Wynn would also see action with Cleveland as well as the White Sox. Wynn (24) would lose 244 games to go with his 300 wins and was elected to the Hall of Fame in 1972.

July 14

1934 — Lou Gehrig plays shortstop for one inning to keep his 1,427 consecutive games-played streak alive. In Detroit, the day before, he had taken himself out of a game against the Tigers. In the second inning after singling to center (while running to first) he doubled over complaining of a terrible back pain. Overnight treatment to his back didn't help. Gehrig, quite conscious of keeping his streak alive and not able to play the entire game, asked manager Joe McCarthy to place him in Frankie Crosetti's lead-off spot as the Yankees shortstop, and to take one time at bat then leave the game. McCarthy agreed.

Although unable to take a full swing, Gehrig got a piece of the ball and singled to right field. McCarthy, in the meantime, had discovered that Crosetti also wasn't feeling well so Red Rolfe ran for Gehrig and remained in the game at short. Gehrig, having taken one turn at bat and retiring from the game ensured his streak was uninterrupted and the incident soon forgotten – but not by everyone. Shortly after Gehrig died in 1941, James M. Kahn wrote in the *New York Sun*:

> *"This was Gehrig's closest escape from having his endurance mark broken, and it is given in detail because it may hold an additional interest for medical men. These attacks occurred occasionally and escaped accurate diagnosis, invaribly doubling him over and making it painful and difficult for him to breathe until they wore off in a couple of days. For convenience in reporting them and because of the absence of anything more definite, the sports writers referred to the attacks as lumbago. Gehrig became quite sensitive to the curiosity of the reporters after a while when these attacks hit him, which they did three or four times over a period of four or five years."*

1939 — A.G. Spalding & Bros. advertise in *The Sporting News*, "Another Achievement of the Spalding Research Laboratory – The New Baseball Batters'

Head Protector." It resembles headphones with a spring steel band that fits over the cap to hold a hard fiber cover with sponge strips —"shock absorbers" — to protect the temples and ears. It was produced at the request of Frank Shaughnessey, president of the International League and was immediately put to use in that circuit.

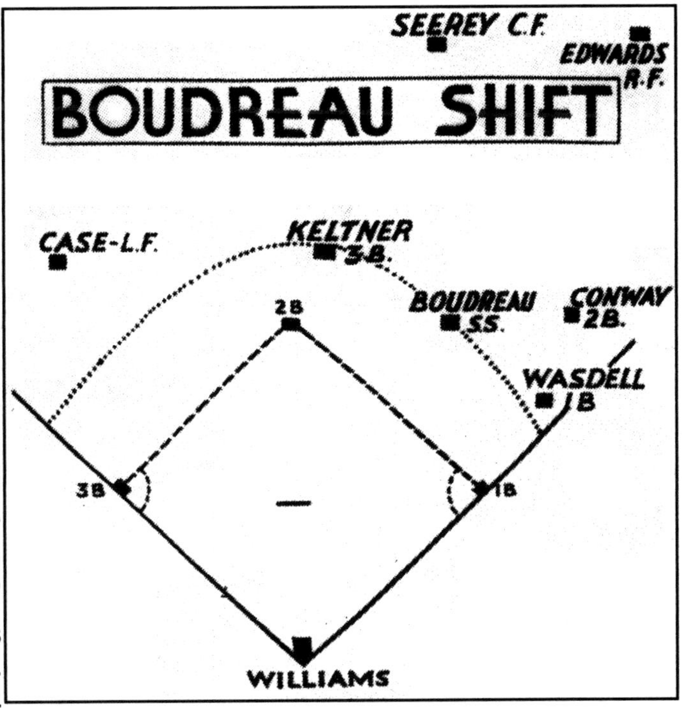

1946 — Cleveland manager Lou Boudreau creates the "Boudreau Shift" against Ted Williams in the second game of a doubleheader at Fenway Park. He had toyed with the idea of using a shift against Williams for days and had sketched the defensive move on a hotel napkin. After Boston beat Cleveland 11-10 in the first game with Williams hitting three homeruns, a single and driving in eight runs the "Boudreau Shift" is born. In an effort to hold down Williams' production, Boudreau shifts his entire defense, except left fielder George Case, to the right side of the infield. Third baseman Ken Keltner moves a bit to the right of second base and deep; shortstop Boudreau plays in the normal second baseman's position; second baseman Jack Conway moves to shallow right field near the foul line; first baseman Jimmy Wasdell plays deep back of first on the grass – tight to the foul line; center fielder Pat Seerey moves about ten steps into right and right fielder Hank Edwards plays deep in right center. This leaves only Case shallow in left, a bit closer to the left field line than second base, but still the only player on the left side of second base.

In the second game Williams went one-for-two with two walks against the shift. His one hit was a double over Wasdell's head down the right field line. Other good hitters before Williams had to face shifts but probably not as exaggerated as Boudreau's. The Chicago White Sox used a shift against Babe Ruth in 1920. Another left handed hitter, against whom foes regularly used the shift to right, was Cy Williams with the Cubs and Phillies (1912-1930). He hit .345 against it in 1926. One of the most interesting shift stories unfolded during the 1932 season when Dale Alexander (1929-1933), who began the season with Detroit and was traded to the Red Sox in June, won the American League batting championship with an average of .367. Everything he hit was to the right of second base. Alexander is probably the only *right-handed* hitter that that had to face the "Ted Williams Shift."

July 15

1901 — 22 year-old Christy Mathewson pitches the New York Giants to a 5-0 no-hit win over the Cardinals at League Park in St. Louis before an estimated 5,000 fans. He struck out four, walked four and a third batter reached on an error. Mathewson debuted with the Giants in 1900 and lost all three of his decisions. This season he would wind up with a 20-17 mark.

1928 — The Hollywood Stars of the Pacific Coast League become one of the Pioneers of air travel when they fly from Seattle to Portland in order to make train connections to Los Angeles following a Sunday doubleheader to keep a scheduled game on Tuesday with San Francisco. The Stars regulars and two or three pitchers took the flight while the rest of the team and equipment trucks left Seattle by train on Saturday.

1973 — With the New York Mets brass slowly shaking their heads over the deal that sent Nolan Ryan to the California Angels in December 1971, the 26-year old fireballer chalks up his second no-hitter with a 6-0 gem over Detroit at Tiger Stadium before 41,411 Cap Day fans. True to form, he walked four batters but struck out a whopping 17 – 12 of them in the first five innings. Just two months earlier on the same day, Ryan had thrown his first no-hitter at the Royals in Kansas City.

July 16

1970 — After playing their home games for 61 seasons at Forbes Field, the Pirates play their first game near downtown Pittsburgh at Three Rivers Stadium. The Cincinnati Reds squeeze out a 3-2 win before 48,846 as Tony Perez hits the first homerun in the new stadium off Dock Ellis. Accompanying the team to their new home was a portion of the brick outfield wall at Forbes Field, the Honus Wagner statue, and the Babe Ruth plaque indicating where Ruth had hit his 714th homerun as well. All were placed in the Allegheny Club. This move was also historic when the Pirates became the first major league team to go to double-knit polyester pullover uniforms. No buttons or zippers on jerseys, or belts on pants. The new uniform featured a crew neck and the pants had a built-in elastic waist with snaps. By the middle of the 1970s most clubs had followed suit, but by the early 1990s teams were back to where they had been – except for the flannels.

July 17

1924 — Jesse "Pop" Haines spins a no-hitter for the Cardinals at Sportsman's Park against the Boston Braves in a 5-0 win. He walked three and struck out five and had help on three occasions when his defense came through on difficult plays. Haines' no-hitter is the first ever pitched by a Cardinal pitcher in St. Louis. Two Browns pitchers, Ernie Koob and Bob Groom, had previously turned the trick on back-to-back days on May 5 and 6 in 1917. Haines finished the 1924 season with a record of 8-19, the only time he failed to win in double figures in 12 consecutive years. Haines, a knuckleballer-fast ball pitcher, made his major league debut in 1918 with Cincinnati but pitched in only one game. He spent the 1919 season in the minors with Tulsa (Western League) and Kansas City (American Association) then returned to the majors with the Cardinals in 1920 and stayed for 18 years. It was the persuasion of Branch Rickey, then St. Louis manager, which led to Haines' purchase for $10,000 after a 21-win season with Kansas City. Haines would pitch through his 44th birthday in 1937, appear in four World Series with a 3-1, 1.67 ERA and was a member of the 1934 Gas House Gang in one of those fall classics. Haines' (16) no-hit game in 1924 would be his only no-hitter, finishing with a mark of 210-158 and entering the Hall of Fame in 1970.

1941 — Cleveland pitchers Al Smith and Jim Bagby combine to stop Joe DiMaggio's 56-game hitting streak before 67,168 fans at Cleveland stadium. Ken Keltner makes two brilliant stops at third base and another hot smash by DiMaggio in the eighth inning results in a double play started by shortstop Lou Boudreau. Going 3-for-4 the night before against the Indians, DiMaggio ended his streak with 91 hits in 223 at-bats, an average of .408, scored 56 runs, 15 homeruns with 55 RBI while striking out only seven times. He started his two-month streak on May 15 with a single off Eddie Smith of the White Sox. The day following the end of his streak DiMaggio would start a string of 17 more games in which he would hit safely. Nine years earlier as an 18-year old with the San Francisco Seals of the Pacific Coast League he rolled up a 61 game hitting streak.

2000 — Chris Richard of the St. Louis Cardinals looks at the first pitch thrown to him in the majors and hits it into the stands at the Metrodome. Another rookie, the Twins' Mike Lincoln, serves up the pitch. Richard is the 15th player to waste no time getting in the homerun category and he follows Tampa Bay's Esteban Yan to become the first two rookies in the history of the to turn the trick in the same season; Yan hit his on June 4.

July 18

1882 — Tony Mullane pitches both right and left handed for the Louisville Eclipse in an American Association game at Baltimore to become the first major league pitcher to perform the feat. Normally a righty, he begins pitching left-handed in the fourth inning against lefty hitters and does quite well until the ninth when Charlie Householder beats him with a homerun that turns into a 9-8 Baltimore victory. The *Baltimore American* reported the incident: "During the game when the Baltimore group of left-handed hitters, Whiting, Householder and Pearce, were coming to bat, Mullane, the Louisville pitcher, changed his delivery from right hand to left hand, and puzzled the batters considerably. This was a novelty in pitching and excited much interest. He was not, however, able to keep the left-handed delivery up for any length of time, but it was very effective while it lasted."

On July 14, 1893 the right-handed Mullane would do it again and pitch the 9th inning left-handed in a losing cause for Baltimore against the Chicago Colts in a National League game. Trailing 7-2 going into the final inning Mullane gives up three more runs as the Orioles lose 10-2. Quoting from the *Chicago Tribune*, "So hard did they hit Mulane that he lost his baseball sense and tossed up left hand lobs to the Colts." Mullane would pitch 13 years with a record of 285-215.

1948 — Pat Seerey of the Chicago White Sox becomes the fifth player in history to hit four homeruns in a game. They come in a White Sox victory 12-11 at Shibe Park in the first game of a doubleheader against Philadelphia. After striking out in his first at-bat, Seerey homers in the fourth, fifth and sixth innings, the first two off Carl Scheib and the third off Bob Savage. After fouling out in the seventh and drawing a walk in the ninth he hits number four in the 11th off Lou Brissie. Cleveland had traded the chunky outfielder, 5'-10" and 200 pounds, to Chicago in June. This season he would hit 19 homeruns and during his seven-year major league career would total 86 and hit .224. In four of his seven seasons he led the American League in strikeouts. Seerey played in only four games with the Sox in 1949 and was sent down to Chicago's Class-A Western League club at Colorado Springs.

1960 — The formation of the pesky Continental League and their delays to begin operation as a third major league forces the National League to act and vote for expansion. Behind a solid vote of league leaders in Chicago the circuit warns Continental brass that if they did not show an intention of entering organized ball, and paying indemnities for the minor league territories to be invaded, both majors would take in several of their cities. After two weeks of intensive haggling over indemnities to the American Association, which had five clubs committed to the new league, the Continental League bows out of the picture, opening the door for New York and Houston to enter the National League in 1962.

1970 — San Francisco's Willie Mays bounces a single through the left side of the infield for his 3000th hit. The hit comes off Mike Wegener in the second inning as the Giants rout Montreal 10-1. The 39-year old Mays is the tenth player to reach the three- thousand mark and would go on to total 3,283 hits in his career.

1999 — Spooky? Prior to the New York-Montreal game at Yankee Stadium before 41,930 fans Don Larsen and Yogi Berra recreate the final out of Larsen's World Series perfect game in 1956 against Brooklyn. Larsen then went to the mound and shook the hand of Yankee starting pitcher David Cone who then proceeded to pitch his own perfect game, a 6-0 win over the Expos, the 14th in the history of major league baseball. Larsen had pitched the fourth, and nearly 43 years had elapsed between the gems of Larsen and Cone.

July 19

1909 — Shortstop Neal Ball of the Cleveland Indians executes the first unassisted triple play in major league history. This feat occurred In the top of the second inning of the first game of a double header against the Red Sox at League Park. With Heinie Wagner on second and Jake Stahl on first, Amby McConnell hits a line drive to Bell, who touches second to double Wagner then tags Stahl coming down from first. In the bottom of the second, obviously still pumped up by his defensive play, Ball hits an inside the park homerun, his only homer of the season.

1910 — Cy Young registers his 500th victory at age 43 as Cleveland defeats Washington in 11 innings 5-4. Going into 1911 Young had 504 victories and would win three games for the Indians that year before being waived in July. After being claimed by the Boston Braves, Young picked up wins 508, 509, 510 and 511 then retires with a record of 511-316.

July 19

1911 — One of the most unusual and outstanding defensive plays in minor league history — an unassisted triple play by an outfielder — takes place in Los Angeles by center fielder Walter (Rosy) Carlisle of Vernon in the Pacific Coast League. In the sixth inning with the score tied 3-3 and the Angels' Charles Moore on second base and George Metzger on first, batter Roy Akin hits a low liner over second base; the runners are off without hesitation. Carlisle, who was playing in shallow center, catches the ball off the grass and turns two or three somersaults and lands on his feet while hanging onto to the ball. Moore had rounded third by this time and Metzger had passed second. The rest was easy. Carlisle ran and touched second to retire Moore then trotted to first to triple-up Metzger. Carlisle was a minute 5'-9" 150-pounder who played 19 seasons in the minors with a three-game stint with the Red Sox in 1908.

1927 — Just shy of seven years after he registered his 3000th hit, Ty Cobb becomes the first to reach the 4000 mark and he does it against the team he played with for 22 years, the Detroit Tigers. Now with the Philadelphia Athletics, and 40 years old, Cobb doubles off the glove of another future Hall-of-Famer, right fielder Harry Heilmann. Detroit wins 5-3 as Tigers pitcher Sam Gibson serves up the historic pitch that would lead to Cobb's final total of 4,191.

1938 — Larry MacPhail hires Babe Ruth as a coach with Brooklyn. Following his release by the Braves after the 1935 season, Ruth had been out of baseball but still hoped to someday manage in the majors. He, of course, jumped at the chance to join the Dodgers even though his salary would be only $15,000 (down from a high of $80,000 in 1932). Ruth coached first base, helped the younger players with their hitting and his presence on the club helped boost attendance at Ebbets Field. There was one negative for Ruth, Leo Durocher was the Brooklyn shortstop. While both were with the Yankees, Ruth and Durocher had disliked each other and their feelings had not changed. Also, their mutual contempt for each other was no secret around the team. When the season ended MacPhail fired manager Burleigh Grimes, and Ruth read about the change in the newspapers. He was devastated to learn the job had gone to – Leo Durocher!

1976 — 24 year-old pitcher Steve Busby of the Kansas City Royals is the first player to undergo rotator cuff surgery. In only his fourth full season in the majors and after winning 16 games in 1973, 22 in 1974, 18 in 1975 (including no-hitters against Detroit on April 27, 1973 and June 19, 1974 against Milwaukee), Busby goes under the knife in a procedure that in two years would become commonplace. Busby was 3-3 in 1976 when he had his operation and would miss the entire 1977 season; he would never return to his pitching excellence. Busby retired in 1980 with post-surgery records of 1-0 in 1978, 6-6 in 1979 and 1-3 in 1980.

July 20

1858 — Fans are charged for the first time to see a baseball game. Approximately 1,500 fans each pay 50 cents to see the New York All-Stars play Brooklyn. The game is played on Long Island at the Fashion Race Course and results in a 22-18 New York victory.

1916 — Cincinnati and the New York Giants pull off a five-player trade that involves three future Hall-of-Famers as well as a change in managers. The Giants send Christy Mathewson, Edd Roush and Bill McKechnie to the Reds for Buck Herzog and Red Killefer. Mathewson takes over as manager of the Reds, replacing Herzog, who had been fired a few days earlier. This would mark the end of Mathewson's pitching career, but he would continue to skipper the Reds through 1918. Until his move to Cincinnati, Mathewson had spent his entire 17 years with the Giants, pitching two no-hitters and playing in four World Series. He had an excellent .665 winning percentage (373-188), an earned run average of 2.13, won 20 or more games in 13 seasons for New York and in five of those cranked out 30 or more victories. Mathewson completed 79% of the 551 games he started and was one of the first five players and the first pitcher to enter the Hall of Fame in 1936. Outfielder Edd Roush was only 23 years old and in his fourth major league season at the time of the trade and after playing for 18 years would be inducted into the Hall of Fame in 1962. McKechnie, a journeyman infielder for 11 years, would go on to carve his niche in baseball as one of the best managers in history. For 24 years McKechnie (65) would manage Pittsburgh, the St. Louis Cardinals, the Boston Braves and Cincinnati to a winning percentage of .524 and join Roush in the induction ceremonies at Cooperstown in 1962.

1958 — Detroit right-hander Jim Bunning throws a 3-0 no-hitter at the Red Sox before 29,524 at Fenway Park in the first game of a double header. He struck out 12 batters, and the only men to get on base were walks to Gene Stephens and Jackie Jensen (who was hit by a pitch). On June 21, 1964 Bunning, now pitching for the Phillies, would throw a perfect game against the Mets.

1976 — Hank Aaron hits his 755th and final homerun while playing for the Milwaukee Brewers in a 6-2 victory over California. The homer comes with no one on base in the seventh inning off Angels pitcher Dick Drago.

July 21

1970 — San Diego pitcher Clay Kirby has a no-hitter against the New York Mets through the eighth inning. The Padres are behind 1-0 and Kirby is due to bat third in the bottom of the eighth. San Diego manager Preston Gomez has a decision to make — leave Kirby in with a chance for a no-hit game or try and win with a pinch-hitter. With two outs and the bases empty Gomez elects to go for the win and sends Cito Gaston up to hit for Kirby. Gaston flies out. Jack Baldschun replaces Kirby in the ninth, gives up two runs and the Padres lose 3-0. The odds against this happening again are astronomical but four years later, September 4, 1974, Gomez, now managing the Houston Astros, is faced with the same situation. Don Wilson has a no-hitter through the top of the eighth and the Astros are trailing Cincinnati 2-1. Wilson is the lead batter in the bottom of the eighth and Gomez makes the same move – he lifts Wilson for Tommy Helms and Helms grounds out to short. Greg Gross and Roger Metzger follow with singles but Cesar Cedeno strikes out and Metzger is thrown out at second by Johnny Bench to complete the inning-ending double play. Mike Cosgrove relieves Wilson and pitches a scoreless ninth but the Reds win 2-1. Gomez later summed up the two games when asked if he would do it again, he replied: "I would. To me you can't set a record at the expense of 24 other players. You play to win."

July 22

1876 — The Chicago White Stockings defeat the Louisville Grays in a National League game in which Louisville is charged with 37 errors. There were 88 runs scored in the game of which only 37 were earned. Scorekeepers in this era did not consider any ball to be "too hot to handle" and fielders wore no gloves.

1935 — Bob Feller, fresh off the farm in Van Meter, Iowa and still in high school, signs a minor league contract with Fargo-Moorhead of the Northern League. The contract was scrawled out in long hand and read:

Agreement -
This agreement entered into this day (July 22nd, 1935) by and between the Fargo Baseball Club and Robt. Feller and his legal guardian W.A. Feller agree to as follows. The Fargo club agrees to pay Robt. Feller or his legal guardian $500 if he is retained on the roster of the Fargo Baseball Club on Sept 15th 1936. The Fargo club agrees to allow Robt. Feller to visit his folks at any time during the 1936 season, also to invite Robt. Fellers' folks to visit him at Fargo during the summer of 1936 at the expense of the Fargo base Ball Club. The Fargo club has no objection to Robt. Feller playing Basket Ball at any time. For a consideration of one dollar paid to Robt Feller this agreement is declared valid.

Cy Slapnicka - Representing Fargo Club
Robt Feller - Player
W.A. Feller - Legal Guardian

COPY OF BOB FELLER'S CONTRACT, SIGNED JULY 22, 1935

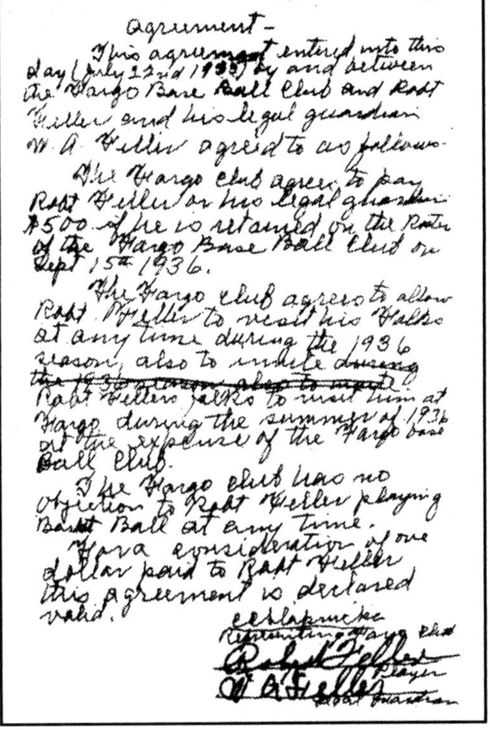
Agreement -
This agreement entered into this day (July 22nd 1935) by and between the Fargo Base Ball Club and Robt Feller and his legal guardian W.A. Feller agreed to as follows.
The Fargo club agrees to pay Robt Feller or his legal guardian $500 if he is retained on the roster of the Fargo Base Ball Club on Sept 15th 1936.
The Fargo club agrees to allow Robt Feller to visit his folks at any time during the 1936 season, also to invite during ~~the 1936 season also to invite~~ Robt Fellers folks to visit him at Fargo during the summer of 1936 at the expense of the Fargo base Ball Club.
The Fargo club has no objection to Robt Feller playing Basket Ball at any time.
For a consideration of one dollar paid to Robt Feller this agreement is declared valid.
C C Slapnicka
Representing Fargo Club
Robert Feller Player
W A Feller Legal Guardian

This agreement, however, was illegal. Under a regulation at the time, major league clubs had agreed not to sign free agents other than college players. Minor league teams were supposed to sign high school talent and sandlot players and then sell them to big league clubs. Slapnicka, in reality, was representing Cleveland and Feller's contract had been transferred to New Orleans, another Indians farm club. Meanwhile, while pitching for Des Moines in a National semipro tournament, Feller caught the eye of numerous major league scouts, which led Detroit to check with baseball's minor league offices as to his status. It was then revealed that Feller was the property of the Cleveland Indians. This led to the Des Moines Western League club filing a complaint with commissioner Landis claiming violation of the major-minor league agreement. Landis, who could have declared Feller a free agent, instead ordered Cleveland to pay Des Moines

$7,500. The commissioner, not liking the rule, moved to eliminate the clause that theoretically kept the majors from competing with the minors for free agents. Feller was well satisfied with his association with Cleveland and in July of 1936 made his professional debut with the Indians against the St. Louis Browns at League Park in Cleveland.

July 23

1944 — Bill Nicholson of the Chicago Cubs is ordered intentionally walked with the bases loaded. The order comes down from New York manager Mel Ott in the eighth inning of the second game of a doubleheader at the Polo Grounds. Nicholson had hit three homeruns in the Cubs' 7-4 first game win and connected for another in the second game. Despite a Chicago rally the Giants pull out a 12-10 victory in the second game for a split. Nicholson hit six homeruns in the four game series – one each on Friday and Saturday and four in the Sunday doubleheader. Where documentation exists, the intentional walk with the bases full happened only one other time – May 23, 1901 – Chicago White Stockings pitcher/manager Clark Griffith gave the walk to Philadelphia's Nap Lajoie.

1964 — Bert Campaneris of the Kansas City Athletics connects for a homerun on the first pitch thrown to him in the majors. It comes off Jim Kaat of the Minnesota Twins as Campaneris becomes the seventh big leaguer to accomplish this. He would waste little time hitting his second homer, getting another in the same game. Before the year was out he would have four homeruns in his rookie season. During his 19 years in the majors the shortstop would hit only 79 homers; 22 of those came with Oakland in 1970. That season Campaneris hit just one less than the club leader Reggie Jackson who finished with 23.

July 24

1942 — Dave Barnhill was only 5'-7" and 150 pounds but the right-hander threw as hard as anyone in the Negro leagues — including Satchel Paige and Slim Jones. Most of his career was spent with the New York Cubans of the Negro National League and one of the highlights of his years of pitching came on this day when he received the following telegram that gave him hope of becoming the first black player to appear in the major leagues in this century. The following was sent by sports editor Nat Low:

HAVE JUST ARRANGED WITH WILLIAM BENSWANGER, PRESIDENT OF

THE PITTSBURGH PIRATES, A TRYOUT FOR YOU WITH TEAM IN PITTSBURGH SOON. CONGRATULATIONS, WON'T YOU PLEASE GET IN TOUCH WITH ME SO WE CAN MAKE FULL ARRANGEMENTS?

Three days later, July 27, the *New York Daily Worker* reports that Benswanger would arrange tryouts not only for Barnhill but also for Roy Campanella and Sammy T. Hughes. It never came to pass and Barnhill's only comment later was: "He (Benswanger) was scared to take a chance." Dave Barnhill never pitched in the majors.

1948 — The manager and four players with the Duluth Class-C Northern League team are killed and 13 others injured when their bus is struck head-on by an out-of-control truck laden with chemicals; both vehicles are engulfed in flames. The accident happens near the northern city limits of St. Paul as the Duluth team is en route from Eau Claire, Wisconsin to St. Cloud, Minnesota. The victims are manager and driver George Treadwell, 42; pitcher Don Schuchmann, 20; outfielders Gil Trible, 19; and Gerald Peterson, 23; second baseman Steve Lazar, 23 and the driver of the truck. Among the survivors is first baseman Mel McGaha who would later manage Cleveland and Kansas City. Two years earlier on June 19, 1946, nine members of the Spokane club of the Western Association died when their bus went off the road and plunged down a gorge.

July 25

1910 — After struggling through his first two seasons in the majors with the Philadelphia Athletics and an average of .150 (6-40), Shoeless Joe Jackson is traded to Cleveland. The Indians give up outfielder Bris Lord who would go on to hit .256 for the A's and Braves through 1913. Jackson went 29-for-75 (.387) the remainder of the 1910 season for Cleveland and in his first full year in 1911 hit .408. Before being banished from the game following the 1920 season for his involvement in the 1919 Black Sox scandal, Jackson would accumulate a career batting average of .356 in 13 years.

1933 – 18 year-old Joe DiMaggio of the Pacific Coast League San Francisco Seals hits safely in his 61st consecutive game. The string would end the next day with DiMaggio going 0-for-5 at Seals Stadium against Oakland's Ed Walsh, Jr. son of the famed Chicago White Sox spitballer and Hall-of-Famer. Although he eclipsed the old PCL record of 49 straight games set by Oakland first baseman Jack Ness in 1915, DiMaggio fell short of the professional baseball record of 69 in a row set by Joe Wilhoit of the Wichita Witches in the Class-A Western League in 1919.

1941 — Lefty Grove chalks up his 300th and last career victory, pitching a complete game win for Boston 10-6 over the Cleveland Indians at Fenway Park. He would make six more starts for the Red Sox, but not win another and finish the season at 7-7. Grove started only 456 games on the way to his 300 wins, but made 160 relief appearances and picked up 33 victories out of the bullpen. He retired after 17 years in the majors with a 300-141 record. His winning percentage of .680 is one of the best in history, and it all began with his first win for the Philadelphia Athletics in 1925 and culminate with is 300th at age 41. He becomes the 12th major leaguer to win 300 (winning a high of 31 in 1931 and 20 or more in seven other seasons). Grove (10) was voted into the Hall of Fame in 1947.

1987 — The Salt Lake City Trappers of the Pioneer League, a rookie classification circuit, win their 29th straight game to set a professional baseball record. The club, made up primarily of free agents passed over by pro scouts in the draft, racks up number 29 with a 13-3 win over Pocatella. The game drew a standing-room-only crowd of 9,968 at Derks Field in Salt Lake City, many of whom paid scalpers up to $50 for the privilege of seeing baseball history made. The victory takes the old record of 27 out of the books, originally set in 1902 by Corsicana (Texas League) and tied by Baltimore (International) in 1921. Two days after their 29th win the Trappers would lose to Billings 7-5. Salt Lake City would go on to finish first in the Southern Division with a record of 49-21 and defeat Billings three games to one for the Pioneer League pennant.

The Trappers were managed by Jim Gilligan, also in his first pro season after spending 14 successful years at Lamar University in Beaumont, Texas. Gilligan would eventually return to Lamar for his second tenure as the Cardinals coach. Salt Lake City would set another record at season's end by drawing 170,134 to eclipse the old mark for short-season attendance set in 1975 (119,253) by Portland (Northwest League).

July 26

1928 — Outfielder Chuck Klein, playing with Fort Wayne in the Class-B Central League, is spotted by Phillies manager Burt Shotton and promptly purchased for $7,500. At the time Klein was hitting .331 with 26 homeruns in 88 games, and went on to finish the season with Philadelphia batting .360 with 11 homers in 64 games. Although Klein had five tremendous seasons with the Phillies (.359 and

180 home runs), the team finished in the second division four times. Not only was Shotton fired but Klein was traded to the Cubs. In 1936 Chicago traded Klein back to Philadelphia and before his career ended he would also play with Pittsburgh then serve his third term with the Phillies. Klein spent 17 years in the majors with a .320 batting average, winning the National League batting Championship in 1933, one year after he was honored as the league's Most Valuable Player in 1932. Klein (32) was elected to the Hall of Fame in 1980.

1951 — Granite Falls of the Class-D Western Carolina League breaks their 26-game losing streak with a 5-4 win over Marion. It would be the final win of the season for the Graniteers as they lose their final 33 games and finish the season 14-96 – 57 games behind first place Morgantown.

July 27

1960 — The first announcement of the Fireman Trophy is made by columnist Jerome Holtzman in *The Sporting News*. Within the next few weeks numerous stories would be run in the publication quoting baseball executives, managers and players, all of whom endorsed Holtzman's idea. With relief pitchers growing in importance and with no accurate statistic to measure their effectiveness, Holtzman scratched out a formula to determine saves, a formula that is the basis for the *save* as we know it today. This was the beginning of *The Sporting News* Fireman Trophy that would be awarded to the top reliever in each league continuing through the 1968 season. In 1969 the save became an official baseball statistic, with Holtzman's original formula almost completely intact.

The first winners were Lindy McDaniel of the Cardinals and Mike Fornieles of the Red Sox. Rolaids took over the award in 1976 employing a unique scoring system. The first winners of that award were Rawley Eastwick of Cincinnati and Mike Campbell of Minnesota. Due to intensive research of games played before saves (and other pertinent statistics) were recorded the Society for American Baseball Research (SABR), as well as other independent baseball buffs, have made it possible to bring the past to the present for comparative purposes. In the case of saves, Bob Tiemann of SABR, after exhaustive digging, concluded that the first save was recorded by Harry Wright of the Boston Red Stockings when he relieved Al Spalding on May 20, 1871 against the Philadelphia Athletics in a National Association game.

July 28

1890 — 31 year-old Mickey Welch wins his 300th game with a 4-2 complete game victory for the New York Giants against Pittsburgh. Welch pitched his entire 13-year career with the same franchise – starting in 1880 with the Troy, N.Y. Trojans, a club that in 1883 was moved to New York City and became known as the Gothams, then renamed the Giants in 1885. The 5'-8" 160-pound right-hander is the third 300 game winner in baseball's short history – the first two being Pud Galvin of the Pirates in 1888 and Tim Keefe of the Giants in 1891. Both Welch and Galvin worked their entire careers at the 50-foot pitching distance while Keefe won only ten of his 327 games at the longer distance. 44 of Welch's 300 wins came in 1885 and he finished his career in 1892 with a 307-210 record and was voted into the Hall of Fame in 1973. It is interesting to note that in 1887 the rule allowing the batter to call for a high or low pitch was abolished, but new wrinkles to help the batter were added. The batter was struck out on four strikes and walked on five balls and those walks entered the record as base hits and a time at bat. The 60' 6" rule was put into effect in 1893.

1991 — Dennis Martinez pitches the 11th perfect game in history as Montreal defeats the Los Angeles Dodgers 2-0. A Dodger Stadium crowd of 45,560 watched as Martinez threw only 96 pitches (66 strikes and 30 balls) in registering the second perfect game pitched in Los Angeles. Sandy Koufax tossed the other in 1965 when the Dodgers beat the Cubs 1-0. Martinez' catcher was Ron Hassey and it was the second perfect game he caught in his career – also working Len Barker's "el perfecto" for Cleveland over Toronto on May 15, 1981.

1994 — 46,580 Rangers fans at the Ballpark in Arlington are treated to Kenny Rogers' perfect game, a 4-0 gem over the California Angels with Andrew Lorraine the losing pitcher. It got a little touchy when Rex Hudler opened the ninth with a liner to center but Rusty Greer made a diving catch and Rogers then disposed of Chris Turner and Gary DiSarcina to wrap it up. Rogers struck out eight of the 27 batters he faced while throwing only 98 pitches (34 balls and 64 strikes). It was the 12th perfect game in the majors since Cy Young threw the first for the Red Sox in 1904. Ever wonder what the odds are against a perfect game? It has been estimated they are about 20,000 to one.

July 29

1911 — Cy Young, overweight and 44 years old, pitches his last game for the

Cleveland Indians. After giving up five runs to Washington, Young is taken out after three innings in a 7-1 loss. His next appearance with the Tribe would be on the coaching lines and his unconditional release would come on August 15. This was the beginning of the end of 22 years with Cleveland, the Cardinals, and Red Sox that netted him 507 victories. Six days after his release Young would sign with the National League Boston Rustlers and win his 511th game on September 22nd, a 1-0 shutout over Pittsburgh. Although he reported to spring training with Boston in 1912 he did not pitch in a single game and retired on May 24.

July 30

1936 — The Boston Red Sox take to the air and fly from St. Louis to Chicago aboard one plane accompanied by owner Tom Yawkey and American League president Will Harridge. This is believed to be the first flight carrying an entire team. In 1934 the Reds used three planes for a trip from Cincinnati to Chicago. Other known early flights were made by the Cardinals in 1938, the Yankees in 1946, the Phillies in 1950, Detroit in 1956 with others falling in line during this period. Perhaps the first flight was made in 1914 when the entire St. Louis Browns team was shuttled across Tampa Bay during spring training. There is no mention as to how many trips it took to transport the team since the seating capacity was very limited. The St.Petersburg-Tampa Airport Line lasted only a few months, primarily because of the war. The aircraft was a Benoist Type XIV aircraft number 43 powered by a two-cycle, 75-horsepower Roberts engine that could reach speeds of 65 MPH. Flights between Tampa and St.Petersburg lasted 20 minutes; the trip took two or three hours by steamship.

1968 — Washington shortstop Ron Hansen executes the eighth unassisted triple play in history in the first inning of the Senators game with the Indians at Cleveland Stadium. With the Indians' Dave Nelson on second and Russ Snyder on first, both breaking on a 3-2 pitch to Joe Azcue, Hansen spears Azcue's line drive, steps on second to double Nelson then tags Snyder coming into second. This is the first unassisted triple play pulled off in the majors in 41 years, or since 1927 when two were completed in back-to-back days May 30 and 31. The first inning was the only highlight for Washington as Cleveland ended up beating the Senators 10-1.

July 31

1909 — For the second time in fourteen months pitcher Bill Burns has a no-hitter broken up with two outs in the ninth inning. This time pitching for the White Sox, Burns gives up a single to Washington's Otis Clymer in the second game of a doubleheader but holds on to give Chicago a 1-0 victory. On May 25, 1908 Burns tasted disappointment of the same variety when Germany Schaefer of Detroit broke up his no-hit bid. Burns was throwing for the Senators at the time and lost 1-0.

1932 — The Cleveland Indians play their first game at Municipal Stadium with Philadelphia's Lefty Grove pitching a 2-0 shutout against the Tribe's Mel Harder before a crowd of 76,979. It would be 15 years, in 1947, before the Indians would make this park their permanent home. In April 1934 Cleveland would be back at League Park for all of their games except on Sundays and Holidays, which would be played downtown. The Indians added night games to the new park in 1939 and would play their final game at League Park on September 21, 1946. In 1987 the stadium became the first baseball park to be listed in the National Register of historic places. On October 3, 1993 the Indians would lose to the White Sox 4-0 in the final game played in Cleveland Stadium. On April 4,1994 Cleveland would open its new park in the Gateway Sports and Entertainment Center with a come from behind win over Seattle in eleven innings.

1954 — Joe Adcock becomes the seventh player in the game's history to hit four homeruns in a game, three of them consecutively. The Milwaukee first baseman rolled up some impressive numbers in the Braves 15-7 win over Brooklyn – he also doubled for five extra base hits and 18 total bases. The downside came the next day at Ebbets Field when Adcock was beaned by the Dodgers Clem Labine. The Braves' Gene Conley reciprocated by knocking down Jackie Robinson who ended up in a fight with Eddie Mathews.

1990 — Twenty-three years after his first major league win in 1968, and now 43 years old, Nolan Ryan, making his second attempt to win his 300th game, succeeds with an 11-3 victory over the Milwaukee Brewers. Leading 5-3 with two outs in the eighth inning, Texas manager Bobby Valentine is soundly booed by 55,097 Milwaukee fans at County Stadium as he lifts Ryan and brings in Brad Arnsberg who gets the final four outs. Ryan is the 20th pitcher to record 300 wins but is only the fourth to not complete his game. The others were Walter Johnson, Steve Carlton and Early Wynn. The Rangers scored six runs in the ninth to make it an easy Texas victory. In Arlington, 7,828 Texas fans had the opportunity to watch the historic game on the Diamond Vision screen at Arlington Stadium as team officials had opened the gates for a $3 parking charge.

"For this relief much thanks" – Shakespeare, *Hamlet*

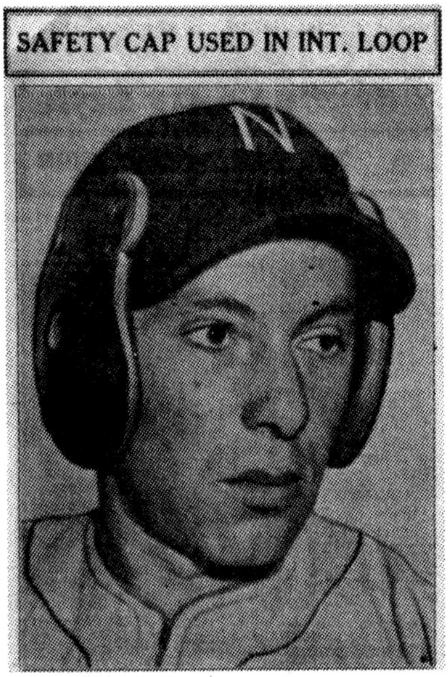

Safety cap for use in the International League, 1939

Lou Gehrig

Chapter Eight

"The other day Willie Mays hit his 522nd homerun. He has gone past me, and he's pushing, and I say to him, 'Go get 'em, Willie.' Baseball gives every American boy a chance to excel. This is the nature of man and name of the game. I hope that someday Satchel Paige and Josh Gibson will be voted into the Hall of Fame as symbols of the great Negro players who are not here only because they weren't given the chance."

From Ted Williams' induction into the Hall of Fame, 1966

August 1

1950 — The owners of the Fort Lauderdale club of the Class-B Florida International League attempt to sign Dottie Kamenshek, 26-year old star first baseman for the Rockford Peaches. The president of the All-American Girls Baseball League refuses to approve the sale. The AAGBL, founded by Philip K. Wrigley, operated in the Midwest 1943-1954. Kamenshek was considered by many as the league's best hitter, compiling a league high .292 lifetime average while striking out only 81 times in 3,736 at-bats with 515 walks.

August 2

1938 — A yellow baseball is used in the first game of a doubleheader at Ebbets Field as the Dodgers beat the St. Louis Cardinals 6-2. The motivating force behind the introduction of this colored ball is scientist Frederic H. Rahr who made an agreement with the Spalding Baseball Company to manufacture the balls if Rahr would arrange to have the hides dyed. Larry MacPhail, Brooklyn's general manager, took it from there and persuaded National League president Ford Frick to sanction the test. Rahr's principal purpose was safety – better visibility than the conventional white ball – both for the fans and for the batter. Both the fans' and owners' reaction was so positive that four months later the National League voted to permit its use in future games. The only drawback was the dye showed a tendency to come off on perspiring fingers making the ball soggy and harder to grip. The colored ball would be used in three more National League games in 1939, but for reasons unknown (unless it was to use up the leftover yellow balls from the first game), never appeared in the major leagues again.

August 3

1906 — Pitchers Tom J. Hughes of Washington and Fred Glade of the Browns are locked in a scoreless tie after nine innings at St. Louis. Hughes, the first man up in the tenth, hits a shot off Glade into the centerfield bleachers for a 1-0 lead. The Browns stormed back in the bottom of the inning on Branch Rickey's single, an error and passed ball, but Hughes hangs on for the 1-0 victory for the Senators. There have been three Tommy Hughes to pitch in the majors. This Tommy was best known as "Long Tom" who had six homeruns in his career and 25 shutouts.

1930 — In an outstanding Negro League game between the Kansas City Monarchs and the Homestead Grays of Pittsburgh, Smokey Joe Williams of the Grays beats Chet Brewer 1-0 in 12 innings. Williams gives up only one hit and fans 27. Josh Gibson was Williams' catcher and Oscar Charleston scored the winning run at Kansas City. Gibson, Charleston, and Williams would eventually be inducted into the Hall of Fame. Negro players began playing their own game in 1862, and the first Negro Leagues were formed in 1886 and continued through 1955. Gibson (20) played from 1930-46 and was inducted in 1972.

Charleston's career lasted from 1915-54 with induction in 1976 while Williams pitched from 1924 through 1934 and was inducted in 1999. Other Negroes in the Hall of Fame with years-played and induction years: Satchel Paige (1924-55) 1971; Buck Leonard (32) (1933-53) 1972; Monte Irvin (20) (1937-48) 1973; Cool Papa Bell (17) (1922-46) 1974; Martin Dihigo (1923-45) and Pop Lloyd (1905-31) both in 1977; Judy Johnson (5) (1918-38) 1975; Rube Foster (1902-1926) 1981; Ray Dandridge (38) (1933-53) 1987; Leon Day (1934-53) 1995; Bill Foster (1923-37) 1996, Willie Wells (1924-1954) 1997 and Bullet Joe Rogan (1917-46) 1998.

1960 — Two general managers, Frank Lane of Cleveland and Bill DeWitt of Detroit, make a novel move and trade managers. Lane trades Joe Gordon to the Tigers and DeWitt sends his skipper, Jimmy Dykes, to Cleveland. At the time Dykes' record was 44-52 (fourth place) and Gordon was 49-46 (sixth place). At the end of the season Dykes' record with the Indians was 26-32 and Gordon finished 26-31 at Detroit. Both managers were winding down their careers and Dykes' would spend his final season in 1961 with the Indians. Interestingly, Gordon was fired by the Tigers at the end of the season and became manager of Kansas City in 1961, and Lane would leave Cleveland early in 1961 to become general manager at Kansas City and be re-united with Gordon. This whole scenario began when DeWitt facetiously suggested during player trade talks, "Frank, we're getting nowhere on this, so let's trade managers."

August 4

1971 — Dallas-Fort Worth right-hander Tommy Walker pitches a 15-inning no-hitter in a Class-AA Texas League game against the Albuquerque Dukes. Walker faced only two batters over the minimum 45, yielding just four walks in a 1-0 victory for the Spurs.

1985 — Rod Carew registered his first major league hit with the Minnesota Twins in 1967, and Tom Seaver picked up his first victory while pitching for the New York Mets the same year. Carew, at 39 years old, collects his 3,000th hit just hours after the 40-year old Seaver wins his 300th game. Seaver, in his second season with the White Sox throws a six-hitter – all singles – against the Yankees before 54,032 fans at Yankee Stadium in a 4-1 Chicago victory. Seaver becomes the 17th pitcher in history to win 300, striking out seven and walking only one.

Across the country at Anaheim Stadium a short time later the Angels' Rod Carew bloops a single off the Twins Frank Viola in the third inning to become the 16th player to hit the 3000 mark. Carew would finish with 3,053 hits (including 94 hits as a designated hitter) and Seaver with 311 victories and the two would enter the Hall of Fame in back-to-back years –Carew in 1991 and Seaver in 1992.

1989 — Toronto Blue Jays pitcher Dave Stieb has his third potential no-hitter broken up with two outs in the ninth inning – all three coming in less than a year. On September 24, 1988 Cleveland's Julio Franco singles and seven days later, September 30 Baltimore's Jim Tabor hits safely on a 2-2 count. In this game, Stieb was within one out of a perfect game against the Yankees at SkyDome when Roberto Kelly doubled. Stieb would settle for a 2-1 win over new York as 48,789 fans looked on.

August 5

1921 — In 1920 the world found itself a little smaller as commercial radio made its official debut. It happened on KDKA Pittsburgh, and it started a fad of building ones' own radio out of an oatmeal box wrapped in galena ore. The "Roaring Twenties" were swinging into high gear as radio began featuring orchestra music, comedy, as well as discussion programs and public service.

The first sports broadcast hit the airwaves on July 2, 1921 when KDKA carried the World's Heavyweight Boxing Championship between Jack Dempsey and

Georges Carpentier. Then, on August 5, 1921, baseball's first play-by-play radio coverage was aired on KDKA as Harold Arlin described the Pirates 8-5 victory over Philadelphia from Forbes Field. Arlin, an electrical engineer with Westinghouse – the parent company of KDKA – became an announcer by chance when wandering into the studios to satisfy his curiosity and ended up applying for, and getting, the open announcer's job. Using a microphone that looked like a tomato can with felt lining, Arlin spearheaded radio's entry into baseball with the game's first broadcast. Surprisingly, neither the *New York Times* nor any of the Chicago newspapers made mention of the broadcast.

1955 — It is impossible to figure how many games the New York Yankees would have lost had the designated hitter been in effect during the years Red Ruffing was pitching for the Bronx Bombers. On this day against Cleveland, Ruffing homered and singled in his first two at-bats against Harry Eisenstat, and when he came up in the seventh inning with the scored tied 1-1, the Indians walked him intentionally. Ruffing was inducted into the Hall of Fame in 1967 mostly for his work on the mound where he won 273 games. However, his contributions in the batters' box might have been factored in. In 12 of his 22 years in the majors Ruffing went to bat officially over 100 times, and hit in excess of .300 in seven of those years. The homerun he hit off Eisenstat was one of the 35 homers Ruffing would hit during his career, one less than the all-time record of 36 hit by pitcher Wes Ferrell. Ruffing did, however, set a career RBI record for pitchers with 273 (matching his 273 wins) and finished with a lifetime batting average of .269.

1973 — Phil Niekro, who started the season in the Atlanta bullpen because of arm problems, puts all his pitches to work as a starter and throws a 9-0 no-hitter against San Diego. Niekro struck out four Padres and walked three while receiving a favorable call from the official scorer in the third inning when shortstop Marty Perez' high throw pulled first baseman Frank Tepedino off the bag. For the first six innings Niekro relied on fastballs and sliders but went exclusively with knucklers in the last three frames. Only 8,748 fans were in attendance, but they gave the 34-year-old right-hander a standing ovation as he headed for the mound in the ninth and proceeded to retire Dave Roberts, Nate Colbert and Cito Gaston to rack up the first no-hit game in Atlanta Stadium since the park opened in 1966.

August 6

1930 — Gene Rye, a 5'-6" 170-pound outfielder for the Waco Cubs in the Class-A Texas League, hits three homeruns in the eighth inning against the Beaumont

Exporters in a 20-7 Waco victory. Waco trailed Beaumont 6-2 going into the bottom of the eighth at Katy Park and Rye poled a leadoff homer off Jerry Mallet that would trigger a 18 run explosion for the Cubs. Rye's next two round-trippers, one a grand slam, came off Walter Newman. Better known as Half-Pint, Rye would hit 26 homeruns in 1930 and finish second in the Texas League batting .367. His outstanding season rated a call from the Boston Red Sox in 1931 but his major league stay lasted only 17 games with no homeruns and a batting mark of .179. One other note on this game – Waco was one of the pioneers in night games and this one was the first night game to be broadcast in the Texas League.

1933 — Perhaps the single most important factor in the integration of baseball was the establishment of the annual Negro League East-West All-Star games. This is the first of the 19 games played through the 1950 season, all of which were played at Chicago's Comiskey Park with one exception. In 1946 two games were played, one in Chicago and the other in Washington. Players were selected by fan voting through two of the largest black newspapers, *The Chicago Defender* and *The Pittsburgh Courier.* The opening game in 1933 drew 19,568 as the West won 11-7. For the next 18 years the West would win 11 of the 19 games and attendance would swell to 51,723 for the 1943 game. Average attendance for this classic would be 34,253.

1962 — The first 1-0 National League game won on a pitcher's homerun since 1879 is a 13-inning Cincinnati win over Houston at Colt Stadium. Reds starter Bob Purkey pitched the first ten innings and Colt .45s starter Turk Farrell worked twelve innings before being relieved in the 13th by Don McMahon. McMahon then served up a pitch to Johnny Klippstein, who had taken over for Purkey in the 11th inning, and Klippstein deposited it 390 feet into the left field pavilion for the only run of the game. Klippstein would have only three hits during the 1962 season and only five career homeruns.

1981 — As a result of a seven-week strike, baseball decides to go to a split-season format with the Yankees, Oakland, Phillies and Los Angeles declared division winners for the first half to qualify for the divisional series at season's end. The second half winners were Montreal, Houston, Milwaukee and Kansas City. This is not the first year that baseball employed this system. In 1892 the National League picked up four cities from the collapsed American Association and would operate as a 12-club circuit. To add to the novelty it was decided that the season would be divided into two championships with the first half ending on July 15. This was the year — 1892 — that the 154 game schedule made its debut with each team playing its 11 rivals 14 times. The first half was won by Boston and the second half by Cleveland. Overall it was not a success, and the double championship was not repeated until the mid-season strike in 1981.

1985 — True to their announced plans to strike on August 6, the players walk out and all games are cancelled. However, the two sides settle their differences the next day and the season resumes on August 8. The two-day walkout caused 25 games to be postponed, all of which were made up. The new five-year agreement extended the eligibility period for salary arbitration to three years with the owners dropping their salary cap demand and increasing the annual pension of a 10-year major leaguer to $91,000. The minimum pay was raised from $40,000 to $60,000.

1999 – 22 year-old San Diego outfielder Tony Gywnn had two hits in his major league debut against Philadelphia on July 19, 1982, and 17 years later he becomes the 22nd player to move into the 3,000 hit club. Needing one hit to reach that mark at Olympic Stadium in Montreal he sends a soft line drive past second base off Expos rookie right-hander Dan Smith in his first at-bat. Smith failed to last the inning and Gwynn went on the lead the Padres to a 12-10 win with three more singles.

August 7

1938 — In one of the "wildest" nights in baseball history, Alex Swails, pitching for Muskogee in the Class-C Western Association, issues 32 bases on balls in eight innings to Ponca City. Ponca City wins the game 16-7 while leaving 22 runners on base. To top off the evening, Ponca City hurler Hub Kittle walked 11 to swell the total of free passes in the game to 43. Kittle, incidentally, would have one of the longest tenures in baseball history as a major and minor league coach that spanned nine decades.

1950 — The Chicago American Giants of the Negro American League carried three white players on their roster – pitcher Lou Chirban, pitcher-second baseman Stan Miarka and shortstop Frank Dyll. When the Giants came into Birmingham to play the Black Barons, police barred the trio from participating in the double header. This would be the only season the three would play in the Negro leagues.

1999 — One day after Tony Gwynn picked up hit number 3,000, Wade Boggs follows with his 3,000th and becomes the 23rd player to reach the plateau. The 41-

year old Boggs best known for spraying singles to the opposite field pulls a homerun off Cleveland's Chris Haney in the sixth inning. He is the first player to homer for his 3,000th hit. Boggs started his hit parade with the Red Sox in 1982 and highlighted the event by kissing home plate in front of 39,512 home fans at Tropicana Field in Tampa Bay's 15-10 loss to the Indians. He would go on to log 3,010 hits before his retirement, have seven 200 hit seasons with 123 hits coming as a designated hitter. Gwynn and Boggs came close to reaching the magic number on the same day – sometimes it takes longer – between Eddie Collins' in June 1925 and Paul Waner's in June 1942 it took 17 years.

August 8

1931 — It took 20 years before a no-hitter was pitched in Washington's Griffith Stadium that opened in 1911. The Senators' Bobby Burke pulls it off against the Boston Red Sox in a 5-0 victory. The last game in the stadium would be played on October 2, 1960 and over that period of 50 years Burke's no-hit game would be the only one pitched in the venerable park. Burke, a 24 year-old left-hander, ended his 10-year career with a 38-46 record. Not many fans over the history of Washington baseball saw a no-hit game in the Nation's Capitol since only 3,000 were on hand to watch Burke reel off his gem in one hour and 35 minutes.

August 9

1921 — Scheduled for a game in Woodland, California 45 miles away the Marysville California Merchants, a semipro team, becomes one of the first baseball teams to fly when part of the team boards a 12-passenger plane. The rest of the team took cars and the split squad that drove to Woodland would fly back. The plane was called the Falcon and was owned by the Friesley Aircraft Corporation that later was sold to the Chinese government. Following the highway, the Falcon flew at an altitude of 1,500 feet at around 80 miles an hour and landed on a makeshift runway in a hay field. The team made the round-trip with some anxious moments and lost their game to the Woodland Legionnaires 15-5.

1976 — Only 9,860 fans are on hand at Three Rivers Stadium to see the first no-hitter pitched in Pittsburgh by a Pirates pitcher since 1907. John Candelaria snuffs out the Los Angeles Dodgers 2-0 to become only the second Buc in history to throw one in the city. Nicolas Maddox threw the other on September 20, 1907 when he beat the other Dodger's team (Brooklyn) 2-1 at Exposition Park. The Cardinals Bob Gibson no-hit Pittsburgh one year after the opening of Three

Rivers, and Candelaria's no-hitter would be only the third in Pittsburgh's National League history that began in 1891.

1988 — The first official night game at Wrigley Field in Chicago goes into the record books as the Cubs knock off the New York Mets 6-4. The pre-game fanfare and festivities had already been held the evening before when the scheduled game with Philadelphia was postponed because of rain during the fourth inning. Although many of the politicians and celebrities were missing on this historic night, 36,399 fans (39,008 were on hand for the washed out game) watched the Cubs rally for the victory. Wrigley Field had been without lights for 74 years since the park opened in 1914 as Weeghman Park. The first major league night game was played in Cincinnati May 24, 1935.

August 10

1944 — Boston Braves pitcher Red Barrett subdues the Cincinnati Reds 2-0 in one hour and 15 minutes. The game time is held down as Barrett throws only 58 pitches to 29 batters – an average of 6.4 pitches per inning. Barrett pitches a 2-hitter without walking or striking out a single batter. The performance parallels his 11-year career in which he won 69 games and lost 69. During this period Barrett pitched 1,263 innings, walking an average of two batters per nine innings while striking out the same number.

1971 — The Society for American Baseball Research (SABR) is formed as sixteen baseball researchers gather at Cooperstown, with founder L. Robert Davids named president.

August 11

1938 — The Newark Bears ran rough-shod over the rest of the International League in 1937 winning the pennant by 25 and-a-half games over Montreal, with last place Jersey City finishing 58 games behind. On this date in 1938 the Bears were holding a 12 and-a-half lead in the standings printed in all International League cities except the *Buffalo Times*. News Editor Joseph Cummiskey of the *Times* had ordered the Bears out of his newspapers' standings with the statement: "Once there were three little bears — a momma bear, a daddy bear and a baby bear. And once there were 20 Newark Bears, and they were big bad bears. They ate up everything in the league. Times are hard and we figure someone else should have a bite once in a while, so we are kicking Newark out of the league. Who wouldn't? Besides, I'm against monopolies." Newark would win again in 1938 by 18 games over Syracuse with Baltimore finishing last 51 games out.

1940 — Pitcher-outfielder Stan Musial of the Daytona Beach club of the Class-D Florida State League lands on his left shoulder making a shoestring catch while playing centerfield, and it proves to be the end of the pitching phase of his career. Musial finished the 1940 season with a .311 average and 1941 would see him make his meteoric rise to St. Louis. Opening in Class-C and batting .379 with 26 homeruns, the Cardinals moved him to Triple-A Rochester where he posted a .326. He finished the season playing 12 games with St. Louis hitting .426. 1942 established his Cardinals career when he hit .315 and went on to play 22 seasons through 1963, missing only 1945 when he was in the service. Musial would be the National League's Most Valuable Player in 1943, 1946, and 1948. The 1948 season would be his most productive, leading the league in eight offensive categories — average, runs, hits, RBI, doubles, triples, on-base percentage and slugging average. He would be NL batting champion seven times, lead the league in hits five years, runs four seasons and runs batted in twice. Musial (6) was inducted into the Hall of Fame in 1969 in his first year of eligibility, following career marks of .331, 3,630 hits and 1,951 RBI.

1953 — Monte Stratton's major league pitching career with the Chicago White Sox was cut short following the 1938 season when he accidentally discharged a .22 caliber pistol into his right knee while hunting. The slug severed the main artery and necessitated amputation of the leg. On this date, Stratton makes his final professional comeback try. This would be his second signing with Greenville, Texas (his home town), of the Class-B Big State League. He would be released after one appearance and shortly thereafter would be signed as a gate attraction for one game with Sherman-Denison of the Class-D Sooner State League. At this point he admitted the artificial leg turned out to be too much of a handicap in fielding and running and his baseball career ended. In 1939, one year after his accident, he had accepted a coaching position with the White Sox, and by 1946 he thought he was ready to pitch again. He signed on with Sherman (at that time in the Class-C East Texas League) where he won 18 and lost eight for the second-division team. After pitching briefly with Waco (Big State) in 1947 Stratton made the first of his two comebacks with Greenville in 1950. When he was released he finished the season with Brownsville of the Class-C Rio Grande Valley League going 4-0.

1961 — 40-year-old Warren Spahn becomes the 13th pitcher to win 300 games as he scatters six hits in a 2-1 victory over the Chicago Cubs at County Stadium. The left-hander won his first game in 1946 and hits the 300 mark at age 40. This would be one of 13 seasons he would win 20 or more games, posting a record of 21-13 and finishing his major league career with 363 victories at the age of 44.

August 12

1994 — With the conclusion of the Seattle Mariners 8-1 victory over the Oakland Athletics on August 11 major league players walk out in a strike that will lead to the cancellation of 669 regularly scheduled games and the World Series. The major stumbling block in the negotiations to obtain a new Basic Agreement that expired on December 31, 1993 is the owner's insistence on a salary cap. Richard Ravitch, the owner's negotiator, emphasized the need for a salary cap in order to keep small market teams competitive. The union is seeking to reduce salary arbitration eligibility to two years of major league service and is also seeking to increase the minimum salary from $109,000 to $200,000. Players struck in 1985 and owners locked their training camps in another labor dispute in 1990.

August 13

1906 — On June 13, 1901 right-hander Jack Taylor of the National League Chicago Orphans is knocked out of the box after four innings in a 9-4 loss to the New York Giants. It would be the only time he was relieved in 31 starts during the 1901 season. Taylor's next start would be the beginning of his 187 consecutive complete games over the next five years. On this date that streak would come to an end when the Brooklyn Superbas knocked him out in the third inning. In Taylor's first two major league seasons with Chicago (1898-1899) he completed all 44 of his starts and in 1900 started 26 and completed 25 of them. During his run of 187 complete games he made 15 additional appearances in relief. Taylor, in ten seasons with Chicago and the St. Louis Cardinals, racked up 278 complete games in 286 starts – a completion percentage of 97.2. His career won-lost record was 152-139, but his complete game performance by today's standards is one of the most unbelievable achievements in baseball history – a record that will never be broken.

1910 — In a unique statistical game, the Brooklyn Superbas (they would become the Dodgers in 1911) and Pittsburg (the "h" was often omitted during this era) Pirates play to an 8-8 tie in the second game of a doubleheader called at the end of nine innings because of darkness. Each team had 38 at-bats, 13 hits, eight runs, five earned runs, one double, 13 assists, 27 put outs, two errors, five strike-outs, three walks, one hit batsman and one passed ball. The game was played at Brooklyn's Washington Park.

1926 — Pittsburgh outfielder Max Carey, in his 17th season with the Pirates, is waived and claimed by Brooklyn. Carey's exit from Pittsburgh is the result of the so-called "ABC Mutiny" that resulted in the moving of three of the Bucs' best players – Babe Adams, Carson Bigbee and Carey. Former Pirates manager Fred Clarke had been occupying a seat in the dugout to assist manager Bill McKechnie, and when Bigbee and Adams overheard Clarke suggest McKechnie bench Carey in favor of "anybody, even the batboy", Carey called a secret meeting for the purpose of ousting Clarke from the dugout. Carey was outvoted in his request and upon hearing of the minor uprising owner Barney Dreyfuss ordered the removal of the trio. Adams and Bigbee were released and never played again and Carey was claimed by Brooklyn for $4,000.

In order to protect his amateur status at Concordia College in Fort Wayne, Indiana, where he was studying to be a Lutheran minister, Maximilian Carnarius made his pro debut as Max Carey and it would forever remain that way. Best known for his speed and arm in the outfield as well as stealing bases, Carey broke in with Pittsburgh in 1910 following one season with South Bend in the Class-B Central League where he first adopted his pseudonym. He played 20 years with the Pirates and Dodgers hitting .285 as a switch hitter while leading the National League for ten seasons in stolen bases and accumulating 339 outfield assists and 86 double plays. Following his final season in 1929 he returned to Pittsburgh as a coach and later was appointed Brooklyn manager in 1932. Joining Carey as one of his coaches was Casey Stengel who would take over as Dodgers manager when Carey was fired following the 1933 season. Carey (22) was inducted into the Hall of Fame in 1961.

1932 — Future Hall-of-Famer Red Ruffing breaks up a scoreless tie in the top of the tenth when he lines a homerun over the 407-foot left field fence at Griffith Stadium to give the Yankees a 1-0 win over Washington. The winning hit was the third of the day for Ruffing; his own future Hall of Fame teammates, Earle Combs, Lou Gehrig, Babe Ruth, and Bill Dickey were being held hitless by Senators' pitcher Tommy Thomas.

1969 — Just four days removed from the disabled list because of a torn back muscle suffered in June and experiencing two seasons with career threatening arm problems, Jim Palmer no-hits the Oakland Athletics 8-0 at Memorial Stadium. He struck out eight batters but walked six, including three in the ninth, and although he also gave up two hard-hit balls in the inning, both were turned into outs to the relief of an anxious crowd of 16,826 fans. The Orioles also committed two errors behind Palmer in the third and sixth innings. With an eight run lead in the ninth manager Earl Weaver wasn't about to lift Palmer but he did have Eddie Watt warming in the bullpen.

1979 — The Cardinals Lou Brock beating out an infield hit off pitcher Dennis Lamp in a 3-2 victory over Chicago becomes the 14th player to record his 3,000th hit, and it comes against the team he broke in with in 1961. As a 22-year old, Brock went 1-for-11 with the Cubs in four games before becoming a regular in 1962 and moving on to St. Louis in 1964. This would be Brock's final season and before the year ended the 40-year old outfielder pushed his career total to 3,023.

August 14

1922 — In an exhibition game between an American League All-Star team and the Boston Red Sox, Lizzy Murphy plays first base for the Stars and thus becomes the first woman to play for a major league team.

1937 — He was a native of Massachusetts, a fan of the Red Sox, was scouted by that club as well as the A's and Braves, but all three of those teams were outbid when he was purchased by Pittsburgh for $10,000. His first game with the Pirates was on September 15, 1920 and his last was on this date when he was sent into his final game as a pinch runner by manager Traynor. For 17 years, all with Pittsburgh, Pie Traynor was known as the King of Third Basemen. He used a special glove that contained a felt pocket replacing the leather – he maintained hard hit balls had less tendency to bounce out of the pocket. Traynor hit .320 with 2,416 hits, played in two World Series with an average of .293 (11 games 12-41) and was playing manager for the Bucs 1934 through 1937 and continued as the clubs' skipper through 1939. Traynor (20) entered the Hall of Fame in 1948.

1971 — St. Louis right-hander Bob Gibson says after his 11-0 no-hitter over the Pittsburgh Pirates: "This was the greatest game I've ever pitched anywhere." This after he blew a called third strike past Willie Stargell to end the game with his 10th strikeout. Gibson walked three, and one batter reached on a strikeout-wild pitch but none got beyond first base. 30,678 fans saw the first no-hitter pitched in Pittsburgh since 1907.

Two fine plays helped Gibson when Jose Cruz hauled down a 400-foot drive to center by Milt May in the seventh inning and Joe Torre made a leaping stab of Dave Cash's bad-hop grounder in the eighth. Working all of 17 of his major league years with the St. Louis Cardinals, Gibson would pitch many great games in which he would compare this one. He had five 20-win seasons chalking up a high of 23-7 in 1970 while winning his second Cy Young Award. In 1968 he would go 22-9 and finish with a 1.12 earned run average, 13 shutouts and his first Cy Young as well as being honored as the National League's Most Valuable Player. In three World Series (1964-67-68) Gibson would start nine games, pitch nine complete games, win seven and lose two with an ERA of 1.89 and average 10.2 strikeouts per nine innings (92K-81IP). To point up his outstanding athleticism he was the recipient of nine Gold Gloves. Gibson (45) was elected to the Hall of Fame in 1981 in his first year of eligibility.

August 15

1902 — Pierce Nuget Chiles was an outfielder, first and second baseman for the Philadelphia Phillies in 1899 and 1900. He played in 130 games with a batting average of .296 in his two National League seasons. Chiles major league career was cut short in 1901 when he was sentenced to the Texas State Penitentiary in Huntsville for an unknown crime. On this date Chiles escaped incarceration and was never heard from again. Also unknown is how he acquired the nickname "What's the Use."

1989 — San Francisco pitcher Dave Dravecky, making his second start following treatment for cancer, and pitching a 3-hit shutout in the sixth inning against Montreal, breaks his pitching arm while throwing to Tim Raines. Dravecky was found to have suffered a stress fracture in his upper arm. The left-hander had undergone surgery at the end of the 1988 season to remove a cancerous tumor from the upper part of his pitching arm. Because the tumor was attached to the bone, half of the deltoid muscle had been removed. Dravecky would never pitch again. Interestingly, in 1912 also on August 15, William Craig while pitching for Steubenville in the Class-D Ohio-Pennsylvania League died from injuries received while throwing a curve ball. The swing of the body broke one of his legs causing an internal rupture.

August 16

1870 — Although pitcher Candy Cummings was inducted into the Hall of Fame in

1939 for inventing the curve ball, it was on this date that 18-year old Fred Goldsmith, a semi-pro pitcher, held a demonstration at the Capitoline Grounds in Brooklyn showing that a thrown ball could actually curve. In an account written by Henry Chadwick in the *Brooklyn Eagle* he reported "what had been considered an optical illusion and against all rules of philosophy is now an established fact." However, Chadwick would later credit Cummings with the discovery.

Some 30 years later, in the early 1900s, *Colliers* magazine claimed that Cummings originated the curve when he was a boy, idly throwing clamshells. Cummings, in the article, placed 1864 as the year he threw his first curve ball for the Excelsior Juniors in Brooklyn, but there were no dates or written accounts of the exhibitions. According to baseball records, Cummings did not join that independent team until 1866. Cummings' Hall of Fame plaque reads: "Pitched first curveball in baseball history. Invented curve as an amateur. Ace of Brooklyn Stars. Ended long career as Hartford pitcher in National League's first season (1876)."

Actually, Cummings finished a 'short' National League career pitching one year each with Hartford and Cincinnati with a combined won-lost record of 21-22. Furthermore, the Brooklyn Stars was another independent team, known as Star of Brooklyn, for whom Cummings pitched for four seasons. His "Ace" status was evidently based solely on his appearing in 80 games over those four years with no mention of a won-lost record. Goldsmith's curve ball demonstration was held two years before Cummings pitched his first professional game in 1872 in the National Association.

Goldsmith started his professional career at age 27 in the National League with the Troy, New York, Trojans in 1879 (later to become the New York Gothams, then Giants). He later joined the Chicago White Stockings in 1880 and for the next four seasons won 21-24-28-25 games, finishing his six year major league career with 112 wins and 67 losses. Cummings may have invented the curve ball when he was 16 years old but there appears to be little, if any, documentation. On the other hand, if he did, Goldsmith's was much better. Cummings was inducted into the Hall of Fame in 1939.

1893 — The first no-hitter, following the change of the pitching distance from 50 feet to 60 feet six-inches, is thrown in a National League game by William Hawke of Baltimore in a 5-0 win over the Washington Senators. Hawke pitched only three years with the St. Louis Browns and Orioles and ended his career with a 31-31 record.

1920 — Shortstop Ray Chapman of the Cleveland Indians is hit in the head with a pitch thrown by New York right-hander Carl Mays. It was not known whether Chapman saw the pitch, although he appeared to duck away before it hit him in the temple. After crumpling to the ground, he was helped back to the Indians' clubhouse and then removed to a hospital where the 29-year old Chapman lapsed into a coma and died early the next morning. There was an outcry by Boston and Detroit players demanding that the side-arming Mays be banished from baseball. A week later the Cleveland club petitioned the other American League teams not to play the Yankees if Mays were pitching. Both the banishment and the petitions failed. Mays continued pitching for New York through the 1923 season, played for Cincinnati for five years and would wind up his major league career in 1929 with the Giants. Reserve shortstop Harry Lunte went in to play for Chapman and played that position until September 6 when he went down with an injury and was replaced by Doc Evans. The pennant-bound Indians purchased 22-year old Joe Sewell from New Orleans and he became the everyday shortstop on September 12. It was the beginning of 14 years in the majors for Sewell who ultimately would be inducted into the Hall of Fame.

1948 — Babe Ruth dies of throat cancer at age 53 in New York. One writer put it this way –"The big and the little people of a great nation paused today to mourn the passing of Babe Ruth, one of the most beloved Americans of all time. His big heart, the fighting heart that put the hearts of a million kids into the great American game of baseball, stopped beating."

August 17

1903 — The first known mid-season All-Star game in organized baseball is played in the Class-D Hudson River League. The stars were called the All-Leaguers, and they defeated Poughkeepsie 7-0. Five of the stars were from the eventual pennant winning Kingston Colonials with one each from Catskill, Peekskill, Hudson and Saugerties. The only club not represented was the Newburgh Hillsides.

1967 — After spending 15 seasons with the Braves and joining Houston for only 101 games at the start of the 1967 season, Eddie Mathews is traded to Detroit for pitcher Fred Gladding and cash. He would finish his career following the 1968 season with a batting average of .271 and 1,453 runs batted in. Mathews (41) hit 47 homeruns in 1953 and 46 in 1959, ending his play in the majors with 512 homers and a berth in the Hall of Fame in 1978.

August 18

1915 — After spending the first 39 years of their existence in The South End Grounds and going through numerous nickname changes (Red Caps, Bean-eaters, Doves, Rustlers and Braves) the Boston National League franchise opens Braves Field. The new park was opened five months following ground breaking at a cost of $1 million. Located off Commonwealth Avenue, the park bordered the Boston and Albany railroad tracks and the gala opening drew an estimated crowd of 40,000. Dick Rudolph pitched the Braves past the St. Louis Cardinals 3-1. Rudolph was a 27 game winner for the 1914 "Miracle Braves" as they swept the Athletics in the World Series with Rudolph winning two of the four games. The new park became famous for its deep fences – 402 to left and 550 to center and the first homerun was not hit until a week after the opening; it was hit inside the park by the Pirates' Doc Johnston. It would be May 26, 1917 before a homerun was hit into the seats when Cardinals outfielder Walton Criuse hit one into the right field "Jury Box" located beyond the 402 mark. For the next 37 years, an average of only 52 home runs would be hit each season with the last coming on September 21, 1952 by Brooklyn's Roy Campanella just prior to the Braves' move to Milwaukee and the sale of the grounds to Boston University.

August 19

1915 — Future Hall of Fame pitcher Eddie Plank, after spending 14 seasons with the Philadelphia Athletics and winning 284 games, elects to jump to the "outlaw" Federal League in 1915. As a member of the league's St. Louis Terriers, he would win his 300th game 4-3 over the Brooklyn Tip Tops. Plank is the only pitcher to win number 300 while pitching in a league that was never recognized by professional baseball as a major league. Be that as it may, he becomes the ninth pitcher in history to reach that coveted mark. Subtracting the 21 victories he registered in his one season in the Federal League, Plank would have won his 300th game at age 41 when he posted his 16th and final victory of 1916. He was awarded to the St. Louis Browns of the American League as part of the peace agreement between the three leagues in January of 1916.

Plank won his first game with the Athletics in 1901 and was 12 days short of his 40th birthday when he won his 300th with the Terriers. The Federal League operated in 1914 and 1915 as a third "major league" (although it was never recognized as such) before it collapsed. Most statistical books list the records of players who jumped to the outlaw circuit along with those of games played in the American and National leagues. One exception is *The Sporting News* which credits Plank with 305 career wins as opposed to the more widely accepted 326.

1921 — Ty Cobb, just four months shy of his 35th birthday, singles off Boston Red Sox pitcher Elmer Myers and becomes the fourth player in history to reach the 3,000 hit mark. The Detroit outfielder registered his first hit in 1905 with the Tigers and for eight of the next 17 seasons led the American League in hits. When his career ended with the Philadelphia Athletics in 1928 his total had reached 4,190. Cobb is the youngest in history to reach the 3,000 mark.

1935 — Baseball has always been the most widely and popularly acclaimed family spectator sport in the United States. In the thirties the game went one better and fielded family teams of all brothers. On August 19, 1935 nine Diekes brothers ages 14 to 33 from Hye, Texas played for the All-Brothers Champion-ship against the 10 Stanczak brothers ages 20 to 40 from Waukegan, Illinois. Father Dieke owned a farm, the cotton gin and the mercantile store in the Central Texas town with a population of 105. The brothers stayed busy all week in the family's various ventures but when Sunday rolled around it was all baseball, playing all teams within a 30-mile radius of Hye. The more cosmopolitan Stanczak brothers were well known for their play along the shores of Lake Michigan, winning some amateur and semi-pro league championships as well as four victories over another all-brothers team from Cheyenne, Wyoming.

The confrontation between the Diekes and Stanczaks was played as an exhibition on the final night of the National Semi-Pro Baseball Tournament at Lawrence Stadium in Wichita, Kansas. Despite an 11-5 loss to the Stanczaks it is the Diekes' team photo in the Hall of Fame Museum in Cooperstown, New York, proclaiming them as the greatest brothers baseball team of all time.

1950 — The Class-AA Texas League experiments with a "strike zone" uniform worn by the Fort Worth Cats against Oklahoma City. The regular red and white uniforms worn by Fort Worth had a one-inch royal blue stripe across the arm-pit area and at the knees to designate the strike zone. The uniform change was made with the sanction of league officials and the three umpires working the game. President John Reeves said following the one-game trial, "I don't think much of its future. The umpires can't look at both the stripes and the ball at the same time. This move showed a gesture toward modernization, but without practicability."

1951 — St. Louis Browns owner Bill Veeck pulls off one of the greatest promotional stunts in baseball history when 3-foot, 7-inch, 65-pound Eddie Gaedel, wearing number 1/8 on the back of his uniform, enters the second game of a doubleheader at Sportsman's Park against Detroit as a pinch hitter. Veeck had hired the midget and signed him to an official American League contract, with strict orders, "Don't take the bat off your shoulder!"

Gaedel entered the game as the lead-off hitter in the bottom of the first inning batting for Frank Saucier who had started in right field for the Browns. When the umpires protested, Veeck produced the contract and Gaedel proceeded to draw a four-pitch base on balls from Tiger pitcher Bob Cain with Bob Swift catching on his knees. Jim Delsing then entered the game as a pinch runner and remained in the game to play right field. This would be Gaedel's (who was paid $100 for his appearance) first and only major league game since the league would later pass a rule preventing such "stunts."

With 20,000 fans in the stands, Gaedel popped out of a huge birthday cake at home plate denoting the 50th anniversary of the American League. This took place before the opening game of the twin bill, but the fans were yet to see the climax of the promotion in the first inning of the second game. Gaedel would die from a beating by muggers on a street in his native Chicago ten years later. Although the league president said he was not to be listed in the official baseball records – he's in there!

GAEDEL, EDWARD CARL
B. June 8, 1925 Chicago D. June 18, 1961 Chicago B/R T/L
1951 STL A 1G 1W

1965 — Cincinnati's Jim Maloney and the Cubs Larry Jackson pitch shutout ball at Wrigley Field for nine innings before the Reds Leo Cardenas homers off the flag pole at the left field line for a 1-0 Cincinnati lead. That would be the only run of the game as Maloney rings up a weird 10-inning no-hitter. Maloney threw 187 pitches while striking out 12 and walking 10 along with one hit batter. And that wasn't all – he had a full count on 14 batters and stranded 10 runners while twice leaving the bases loaded. Maloney's no-hit game was only the fourth pitched at Wrigley Field in 49 years and only the second by a visiting pitcher — the other was also pitched by a Red – Fred Toney and it too was won by Cincinnati 1-0 in 10 innings with both Toney and the Cubs' Hippo Vaughn pitching into the 10th without allowing a hit. Wrigley Field was known as Cubs Park at the time – May 2, 1917.

1969 — The Cubs' Ken Holtzman treats 41,033 fans at Wrigley Field to a 3-0 no-hitter against the Atlanta Braves as Ron Santo blasts a three-run homer in the first inning. Holtzman walked three batters and he had two spectacular plays behind him by second baseman Glenn Beckert – both of them robbing Felipe Alou. He did not strike out a single Braves batter to become only the third no-hit pitcher in history without a strikeout (the Browns Earl Hamilton vs. Detroit August 30, 1912 and the Yankees Sam Jones vs. Philadelphia September 4, 1923).

August 20

1919 — Outfielder Joe Wilhoit playing with Wichita in the Class-A Western League has his consecutive game hitting streak stopped. After running his string to 69 games the night before, Wilhoit is held hitless by Elmer Vangilder of Tulsa on a fly out, ground out and strikeout. He had another chance to keep the streak alive in the seventh inning but rookie Tulsa relief pitcher Jack Williams walked Wilhoit to end his run. Vangilder would join the St. Louis Browns later in the season and spend the next eleven years in the major leagues.

Wilhoit had played for the Braves, Pittsburgh and Giants in 1916-18 but started the 1919 season with Seattle in the Pacific Coast League hitting .165 in 17 games and was sent to Wichita. After a slow start he began his streak on June 14 and when it ended he had hit a phenomenal .505 (151-299) and closed out his season batting .422 with 222 hits. Wilhoit would join the Boston Red Sox to finish the 1919 season but would be back in the minors with Toledo and Salt Lake City before he retired in 1923. He would hit .257 in the majors and .336 in the minors.

1938 — Before an estimated gathering of 25,000, Indians' catchers Hank Helf and Frankie Pytlak catch baseballs dropped from the top of the 52-story (708 foot) Terminal Tower in Cleveland. The catchers break the altitude catching record set on August 29, 1894 by Chicago Cubs catcher William "Pop" Schriver when he caught a ball thrown off the 550 foot Washington monument. This catch was duplicated in 1908 by Washington catcher Gabby Street and again in 1910 by White Sox catcher Billy Sullivan, Sr.

Several failed attempts have been made to catch balls dropped from airplanes and helicopters as well as one drop from a blimp 1,200 feet over the Treasure Island baseball field in San Francisco during the 1939 World's Fair. The would-be recipient was San Francisco Seals catcher Joe Sprinz who got a portion of his hand and mitt on the ball but didn't catch it. What he did get was three months in the hospital as a result of the ball knocking out five of his teeth and fracturing his upper jaw in 12 places.

August 21

1926 — 25-year old Ted Lyons throws a 6-0 no-hitter for the Chicago White Sox at Fenway Park against Boston. Lyons struck out two batters while walking only one and one Red Sox reached on an error. The ninth inning brought to mind the game less than a year before on September 19, 1925 when Lyons lost a no-hit bid on a two out ninth inning single by Washington's Bobby Veach. Now facing Boston shortstop Topper Rigney in the same situation, Lyons got him on a hot grounder to first baseman Earl Sheely's right. The big first sacker jumped on the ball, dug it out and threw to Lyons covering first to complete the no-hitter. Some accounts reported the time of game was 1 hour and seven minutes, however the *Chicago Tribune* box score listed a time of 2 hours. Lyons would go on to pitch 21 years with the White Sox, win 260 games and manage the team for three seasons – all of which would lead him into the Hall of Fame.

1947 — The first Little League World Series is held in Williamsport, Pennsylvania. The Maynard Midgets of Williamsport take the final game 16-7 to win the Championship.

August 22

1933 — William Veeck, president of the Chicago Cubs, suggests a mid-summer series of interleague games, at the same time proposing a split-season. While getting a favorable response from some on interleague play, Washington owner Clark Griffith is opposed and wisely sums up the proposal, "We're not going for any Hippodrome stuff. The American League is a big league."

1949 — Leo Durocher, in his first full season with the New York Giants after he left Brooklyn as manager, sells first baseman Johnny Mize to the Yankees for $40,000. Mize's homerun total had dropped off dramatically with the Giants from his 1948 season and Durocher was getting impatient with his new club in the middle of the National League pack. Mize was just one of many moves he was making to upgrade his team. Mize helped the Yankees into the first of six consecutive World Series and would play in five of them before retiring in 1953. Mize began his career in 1936 with the Cardinals, winning the 1939 batting title with a .349 average. He also led the league in homeruns in 1939 and 1940 before being traded to the Giants in 1942. Mize would spend the next three years (1943-45) in the Navy and in 1947 and in 1948 would tie Pittsburgh's Ralph Kiner for the league home run title, each hitting 51 and 40. He ended up with 359 homeruns, 1,337 runs batted in and a .312 average. Mize, who wore number (10) with the Cardinals, (15) with the Giants and (36) with the Yankees, was inducted into the Hall of Fame in 1981.

1965 — It was Sunday afternoon and 42,807 fans were on hand at Candlestick Park to see the Dodgers and Giants battle for first place in the final game of their four game series. Juan Marichal and Sandy Koufax were the pitchers and after Maury Wills had beaten out a bunt for a base hit and scored in the first inning, Marichal buzzed him in the second inning with a fastball and sent Wills sprawling. Koufax, attempting to retaliate, threw a pitch over Willie Mays head that sailed all the way to the screen.

Marichal was the first batter in the third inning and following two pitches, Dodgers catcher John Roseboro dusted Marichal's ear with his return throw to Koufax. Marichal promptly turns and begins striking Roseboro on the head with his bat. Roseboro suffers a considerable cut to the head and his bleeding kept the situation from becoming a free-for-all. National League president Warren Giles terms the attack "unprovoked and obnoxious," slaps Marichal with a $1,750 fine and suspends him for eight playing dates, a sentence that drew overwhelming criticism for its leniency.

August 23

1949 — The Oshkosh Giants of the Class-D Wisconsin State League play before a crowd of 4,101 against the Green Bay Blue Jays while the parent New York Giants attract only 3,845 at the Polo Grounds against the Chicago Cubs. The New York club had been struggling on the field and at the gate since they last won back-to-back pennants in 1936 and 1937. In the last eleven years the Giants had finished in last place twice and had only three first division finishes.

August 24

1937 — The team universally recognized as the greatest in minor league history, the Newark Bears, clinch the International League pennant by 25 and one-half games over second place Montreal and finish the season with a record of 109-43. Newark was a Yankees farm team at a time when major league baseball consisted of only 16 teams; this caused many talented players to be relegated to longer stays in the minors. Of the 21 players on the Bears roster in 1937, pitcher Jack Fallon was the only one never to reach the major leagues.

Oscar Vitt, who went on to manage Cleveland the next season, managed the team. He remained as the Indians skipper for three years before becoming the target of a player demand that he should be fired in 1940 – apparently because of his fierce drive. The Newark club's pitching staff had Atley Donald, Joe Beggs, Steve Sundra and Vito Tamulis who combined for 73 of the 109 victories. Also, Spud Chandler, sent down by the Yankees due to arm trouble, pitched briefly with the Bears, as did Johnny Niggeling. Seven players hit over .300 – Charlie Keller (.353), Babe Dalhgren (.340), Buddy Rosar (.332), George McQuinn (.329), Willard Hershberger (.325), Francis Kelleher (.305), and Bob Seeds (.303). Jimmy Gleeson hit .299 and Joe Gordon .279.

After winning eight straight games in the first two playoff series in 1937, the Bears lost the first three games in the Junior World Series to the American Association Columbus Redbirds (4-5, 4-5 in 11 innings and 3-6). Newark then came back to take four straight (8-1, 1-0, 10-1 and 10-4). The Newark Bears would win the International League pennant again in 1938 with 104 victories but lose the Junior World Series in seven games to Kansas City. That would end their two-year dominance of the International League.

1989 — Commissioner Bart Giamatti banishes Cincinnati Reds manager Pete Rose from baseball for illegal sports betting and tells reporters at the news conference he believes Rose bet on the Reds and other baseball games. However, this accusation isn't included in baseball's official agreement with Rose. In the conclusion of The Agreement Section C states:

> "Nothing in this agreement shall be deemed either an admission or a denial by Peter Edward Rose of the allegation that he bet on any major league baseball game . . . Neither the commissioner nor Peter Edward Rose shall be prevented by this agreement from making any public statement relating to this matter so long as no public statement contradicts the terms of this agreement and resolution."

August 25

1952 — After throwing his first no-hitter on May 15 against the Washington Senators, Detroit's Virgil Trucks tosses up another with a 1-0 win over New York before a small crowd of 13,442 at Yankee Stadium. Lack of a definitive official scorer's decision on a play in the third inning kept the no-hit possibility in doubt until late in the game. The play in question came on a ground ball off the bat of Phil Rizzuto that Johnny Pesky fielded, dropped and threw late to first baseman Walt Dropo. Scorer John Drebinger ruled it an error but shortly thereafter changed it to a hit.

As the game progressed with the possibility of a no-hitter hinging on that call and constant input by other writers to change the decision, the Tigers take a 1-0 lead in the top of the seventh, the pressure got to Drebinger. He called the dugout and Pesky told him he messed up the play that led Drebinger to change the call back to an error. Trucks walked one batter and struck out eight and Detroit scored the only run of the game on a double by Dropo and Steve Souchock's single. It was only the fifth win of the season for Trucks along with 15 defeats and left the last place Tigers 29 games behind the leading Yankees.

1956 — Two future Hall-of-Famers cross paths with the Yankees as Enos Slaughter is waived by Kansas City and claimed by New York. To make room on the roster for Slaughter, Phil Rizzuto is released. This is the second tour of duty with the Yankees for Slaughter who just a year before was traded to the Athletics along with Johnny Sain. Slaughter played in three World Series for New York before being waived in 1959 and claimed by the Milwaukee Braves. He was inducted into the Hall of Fame in 1985. For Rizzuto, it was the end of 13 years as the Yankees' shortstop and the beginning of a long career as a broadcaster for the Yanks. Rizzuto (10) hit .273 during his career, was the American League Most Valuable Player in 1950, participated in nine World Series with the Bronx Bombers and entered the Hall of Fame in 1994.

1996 — 50,000 fans pack Yankee Stadium to see a red granite monument unveiled in honor of Mickey Mantle. The Monument is only the fourth to be erected by the Yankees and the first in 47 years. The 5-foot, 4,500-pound monument joins those of New York legends Babe Ruth and Lou Gehrig who were honored in the same ceremony on opening day April 19, 1949. The Yankees had erected the first monument for manager Miller Huggins in 1932.

August 26

1939 — Major league baseball is televised for the first time as the first game of a doubleheader between Brooklyn and Cincinnati is shown on NBC's experimental station W2XBS. Only viewers living within a radius of 50 miles of Ebbets Field could pick up the game and only a very few within that area had sets. There were fewer than 500 sets in all of the United States and NBC executives owned most of those in the New York metropolitan area.

Two cameras covered the game, one at ground level behind the plate and the other in the upper deck stands back of third. Red Barber was the announcer and Proctor and Gamble, Socony-Vacuum and General Mills sponsored the game. Barber did the commercials live, holding up a bar of Ivory Soap, then donning a service station attendant's cap, holding up a can of Mobil Oil and topping it off by pouring Wheaties into a bowl with sugar and cream and proclaiming it was "the Breakfast of Champions."

Following the game, Barber left his post in he upper deck and went to the field to interview Dodgers manager Leo Durocher, Cincinnati skipper Bill McKechnie, Reds winning pitcher Bucky Walters and Dodgers first baseman Dolph Camilli. The Reds won the game 5-2 and Brooklyn took the nightcap 6-1, which was not televised. There, of course, was no Instant Replay, however it was envisioned by a Washington, D.C. baseball fan in 1884. He proposed that an arrangement be constructed to take instantaneous views of the ball as it passes over the plate, then the picture could be thrown on a screen so that the spectators might see if the umpire calls balls and strikes with good judgement.

August 27

1911 — After pitching five one-hitters since breaking into the majors with the White Sox in 1904, Ed Walsh misses a perfect game with a fourth inning walk, but goes on to no-hit the Red Sox 5-0. Using his famed spitter, Walsh struck out eight Boston batters with the final one coming in the ninth inning when he struck out pinch hitter Les Nunamaker to pitch the first no-hitter in recently opened Comiskey Park. This win would be one of his 27 victories to go along with 18 defeats in 1911. In 1912 Walsh would almost duplicate that record (27-17) before falling on hard times in the next five years, winning only 13 of his last 21 decisions in the majors. Walsh spent 13 of his 14 years with Chicago and pitched the 1917 season with the Braves. He posted a 40-15 mark in 1908 on his way to 195 career wins against 126 losses, pitching over 400 innings in two seasons and more than 300 in three others. However, the most impressive mark he left in baseball was his career earned run average of 1.82, posting an ERA of less than 2.00 in six of his 14 seasons. Walsh was voted into the Hall of Fame in 1946.

1912 — Looking for more statistical categories to rate pitchers' effectiveness, the National League officially adds the earned run average. The first to receive recognition in 1912 is Jeff Tesreau of the New York Giants with an ERA of 1.96. The American League would follow suit in the 1913 season with Washington's Walter Johnson leading the pack with 1.14.

1938 — The New York Yankees, on their way to another American League pennant, play their fifth consecutive doubleheader at Yankee Stadium before 40,959 and sweep the twin bill. In the nightcap, right-hander Monte Pearson throws a no-hitter against his ex-teammates, the Cleveland Indians in a 13-0 rout. Because of the heavy schedule of games, Yankees manager Joe McCarthy was pitching Pearson on two days rest hoping to get five or six innings out of the 6-foot, 175-pounder. Pearson was coming off his ninth straight win when he beat the White Sox in the second game of a doubleheader two days earlier.

Although he walked the first two Indians in the fourth inning, McCarthy stayed with him and Pearson went on to retire the last 18 batters he faced. His final year in the majors was 1941 with Cincinnati. He finished his ten years with the Yankees, Cleveland and the Reds with a record of 100-61. He pitched one game each in the 1936-37-38-39 World Series winning all four games for New York with an earned run average of 1.01.

August 28

1926 — Cleveland right-hander Emil "Dutch" Levsen is the starting pitcher in both games of a doubleheader against Boston winning both games 6-1 and 5-1 going the distance in both. He is the last pitcher in baseball history to win two complete games in one day. Levsen allowed four hits in each game, walking one batter in the first and two in the second game and oddly did not strike out a single batter during the entire afternoon. The Indians used the same identical lineup in each game. 1926 was Levsen's only prolific year in the six he spent in the majors. That season he won 16 and lost 13; his career total was 21-26. 51 of his 81 games were starts in which he pitched 23 complete games.

August 29

1925 — Babe Ruth's many off-field antics such as his womanizing, drinking, refusing to travel with the team and his generally bad attitude, finally comes to a head when he is fined and suspended. He had mellowed mildly by agreeing to stay in the same hotel with the team but still had his occasional training lapses. Although he showed up for games, he usually reported late and rarely stayed in his hotel suite. After a night on the town in St. Louis, Ruth shows up late for batting practice and manager Miller Huggins lowered the boom on the Babe. He had broken a 1 a.m. curfew and didn't get back to the hotel until two-thirty. Upon Ruth's late entry into the clubhouse, Huggins snapped: "Don't bother getting dressed, Babe. You're not playing today. I'm suspending you, and I'm fining you $5,000. You're to go back to New York on the five o'clock train."

The two engaged in a shouting match with the Babe's tirade against Huggins laced with obscenities. But Huggins got the last word: "And I'll tell you something else, mister, before you get back in uniform, you're going to apologize for what you've said and apologize plenty. Now go on. Get out of here." Little did Ruth know that Huggins had prior approval from owner Jacob Ruppert for both the fine and suspension. Needless to say, Ruth wasn't on the five o'clock train. The next morning he was on his way to Chicago to plead his case to commissioner Landis, but the judge was away in Michigan at his summer place.

Ruth arrived in New York two days after his suspension and following a meeting with Ruppert, the Babe learned his fate. In answer to a question from the press, Ruppert said Ruth had not been reinstated and Huggins was in absolute command of the ball club and Babe would have to admit to his errors and apologize to the manager. It was now Tuesday; the Yankees were back in New York and Ruth had been suspended on Saturday, Ruth was now eager to get the apology over with but Huggins wasn't eager to listen to it, let alone accept it. Ruth contacted or saw Huggins four times through Saturday, but finally on Sunday after eight days on suspension, Ruth was allowed to apologize to Huggins and the entire team. The Bambino would never again challenge Huggins' authority but in time would resume his lust for drink, food and women.

August 30

1912 — It was "Ty Cobb Day" at Navin Field in Detroit in celebration of the seventh anniversary of Cobb's big league debut in 1905, but St. Louis Browns lefty Earl Hamilton steals the show with a 5-1 no-hit effort against the Tigers. "Ty Cobb Day" was not a success at the gate as rain helped hold the crowd down to 1,704 but Cobb did score the only run for Detroit after drawing one of the two bases on balls issued by Hamilton. The left-hander did not strike out a batter, thus becoming the first pitcher in history throwing a no-hitter without a strikeout. Cobb's first major league game on August 30, 1905 was more successful as Detroit won 5-3 with Cobb getting his first hit, a double, off Jack Chesbro of the Yankees.

1916 — Boston lefthander Hubert "Dutch" Leonard allows only two walks in pitching the Red Sox to a 4-0 no-hit win over St. Louis at Fenway Park before 8,500 fans. The Browns complained of the watered-down-base-lines that minimized the speed of the fastest team in the league, as well as the constant bean-balling of Leonard that kept St. Louis batters on their backs most of the afternoon. Leonard would go on to an 18-12 season and help the Red Sox to their second straight pennant. On June 3, 1918 he would pitch his second no-hitter against Detroit. He would pitch eleven years in the majors with Boston and Detroit and wrap up his major league career with a 139-112 record.

—

Both Asheville and Winston-Salem were out of the running in the Class-D North Carolina League, and in this era it was not uncommon late in the season to play fast games. However, on this date the two clubs outdid themselves and played their official league game – the full nine innings – in 31 minutes. The day started when the visiting Winston-Salem club informed Asheville Tourists' manager Jack Corbett they would like to catch the last train out of town leaving at three o'clock. Since this was the last home game for Asheville, Corbett agreed to get the game over as soon as possible.

The game began at 1:28 p.m., 32 minutes before the scheduled game time, and at 1:59 it was over, with Winston-Salem winning 2-1. Both teams cooperated fully – hitting the first pitch and changing sides in record time. Because of the early start, umpire Red Rowe didn't arrive until the fourth inning, and Asheville's club president, L.L. Jenkins, later informed those in attendance they would receive a refund if they wished. One of the spectators was 18-year-old Thomas Wolfe, an Asheville boy, whose *Look Homeward, Angel* would turn him into a literary giant. Wolfe and Corbett were fast friends and Wolfe would often shag flies before games as well as take an occasional turn as batboy. Wolfe later would draw heavily on the game of baseball to create atmosphere and characterization in his novels.

The players in this game did not know they would be setting a record for the fastest game played in professional baseball history. The old record was set on September 19, 1910 in a Class-A Southern Association game in which Mobile defeated Atlanta 2-1 in 32 minutes. That same day, in another late-season game in the same league at Nashville, New Orleans and the home club rushed through play in 42 minutes.

1965 — 75-year-old Casey Stengel, following his doctor's advice, retires as manager of the New York Mets. He had suffered a fractured wrist in May and later underwent surgery for a displaced fracture of his left hip in July. Stengel entered the big leagues in 1912 and played 14 seasons through 1925 with a batting average of .284. He played in three World Series (12 games) and hit .393. However, it was in the managing department that he gained his greatest baseball fame. His new career, which began in 1934 with Brooklyn for three seasons and followed with the Boston Braves for six, was a disaster; he won only 581 and lost 742 in those nine years. However, things turned around for him in 1949 when he moved to the American League and became skipper of the Yankees. For the next 12 seasons his New York clubs would win 10 pennants with 1,149 victories and only 696 losses – a win percentage of .633. Ironically, the year the Yankees won their most games, 103 in 1954, they finished second. After being fired by the Yankees following the 1960 season, Stengel took on the expansion New York Mets in 1962 and his clubs finished last the next four years. Stengel was 175-404, a .302 win percentage with the Mets. His managing record for his full 25 seasons was 1905-1842. Stengel (37) was elected to the Hall of Fame in 1966.

August 31

1903 — Iron Man Joe McGinnity, the first submarine pitcher in baseball, winds up the month of August by pitching his third straight doubleheader, all complete games and all victories. McGinnity started his run on the first of the month when he led his Giants teammates to 4-1 and 5-2 wins over the Boston Beaneaters. On August 8 he tantalized Brooklyn 6-1 and 4-3, and to wrap up his fabulous and unbelievable August, McGinnity subdued Philadelphia on this date 4-1 and 9-2. In those 54 innings he won all six games, allowed 30 hits, struck out 28 and walked only ten. In the history of the game two pitchers had two complete game doubleheader wins – Ed Walsh of the White Sox in 1905 and 1908 and Grover Cleveland Alexander in 1916 and 1917 for the Phillies. Eighteen other pitchers accomplished the feat only once.

1909 — The A.J. Reach Company is awarded the patent that will replace the hard rubber-cored center in baseballs with a cork center. The new balls will be much livelier in 1910 and 1911. In 1909 the league batting average was .244 with 160 homeruns, in 1910 .256-214 and 1911 .260-316.

1950 — Brooklyn's Gil Hodges hits four homeruns off four different pitchers with all four going out over the left field fence at Ebbets Field. Before 14,226 fans Hodges becomes the sixth player to hit four homers in a game as the Dodgers trounce the Boston Braves 19 to 3. The Brooklyn first baseman connected off Warren Spahn in the first inning, Norman Roy in the third, Bob Hall in the 6th and finished with an eighth inning homerun off Johnny Antonelli. Hodges also sandwiched in a single during the evening and had nine runs batted in.

1957 — What real baseball fan can forget lefthander Steve Dalkowski, even though he never reached the majors? In this his first year in the minors, while pitching a 7-5 winning effort for Kingsport in the Class-D Appalachian League, he strikes out 24 Bluefield batters while walking 18, hitting four and throwing six consecutive wild pitches. In 1960 Dalkowski pitched for Stockton in the Class-C California League and finished the season with 262 strikeouts and 262 walks in 170 innings. While spending nine seasons in the minors Dalkowski averaged 12.2 walks and 12.6 strikeouts per nine innings. One other stat points out he certainly wasn't hit very hard, giving up an average of only six hits per nine innings during his career.

"You may go walk"
– Shakespeare, *Taming of the Shrew*

Stan Musial

Joe Medwick

Chapter Nine

The inscription on Lou Gehrig's monument behind the centerfield fence at Yankee Stadium reads:

"A man, a gentleman, and a great ball player whose amazing record of 2,130 consecutive games should stand for all time."

—

On September 6, 1995 in Baltimore, Cal Ripken's streak reached 2,131. Gehrig's unbreakable record was broken — by a man, a gentleman, and a great ball player.

September 1

1902 — Joe Tinker, Johnny Evers and Frank Chance appear in the same lineup for the first time with the Chicago Cubs, but not in the same positions for which they later would gain baseball immortality. Chance did play first but Tinker was at third and Evers at short. Rounding out that infield was Bobby Lowe at second base. The three Future Hall-of-Famers would begin their seven-year run as the Cubs' regular infield in 1904 and it would last through the 1910 season. Five of those seven years (1906-1910) their regular third baseman was Harry Steinfeldt who was acquired from Cincinnati in March of 1906. For three seasons (1903-05) Doc Casey played third for Chicago before being traded to Brooklyn to make room for Steinfeldt. 1911 saw the complete breakup of the famed infield with Chance leaving the Cubs in 1912 and Evers departing in 1913.

1906 — 23-year-old rookie Jack Coombs of the Philadelphia Athletics and 24 year old Joe Harris of the Boston Pilgrims each pitched the distance in a 24-inning A's win 4-1. Under the circumstances the game can be considered speedy (4 hours and 47 minutes), with Coombs allowing 14 hits, 18 strikeouts and finding enough energy to steal two bases. Harris gave up 16 hits and fanned 14. The two pitchers' careers would go in opposite directions following this titanic struggle. Coombs would go 10-10 in his first season, spend 14 years in the majors with Philadelphia, Brooklyn and Detroit and wind up with a 157-110 record. Harris' defeat in this game would be one of 21 games he would lose while winning only two during the 1906 season. His career would end following 45 pitching appearances in three years with Boston and a 3-30 major league mark.

2000 — Baseball and the new World Umpires Association end six months of negotiations and agree on a labor contract running through 2004. The deal does not contain any provisions for rehiring the 22 umpires terminated a year before after their mass resignations. The turmoil began following the 1999 All-Star game when the old union, the Major League Umpires Association led by Richie Phillips, called for mass resignations as a way to start negotiations. The strategy collapsed leading to the formation of the new union.

September 2

1990 — Toronto's Dave Stieb throws the first no-hitter in Blue Jays history – a 3-0 win over the Indians before 23,640 at Cleveland Stadium. There were no tough plays behind Stieb as he struck out nine and walked four. Fred McGriff belted two solo homers and Manny Lee doubled in the other Toronto run. In the past, Stieb had gone three times in games with two-outs in the ninth inning before his no-hitters were spoiled – one an almost perfect game.

September 3

1906 — Philadelphia had one of the longest histories in Negro baseball, dating back to 1867; the Philadelphia Giants the most dominant team in the early part of the century. They had been Colored World Champions in 1902 and 1904 and on this Labor Day before some 10,000 fans (at the time black baseball's largest crowd), the Giants won their third title with a 3-2 victory over another Philadelphia team, the Cuban X-Giants. Two future Hall-of-Famers played in that game. Rube Foster pitched the win for the Giants and John Henry "Pop" Lloyd played second base for the Cuban X-Giants. As a pitcher Foster had a nasty screwball and unique submarine delivery. He also etched his niche in baseball as a manager and owner, but his most impressive fulfillment was his creation of the Negro National League in 1920. Attempts had been made as early as 1887 and again in 1906 and 1911 to achieve a viable league, but all had failed before the NNL. Foster was voted into the Hall of Fame in 1981. Lloyd was a great hitting infielder whose career started in 1905 and didn't end until 1931 when he was 47 years old. Lloyd entered the Hall of Fame in 1977.

September 4

1923 — Yankee right-hander Sad Sam Jones, in his second season with New York following a trade with the Red Sox, slams the door on the Athletics for a 2-0 no-hitter. Jones faced only 29 Philadelphia batters — one walk and an error produced the only base runners at Shibe Park. He did not strike out a single batter, thus becoming the second to pitch a no hit game without posting a strikeout. (Earl

Hamilton of the St. Louis Browns was the first on August 30, 1912 against Detroit). The 31-year-old Jones would finish the 1923 season with the pennant winning Yankees as their winningest pitcher with a 21-8 mark, and he was still pitching in 1935 at age 43.

Jones threw for Cleveland, the Red Sox, Browns, Yankees, Washington and the White Sox in his 22 seasons in the majors and appeared in four World Series. Five pitchers on the Yankees staff in 1923 would win 92 of New York's 98 pennant-winning victories and contribute nine saves. These five pitchers would finish their major league careers with a total of 1,096 wins – Herb Pennock (240), Waite Hoyt (237), Jones (229), Bob Shawkey (196) and Joe Bush (194).

September 5

1914 — 19-year-old Babe Ruth pitches the Providence team of the International League to a 9-0 win over Toronto. The youngster allowed only one hit, struck out seven and walked three. With Providence leading 1-0, Ruth comes to bat in the sixth inning with two men on base and hits the only homerun he would hit in the minor leagues. In this, his only season in the minors, pitching for both Baltimore and Providence, Ruth would be more dominate on the mound than at the plate. As a pitcher he went 22-9 allowing only 219 hits in 245 innings. He batted only .231.

September 6

1905 — The Chicago White Sox sweep a doubleheader with a double shutout of the Tigers at Bennett Park in Detroit 2-0 and 15-0. The day is highlighted in the nightcap when Sox right-hander Frank Smith spins a no-hitter with only three walks and eight strikeouts. The 5-11, 195 pound Smith had the strange nickname "Piano Mover" and at one time sought to fight Jim Jeffries in the ring. 1905 would see Smith finish with a 19-13 record in helping the White Sox to a second place finish in the American League. He had a creditable 10 seasons in the majors with a 120-97 record then pitched the 1914-15 seasons in the outlaw Federal League. On September 20, 1908 Smith would chalk up his second no-hit game for the White Sox, a 1-0 win over the Philadelphia Athletics.

1948 — Wes Ferrell, now 40 years old, former American League pitcher and now manager of Marion in the Class-D Western Carolina League, wins the circuit's batting championship with an average of .425. Playing in the outfield most of the season, Farrell collected 162 hits, 24 home runs, 14 triples and 30 doubles while driving in 119 runs. In 15 seasons in the majors with Cleveland, the Red Sox, Washington, the Yankees, Brooklyn and Boston Braves, pitcher Ferrell hit .345 with 38 homeruns.

1995 — Cal Ripken of the Baltimore Orioles breaks one of the most revered records in all of sports – Lou Gehrig's legendary streak of 2,130 consecutive games played. With 46,012 looking on at Camden Yards in Baltimore, the record – 2,131 – becomes Ripken's after the top of fifth inning was played and the game became official. Ripken's streak started May 30, 1982 with 27 games at third base. He began his string at shortstop July 1, 1982.

September 7

1923 — Boston Red Sox pitcher Howard Ehmke had a no-hitter going with two outs in the sixth inning when his opposing pitcher Slim Harriss of the Athletics lines a shot over shortstop Johnny Mitchell's head. The ball ends up at the base of the left center field wall, and Harriss is standing on second base. Boston left fielder Mike Menosky fires the ball back to Mitchell, and he lobs a toss to first baseman Joe Harris who tags first. Umpire Red Ormsby throws up his right thumb and declares Harriss out for failure to touch first base. That was the hit that wasn't as Ehmke goes on to pitch a 4-0 no-hit game. Ehmke was the leading pitcher for the Red Sox in 1923 with a 20-17 record despite his club's last place finish in the American League. His career record would even out at 163-163. As for Slim Harriss, he was a no-hitting machine, even for a pitcher, and that one hit that was taken away from him didn't change his .146 lifetime bat mark at all.

1936 — Frances (Sonny) Dunlap, All-America girl's AAU basketball player for the Tulsa Stenos, becomes the first woman to play an entire game in organized baseball. Dunlap played right field for Fayetteville against Cassville in the Class-D Arkansas-Missouri League. She had no fielding chances and no hits in three at-bats, but did hit the ball in each trip to the plate. Had there been advance publicity and had league officials or the National Association (minors) been advised of the club's intent, Dunlop's appearance would never have been allowed.

1945 — Washington first baseman Joe Kuhel hits the only homerun by a Senator in Griffith Stadium all season. It was one of only two he would hit all year, and this one was hit inside the park. Opponents would connect for only six in Washington during the 1945 season, and the Senators homerun total for the year was only 27. Despite their lack of power, Washington finished second, only a game and-half behind the pennant winning Detroit Tigers.

1974 — 27-year old Nolan Ryan, pitching for the California Angels against the Chicago White Sox, is clocked on the radar gun at 100.8 mph. Although movement and location are the most important elements of fastball pitchers, speed has fascinated the average fan more then the other elements. Determining the MPH results in this scientific era vary from gun to gun. Furthermore, no one can really prove that the "primitive" devices used to measure the speed of pitches in the early years of the game were any less reliable or less accurate than today's radar guns. Walter Johnson's fastball was measured in the 1910s at 99.7, and in 1946 Bob Feller was clocked at 107.9 (with a U.S. Army device used for measuring the speed of projectiles), and J.R. Richard at 100.0 in 1978. Since then many pitchers have topped the 100 mark. Fastballs in-and-around 100 mph reach the plate in about 0.38 seconds which cuts down the batter's decision-time to swing from 1/10th to 1/8th of a second.

1993 — Mark Whiten of the St. Louis Cardinals becomes the 12th player in history to hit four homeruns in a game, racking up 12 RBI in the second game of a doubleheader at Riverfront Stadium in Cincinnati. Whiten went 0-4 in the first game and 4-5 in the nightcap. The Reds won the opener 14-13 and St. Louis took the second game 15-2. Whiten connected for a grand slam in the first inning off Larry Luebbers and homered twice off Mike Anderson in the sixth and seventh innings, each with two men on base. His fourth homer came with one man on in the ninth off Rob Dibble.

September 8

1965 — Bert Campaneris, a shortstop by trade and in his second season in the majors with the Kansas City Athletics, plays all nine positions – one each inning – against California. He was taken out of the game following a ninth inning collision with Angels' catcher Ed Kirkpartick. California went on to win 5-3 in 13 innings. Kansas City manager Haywood Sullivan, probably at the behest of owner Charlie Finley, allowed the 21-year old Campaneris to perform the stunt. After all, the Athletics were suffering through another disastrous season and well on their way to 103 defeats and the lowest attendance (528,344) in the American League.

Three years later, on September 22, 1968, Minnesota's Cesar Tovar would also play all nine positions against the Oakland Athletics. This would not be duplicated for the next 32 years until two players pulled it off in 2000. Scott Shelton (Texas) did it on September 6 against the White Sox and Shane Halter (Detroit) on October 1 against Minnesota. This record will not be broken until some enterprising manager allows a player to add the tenth position with an appearance at designated hitter.

September 9

1899 — The date was 9/9/99 and it was the 9th inning with two outs that right-hander Doc McJames of the Brooklyn Superbas had his potential no-hitter spoiled. Hugh Duffy of the Boston Beaneaters breaks it up, but McJames and Brooklyn hold on for a 4-0 win.

1914 — A young pitcher for the Boston Braves, with a newfound spitball, controls the pitch just enough to throw a 7-0 no-hitter against the Philadelphia Phillies. His name was George Davis, and he won the second game of a doubleheader following a 10-3 Philadelphia victory in the first game. Davis lost his control in the fifth inning and walked three men in a row, but he rose up and struck out a batter and got an inning-ending double play. Davis, a Harvard law student, was a nondescript member of the team that was later dubbed "The Miracle Braves" and would go on to win the World Championship. Davis won only three games during the 1914 season and was 7-10 in his four years in the majors. One distinction came out of this game. Davis went down in history as the first pitcher to toss a no-hit game at newly opened Fenway Park (1912), and the only National League player ever to do so in the American League stadium; in 1914 the Braves were in transition between their old park — The South End Grounds — and the opening of Braves Field in 1915.

1965 — In probably the most immaculate game ever pitched, the Dodgers' Sandy Koufax throws a perfect game against Chicago while the Cubs Bob Hendley allows Los Angeles only one hit. In hurling the fourth no-hitter of his career, Koufax struck out 14 and the Cubs never came close to getting a hit. On the other hand, Hendley had held the Dodgers hitless until Lou Johnson aimed a double to right with two outs in the seventh inning; Johnson would be the only man to reach base. Hendley walked Johnson to lead off the fifth inning, and following a sacrifice bunt by Ron Fairly, Johnson stole third then scored when Cubs catcher Chris Krug's throw sailed past third baseman Ron Santo into left field giving Los Angeles the 1-0 victory. The entire spectacle was reeled off in 1-hour and 43-minutes before a crowd of 29,139 at Dodger Stadium.

1992 — Milwaukee's Robin Yount, hitless in his first three at-bats against

Cleveland at County Stadium, lines a single into right center in the seventh inning off Jose Mesa and becomes the 17th player to record 3,000 hits. Yount began his career when he was 18 and was seven days short of his 37th birthday when he reached the coveted mark. Always a fan favorite, 47,603 were on hand to see Yount become the third youngest player to reach 3,000; Ty Cobb was the youngest at age 34. Yount's first year in the majors was 1974, and he spent his entire 20-year career with Milwaukee totaling 3,142 hits, 1,406 runs batted in, 251 home runs and an average of .285. After spending his first eleven years at shortstop he moved to the outfield for his final nine seasons. In 1982 and 1989 he was the American League's Most Valuable Player and was honored with one Gold Glove. Yount (19) entered the Hall of Fame in 1999.

September 10

1919 — After nine seasons with the Yankees, a 1918 trade to the Red Sox, and a mid-season move to Cleveland, Ray Caldwell gets back at New York with a 3-0 no-hitter in the first game of a doubleheader at the Polo Grounds. Caldwell was 7-4 with Boston and following his move to the Indians had been knocked unconscious by a bolt of lightning just two weeks prior to his win over the Yankees. We assume the electricity his body consumed when he was struck had nothing to do with his pitching on this day, but he did use a very effective spitball for the first time in his career. He faced only 29 batters, walked only one and struck out five. He finished the 1919 season with a 5-1 mark for Cleveland and pitched through 1921, working in the World Series of 1920 for the Indians and finishing his career with a record of 133-120. Caldwell's no-hitter would be the only American League no-hit game pitched in the Polo Grounds. The Yankees leased the park from the Giants for ten years (1913-1922) during which time the two teams shared the facility.

1995 — The National League honors their three Hall of Fame umpires in a special ceremony at Wrigley Field before the Cubs game with San Francisco. Conducted by National League President Leonard Coleman and Richie Phillips, the general counsel of the Major League Baseball Umpires Association, numbers one, two and three are retired on behalf of Bill Klem, Jocko Conlan and Al Barlick, respectively. Klem was elected to the Hall of Fame in 1953 — he umpired from 1905 to 1940; Conlan entered in 1974 — serving the league from 1941 to 1965 and Barlick was voted into the hall in 1989 – with three tenures – 1940-1943, 1946-1956 and 1958-1971. There are five other umpires in the Hall of Fame and one of them, Tom Connolly (inducted in 1953), served in both circuits AL (1888-

1899 and NL 1901-1931). The other American League arbiters in the Hall of Fame and their year of induction are: 1973 Billy Evans (1906-1927), 1976 Cal Hubbard (1936-1951 and 1954-1962), as well as 1992 Bill McGowan (1925-1954) and 1999 Nestor Chylak (1954-1978).

September 11

1946 — Cincinnati and Brooklyn play 4 hours and 40 minutes through 19 scoreless innings before darkness halts proceedings at Ebbets Field. The Reds had two runners cut down at the plate, one in the fifth when Eddie Lukon tried to stretch his triple into an inside-the-park homer — Pete Reiser to Pee Wee Reese to Bruce Edwards, and in the 19th when Bert Haas singled and Dane Clay was thrown out by Dixie Walker. Johnny Vander Meer pitched the first 15 innings for Cincinnati with Harry Gumbert finishing for the Reds. Hal Gregg worked the first ten for the Dodgers with Hugh Casey, Art Herring and Hank Behrman finishing. 25 runners reached base on 18 hits and seven walks.

1985 — Cincinnati's Pete Rose becomes the all-time hit leader with number 4,192, breaking Ty Cobb's record. Rose lines a 2-1 pitch off San Diego pitcher Eric Show to left-center for a single in the first inning. The Reds win the game 2-0 before 47,237 fans at Riverfront Stadium. Ironically, it was on this date in 1928 while playing in his second season with the Philadelphia Athletics (after 22 years with Detroit) that Cobb came to bat for the final time in his career. With 50,000 fans looking on at Yankee Stadium and New York leading 5-3 in the top of the ninth, A's manager Connie Mack sends Cobb up to pinch hit for Jimmy Dykes. Cobb lifts a pop fly to shortstop Mark Koenig. The final pitch to Cobb is thrown by Yankees pitcher Henry Johnson.

September 12

1911 — Boston Rustlers' Cy Young and the Giants' Christy Mathewson face each other for the only time in their careers. Young, in his final major league season, is 43 years old and Mathewson is 30. Young allows three homers and nine runs in less than three innings and with a 9-0 lead New York manager John McGraw lifts Mathewson to save him for a later game as the Giants are in the thick of a pennant race. 10,000 fans (the largest crowd of the season) show up for the game at Boston's South End Grounds in anticipation of a pitchers' dual, but the highlight of the game turns out to be a steal of home by Mathewson.

1930 — The last "bounce homerun" is recorded with Brooklyn catcher Al Lopez lining a hit over the head of Reds left fielder Bob Meusel that bounces into the bleachers at Ebbets Field. The National League would rule following the 1930 season that such a hit would henceforth be a double. The American League had made such a change after 1929.

1965 — First baseman Brant Alyea in his first major league at-bat hits the first pitch thrown to him for a homerun. Another rookie, Rudy May of the California Angels, throws the pitch, in a 7-1 Senators win. Alyea would play only eight games with Washington in his first season and hit one more home run before being sent back to the minors. Alyea did not resurface in the majors until rejoining the Senators in 1968 playing six seasons with Washington, Minnesota, Oakland and the Cardinals. He was the eighth player in history to homer on his first pitch and would finish his career with a total of 38 homeruns.

1974 — Frank Robinson is traded by the California Angels to Cleveland for Ken Suarez, Rusty Torres and cash. It is the third time he has been traded in the past three years since leaving Baltimore in 1971. After ten years with Cincinnati he was traded to the Orioles following the 1965 season for Milt Pappas, Jack Baldschun and Dick Simpson. 1966 would turn out to be his premier major league season. Robinson won the Triple Crown with Baltimore hitting .316 with 49 homeruns and 122 RBI. He also was the Most Valuable Player that year gaining his second MVP award having won the National League title with the Reds in 1961. He finished his 21-year major league career with a .294 average, 586 homeruns and 1,812 runs batted in. In 1975 he took over as player-manager of the Indians and went on to manage eleven years with Cleveland, San Francisco and Baltimore. Robinson (20) was elected to the Hall of Fame in his first year of eligibility in 1982.

1979 — The Red Sox Carl Yaztrzemski becomes the 15th player in baseball history to get 3,000 hits when he rips an eighth inning single off Yankees pitcher Jim Beattie at Fenway Park. Boston goes on to win 9-2. Interestingly, the 40-year-old Yaztrzemski is the first player to reach the 3,000 mark without a 200-hit season since Cap Anson in 1897. Yaz would continue playing through the 1983 season and finish with 3,419 hits, 452 homeruns and 1,844 runs batted in. He won the Triple Crown and the American League's Most Valuable Player Award in 1967 batting .326 with 44 homers and 121 RBI. Yaztrzemski was a one-club player spending all 23 years with the Red Sox and was elected to the Hall of Fame in 1989 in his first year of eligibility.

September 13

1908 —Lancaster pitcher Walter (Smoke) Justis pitches his fourth no-hitter of the season in the Class-D Ohio State League in a 3-0 victory over Marion. In his last start, on September 8, he had thrown a no-hit game over Lima in a 5-0 win and also posted no-hitters on July 19 against Mansfield 6-0 and on August 3 beat Portsmouth 6-0. Lancaster won the pennant in 1908 by eleven games and the team tossed a total of six no-hitters with Justis leading the league with 298 strike-outs. Justis had appeared in two games with Detroit in 1905 pitching three innings and allowing four hits and six walks in his only season in the majors.

1925 — Dazzy Vance of the Brooklyn Robins spins the first no-hit game pitched at Ebbets Field (it opened in 1913), a 10-1 win in the opening game of a double-header against Philadelphia. Only two batters reached first off Vance, a first inning leadoff walk to Heinie Sand and Chicken Hawks scored the only run when he reached on a error. Just five days earlier Vance pitched a one-hit win over the Phillies with the only hit coming in the second, giving Vance a string of 16 no-hit innings. Vance struck out nine in winning his 22nd and final victory of the year against nine defeats for 6th-place Brooklyn. Thirty years following his only no-hitter Vance would enter the Hall of Fame.

1964 — The St. Louis Cardinals become only the second team in major league history to score in each of nine innings in a game. The Redbirds pounded the Cubs 15-2 at Wrigley Field with 18 hits; their line score read: 2 1 2 2 2 1 3 1 1. Every non-pitcher except Bill White scored a run for St. Louis and only Dal Maxvill and Bob Uecker failed to bat in a run. In the only other such game the Giants accomplished the feat against the Phillies in 1923 at Baker Bowl winning 22-8. Ironically, both the Cardinals and Giants would go on to win pennants and beat the Yankees in the World Series.

September 14

1923 — George Burns of the Boston Red Sox becomes the third player in history to execute an unassisted triple play. He is the first to execute the play as a first baseman – the first two were pulled off by a shortstop and a second baseman. In the second inning at Fenway Park with Indians on first and second, Burns catches Frank Brower's line drive, tags rookie Rube Lutzke off first base, then runs to second and reaches the bag before Riggs Stephenson can return from third base. Cleveland has been involved in all three unassisted triple plays, with Neal Ball turning the first against the Red Sox in 1909 and the Indians' Bill Wambsganss against Brooklyn in the 1920 World Series.

1951 — The list of players hitting homeruns in their first major league at-bat is very long, but rookie outfielder Bob Nieman of the St. Louis Browns not only hit one in his first trip to the plate, but connected again in his second at bat. Both were hit off Mickey McDermott of the Red Sox. These would be the only homeruns Nieman would hit in his debut season while playing only 12 games with the Browns. Nieman played 17 seasons with seven different teams, finishing with 125 homeruns and hitting .295. He hit a career high 21 homers with Baltimore in 1959 and in his final plate appearance in the majors drew a walk in the 1962 World Series with San Francisco.

1994 — Major league owners cancel the remainder of the season after failing to reach a contract agreement with striking players. The Division Series, the Championship Series as well as the World Series were scrapped. All but two of the 28 owners, Peter Angelos of Baltimore and Marge Schott of Cincinnati, signed the resolution calling for the cancellation of the season. 433 games had been lost due to the strike that started on August 12; this edict would bring the total of regular season games cancelled in 1994 to 669.

September 15

1894 — Bobby Wallace wanted to play shortstop but after being rejected by Connie Mack because he was too small (5'-8"), he jumped at the chance to join the Cleveland Spiders, who were desperate for a pitcher. On this date he made his major league debut. He lost 7-2 to Boston in a six-inning outing called because of rain – he gave up 14 hits. Despite this, he stuck with the mound for four years and had a record of 24-22. In 1899 he got his chance to play shortstop when he joined the National League's St. Louis Perfectos and sparkled at that position for the next 20 years. He pioneered the scoop and toss pickup – throwing in one continuous motion instead of coming up to throw. Wallace hit only .267 but it was his glove that got him into the Hall of Fame in 1953.

1949 — The first death benefits of the player pension plan are paid to Mrs. Ernie Bonham, widow of the Pittsburgh pitcher who died just 18 days after pitching the Pirates to an 8-2 win over Philadelphia. The 36-year-old hurler died following an appendectomy and other abdominal surgery. Benefits amounted to $90 monthly for ten years. Bonham spent ten seasons in the majors with the Yankees and

Pirates, appearing in three World Series with New York, finishing his career with a 103-72 mark.

1971 — In the ninth inning of a 4-2 Atlanta win over Houston, Astros manager Harry Walker summons rookie pitcher Larry Yount in from the bullpen. Yount had been called up to the majors two weeks earlier from Triple-A Oklahoma City but had yet to make his big league debut. After throwing several warm-up tosses, pain in his right elbow forced his removal without throwing a pitch. Yount would go into the record books as a one-game pitcher without throwing a single pitch. Over the long history of the game hundreds of players have participated in just one game, but Yount's lack of action is one of the most unusual. Many played on defense without getting a single chance in the field and several were used as pinch runners without scoring. Yount would never again appear in the majors; he finished his career in the minors before retiring in 1976.

1999 — Baseball's ownership committee meeting in Cooperstown approves the sale of the Cincinnati Reds that ends the turbulent tenure of Marge Schott. At the same time baseball finalizes plans to consolidate functions of the American and National Leagues into the office of the commissioner. Both league presidents will lose their power and National League president Leonard Coleman immediately announces his resignation at the end of the season. Coleman will remain with baseball as a senior advisor to the commissioner and as president of Major League Baseball Charities. American League president Gene Budig would later accept a position as senior advisor to the commissioner. Schott, who had served as president and chief executive officer of the Reds since 1985, had agreed earlier to sell between five and six percent of her partnership units for $67 million.

September 16

1960 — In his 16th season with the Braves, Warren Spahn registers his first no-hitter, a 4-0 victory over Philadelphia. At the same time the 39-year old becomes a 20 game winner for the eleventh time on his way to a 21-10 season with 18 complete games. Only two Phillies, both on walks, reached base and neither got beyond first. Spahn struck out 15 batters and the only tough play came on the final out. Bobby Malkmus lined a pitch off Spahn's glove and shortstop Johnny Logan reacted with a great pickup, followed by first baseman Joe Adcock's equally fine backhand stab of Logan's low-wide throw to seal the no-hitter. An all-day rain and further threat of showers held the County Stadium attendance to 6,117. Less than a year later, on April 28, 1961, Spahn would spin his second no-hit game against San Francisco.

1971 — Cubs lefthander Juan Pizarro, throwing a 6-hit 1-0 shutout against New York at Shea Stadium, homers for the only run of the game. The homerun hit over the right field fence in the 8th inning off Tom Seaver was the only homer hit by Pizarro all season. He had eight during his career. Pizarro walking two batters and striking out eight finished with a flourish by striking out pinch-hitters Ken Singleton and Tommy Agee in the ninth.

1988 — For the 16,591 fans who sat through a 2-hour and 27-minute rain delay at Riverfront Stadium in Cincinnati, the wait was worth it. The show finally started at 10:02 p.m. and when it ended the Reds Tom Browning had thrown the 10th perfect game in baseball history. The lefthander didn't come close to allowing a base runner to the Dodgers, beating Tim Belcher 1-0. Browning striking out seven, never reached a 3-ball count to any batter with 72 of his 102 pitches strikes.

1993 — At the Metrodome, Minnesota's Dave Winfield playing with his fifth major league team in his 20th season, drives an RBI-single to left field in the ninth inning off Oakland's Dennis Eckersley for his 3,000th hit. His first hit came in 1973 with San Diego – fresh out of the University of Minnesota at age 21. Now 41 years old he becomes the 19th player to reach the coveted mark. Winfield would finish with 3,110 hits without a single 200-hit season. 399 of Winfield hits came as a DH.

1996 — Three years to the day after Winfield's historic 3,000th hit, the Twins' Paul Molitor becomes the 21st to reach the plateau and the first to do it with a triple. The hit, into right center, came in the fifth inning at Kauffman Stadium in Kansas City off rookie pitcher Jose Rosado in a 6-5 loss to the Royals. The 40-year old Molitor was 22 years old in 1978 when he joined the Milwaukee Brewers with whom he collected 2,212 of his hits before joining Toronto and then Minnesota to finish his career with 3,319. He had four 200 hit seasons and was the most prolific user of the designated hitter position, seeing action in that spot to some extent in most of his seasons and had 1,457 hits as a DH.

September 17

1968 — The Giants Gaylord Perry out duels Bob Gibson of St. Louis 1-0 but it took a no-hitter by the San Francisco right-hander before a small crowd at Candlestick Park to win the game. Gibson entered the game with a 21-7 record and an ERA of 1.13, but he allowed four hits and the only run of the game in the first inning on a homerun by Ron Hunt. Perry walked four batters, struck out nine and allowed only two balls to be hit out of the infield. Perry attributed his success on an overpowering fastball, but Cardinals manager Red Schoendienst was quoted: "Perry was throwing the same old sinker, but it was wet and it sure dipped." St. Louis batters felt that 75% of Perry's deliveries were "loaded."

1998 — The oldest former major league player, Chet "Red" Hoff dies at age 107 at a nursing home in Daytona Beach, Florida. Hoff was born May 8, 1891 in Ossining, New York and was signed off the semi-pro sandlots at age 20 by the New York Highlanders (Yankees) in 1911. The small 5-9, 162 pound lefthander made his major league debut on September 6, 1911 pitching in only twelve games for New York in 1911-13 with no decisions. Hoff played the entire 1914 season with Rochester in the International League where one of his teammates was Wally Pipp. His fourth and final season in the majors was 1915 with the St. Louis Browns where he went 2-2. In 1993 he returned to the site of his first big league appearance. The 102-year-old Hoff said at a dedication of a home plate-shaped plaque on the site of Hilltop Park, "This is a great memory for me." Hilltop Park was located at 168th Street and Broadway, now the location of the Columbia-Presbyterian Medical Center.

September 18

1897 — Pitching for the Cleveland Spiders in the 12-club National League, Cy Young racks up the first no-hitter of his career, a 6-0 win over the Cincinnati Reds. The game is played at the original League Park in Cleveland. This was a nightmare in scoring, with two previous decisions scored as hits later changed to errors. Cincinnati's Bug Holliday hit both balls in the fourth and sixth innings and each to the Spiders third baseman Bobby Wallace, but both plays, scored as hits, were changed to errors in the eighth inning. There was one other Cleveland error behind Young who also walked one but faced only 29 batters for his no-hit win.

1963 — The last official major league game is played at the historic Polo Grounds, home of the Giants from 1891 through 1957. Following the New York Giants' move to San Francisco the park was empty for five seasons before the expansion New York Mets made the Polo Grounds their home field in 1962 and 1963. The Giants shared the park with the Yankees from 1913 through the 1922 season until the opening of Yankee Stadium. Even though the last place Mets won only 56 home games at the Polo Grounds in their two years and lost their final game 5-1 to the Phillies, the venerable stadium deserved better than the attendance for its swan song – only 1,752 showed up.

1968 — The Cardinals' Ray Washburn pitches a 2-0 no-hitter at Candlestick Park – one day after the Giants' Gaylord Perry tossed a no-hit game against St. Louis. It is the first time in the history of major league baseball that no-hitters have been pitched in successive games involving the same teams. Washburn was wild in his 138-pitch effort, walking five while striking out eight. The Cardinals didn't score until the eighth inning off losing pitcher Bob Bolin who allowed seven hits. Bob Gibson had pitched a 4-hitter the night before in losing to Perry's no-hitter 1-0. In the two games there was a total of only eleven hits and three runs; the total attendance for the two-game history-making event was only 14,249. This history-making event would soon be duplicated – on April 30, 1969 Cincinnati's Jim Maloney would no-hit Houston and the next night Don Wilson threw a no-hitter against the Reds.

1977 — With the largest regular season crowd on hand in Baltimore history 51,798 gather on "Thank Brooks Day." This was Brooks Robinson's last of 23 seasons as an Oriole that had its beginning in 1955 when he was 18 years old. He sparkled at third base winning 16 Gold Gloves at the hot corner. Those 16 are more than any other position player in the history of the game – only pitcher Jim Kaat also had 16. Robinson hit .267 with 268 homeruns, and in 2,896 games had 2,848 hits. In 1964 he was the American League's Most Valuable Player (.317, 118 RBI, 28 homeruns) and his performance in the 1970 World Series was a defensive clinic at third base. Robinson (5) was honored with his selection to the Hall of Fame in his first season of eligibility in 1983.

September 19

1954 — Philadelphia loses to the New York Yankees 4-2, and when the season ended the Athletics were in last place with 103 losses. In the stands on this day are only 1,715 fans, and they would be the last to see the Athletics in action at Shibe Park – on Monday September 20, 1954 the A's would go on the road and never come back. The franchise was sold and would be moved to Kansas City. In 1948 the Athletics drew 945,076 but attendance began falling off in the early 1950s, drawing only 362,113 in 1953 and 304,666 in 1954. Athletics fans would now have only memories of Elmer Valo, Gus Zernial, Bobby Shantz, Eddie Collins, Frank "Home Run" Baker, Jimmie Foxx, Lefty Grove, Mickey Cochrane and many others going back to Connie Mack's tenure as manager and owner that began in 1901.

September 20

1907 — Just 21, rookie right-hander Nicholas Maddux throws a 2-1 no-hitter for the Pittsburgh Pirates against the Brooklyn Superbas in a dandy pitching duel with Elmer Stricklett. Brooklyn took a 1-0 lead in the fourth on a two-base throwing error by Maddux and another misplay, however, the Pirates tallied single runs in the fifth and seventh for the win. Maddux struck out five, hit a batter and walked three while Stricklett was giving up only two hits to Pittsburgh. Pirates' manager Fred Clarke struck those hits, the only ones of the entire afternoon. This no-hit game was played at Exposition Park in Pittsburgh and there would not be another no-hitter in the city until 1971 when Bob Gibson tossed one for the St. Louis Cardinals. John Candelaria would be the next Pirate to pitch a no-hitter in Pittsburgh in 1976.

1908 — Frank Smith of the White Sox pitches the second no-hitter of his career, a 1-0 win over the Philadelphia Athletics at Chicago's South Side Park. With Eddie Plank pitching a 3-hitter for the A's there was no score going into the bottom of the ninth. Frank Isbell singled to open the inning, stole second and moved to third on a passed ball. Freddy Parent then scored Isbell on a sacrifice fly to shallow right as Smith watched from the bench. His other no-hitter was much easier — a 15-0 win for the White Sox over the Tigers on September 6, 1905. It was the first no-hit game pitched in Detroit.

1924 — Grover Cleveland Alexander registers the 300th win of his Hall of Fame career while pitching for the Chicago Cubs. He becomes the 11th in major league history to reach that mark. It was a long afternoon on the mound for the pitching great as he went the distance in his 12-inning 7-3 victory over the New York Giants. Alexander made a fast start toward 300 wins when he was a rookie with the Phillies in 1911. He won 28 games in his first year and for the next seven seasons averaged 27 victories before his trade to the Cubs following the 1917 season. Alexander joined the Army in April of 1918 and saw duty in France. Upon his return he suffered fits of epilepsy for the rest of his life, although he did win 27 games in 1920, 22 in 1923 and 21 in 1927. Alexander was 37 years old and in his 14th big league season when he picked up number 300. He would win 73 more games with number 373 coming with the St. Louis Cardinals in 1929.

1952 — National League president Ford Frick is elected as the third commissioner of baseball. With the final balloting deadlocked between Frick and Warren Giles, Giles withdraws and the owners give Frick a 7-year contract at $65,000 a year. Giles, who had been general manager of the Cincinnati Reds since 1936 and the team's president since 1946, is elected as the new president of the National League. Frick would be elected to the Hall of Fame in 1970.

1958 — 35-year-old knuckleballer Hoyt Wilhelm who had appeared in 361 games – all in relief – while pitching for the Giants, Cardinals, and Indians, makes his ninth career start and pitches a no-hitter for Baltimore over the New York Yankees. The Orioles had acquired Wilhelm only three weeks earlier (August 23) from Cleveland off waivers for $20,000. Don Larsen was opposing Wilhelm on the mound for the Yankees and allowed only three hits with a seventh inning homerun by Gus Triandos winning it 1-0. Wilhelm struck out eight and walked two.

1992 — Second baseman Mickey Morandini of the Philadelphia Phillies pulls off an unassisted triple play – the ninth in major league history – against the Pittsburgh Pirates. This is only the second ever turned in by a second baseman – Bill Wambsganss executed the other for Cleveland in the 1920 World Series against Brooklyn. Jeff King's line drive in the sixth inning triggered the triple-killing with Morandini stepping on second base to double Andy Van Slyke and tagging Barry Bonds coming down from first. The first unassisted triple play was pulled off in 1909 by Red Sox shortstop Neal Ball, and through 2000 only eleven have been executed, probably making it one of the rarest feats in major league history occurring approximately only once in every 30,000 games.

1998 — Cal Ripken walks into Baltimore manager Ray Miller's office at 7:45, sits down, looks at his skipper and says, "Today is the day!" This ended a streak of playing in every Baltimore game for more than 16 years – 2,632 consecutive games. Ripken had broken Lou Gehrig's record of 2,130 games on September 6, 1995, a streak that began when manager Earl Weaver first wrote Ripken's name on an Orioles lineup card on May 30, 1982; that streak that would outlast seven managers.

September 21

1934 — Dizzy and Paul Dean pull off pitching magic at Ebbets Field against the Dodgers - Dizzy throws a three-hit shutout for the Cardinals in the opener of a double header to win 13-0, then is up-staged by younger brother Paul as the rookie tosses a 3-0 no-hitter at Brooklyn. Paul Dean issued a base on balls to Len Koenecke in the first inning then retired the next 25 in order including six on strikes – Dizzy had pitched no-hit ball through one out in the eighth in the opener. This was not only a memorable afternoon for the Dean brothers as Dizzy won his 27th game (he would finish with 30) and Paul his 18th (he would win 19). The 1934 and 1935 seasons would see the brother combination win 96 (50.3%) of the 191 Cardinal victories in winning the pennant in 1934 and finishing second in 1935. Paul Dean would develop a sore arm in early June of 1935 but the extent of the injury (a torn piece of cartilage in the upper side of his arm joint) would not be known for some time; it was the injury that finished him. For the next five seasons he would win only 12 games, eight with St. Louis and four with the Giants through the 1940 season. He pitched in five games with New York in 1941, sat out the 1942 season and worked in only three games with the Browns in 1943.

1946 — The last game is played at League Park in Cleveland. The park was opened and occupied by the Cleveland Spiders of the National League from 1891 through 1899. In 1901, the inaugural season of the American League, the Indians took over the stadium. From 1932 through 1946 the Tribe used both League Park and the downtown Cleveland Stadium as their home base. In the final game at League Park, Detroit beat the Indians 5-3 in 11-innings.

1952 — Although the 8,822 fans attending the Boston-Brooklyn game did not know it at the time, they saw the final game to be played at Braves Field, which opened in 1915. By the opening of the season in 1953, the Braves had moved to Milwaukee. In the National League's final game in Boston, Brooklyn chalked up an 8-2 win.

September 22

1904 — Jim "Orator" O'Rourke, who had been out of the majors for 11 seasons while managing, playing and umpiring in the minors, returns to the New York Giants and winds up his 18-year major league career by catching the entire game of a 7-5 victory over Cincinnati. This was a special game for O'Rourke who at 52 years old is catching future Hall of Fame pitcher Joe McGinnity, and catching the 100th win for the Giants who were clinching the first pennant for John McGraw. O'Rourke was charged with an error, had one hit and scored a run as he became the oldest position player to play an entire game. While catching most of his career, he played all positions including pitcher and hit .314. He managed Buffalo and Washington when those cities were in the National League and played with

Boston, Providence (also a NL team), the Giants and Washington; he was voted into the Hall of Fame in 1945.

1911 — 44-year old Cy Young racks up his final victory (511) pitching the Boston Rustlers to a 1-0 shutout of the Pittsburgh Pirates at Forbes Field before a small crowd of 1200. Young was opposed on the mound by Babe Adams, the star of the Bucs pitching staff. Young gave up nine hits and had three errors behind him, but he stranded nine of the twelve runners while the other three were caught stealing. Young struck out Honus Wagner three times and ended the game fanning pinch hitter Tommy Leach with a runner on second. The future Hall-of-Famer would end the season by losing his last three games for Boston. And, although he went to spring training in 1912, he would not pitch in a regular season game and retire on May 24.

September 23

1845 — The first official notation goes into the baseball history books as the Knickerbocker Baseball Club of New York is organized and its trailblazing rules adopted. Led by Alexander Cartwright and Dr. Daniel L. Adams, the Knickerbockers launch the game as we know it today. These rules would distinguish this brand of baseball from other forms played throughout the country – including longer base paths, outlawing the practice of retiring a base runner by hitting him with a thrown ball, turning rectangular base paths into a diamond and creating foul lines. What set this apart from other versions of bat and ball games was the fact that the rules were written down and printed by an organized club giving them an authority found in rules of other established sports.

1983 — Steve Carlton was 21 years old when he won his first major league game in 1966 while pitching for the St. Louis Cardinals. 17 years later at Busch Stadium the Phillies left-hander beats the Cardinals 6-2 for his 300th win. At age 38 he becomes the 16th pitcher to post number 300 and goes on to win a total of 329.

September 24

1934 — Babe Ruth plays his last game as a Yankee although it is not billed as such. However, Ruth knew it would be his last. He had been trying to acquire the managerial position and was upset in 1932 when the Yankees offered him the Newark job in the International League. In 1931 Joe McCarthy replaced Babe's good friend Bob Shawkey as Yankees manager – the job Babe thought he should have been given. Ruth was paid $35,000 in 1934 and the Yankees obeyed baseball law by sending him a registered letter containing their 1935 offer prior to January 1 of that year. The contract called for one dollar.

1957 — The Brooklyn Dodgers close out Ebbets Field after 44 years on the left arm of rookie Danny McDevitt's 3-0 shutout of the Pittsburgh Pirates. In this game Gil Hodges drove in the final run. Only 6,702 of the Flatbush Faithful show up to say their goodbyes. Two days earlier (September 22) Duke Snider hit the final two homeruns in the storied stadium, both off the Phils' Robin Roberts. Ebbets Field opened in 1913 and was demolished in 1960.

1974 — Detroit's Al Kaline doubles down the right field line off Dave McNally in the fourth inning for his 3,000th hit. The 39-year old is the 12th player to hit the 3,000 mark. As an 18-year old rookie in 1953 he had his first seven hits for the Tigers and ironically would hit safely seven more times in his final season, to run his career total to 3,007. Kaline was the first beneficiary of the designated hitter rule to reach the 3000 mark, racking up his final 146 hits as a DH in 1974. He was a native of Baltimore and his historic hit came at Memorial Stadium in a 5-4 losing cause to the Orioles. He played his entire 22 years with Detroit hitting .297 with 399 homers, 1,583 runs batted in and 10 Gold Gloves in the outfield. Kaline (6) won the American League batting title in 1955 at age 20 and was voted into the Hall of Fame in his first year of eligibility in 1980.

September 25

1965 — In one of the club's many promotional stunts, Satchel Paige starts for the Kansas City A's in an official American League game making him the oldest individual to appear in a major league game. His start, which lasted three innings against the Boston Red Sox, comes as Paige is nearing his 60th birthday. The only hit he allows is a double to Carl Yaztrzemski while striking out one batter with no walks on 28 pitches. He left the game with a 1-0 lead but the Red Sox won 5-2. Paige had pitched his first professional game at age 20 in 1926 in the Negro Southern League. He was 42 when he joined Cleveland and 48 when he completed a three-year stay with the St. Louis Browns in 1953. The Kansas City appearance would be his last in the big leagues except for 158 days as a coach for the Atlanta Braves – this qualified him for a major league pension.

September 26

1976 — The first home of the Montreal Expos – Jarry Park – sees its final major league action as the Phillies sweep a doubleheader 4-1 and 3-1 and clinch the National League East title. Jarry Park was a stopgap for the Expos, but the stopgap lasted eight years. In the final season, with a home record of 27-53, the club drew only 646,704 to the playground Montrealers came to know as "the world's only bilingual outdoor insane asylum". If Jarry Park did nothing else it allowed Montreal to acquire a major league franchise in 1969 with only a city park to play in, leaving Denver and Dallas-Fort Worth still looking for big league play. As writer Bob Dunn so graphically wrote of its swan song in *The Sporting News*, "In the end almost everyone was more grateful to her for leaving than for being."

1981 — Nolan Ryan pitches his fifth no-hitter, his first in the National League, wiping out Los Angeles 5-0 with 11 strikeouts. The 34-year-old walked three, all in the first three innings, then retired the next 19 batters in order. Ryan had defensive help from second baseman Phil Garner and right fielder Terry Puhl, both coming up with spectacular plays in the seventh inning to the delight of 32,115 fans in the Astrodome. This is Ryan's first no-hit game since 1975 after pitching two in 1973, his third in 1974, and his fourth in 1975.

1983 — Cardinals pitcher Bob Forsch, who hadn't won a starting assignment in over two months, brings a record of 8-10 and an ERA of 4.61 into the game against Montreal and pitches the second no-hitter of his career 3-0. The 33-year old threw only 96 pitches, struck out six, hit a batter, had an error behind him and walked no one. Forsch pitched his first no-hit game against Philadelphia on April 16, 1978.

September 27

1914 — Cleveland's Nap Lajoie becomes the third player to register 3,000 hits when he doubles off Yankees pitcher Marty McHale in a 5-3 win over New York. Lajoie was 21 years old in 1896 when he picked up his first major league hit with the Phillies and was 39 when he hit number 3,000. He became manager in 1905, and the nickname of the Cleveland club was changed from Blues to Naps in honor of the new skipper. He remained manager until late in the 1909 season but stayed on as a player. Cleveland continued to be called the Naps through 1914 then became the Indians in 1915 when Lajoie was waived to the Athletics. The future Hall-of-Famer would accumulate 3,242, 3,244 or 3,252 hits depending upon which record book is consulted.

1928 — Lefty Grove of the Philadelphia A's strikes out all three batters in the seventh inning on nine pitches to become the first pitcher in history to do it twice in his career. It was less than a month before, on August 23 in the second inning, when he pulled off this rare feat for the first time. He was the only pitcher to do twice in one season.

1936 — In a game against the Cubs, the Cardinals' Johnny Mize is ejected for arguing in the seventh inning and is replaced at first base by 24-year old rookie Walter Alston. Alston, a late-season call-up by St. Louis, would be making his first-and-only major league appearance. It was not a good debut. He was fanned by Chicago pitcher Lon Warneke in his only at-bat and made one error in two chances in the field.

Alston spent 12 seasons in the minors playing for 10 different teams in eight leagues with a career bat mark of .287, but his career took a turn when he was appointed the new manager of the Dodgers in 1954 – a position he would hold for 23 years. When Chuck Dressen was fired by Brooklyn following the 1953 season, and Alston was hired, the *Brooklyn Eagle* bannered the announcement with: "WALTER WHO?" Alston was coming off 13 years of minor league managing and was finishing six seasons at Triple-A in the American Association and International Leagues. He had won one pennant at St. Paul in two seasons and finished third in the other.

As skipper of the Montreal Royals he took two flags and finished second twice. Before retiring following the 1976 season, Alston would compile a .558 winning percentage for the Brooklyn/Los Angeles Dodgers, and appear in seven World Series and win four of them. Alston (24), who played in only one major league game, was inducted into the Hall of Fame in 1983.

1953 — The St. Louis Browns play the last game in the history of the franchise and lose 2-1 to the Chicago White Sox in 10 innings. The Milwaukee Brewers American League franchise had been moved to St. Louis following the 1901 season, and the Browns began their 52-year stay at Sportsman's Park. Johnny Groth scored the final franchise run in the fourth inning when Ed Mickelson drove him in. Billy Pierce was the White Sox winning pitcher, hanging the 100th loss on the last place Browns. St. Louis won its only American League pennant in 1944 with an 89-65 record, one game in front of Detroit, and finished with 100 or more losses in eight of their 52 seasons with a high of 111 defeats in 1939. The franchise was moved to Baltimore in 1954 to become the Orioles.

1963 — The Houston Colt .45s, in their second season following expansion in the National League, field an all-rookie starting lineup against the New York Mets and lose 10-3. Houston manager Harry Craft's opening lineup averages 19.4 years. The youngest is pitcher Jay Dahl at 17. He would be tragically killed in an auto accident in 1965. Jimmy Wynn cf and Aaron Pointer rf are the oldest at 21. Leadoff hitter Sonny Jackson ss is 19, Joe Morgan 2b 20, Rusty Staub 1B 19, Brock Davis lf 19, Glenn Vaughn 3b 19 and Jerry Grote c 20. Other rookies to see action in the game were infielder Ernie Fazio 21, catcher Dave Adlesh 20 and pitcher Danny Coombs 21. Then there were the elder rookies – pitchers Joe Hoerner 26 and Jim Dickson 25, outfielders Johnny Weekly 26 and Mike White 24. Four of the starting nine would go on to become special established major leaguers: Morgan, Wynn, Staub and Grote.

1996 — Baltimore infielder Roberto Alomar spits in the face of umpire John Hirschbeck during an ugly incident in Toronto. The confrontation between the two began as a routine argument by Alomar after Hirschbeck called him out on strikes on a pitch that the Orioles' second baseman thought was outside. A full-blown shouting match ensued after Alomar said Hirschbeck called him "a nasty name", and Alomar spit in Hirschbeck's face. Alomar was given a five-game suspension (the last two games of the 1996 season and the first three of 1997). Alomar appealed but his appeal would not be heard until after the postseason. This incident recalled one involving player-manager George Stovall of the St. Louis Browns who was suspended for three weeks and fined $100 by league president Ban Johnson for spitting on an umpire in 1913. Stovall appealed but Johnson was unmoved, rejected Stovall's appeal and refused to see him.

September 28

1892 — Future Hall-of-Famer John Clarkson becomes the fifth pitcher to win 300 games when the Cleveland Spiders defeat Cincinnati 9-5. The 31-year-old Clarkson was only 21 when he posted his first win with the Worcester Ruby Legs in 1882, a franchise that was in the National League only three seasons. All but 24 of Clarkson's career victories were from the 50-foot pitching distance. Historians disagree on his total major league wins (326-327-328) but all were in the National League with Worcester, the Chicago White Stockings, Boston Beaneaters and Cleveland.

1930 & 1947 – Dizzy Dean begins and ends his major league pitching career on September 28. He made his debut in the last game of the season in 1930, working a complete game 3-1 victory over the Pittsburgh Pirates in St. Louis. He pitched a 3-hitter, struck out five and walked three. Dean also singled in three times at bat. 17 years later on September 28, 1947, and inactive since the 1941 season, Dean returns to Sportsman's Park and works four innings for the St. Louis Browns in a 5-2 loss to the Chicago White Sox. Like his first game in 1930 he gave up three hits in his four innings but was retired from the game when he pulled a leg muscle sliding into second while trying to advance on a teammate's infield grounder. He had reached first on a first-pitch single in his only time at bat. Living up to his Dizzy-Antics the hit was produced with a barber-pole-colored bat.

Dean was the play-by-play broadcaster for the Browns at the time and had commented for weeks: "I could go out there today and do better than a lot of these throwers who are drawing big league salaries as major league pitchers." The Browns management was besieged with requests for Dean to pitch and so he was signed for $1.00 to a 1947 contract. What had been another dismal season for the Browns ended in a blaze of glory as 15,916 turned out to see Dean pitch. St. Louis would lose its 95th game. The Browns attendance had dropped off some 300,000 from 1946 and the average for the 1947 season was just over 4,000 with a season low of 350 fans three days before Dean's appearance.

1932 — Philadelphia A's owner and manager Connie Mack, following eight seasons with three pennants and eight first division finishes, begins dismantling his team for cash. He trades Al Simmons, Jimmy Dykes and Mule Haas to the Chicago White Sox for $100,000. This deal, and further cash transactions, would drop the Athletics from third place in 1933 to seven last-place finishes and two seventh-place finishes over the next nine years.

1938 — Darkness was descending on Wrigley Field after eight innings as Pittsburgh and the Cubs battled for the National League pennant with the score tied 5-5. The Pirates had a one-half game lead on second place Chicago as the umpires debated whether to stop the game or play the ninth inning. 34,000 fans cheered as the umps gave the go-ahead to "play ball." They cheered louder after Cubs pitcher Charlie Root set the Bucs down 1-2-3 in the top of the inning. Then, after Pirates pitcher Mace Brown retired Phil Cavaretta and Carl Reynolds, 38-year old catcher-manager Gabby Hartnett stepped to the plate in the gathering twilight, swung at Brown's first pitch and missed, then fouled off the second pitch. Hartnett made solid contact on the 0-2 pitch and deposited it in the left field bleachers as the famous "homer in the glomin'" took its place in baseball history – the Cubs were in first place – to stay!

Gabby Hartnett played 19 of his 20 major league seasons with Chicago hitting .297 with 236 homeruns, catching 1,790 games and winning the Most Valuable Player Award in 1935. When Hartnett's picture appeared one day in the newspaper signing an autograph for Al Capone – commissioner Landis jumped all over Hartnett. The Cubs catcher had a good answer for Landis, "If you don't want anybody to talk to the Big Guy, judge, you tell him." Charles Leo "Gabby" Hartnett (9) entered the Hall of Fame in 1955.

1951 — New York sweeps a doubleheader at Yankee Stadium against Boston 8-0 and 11-3 to clinch the American League flag. In the process the 39,038 fans watch Allie Reynolds pitch his second no-hit game of the season in the opener. It was the seventh shutout for Reynolds this season and his 17th win as he walked four and struck out nine. The highlight of the tense finish came with two out in the ninth with Ted Williams at the plate. The Splinter fouled off the second pitch by Reynolds and Yogi Berra had it in his mitt but dropped it for an error. Ironically, on the next pitch Williams fouled out to Berra near the Yankees dugout. Reynolds threw his first no-hitter of the season at Cleveland Stadium on July 12 as he bested Bob Feller, who threw a four-hitter, 1-0.

1974 — A sparse gathering of 10,872 was on hand at Anaheim Stadium to see California's Nolan Ryan spin the third no-hitter of his career 4-0 against the Minnesota Twins. Wild in the early part of the game, he walked seven batters in the first five innings, but settled down and allowed only one more the rest of the way. Meanwhile, he was striking out 15 Twins. He ended the game with 367 strikeouts and 202 bases on balls, which mirrored his won-lost record of 22-16 for the 1974 season. This was the first no-hit game at home for the flamethrower, having pitched his first two on the road (both in 1973) at Kansas City and Detroit.

1995 — Greg Allen Harris, who had wanted to pitch ambidextrously during his 15 seasons in the majors with several different teams, but was forbidden to do so, finally gets permission. Harris, normally a right-hander, works the ninth inning for Montreal at Olympic Stadium against Cincinnati pitching with both hands. The 39-year-old Harris, using his specially made six-finger glove faced four batters. Pitching right against right and left against left, retired three on ground balls and walked the other. Harris split his major league time with eight different teams in both leagues with a record of 74-90 – all right-handed. Harris is the first ambidextrous pitcher in the majors in 102 years or since Tony Mullane of the National League Baltimore Orioles in 1893.

September 29

1888 — Pitching for the Pittsburgh Alleghenys in the National League, Pud Galvin enters the baseball history books as the first to record 300 victories. Baseball was still five years away from changing the pitching distance from 50 feet to 60 feet, six inches, thus all of his 361 wins were from the shorter distance. The victory came over the Philadelphia Phillies 4-2. Galvin rolled up his 300 wins in just ten seasons beginning with a 37-27 rookie record with the Buffalo Bisons when he was 21 years old. Galvin pitched in 682 games in his 13 years in the majors and had a decision in all but 12 of them. He was voted into the Hall of Fame in 1965.

1957 — Before 11,606, the New York Giants play and lose their final game at the Polo Grounds 9-1 to Pittsburgh. Johnny Antonelli, who lasted only two innings, is the losing pitcher and Bob Friend the winner. Among the 17 Pirates hits were homeruns by Frank Thomas and Johnny Powers. The Giants had played continuously at the site beginning in 1911, the Yankees were co-tenants 1913-1922 and the expansion New York Mets closed it down 1962 and 1963.

1963 — 18-year-old John Paciorek starts the final game of the season for the Houston Colt .45s in right field. It would be his only major league game. He stroked three singles, drove in three runs, walked twice, scored four times and made two fine running catches in the field. That was his contribution to Houston's 13-4 win over the New York Mets before 5,409 at Colt Stadium. The 6-2, 210 pound Paciorek had been signed in 1962 for a $100,000 bonus out of St. Ladislaus High in Detroit. Opening his pro career and playing well in spring training he eventually was sent to Class-A Modesto of the California League. Before his call-up to Houston in September he suffered a back injury that would ultimately end his career. Paciorek reported to spring training in 1964, was again sent back to the minors where he would undergo back surgery. In 1967 he was released. He was invited to spring training by Cleveland in 1968 was sent to the minors and released in 1969. Paciorek's baseball career was over.

1986 — Cleveland rookie Jay Bell becomes the 10th player in history to hit a homerun on the first pitch thrown to him in the majors, but the Indians lose to Minnesota 6-5. Bert Blyleven serves up the pitch as he gives up his 47th homer of the season, breaking Robin Roberts 1956 record. Bell, a first-round draft choice by the Twins in 1984, was one of four players traded to Cleveland August 1, 1985 in exchange for Blyleven. Bell was called up to the Indians while playing in the Florida Instructional League with Cleveland in the final week of the season in

1986 due to an injury to Julio Franco. Mike Hargrove was his manager and while driving Bell to the Tampa airport the skipper gave Bell a bit of advice: "You've got to swing at the first pitch. You're going to be a rookie, Blyleven is a veteran pitcher, and he's going to throw you a fastball the first pitch. Be sure to swing at it because you can't hit his curveball."

September 30

1917 — "Wahoo Sam" Crawford retires from major league play following 19 years of playing in the outfield for Cincinnati and Detroit. Rated by many as one of the best pure hitters in the game, Crawford was only 19 when he joined the Reds in 1899 out of Wahoo, a hamlet of 1,200 a few miles west of Omaha. Following a four-year stay with Cincinnati, Crawford signed contracts with both the Reds and the Tigers and was awarded to Detroit as part of the peace pact between the American and National Leagues. His lifetime batting average was .309 along with great speed, stealing 366 bases and outstanding outfield ability. He led the league in runs batted in three times with a total of 1,525, and holds a record that may never be broken – 312 career triples. Crawford played in three World Series with the Tigers. After batting only .173 in 61 games in 1917 he left the majors and played with Los Angeles in the Pacific Coast League for four seasons hitting .333. Crawford stopped playing when he was 41, and in 1935, at age 55, he started a run of three seasons as an umpire in the PCL. He was elected to the Hall of Fame in 1957.

1946 — Billy Herman is traded for the third and last time as the Boston Braves send him to Pittsburgh with Elmer Singleton, Stan Wentzel and Whitey Wietelmann for Hank Camelli and Bob Elliott (Elliott went on to win the 1947 MVP Award with Boston). Herman would wind up his 15-year career playing in only 15 games while taking over as manager of the Pirates in 1947 for one year. Herman began his major league career in 1931 with the Cubs and also played with the Dodgers. He also had an unsuccessful three years as manager of the Red Sox in 1964-65-66. Herman (2) had a lifetime average of .304, played in four World Series with the Cubs and Brooklyn and was elected to the Hall of Fame in 1975.

1947 — For the first time the World Series is covered simultaneously by radio and television as TV jumps onboard for the first time. Radio had broadcast the first fall classic in 1921 featuring the Giants' five games to three victory over the Yankees with sports writer Grantland Rice calling the play-by-play. This year, The Gillette Safety Razor Company was the radio sponsor and the Ford Motor

Company would join Gillette on the television side paying baseball the $65,000 rights fee. Commissioner A.B. Chandler stipulated that the telecasts be made available to all video stations. All three networks – NBC, CBS and Dumont – alternated days, plus nine stations in New York, Philadelphia, Schenectady and Washington, and as many radio stations that could be reached by relay or coaxial cable broadcast the game. The Yankees beat the Dodgers four games to three with Mel Allen and Red Barber working radio and Bob Stanton on the television side.

1971 — The New Senators play their final game in Washington before moving to Texas. Although leading the Yankees 7-5 with two outs in the ninth, the game is awarded to New York – one of the few times the losing team wins by forfeit. Most fans attending the game at D.C. Stadium were upset with owner Bob Short moving the team to Arlington, Texas and stormed the field making play impossible. Home plate was dug up, the bases removed, and souvenir hunters dismantled parts of the scoreboard. Professional baseball was first played in Washington in 1871 and over the course of the next 101 years teams were represented in five leagues, including both the National and American.

1972 — In what would turn out to be the final official hit in his 17-year major league career, Pittsburgh's Roberto Clemente, at age 38, picks up number 3,000. He would be killed in December in a cargo plane crash in Puerto Rico while on a humanitarian flight to earthquake-stricken Nicaragua. Clemente's hit, a double, came off Mets pitcher Jon Matlack in the fourth inning to help the Pirates to a 5-0 win at Three Rivers Stadium. He also had four hits in the League Championship Series, which did not count in regular season play. Clemente becomes the 11th player to reach the 3,000 mark reaching the 200 mark in four seasons.

1981 — Minnesota plays its last game at Metropolitan Stadium in Bloomington, Minnesota and loses to Kansas City 5-2. This was the first home of the new Twins when they moved from Washington in 1961. It was originally the home of the Minneapolis Millers of the American Association (1956-1960). The Hubert H. Humphrey Metrodome would open April 6, 1982.

1984 — On the final day of the regular season at Arlington Stadium, California's 6'-7", 185-pound Mike Witt pitches the 9th perfect game in major league history, easily subduing the Texas Rangers 1-0. Only 8,375 fans saw the classic pitching performance – 10 strikeouts on only 94 pitches – 70 of them for strikes, reaching the 3-ball count only twice. The lone run of the game didn't come until the seventh inning with the Rangers' Charlie Hough matching zeros with Witt until then. The Angels scored on an infield hit by Doug DeCinces, a passed ball, an infield out and a roller to first baseman Pete O'Brien, whose throw to the plate was too late to get DeCinces.

1990 — 80 seasons of major league baseball come to an end as the curtain falls on historic Comiskey Park with a 2-1 White Sox loss to Seattle before a crowd of 42,849. Opened July 1, 1910, the Sox will play their next home game on April 18, 1991 across the street in their new Comiskey Park.

1992 — George Brett becomes the 18th member of the 3,000 hit club going 4-for-5 in a Kansas City Royals win over California 4-0. His fourth hit of the night was number 3,000, a first-pitch single past second baseman Ken Oberkfell off 30-year-old rookie lefthander Tim Fortugno. Brett's first career hit was one of the five he picked up for Kansas City as a 20-year-old rookie in 1973. He would finish with a total of 3,154. Brett accumulated 539 hits as a designated hitter most of them in late stages of his career.

"It is not enough to aim, you must hit."
— Italian Proverb

Gabby Hartnett

Dizzy Dean winding up for a pitch, 1930s

Chapter Ten

"I hope to win the pennant next year again. This would make it four in a row, one more than any other team ever won. This done, I will have enough. A baseball team is an expensive luxury, not a source of wealth, as is thought by many. The general impression seems to be that a great fortune is made each year by a winning ball team. I would like to say that if I depended on baseball for my living, I would be hungry often. I will trade my stock at par for a similar amount of stock at par in any good business in Pittsburgh."

Pittsburgh Pirates owner Barney Dreyfuss after the first modern World Series in 1903

October 1

1903 — The first World Series game in major league history is played with the Pittsburgh Pirates defeating the Boston Pilgrims 7-3. This series is also billed as the "Championship of the United States." The game is played at the Huntington Avenue Baseball Grounds in Boston before 16,242. Deacon Phillippe was the winning pitcher in the first game and Cy Young the loser. The first homerun is hit by Pittsburgh right fielder Jimmy Sebring. Boston would go on to win the best-of-nine series five games to three.

Both managers were playing managers — Fred Clarke for Pittsburgh and Jimmy Collins for Boston. Both would be voted into the Hall of Fame in 1945. Clarke, an outfielder, played 21 years with an average of .312, with 220 triples and 506 stolen bases. He managed 16 seasons with four pennants and a win percentage of .576 (Collins' Hall of Fame bio can be found June 7, 1907). Following the series, Pirates owner Barney Dreyfuss tossed his club's share of the gate into the player's pot, creating the curious situation of the losers receiving a larger share ($1,316) than winning Boston ($1,182).

—

The long-since forgotten "City Series" begins its lengthy run in major league baseball when the Chicago White Sox and Cubs play the first of a 15-game series. The game, played at West Side Park (home of the Cubs) results in an 11-0 Cubs win. After the first 14 games the series is even at 7-7; that's where it ended. In those days the contracts of players expired on October 15. One of the most interesting aspects of the series was that 13 of the 14 games were complete games by both Cubs and White Sox pitchers. The only exception was game 13 when Cubs manager Frank Chance used a pinch-hitter for his pitcher in the eighth inning.

Although numerous exhibitions have been played between the two clubs through the years, there has never been the formality of the 26 series played between 1903 and 1942 with the White Sox winning 19 of them. The Sox won 95 games and the Cubs 62; four games ended in ties. Over the years there has been the Ohio championship between Cleveland and Cincinnati, the Browns and Cardinals in St. Louis and the Phillies and Athletics in Philadelphia, but nothing to compare to the Chicago City Series. The last city series was played in 1942.

1932 — The New York Yankees win game three of the World Series at Wrigley Field 7-5 and go on to sweep the Cubs in four games. This is the game in which Babe Ruth, as legend has it, called his homerun against Chicago pitcher Charlie Root in the fifth inning. While Ruth's alleged called shot was taking place, 17-year old Joe DiMaggio would make his professional debut a few hours later with the San Francisco Seals in the Pacific Coast League. DiMaggio had been invited to work out with the Seals and when the regular shortstop Augie Galan was given permission to leave the team early, DiMaggio was inserted at Galan's position handling two putouts and two assists with one hit, a triple, in three times at bat as the Seals defeated the San Francisco Missions 4-3.

1970 — The largest crowd of the season – 31,822 – turns out for the final game at Connie Mack Stadium to watch the Phillies beat Montreal in 10-innings 2-1. They also saw the 61-year-old park almost completely destroyed following the game. Fans ripped up seats, tore off railings, doors, and billboards. The dugouts were ransacked, and the field tarp was torn to shreds in vandalism that reached riot proportions with some 25 post-game casualties, some of them serious enough to require hospital treatment. Some of the long-time baseball fans that had watched the Phillies and Athletics play in what was Shibe Park must have shed some tears as they watched the venerable park die in such a disgraceful manner before their eyes. The park that opened in 1909 had its largest crowd in 1947 when the Phillies played Brooklyn (40,720 paid) and the smallest on September 8, 1916 when only 18 paid and 23 total fans watched the A's and Yankees.

October 2

1908 — In one of baseball's most spectacularly pitched games, Cleveland's Addie Joss goes up against the Chicago White Sox Ed Walsh. Cleveland scored the only run of the game in the third inning on one of the four hits allowed by Walsh, an error and a wild pitch. Joss in the meanwhile was throwing a perfect game against Chicago – the second in major league history following Cy Young's 1904 perfecto for the Boston Red Sox against the Philadelphia Athletics. The first game Joss pitched in the American League was a one-hitter, and he followed that with six more just like it over the next five years – but this was his first no-hitter.

1920 — Only three tripleheaders have been played in major league history – the last one was played on this date when Cincinnati and Pittsburgh played three games in one day with the Reds winning the first two 13-4 and 7-3 and the Pirates taking the third 6-0, shortened to six innings because of darkness. Total playing time was exactly five hours. With the season running out and no makeup dates available, the Pirates had a chance to finish third and win a share of the World Series receipts. Pittsburgh owner Barney Dreyfuss suggested the tripleheader and league president John A. Heydler agreed. Cincinnati would win the pennant and Pittsburgh's try for some take-home pay didn't materialize – they finished fourth. The first tripleheader was played on September 1, 1890 with the Brooklyn Bridegrooms winning all three games against the Pittsburgh Alleghenys. Also in the National League on September 7, 1896 the Baltimore Orioles swept the Louisville Colonels.

1969 — The Seattle Pilots were added to the American League along with the Kansas City Royals in what became known as a political expansion. Following the league's 1967 decision to allow the Kansas City Athletics to move to Oakland, Missouri officials threatened to tie up the AL and Athletics in legal red tape unless Kansas City was guaranteed a replacement team. The 1969 expansion was the emergency solution giving the league two new teams – Kansas City and Seattle. The hurried move to Seattle resulted in the awarding of the franchise to the under-capitalized Dewey Soriano, brothers Milton and Max, and William Daley chairman of the Reading Railroad.

The new Seattle Pilots opened what would be their first and only season April 11, 1969 against the White Sox in rickety Sicks Stadium, originally opened in 1938 as the home of Pacific Coast League's Seattle Rainiers. On this date the team played its final game – overall going 64-98. Seattle became the first major league club since the 1901 Milwaukee Brewers to last only a single season. In third place going into August, the club went 6-22 in the final month and dropped to the bottom of the division. Stadium conditions, injuries, and bickering between ownership, the city, and the press, plus the new owners' failure to live up to original conditions of the contract with the city and the coast league doomed the franchise. However, more than anything it was financial and when Soriano's attempts to sell the team soured, the American League endorsed an agreement that allowed the team to be sold. This came to pass just hours before the start of the 1970 season when the Pilots were sold to Bud Selig and it became the Milwaukee Brewers. Incidentally, the Pilots drew 677,944 for the season; 5,473 showed up to pay their respects in a 3-1 loss to Oakland on the final day.

1972 — Montreal's Bill Stoneman tosses the second no-hitter of his career in a 7-0 win over the New York Mets at Jarry Park. A small gathering of 7,184 saw Stoneman struggle with his control in the first game of a doubleheader in 53-degree weather. He walked seven Mets and one reached on Stoneman's error while he stranded seven runners. Stoneman struck out nine. His first no-hit game came on April 17, 1969 at Philadelphia the first year of the franchise's history. He was an expansion selection from the Chicago Cubs and he went on to pitch eight seasons with a 54-85 record. Stoneman joined the Expos front office in 1983 and was soon elevated to vice-president. In 1999, he would become general manager with Anaheim.

1977 — The "High Five" is born in Dodger Stadium when Dusty Baker takes Houston's J.R. Richard downtown with an historic homerun. It was Baker's 30th. Teammates Steve Garvey, Ron Cey and Reggie Smith also had 30 or more – no other team had ever had as many players who hit that many. When Baker crossed the plate, the first man to congratulate him was the exuberant rookie centerfielder Glenn Burke who had been in the on-deck circle. Burke raised his right hand high above his head and by sheer instinct Baker did the same – they slapped palms. It was the first high five but certainly not the last. Today a player gets that recognition when he moves a runner up a base by executing a sacrifice bunt.

October 3

1947 — The scene is Ebbets Field in the fourth game of the World Series with the Yankees. Without allowing a hit New York pitcher Bill Bevens goes into the ninth inning with a 2-1 lead over the Dodgers. The Dodgers had scored in the fifth inning on two walks, a sacrifice and a ground ball. Brooklyn catcher Bruce Edwards opened the ninth by flying out and Carl Furillo drew a walk. Spider Jorgensen fouled out and Bevens was one out away from a World Series no-hitter. With Al Gionfriddo running for Furillo and Pete Reiser pinch-hitting, Gionfriddo steals second. Despite the fact that Reiser represented the winning run, Yankees manager Bucky Harris ordered an intentional walk – the 10th base on balls issued by Bevens in the game. The wheels continued to turn when

October 3-4

Dodgers manager Burt Shotton inserted Eddie Miksis as a pinch runner for Reiser at first base. The next scheduled batter was Eddy Stanky but Shotton lifted him and sent up Cookie Lavagetto who doubled off the right field wall on Bevens second pitch scoring two runs – Bevens lost his no-hit bid and the game. That evened the series at 2-2 but the Yankees went on to win the championship in seven games.

1993 — The final game is played in two American League parks on the same day – Cleveland Stadium and Arlington Stadium. The Cleveland park was built on a landfill on Cleveland's downtown Lake Erie shoreline, and the first game was played there on July 31, 1932. Pitching that day for the Indians was Cleveland ace Mel Harder in a losing cause to Lefty Grove and the Philadelphia Athletics 1-0. On this day, in a most unusual but brilliant ceremony, the 84-year-old Harder threw out the "last ball" in the stadium's history following the Indians 4-0 loss to the White Sox. 72,390 watched the Old Gal's swan song with 90-year-old Bob Hope causing many baseball tears to flow by singing his amended version of THANKS FOR THE MEMORIES. Then the fitting conclusion – the grounds crew, spiffed out in tuxedos, dug up home plate and it soon would rest at the Tribe's new home in Jacobs Field for the first scheduled game to be played on April 4, 1994.

Only hours later the curtain would fall on Arlington Stadium, the original home of the Texas Rangers following the franchise's move from Washington in 1972. 41,039 saw the Rangers lose to Kansas City 4-1. The park's original name was Turnpike Stadium a minor league park built in 1965 for use in the Class-AA Texas League by the Dallas-Fort Worth Spurs. Following the game home plate was dug up, and under the escort of Nolan Ryan, it was moved to its new location next door to the Rangers new home the Ballpark in Arlington.

October 4

1921 — Two months following the first baseball radio broadcast in history – Philadelphia and Pittsburgh from Forbes Field – the first World Series game is aired. This would be the best-of-nine series, but only the first game would be broadcast. KDKA in Pittsburgh, the station that aired the first game in history, also made the historic first World Series broadcast with a direct wire from the Polo Grounds. The Broadcast was a mere four-station hookup with WJZ Newark, WBZ Springfield, Massachusetts and WYG Schenectady also on the wire. Sports writer Grantland Rice did the play-by-play.

1937 — Leo Durocher is traded by the Cardinals to Brooklyn for Johnny Cooney,

Roy Henshaw, Joe Stripp and Jim Bucher. Durocher began his major league career with the Yankees in 1925 and also played with Cincinnati, but his trade to the Dodgers started him on his way to a long career as a manager. Durocher became player-manager for Brooklyn following the firing of Burleigh Grimes after the 1938 season and ended his playing career in 1945 – ending 17 years as, at best, a mediocre infielder hitting .247. However, he would manage 24 years with Brooklyn, the New York Giants, Cubs and Houston, log 3,739 games, win three pennants and finish with a win percentage of .540. Durocher (2) was voted into the Hall of Fame in 1994.

October 5

1911 — The National Commission, the ruling body of baseball before the naming of a commissioner, sells the motion picture rights to the World Series for $3,500. When the players demand a share of the right's fee, the commission cancels the deal.

1918 — Deep in centerfield at the now-extinct Polo Grounds, home of the New York Giants, there once stood a granite monument with a bronze plaque that read "Soldier, Scholar, Athlete." It was placed there to honor Eddie Grant who had played infield for the Giants in 1913-15 before he became the first player killed in action on this date in the Argonne Forest during World War I. He played his last game in 1915, retiring to enter law practice then enlisted in the army in 1917. On Memorial Day 1921 the monument with its plaque was unveiled at the Polo Grounds. Two other major leaguers were killed in World War I – pitcher Robert Troy and outfielder Alex Barr who were briefly with the Tigers and Yankees respectively.

October 6

1845 — The earliest known scorebook is in the New York Public Library, and within it is the first scorecard for a game of baseball. The game was played on this date and 18 years later the first baseball scorecard was published by Henry Chadwick. A few weeks later The *New York Herald* printed the first box score of a game played on October 25, 1845.

1911 — Cy Young, 44 years old, too fat to field his position but seemingly with an arm as good as ever, had been waived by Cleveland then signed a contract with the Boston Braves on August 21. He had gone 3-4 with the Indians and was 4-4 with Boston where he started and lost his last major league game on this date at Washington Park in Brooklyn 13-3. Young was hit hard in this game but was left in by manager Fred Tenney until the Dodgers had scored eleven runs, seven of them in the seventh inning. Young allowed eleven hits, walked one, hit two batters and struck out three. After going to spring training with the Braves in 1912, he retired on May 12 without appearing in another game.

1923 — Boston Braves shortstop Ernie Padgett pulls off the fourth unassisted triple play in history. In the fourth inning at Braves Field against the Phillies with Cotton Tierney on second and Cliff Lee on first, Padgett catches Walt Holke's liner, runs to second to retire Tierney, then tags Lee before he can return to first. The 24-year old Padgett was in his rookie season with the Braves and this would be one of only two games he would play at shortstop. In two other games he appeared at second base and as a pinch-hitter.

1985 — On the final day of the season Yankees pitcher Phil Niekro becomes the 18th pitcher to win 300 games as he shuts out Toronto 8-0 at SkyDome before a crowd of 44,422. The 46-year-old Niekro hits the mark after having lost his four previous starts going back to win number 299 on September 8. It took Niekro 20 years to get to the magic 300 – having won his first game in 1965 with the Milwaukee Braves. He would go on to win 318 and lose 274, with a career ERA of 3.35. He logged 5,404 innings pitched in 24 seasons and worked 200 or more innings 19 times and in four of those passed the 300 inning mark. Niekro (35) was a five time Gold Glove winner and was inducted into the Hall of Fame in 1997.

1986 — Earl Weaver retires for the second and last time as Baltimore manager, leaving after posting the only losing year in his 17 seasons as the Orioles skipper. Weaver started his pro career in 1948 and spent 14 years in the minors as a second baseman – six of those seasons as a player-manager. His managerial career with Baltimore began in July of 1968, and his first retirement came after the 1982 season. He came back in 1985 for two years before hanging 'em up for good with 1,480 wins and 1,060 losses for a win-percentage of .583. Aside from his winning ways as a manager, he was well known for the number of ejections he received. Weaver was booted out 97 times by 41 different umpires during his career – which is probably a record – this includes one spring training ouster and one game in a World Series. He took the finger ten times in 1975. Weaver (4) went out with a flourish in his final season in 1986 when he was ejected four times. He entered the Hall of Fame in 1996.

October 7

1904 – Right-hander Jack Chesbro registers his 41st win of the season for the New York Highlanders in a 3-2 victory over the Boston Pilgrims. He would finish the season with a 41-12 record, 48 complete games and pitch 454.2 innings. Three of his wins would come in relief. He broke into the big leagues with Pittsburgh in 1899, moved to New York in 1903 and finished his career with the Boston Red Sox in 1909 after he was waived by the Highlanders. Chesbro pitched eleven years and had a 199-131 record with an earned run average of 2.68, winning 20-or-more in five of those seasons and was voted into the Hall of Fame in 1946.

October 8

1912 — When William Frederick "Heine" Heitmuller was stricken with typhoid fever on September 28 he was the second leading hitter in the Pacific Coast League with an average of .335. Leading the league was his Los Angeles Angels teammate Pete Daley with an average of .340. On October 8 Heitmuller died suddenly. In the final three weeks of the season Daley's average fell eight points to .332, which gave a dead man the 1912 Pacific Coast League batting championship.

1939 — Manager Joe McCarthy and the Yankees sweep Cincinnati in the World Series to duplicate the sweep of the Chicago Cubs in 1938. After winning nine pennants, McCarthy rolled up seven World Championships winning 30 games and losing 13 with a .698 winning percentage. As a manager for 24 years with the Yankees, Cubs and Red Sox he finished with a record .614 (2,126-1,335) placing him as the number one winning manager in the history of the game. Marse Joe McCarthy 1926-1950 is elected to the Hall of Fame in 1957.

1956 — Before 64,519 paid at Yankee Stadium, Don Larsen pitches the first perfect game in World Series history as he uses only 97 pitches to wipe out Brooklyn 2-0. The 27-year-old right-hander struck out seven and had a three-ball count on only one batter, Pee Wee Reese, in the first inning. Dodger pitcher Sal Maglie retired the first eleven batters before Mickey Mantle ripped a home run into the lower right field seats. The Yanks scored again in the sixth as Maglie continued his tough pitching allowing New York only five hits and two walks during the afternoon. In the ninth Larsen retired Carl Furillo on a fly to right and Roy Campanella on a ground ball to second. Facing Dale Mitchell, batting for Maglie, Larsen worked the count to 1-2 before veteran National League umpire Babe Pinelli, working the plate for the last time in his 22-year career, called Mitchell out on strikes as Larsen chalks up the majors fourth perfect game.

October 9

1957 — The Brooklyn Dodgers, without holding a press conference, announce the team is moving to Los Angeles. Following the afternoon World Series game between the Yankees and Milwaukee Braves, while baseball writers covering the series were working on game stories in the pressroom in the Waldorf Astoria, Red Patterson, Dodgers publicity chief, walked in and posted a small notice on the bulletin board. It read, "The Brooklyn National League franchise today was transferred to Los Angeles".

1999 — The Houston Astros make the Astrodome obsolete for baseball as they play their final game in the first indoor venue for baseball and football – once called the "Eighth Wonder of the World." The Astros suffer a 7-5 defeat to the Atlanta Braves in their swan song in their home for 35 years. The opening of this first domed stadium in 1965 triggered a building boom of ballparks throughout the majors – some covered, some built for football as well as baseball and most of them with the phenomenon of playing on an artificial surface – Astroturf. Beginning in 1970 both Cincinnati and Pittsburgh opened stadiums for both football and baseball with artificial surfaces and Philadelphia joined them in 1971. In 1973 Kansas City began playing on Astroturf and by 1977 Seattle was playing baseball and football under a dome with an artificial surface, and Minnesota offered the same bill-of-fare beginning in 1982. Montreal inherited a stadium in 1979 from the Olympics (with a park that couldn't make up its mind whether it was open or closed) and Toronto opened a state-of-the-art retractable roof stadium and both Canadian teams installed Astroturf.

In the 1990s a major revolution back to the old began with smaller seating capacity baseball-only stadiums, grass fields and some retractable roofs. It began in Baltimore with Camden Yards, then Cleveland, following with Chicago's new Comiskey Park and Texas' Ballpark in Arlington. By the late 1990s Atlanta and Seattle joined the group. Beginning in 2000 the epidemic continued with Detroit, Milwaukee, San Francisco and even Houston abandoning football and artificial turf in their new homes. Meanwhile, architects were busier than lawyers with San Diego, Cincinnati, Pittsburgh, Philadelphia and Montreal waiting on the drawing boards. Down the line only Wrigley Field appeared safe as Boston's Fenway Park eyeballed the surge that had already devoured Tiger Stadium. As sports writer Frederic C. Klein summed it up, "Now the Astrodome sits derelict, made obsolete by newer versions of itself, but its place in sports history is secure."

October 10

1920 — In one of the weirdest World Series games ever played the best-of-nine series was tied at two wins apiece between Brooklyn and Cleveland as game five started at League Park. In the bottom of the first inning Charlie Jamieson and Bill Wambsganss singled and the Indians manager, Tris Speaker, bunted for a base hit. That brought up outfielder Elmer Smith who hit the first bases loaded homerun in World Series history over the short right field fence (290 feet) to the delight of the 26,884 fans in attendance. The score remained at 4-0 Cleveland, until the fourth inning when the Indians Doc Johnston singled and Steve O'Neill was given a free pass to get to pitcher Jim Bagby. He hit a routine fly ball to right field that would have been caught except for the temporary stands erected for the series. The ball dropped fair into the corner of the stands; Bagby had just hit the first World Series homerun by a pitcher.

But the final drama of the remarkable contest was yet to come. The Indians are now leading 7-0 with the Dodgers batting in the top of the fifth and lead off batter Pete Kilduff singles, Otto Miller follows with another base bit moving Kilduff to second. Brooklyn pitcher Clarence Mitchell is the next batter and he lines a ball just to the right of second base. Second baseman Bill Wambsganss steps to his right, leaps and spears the ball for the first out. Wambsganss, seeing Kilduff racing for third tags second, then Miller, who was running from first base, is tagged out, completing the second unassisted triple play in Baseball history and the first in a World Series. The game ended 8-1 in favor of Cleveland and they would go on to win the series five games to two. Wambsganss, the philosopher, conceded many years later, "Everything is made for by chance – our ancestry, our birth. It's just a matter of chance that you're here at all."

October 11

1896 — If you think free agency and a salary limit have been bones of contention for only the past two or three decades consider this: The National League meeting in Chicago receives a proposal from Brooklyn owner Ferdinand H. Abell to make all players free agents between January 1 and March 1; this would allow all teams to bid on them subject to a salary limit. The plan is studied and ignored.

1911 — The first Most Valuable Players are announced — then known as the

October 11-14
Chalmers Awards. One writer from each team voted with a point system of 8 points for first, 7 for second, etc. giving Ty Cobb a unanimous 64 votes to take the American League award and Frank Schulte of the Cubs winning National League honors. Each received a Chalmers automobile. The Chalmers Award survived through 1914. Starting in 1922 in the American and 1924 in the National, awards were administered by the same vote process with no sponsor connection. The American League discontinued the awards in 1929 and in 1930 the National League followed suit. The Baseball Writers Association of America took over the balloting in 1931.

October 12

1963 — In the first and only Hispanic All-Star game ever played in the United States, the National League whips the American 5-2. The game is also the last game ever played at the Polo Grounds. In a pre-game ceremony, Minnesota's Vic Power receives an award as the number-one Latin player. The Pirates' Al McBean is the winning pitcher in relief and Cleveland's Pedro Ramos is the loser. Among the many players were Washington's Minnie Minoso, Tony Oliva and Zoiles Versalles, Pittsburgh's Roberto Clemente and Manny Mota, San Francisco's Juan Marichal, Orlando Cepeda and Felipe Alou, the Cardinals' Julian Javier and Baltimore's Luis Aparico.

October 14

1908 — At the Hotel Ponchatrain in Detroit, following the World Series, 23 baseball writers put together a rough draft that would lead to the formation of the Baseball Writers Association of America. It wasn't an easy road over the early years of baseball to get the writers together. As early as 1885 the first association of writers was formed in Philadelphia. It was a loose organization for two years, but in 1887 at Cincinnati it was formally organized as the National Baseball Reporters Association. Strong rules were set up and a scoring committee was appointed with Harry Chadwick at the head. However, the group was a fatality of the bitter war between the National League and the Players League, with the writers splitting ranks in support of the two circuits. When peace came and the Players League was disbanded, the writers remained at odds and many were not on speaking terms.

It would be almost 20 years before the 1908 Giants-Cubs playoff game at the Polo Grounds and the Cubs-Tigers World Series would trigger the formation of the BBWAA. It was a cold, wet and snowy series in Detroit and out-of-town writers were given press assignments in the first base pavilion where they had to climb a slippery ladder to get to their seats in the open area. In some cases the writers' seat assignments had been taken by fans who claimed squatter's rights. Chicago writers complained they were treated roughly and discourteously. Indignation arose throughout the entire press corps over their treatment – dirty, un-policed press boxes not only in New York and Detroit, but also in ballparks across the major leagues. The 1908 Chicago-Tigers World Series ended the afternoon of October 14 at Detroit's Bennett Park, and that evening at the Hotel Ponchatrain the BBWAA was temporarily born. Just six weeks later – December 9, 1908 – at the winter meetings of the major leagues at New York's Waldorf Astoria, the first formal meeting was held and a constitution was ratified.

1929 — After spending his first 15 seasons in the majors with Detroit, Harry Heilmann is placed on waivers by the Tigers and sold to Cincinnati. Heilmann broke into the big leagues at age 20 in 1914 then returned to the minors for a year. Following that, he was one of the top hitters in baseball, winning four American League batting titles, topping off with a .403 average in 1923. He didn't miss the .400 mark by much in his other championship years — .394 in 1921, .393 in 1925, and .398 in 1927. Interestingly, beginning in 1907, when Ty Cobb was chalking up batting titles in 12 of the next 13 seasons, the Tigers won 17 of the 21 individual batting championships through 1927 – four by Heilmann and one by Heine Manush. An outfielder, with numerous games at first base, Heilmann played 17 years in the majors, hit .342 with 1,552 runs batted in. He played with the Reds in 1930 and 1932 then retired. Heilmann entered the Hall of Fame in 1952.

October 15

1899 — The worst team of all time in baseball history ends its season with a record 20-134. The National League's Cleveland Spiders finish 84 games out of first place in the 12-club circuit. Cleveland spent two seasons in the National League finishing in 5th place in 1898 with a record of 81-68. Owners Frank DeHaas and Matthew Stanley Robison were upset with the lack of attendance and before the 1899 season bought the National League St. Louis Perfectos and transferred the best of the Cleveland players to St. Louis, leaving the Spiders with a sorry shell of players. The Perfectos would finish 5th in 1899 while Cleveland was floundering so badly the team played only 41 of its 154 games at home, wandering around the league identified by the press as Exiles, Forsakens, Barnstormers and Wanderers. Six different times the club lost 11 or more in a row, including one streak of 24 and only once did the team manage to win two straight. The following year, Cleveland was mercifully expunged from the National League along with Washington, Louisville and Baltimore to make the NL an eight-team league. Cleveland re-entered the majors in 1901 as the American League Cleveland Blues.

October 16

1921 — In defiance of commissioner Landis' ban on World Series participants playing in post-season exhibitions, Babe Ruth, Bob Meusel, and pitcher Bill Piercy conduct a five-day barnstorming tour that starts in Buffalo and ends in Scranton. Ruth openly challenges Landis to act against the move and the commissioner answers with fines rescinding the players World Series shares of $3,362.26 and suspending them until May 20, 1922.

1961 — Following 14 seasons with the Philadelphia Phillies, Robin Roberts is sold to the Yankees. He would be released by New York on April 30, 1962, without appearing in a game, and signed with Baltimore on May 21. Roberts would spend six more seasons in the majors with the Orioles, Houston, and the Cubs with a record of 52-46 before finishing his career in the Eastern League with Reading in 1967, a farm club of the Phillies. Roberts won 20 or more games in six straight seasons (1950-1955), working 300 or more innings each year with a high of 347 in 1953. Known for his impeccable control, he issued only 902 bases on balls in 4,689 innings through his 19 seasons. Roberts (36) finished with 286 wins and 245 losses, an earned run average of 3.41 and was inducted into the Hall of Fame in 1976.

October 17

1885 — At a joint meeting in New York of the two major leagues, the National and American Association, a player salary maximum of $2,000 and a minimum of $1,000 is set for the 1886 season.

1960 — The National League undergoes its first structural change since 1900 as Houston and New York are awarded franchises, to begin in 1962. In 1899 the NL had twelve teams, but the circuit was trimmed to eight with the elimination of Baltimore, Louisville, Washington and Cleveland. Beginning in 1900 the National League would comprise Brooklyn, Pittsburgh, Philadelphia, Boston, Chicago, St. Louis, Cincinnati and New York until 1953 when the Boston franchise moved to Milwaukee. 1958 would see Brooklyn move to Los Angeles and New York to San

Francisco. With the threat of a third major league, the Continental League, looming on the horizon, the National League expanded to ten clubs in 1962.

1979 — Willie (Pops) Stargell leads the Pirates "Family" to a seven game World Series win over Baltimore with a Most Valuable Player performance. For the series Stargell hit .400 (12 for 30) seven of them for extra bases, three homeruns, four doubles and seven RBI. He also shared the National League MVP Award with Keith Hernandez in 1979. During his 21 seasons with the Bucs he hit .282, 475 homeruns and 1,540 runs batted in. Needless to say he was big with the lumber and big on the strikeouts (1,936) — but that went with the territory. Wilver Stargell (8) not surprisingly entered the Hall of Fame in his first year of eligibility in 1988

October 18

1950 — After 50 seasons as manager of the Philadelphia Athletics, 87-year old Connie Mack retires, but maintains his position as president of the team. His successor is Jimmy Dykes. Following three seasons as manager at Pittsburgh (1894-96), and four as skipper of Milwaukee in the Western League, Mack took over the reigns at Philadelphia in 1901, the first year of the American League. He guided the Athletics in 7,517 games with a win percentage of .483, made eight trips to the World Series and won five World Championships. Mack broke into the majors as a catcher in the National League with Washington and played ten years with the Statesmen (Senators) and Pittsburgh. Mack's playing career was not outstanding, but it was his service apart from playing the game that brought him to the Hall of Fame in 1937.

1967 — The American League approves the immediate transfer of the Kansas City franchise to Oakland and votes new expansion franchises for Kansas City and Seattle, both to be operative in 1969. These moves were triggered by the desire of owner Charlie Finley to leave Kansas City, and the league's fear of another anti-trust probe should Kansas City be stripped bare and left without at least the promise of a major league franchise, as happened to Milwaukee the year before. On hearing that Finley had officially moved the Athletics, Missouri senator Stuart Symington declared: "Oakland is the luckiest city since Hiroshima."

October 19

1949 — The Chicago White Sox pull off one of the best trades in their history when they acquire Nellie Fox from the Athletics for catcher Joe Tipton. At 20 years old Fox made his major league debut with Philadelphia, playing in seven games in 1947 and left that club with a batting average of .247 while striking out only nine times in 263 at-bats. He would be the spark for the Go-Go Sox for the next 14 seasons and wind up his career in 1964 as a player and coach with Houston. During 12 consecutive years with Chicago, Fox registered more than 600 at-bats and never struck out more than 18 times in a single season with a total of 216 strikeouts in his career. He led the American League in hits four times while batting .288 and totaled 2,663 hits. Fox (2) was the AmericanLeague MVP in 1959, won three Gold Gloves and was elected to the Hall of Fame in 1997.

October 20

1910 — The liveliness of baseballs has been a topic of controversy for years, but the Rawlings Sporting Goods Company remains steadfast that the 'pill', or nucleus of each baseball has not changed since 1926. It was on this day, October 20, 1910, that cork centers were first placed in baseballs, then refined in 1926 with a red-pellet core, known as cushioned cork which is enveloped within two balanced rubber coverings. The cemented surface of the pill receives a series of three wool and one cotton windings. After being trimmed of excess tailings, the wound ball accepts a film of cement before the cover is hand-stitched together with 88 inches of waxed thread. After the stitching, the seams are machine rolled for about 15 seconds to compress the 108 stitches to produce a consistent surface. The only change in the balls since 1926 was the switch from horsehide to cowhide covers in 1974. The tanners at Rawlings prefer Holstein hides which slowly simmer and bleach to perfection in caldrons teaming with secret chemical concoctions. Since this entire process is machine-produced, the only difference in balls would be the hand stitching. This is a delicate art where each of the 108 stitches must be "perfect" – but since this is a human process, no two balls are exactly alike.

Before 1990 Haitian women were the experts – each sewing only four or five balls a day. Along came the Haitian coup and the United States imposed a trade embargo that halted production in that country. Major league balls are now stitched in Costa Rica. 1990 was a training period of many months for new stitchers and obviously many less than "perfect" balls were produced. Aside from that aspect, and a slight variance in inches and weight, baseballs leave the Rawlings factory free of blemishes, measuring 9 to 9-and-a-quarter inches across two seams, and weighing from 5.00 to 5.25 ounces. The baseball's circumference and weight have been the same since 1872.

October 21

1957 — Minneapolis and St. Paul make their initial overture to acquire the Washington franchise, but the Senators reject the offer. The team was known as the Washington Nationals when it became a charter member of the American League in 1901. Owner Calvin Griffith would eventually express a desire to move to the Twin Cities, and in 1960 the American League would grant his wish by a 6-2 vote to make the league a ten-team circuit by granting Washington and Los Angeles expansion franchises for the1961 season.

1976 — Johnny Bench leads the Big Red Machine to their second straight World Championship – this one a sweep of the New York Yankees. The Reds catcher is the Most Valuable Player with a average of .533 (8-15) two homeruns, a double and triple with six runs batted in. Bench, began his parade of awards after joining the Reds in 1967, winning Rookie of the Year in 1968, and two seasons as the National League's Most Valuable Player and homerun champion in 1970 (45 HR) and 1972 (40 HR). He led the league three times in runs batted in and won ten Gold Gloves behind the plate. Bench (5) hit .267, 389 homeruns with 1,376 runs batted and was voted into the Hall of Fame in his first year of eligibility in 1989.

October 22

1885 — Baseball's first union, the National Brotherhood of Baseball Players is organized by John Montgomery Ward, an attorney as well as a shortstop with the New York Giants. The organization received some concessions, but in 1890, the Brotherhood backed the new Players' League (a share-the-profits-with-the-athletes organization) and the membership jumped to the new circuit. When the Players' League disbanded after one season the Brotherhood went out with it and did not surface again until December of 1900.

1927 — One of the lesser-known members of the Hall of Fame, and a favorite of Giants manager John McGraw, Ross Youngs dies of Brights disease (a kidney ailment) at age 30. His death cut short a 10-year career that started with the New York Giants in 1917 and lasted through only 95 games in 1926. As early as 1924 he was accompanied by a specialist and a nurse when he traveled. Youngs hit .322 during his career and played in four consecutive World Series (1921-1924) with New York. Ross (Pep) Youngs was elected to the Hall of Fame in 1972.

October 22-23

2000 — Yankees pitcher Roger Clemens nearly incites a brawl in the first inning of the second game of the World Series against the Mets. Mets catcher Mike Piazza, jammed by a pitch, breaks the bat in two pieces and the barrel-end is picked up by Clemens and hurled in Piazza's direction as he runs down the first base line. Piazza makes a belated move toward Clemens as the benches empty, but calm is restored by the umpires. In the minds of many baseball people, it was surprising that Clemens' action did not result in his immediate ejection -- but umpires allowed him to continue pitching (Piazza had suffered a concussion after he was hit on the helmet by a Clemens pitch in a July 8 interleague game). Piazza called Clemens' latest action "idiotic" and called for an investigation of the incident. Two days later Frank Robinson, Major League Baseball's vice president in charge of discipline, gave Clemens what amounted to a "slap on the wrist" with a mere $50,000 fine.

October 23

1876 — The *Chicago Tribune* publishes National League season-ending batting averages based on a new method of dividing number of at-bats into number of hits.

1945 — Jackie Robinson, former UCLA football star, who played shortstop for the Kansas City Monarchs, is the center of a bombshell announcement by Brooklyn's Branch Rickey. Baseball's unwritten, but long observed color line had been broken. Rickey had signed two Negroes, Robinson and John Wright. Wright was a pitcher who had played for various Negro League teams since 1937, and was contracted to the Dodgers' farm club at Montreal. This broke the color line that had existed in organized baseball since the 1880s. Within one season Robinson would be playing first base for Brooklyn, while Wright played in only two games with the International League Royals in 1946 and was released.

1973 — Lee MacPhail is elected the fifth president of the American League effective the first of January 1974. He will succeed the retiring Joe Cronin. MacPhail served as player personnel director of the Yankees 1948-58, general manager of Baltimore 1958-65 and returned to the Yankees in 1966 as vice president and general manager. He would serve as AL president for nine years through 1983. Lee MacPhail teams with his father, Larry, as the first father-son combination in the Hall of Fame. Also elected to the hall by the Veterans' Committee in 1998 was switch-hitting shortstop George Davis. He played 20 years (1890-1909) with the Cleveland Spiders, Giants, and White Sox, most of it with New York, where for nine consecutive years he hit .300 or better. Davis played every position except catcher batting .297, 2,688 hits, 1,435 RBI, stole 615 bases and scored 1,544 runs.

1974 — Billy Williams, a fixture at Wrigley Field for 16 years, is traded by the Cubs to Oakland for Darold Knowles, Manny Trillo and Bob Locker. Williams would play two years with the Athletics and wind up with a career average of .290, winning a National League batting title (.333) in 1972 with Chicago. He logged 2,711 hits, 426 homeruns and drove in 1,475 runs. Williams (26) was elected to the Hall of Fame in 1987.

1987 — On September 22, 1987 the Cubs send pitcher Dickie Noles to Detroit for a player to be named. On this date the two teams settle on the player to be named. He is Dickie Noles, who's traded for himself.

October 24

1908 — A baseball song, "Take Me Out to the Ball game", hits the charts as sung by singing sensation Billy Murray. This is the second of three versions to be released within a five-week period since the lyric was first written. The lyricist was a well-known song-and-dance man of vaudeville, Jack Norworth, and the song was inspired while he was riding a New York City elevated train. Spotting a poster advertising the baseball games at the Polo Grounds, he jotted down the words within his 30-minute ride time and later called upon composer Albert von Tilzer to write the music. The two teamed up to produce the most famous sports song ever written. Norworth's plot for the song is written in the verse that precedes the famous chorus. It's about a young girl named Nancy Kelly, whose boyfriend, Joe, suggests that he take her to Coney Island. Nancy has other ideas and replies to the unwelcome suggestion by singing, "Take Me Out to the Ballgame." It would be 40 years before Norworth attended a baseball game and 20 or more years before von Tilzer saw one.

The Baseball Museum at Cooperstown has a display of the first edition of the sheet music, along with a photo of Norworth and a letter he sent to a friend with the original draft of the lyric. The only mention of von Tilzer is his name on the sheet music. This is the National Anthem of baseball and ranks along with "Happy Birthday' as one of the most easily recognized songs – it's peanuts, cracker Jacks and baseball!

1996 – More than thirty years had passed between April 12, 1966, when the

October 24-26

Braves played their first game at Atlanta Fulton County Stadium – and their swan song on this date in 1996 — a 1-0 loss in the fifth game of the World Series against the Yankees. The Braves had their ups and downs following their move from Milwaukee in 1966, and after the first six seasons the club's attendance fell below one million in 1972 and stayed that way for the next eight years. The low point in fan support was 534,672 in 1975 and for the next four seasons the Braves finished in last place. After making their slow recovery in the 1980s Atlanta rose to their glory years winning eight pennants in the 1990s. Fulton County Stadium was replaced by Turner Field, built for both the Olympics and the Braves and opened on April 4, 1997.

October 25

1845 — What appears to be the first box score ever published is printed in the *New York Herald*. It was found by Melvin A. Adelman, an assistant physical education professor at the University of Illinois while researching his dissertation entitled, "The Development of Modern Athletic Sport in New York City, 1820-1870." The game was played between the New York Base Ball Club and the Brooklyn Club on the grounds of the Brooklyn Star Cricket Club. It contains players' names and only two statistical columns headed "Hands out" and "Runs." New York won 37-19 but the number of hands out indicate it was only a four-inning game. Also, the proofreader failed to balance the box as individual hands out for Brooklyn read 13 but totaled 12.

1973 — Following 15 years with the San Francisco Giants, Willie McCovey is traded to San Diego for Mike Caldwell and Bernie (Bernard) Williams. Four years later (1977) he would return to the Giants as a free agent, after a stop-over with Oakland, and play through the 1980 season. McCovey's career would span 22 years in which he hit 521 homeruns, drove in 1,555 runs and hit .270. He was National League homerun champion three times (44-1963 in a tie with Hank Aaron, 36-1968 and 45-1969). He also was the NL Most Valuable Player in 1969. McCovey (44) was the National League Rookie of the year in 1959 and topped off his outstanding career in 1986 when he was elected to the Hall of Fame in his first year of eligibility.

October 26

1931 — Charles (Old Roman) Comiskey, a player, manager and club owner for 49 years, dies at age 72. Comiskey, a player of average ability, broke in with the

St. Louis Browns of the American Association as a pitcher in 1882. A sore arm moved him to first base where he saw most of his action with St. Louis and Cincinnati. He was only 23 in his first major league season but managed the Browns in his second year (1883) and went on to skipper every team he played with for the next 12 seasons. Comiskey, along with Ban Johnson, was instrumental in forming the American League (from the old Western League) in 1901 and for his efforts was awarded the Chicago franchise. He took his hits during the 1919 World Series and for the next 12 years of his life never fully recovered from the betrayal of his White Sox players. Comiskey was voted into the Hall of Fame in 1939.

1960 — A major league expands for the first time in this century as the American League authorizes Calvin Griffith of the Washington Senators to make his long-desired move to Minneapolis-St. Paul. At the same time a new franchise was approved for the nation's capital and a tenth franchise was given to Los Angeles. The moves were passed by only the minimum 6-2 vote with Detroit and Cleveland casting the negative ballots. The franchise shift to the Twin Cities ended a 40-year association of the Griffith family with Washington, beginning with Clark Griffith becoming president of the Senators in 1920.

October 27

1893 — Manager Frank Selee brings the National League's Boston Beaneaters home in first place for the third straight year. Selee was known as a manager who took over struggling franchises in Boston and the Chicago Cubs and turned their fortunes around. In twelve seasons with Boston he won five pennants and although he was not as successful in his four years with the Cubs he did turn the team around making it a contending franchise. He has been credited as the architect of the Tinker to Evers to Chance double play combination. In Selee's 16 seasons with Boston and Chicago his teams finished below .500 only two times and he is the fourth highest manager in winning percentage in the game's history with .598. Selee was voted into the Hall of Fame in 1999.

October 28

1954 — After much haggling, American League owners are deadlocked 4-4 in their effort to come to a conclusion on the fate of the Philadelphia Athletics. When the major leagues approved the Braves' move to Milwaukee and the transfer of the St. Louis Browns to Baltimore (both in 1953), rumors became rampant as to the future of the two teams in Philadelphia. Financial difficulties along with the rift between Connie Mack's two sons, Roy and Earle, who had gained controlling interest in the team in 1950, further fueled the league's problem of whether a local buyer or one from another city would purchase the team. A Chicago industrialist, Arnold M. Johnson and a group of associates were interested in the Athletics with intent to move the team to Kansas City. Four days after the tie vote, the league finally agreed to sell the A's to Johnson and move the team to Kansas City. The American League was anxious to acquire another virgin territory following the Athletics 362,113 attendance in 1953 and only 304,666 in 1954. Johnson's price, as described by him, was a $3,500,000 deal. Kansas City had bounced around in early baseball history, affiliated with the Union Association for one season in 1884, the National League in 1886, and the outlaw Federal League in 1914-15. Having Kansas City in the American League has been no bonanza for the circuit – a transfer to Oakland in 1968, out of baseball for one season and back in 1969 as the expansion Kansas City Royals.

October 29

1981 — The sale of the Philadelphia Phillies is finalized, ending the 38-year ownership by the Carpenter family. The new group of six investors is headed by Bill Giles, and the purchase price is a record-setting $30,175,000, besting the previous high of $21 million paid for the New York Mets in 1980. The purchase of the Phillies for an estimated $400,000 in 1943 by the Carpenter family would be perhaps the most significant move in the club's history. R.R.M. (Bob) Carpenter, Jr. would become president. By 1998 the last of the family-owned franchises (the Yawkeys, Wrigleys, Griffiths) would be gone with the O'Malley's sale of the Dodgers to Robert Murdoch's Fox Group. Along with the ending of the family tradition comes a continuing spiral of purchase prices for baseball franchises – the Dodgers sold for between $311 and $350 million.

October 30

1956 — Ebbets Field in Brooklyn is sold to a real estate tycoon, adding another note to the imminent departure of the Dodgers. Less than one year later, September 24, 1957, the Dodgers would play their final game in the park they had called home for 44 years and take off for Los Angeles. The purchaser of the property is a Dodger fan, Marvin Kratter, for an estimated $3 million with Walter O'Malley signing a lease agreeing to stay until the 1959 season with an option to 1961. With the Dodgers gone following the 1957 season, demolition of Ebbets

Field began on February 23, 1960; the only items salvaged were eight light stanchions that were moved to Downing Stadium on Randall's Island. The area was cleared for a housing development (later renamed the Jackie Robinson Apartments in 1972), along with the Crown Heights Intermediate School, which would be built on the site in 1963. The last vestige of the Dodgers is a two block long brick wall, one block from the Gowanus Canal on Third Avenue between First and Third Streets, once part of old Washington Park where the Dodgers played for 14 years. The building currently houses Consolidated Edison trucks and tools. On a portion of the wall can be seen bricked-in arched windows which had opened into the players' clubhouses. Tom Knight, Brooklyn's official baseball historian says, "It's probably the oldest standing wall of any ball park in the United States.

October 31

1934 — Future Hall-of-Famer Burleigh Grimes, now 41 years old, ends his 19-year career pitching in 10 games with the Yankees. Grimes was one of 17 pitchers throwing the spitball when it was banned in 1920 following its introduction to the majors in 1903, the others were Yancy Ayers and Dutch Leonard of Detroit, Ray Caldwell and Stan Coveleski of Cleveland, Red Faber of the White Sox, Jack Quinn of the Yankees, Allen Russell of the Red Sox, Urban Shocker and Allan Sothoron of the Browns, Bill Doak and Marv Goodwin of the Cardinals, Phil Douglas of the Giants, Dana Fillingim and Dick Rudolph of the Braves, Clarence Mitchell Dodgers and Ray Fisher of Cincinnati. All 17 were allowed to throw the pitch until they retired, and Grimes was the last of those pitchers to throw the legal spitball. As we all know the official banning of illegal pitches was never completely enforced and over the past seven decades attempts have been made to again make the spitball legal. In fact during commissioner Ford Frick's tenure he favored the move. On December 12, 1949 the American League voted 7-1 in rejecting the proposal and on November 26, 1961 the Rules Committee voted 8-1 against bringing it back. Interestingly, the one vote in favor was cast by the National League's supervisor of umpires Hall-of-Famer Cal Hubbard.

The ball no notice takes of ayes or noes
But left or right, as strikes the player, goes.
But, he who threw thee down upon the field,
He knows about it all – he knows – he knows.
—- *The Rubbaiyat of Omar Khayyam*

Chapter Eleven

"The baseball mania has run its course, It has no future as a professional endeavor."

Cincinnati Gazette, 1879

November 1

1914 — Connie Mack starts the house cleaning that will eventually lead to the dispersal of his so-called $100,000 infield. Mack asks waivers on pitchers Eddie Plank and Chief Bender, among others, despite the club's 99-53 record and another pennant in 1914. Lack of attendance (346,641) led to a loss of $50,000 and put Mack in a financial bind. The loss of the two future Hall-of-Famers, Plank and Bender, did not turn out to be too important for Mack as they were nearing the end of their careers. But, the owner-manager would sell second baseman Eddie Collins a month later to the White Sox for $50,000, shortstop Jack Berry to the Red Sox for $8,000 in 1915 and third baseman Frank "Home Run" Baker to the Yankees in 1916 for $37,500. In the first 14 years in the American League, starting in 1901, Philadelphia won six pennants, and from 1910 through 1914 had taken flags every year except 1912. The average yearly attendance at Shibe Park 1909-1913 was 591,524 and the 1914-16 stripping of the club's talent led to last place finishes for the next seven straight seasons (1915-1921) with an average attendance decrease to 158,749.

1916 — Harry Frazee, a theatrical sharpie, buys the Red Sox for $675,000. A big operator and a heavy gambler on extravagant musicals, he was often more broke than rich. He appeared to be sincere at the beginning in owning a baseball club, bringing in good players and manager Ed Barrow, that led to a World Championship in 1918. However, in 1919 a couple of his big shows flopped, and strapped for cash, he sold Ernie Shore, Dutch Leonard and Duffy Lewis to the Yankees for four pitchers and $50,000. He later unloaded Carl Mays, again to New York, for $40,000. Frazee had found an angel for his debts and in January-1920 went to Yankees owner Jacob Ruppert for a $500,000 loan against Fenway Park. But, Ruppert saw him coming. The Yankees owner gave him a $300,000 loan against Fenway Park and another $125,000 for Babe Ruth. From that point on the name of Harry Frazee would forever live in infamy among Red Sox baseball fans.

For the next two seasons New York continued its rape of Frazee's ball club with Wally Schang, Waite Hoyt, Mike McNally and Harry Harper going in one deal and Joe Bush, Sam Jones and Everett Scott in another. Joe Dugan was also shipped to the Yankees, all in deals that involved cash but little in return for talent. The icing to the murder of the Red Sox came when minor league pitcher George Pipgras was forwarded to New York. Within this two-year period the Yankees were in first place and went on to win six pennants in the next eight years – a lot of it accomplished on the blood of the Red Sox. With nothing more to sell, after seven and half years, Frazee sold the club in 1923. The next Boston pennant would be in 1946.

November 2

1974 — Hank Aaron, now 40 years old, is traded by the Atlanta Braves to Milwaukee for Dave May and minor league pitcher Roger Alexander. Aaron had spent his first 21 seasons with the Braves after breaking into the majors when he was 20 years old in 1954. He hit .305 in his 23 years with 3,771 hits, 2,297 runs batted in and 755 homeruns. Aaron (44) was the National League's Most Valuable Player in 1957, the league batting champion in 1959, was awarded three Gold Gloves and was elected to the Hall of Fame in his first year of eligibility in 1982.

November 3

1953 — The sacrifice fly rule, stricken from the books following the 1939 season, is reinstated for the 1954 season and has remained on the books since. Originally introduced in 1908 the SF rule stated the batter is not charged with a time at bat if a runner *scores* after the catch. In 1926 through 1930, a SF was credited to a batter if *any* runner *advanced*. In 1940 the sacrifice fly rule was completely wiped from the rules and remained that way until 1954.

November 4

1935 — The American League announces that pro football great, 6'-3" 253-pound Cal Hubbard, would join their umpiring staff for the 1936 season. Hubbard, a tackle, was an All-America at Geneva College after playing his first two years at Centenary, and went on to play eight seasons in the pros with the New York Giants and Green Bay Packers. While still playing pro football he began his umpiring career in 1928 in the Piedmont League, umpiring in five minor leagues before being advanced to the American from the International League. Hubbard would become one of the most respected umpires in the majors and would work on the field through 1951. Later he would join the AL in a supervisory capacity through

1962. Hubbard would be enshrined in the Hall of Fame in 1976 and become the only person in the Baseball, Pro-Football and Collegiate Halls.

1976 — The first re-entry free agent draft is held as the result of a December 1975 arbitrator's ruling in favor of Andy Messersmith and Dave McNally, abolishing the reserve clause and establishing free agency for players who play out their contracts. This ruling had considerable side effects, among them a 17-day lockout by owners who stated spring training would not open until a new basic agreement was reached. However, commissioner Bowie Kuhn ordered the camps opened and it wasn't until July 12 that the players and owners reached a four-year agreement establishing procedure for free agency – players with a least six years service may become free agents. The draft, held at the Plaza Hotel in New York, involved 23 players and 13 teams. Two days later Minnesota relief pitcher Bill Campbell becomes the first free agent to make a connection, signing a four-year $1 million contract with the Boston Red Sox. Campbell's pay in 1976 was $23,000. Within three weeks some 11 other players signed multi-year deals with Baltimore's Reggie Jackson getting the biggest haul – a five-year $2.9 million contract from the Yankees.

November 5

1997 — The Milwaukee Brewers are moved from the American to the National League by Baseball's Executive Council in what is called the first phase of realignment. The move to the NL Central creates the only six-team division in the majors. The move also sends Detroit to the AL Central and expansion teams Tampa Bay to the American League East and Arizona to the National League West. Following this, Milwaukee has now been in each major league twice. In 1901 the Milwaukee Brewers were one of eight teams in the inaugural season of the American League. The franchise was moved to St. Louis in 1902 and became the St. Louis Browns. Milwaukee next surfaced in the National League when the Boston Braves transferred the franchise to Milwaukee in 1953. The Braves abandoned Milwaukee following the 1965 season and moved to Atlanta. Milwaukee picked up the bankrupt Seattle Pilots in 1970, making their return to the American League.

November 6

1950 — After his contract as Brooklyn Dodgers president is not renewed, Branch Rickey sells his 25 percent interest in the club to Walter O'Malley and Mrs. John

Smith for a reported $1.05 million and signs a five-year contract as executive vice-president/GM with the Pittsburgh Pirates. Probably no one else in the game exercised a more profound impact on baseball, for so long a period, than Branch Rickey. He certainly didn't do this as a player. In his four seasons on the diamond as a catcher-outfielder-first baseman for the Browns and New York Highlanders (Yankees) with a bat mark of .239, or as a manager for 10 years with the Browns and Cardinals. His forte was front office management — enthusiasm and imagination that produced a long list of contributions to further the game – the farm system, the breaking of the color barrier, attempting to establish a third major league that forced the National League to expand, the Knot-Hole gang, plus a highly developed eye for raw baseball talent. He was vice-president of the Cardinals but left that organization at the end of 1942 and joined Brooklyn as president/general manager with a generous amount of team stock. Rickey entered the Hall of Fame in 1967.

1995 — Major League Baseball announces a new five-year television package with Fox, NBC, ESPN and Prime Liberty that will pay each team about $10 million annually for the life of the deal. The package will total $1.7 billion — Fox will be the big spender at $575 million – ESPN will spend $435 million, NBC $400 million and Prime Liberty, soon to be Fox Cable, will chip in about $200 million. Those prices will soothe Major League Baseball's "in house" debacle originally announced on May 28, 1993 with acting commissioner Bud Selig boldly stating at the time of its signing, "We're seizing control of our destiny."

November 8

1934 — Ford Frick, National League publicity director, is named to succeed John Heydler as president of the league. Frick would serve as National League president until his election as commissioner in 1951.

1989 — Pam Postema, who two years previously was on the threshold of becoming the first female umpire in the major leagues, is released by the Class-AAA Alliance, where she had worked the past seven years. Umpire development executive director Ed Lawrence said, "When I first took office (1988) one of the things I quickly took a look at was the adoption of the basic six-year retention policy. That means if, after six years, you haven't been clearly identified as a prospect (for the majors), we would release you." The major leagues fill openings from the reserve list – umpires on minor league contracts who fill major league spots during vacations and illnesses. Postema (according to the Alliance) did not reach that status. At 36 years old she had umpired in the minors since 1977 and stated that the only reason she was denied a chance in the majors was because she was a woman. Postema would file a sex discrimination suit on this date against the American and National Leagues as well as the Triple-A Alliance and The Baseball Office for Umpire Development. Gloria Allred, a prominent women's rights advocate, represented Postema; the suit was settled out of court.

November 9

1950 — After 20 seasons as the Chicago White Sox shortstop, Luke Appling is given his release so he can become manager of the Memphis Chicks of the Class-AA Southern Association. Appling broke into pro ball with Atlanta in the Southern Association when he was 23 years old in 1930. After hitting .323 in 104 games with the Crackers he was purchased by Chicago and played in six games for the White Sox at the end of the season. He was especially noted as possessing one of the sharpest eyes among major league batters with the ability to foul off pitches almost at will. Hall of Fame White Sox pitcher Ted Lyons once said he saw Appling foul 14 consecutive pitches off Yankee pitcher Red Ruffing. He won two American League batting championships in 1936 (.388) and 1943 (.328) and finished with an average of .310. While managing in the minors, Appling won three pennants, two at Memphis, and one with Indianapolis in the American Association. While coaching for Kansas City in 1967 he finished the season as manager after Al Dark was fired; this was his only major league managerial stint, which lasted 40 games. He acquired the nickname "Old Aches and Pains" with his constant complaints of minor ailments, but he played an average of 121 games per season in his 20-year career. Appling (4) coached and scouted for various major league organizations into the late 1980s and was elected to the Hall of Fame in 1964. In 1982 while participating in the first annual Cracker Jack Old Timers Baseball Classic in Washington, D.C., he homered off Warren Spahn. Appling was 75 at the time.

1953 — The United States Supreme Court upholds the special status of baseball as a "sport" exempt from anti-trust actions. This is the second of three challenges that would reach the high court. In this case New York Yankees minor-leaguer George Toolson sued after he was reassigned. Several other players joined the suit, all claiming they were unfairly buried in the minors because they were the property of the better teams. In this case the Supreme Court upheld the exemption, effectively saying that its up to Congress to change it.

The first case began when Major League Baseball made peace with the rival Federal League in 1915. The Baltimore Terrapins were unhappy with the peace pact and brought a $900,000 anti-trust suit against the majors. The Terrapins owners had been offered $50,000 to fold and won triple damages of $240,000 but the verdict was reversed on appeal and the case reached the Supreme Court in 1922. The court ruled unanimously that baseball was not a business engaged in interstate commerce and thus was not subject to federal anti-trust laws.

The third test was by Curt Flood after the Cardinals outfielder was traded to Philadelphia in 1972. In this opinion the Court acknowledged baseball is engaged in interstate commerce, but refused to overturn the exemption. "If there is any inconsistency and illogic in all this, it is an inconsistency and illogic of long standing that is to be remedied by the Congress and not this court." Finally, after three sessions of Congress in October 1998 a bill overturning part of baseball's antitrust exemption became law, thus putting baseball on a par with other professional sports on labor matters. The bill, known as the Curt Flood Act of 1998, overrides part of the 1922 Supreme Court ruling that exempted baseball from antitrust laws on grounds that it was not interstate commerce.

November 10

1975 — Harmon Killebrew's 22 years in the majors comes to an end with his release by Kansas City. He had been a member of the Washington Senators/Minnesota Twins beginning in 1954 and it would be the only big league franchise he would play for until his final season with the Royals in 1975. Killebrew broke in with Washington as a second baseman but would spend most of his career at first, third and would finish his final two years as a designated hitter. He spent a little time in the minors (portions of 1956-58) but also was with the Senators in those three seasons. He was only 18 years old when he participated in nine games with the Senators in his first season and he would not establish himself as a regular until 1959. That year he won the first of his six American League homerun titles with round trippers ranging from 42 to 49. Twice he would hit the 49 mark, the second time in 1969 when he won the league's Most Valuable Player Award with 140 RBI,145 walks, and a bat mark of .276. He finished his career with a .256 average, 1,584 runs batted in and an almost matching 1,559 walks. Killebrew (3) was one of the greatest homerun hitters of all time and was affectionately known as "Killer" for his prolific clouts that totaled 573 – each of which helped pave his way to the Hall of Fame in 1984.

1992 — National League owners reject the relocation of the San Francisco Giants to St.Petersburg, Florida, turning down Giant owner Bob Lurie's sale request by a 9-4 vote. Lurie was prevented from voting and needed 10 of 13 votes to approve his $115 million sale. Bud Selig, owner of the Milwaukee Brewers and chairman of baseball's ruling executive council, said the vote "reaffirmed baseball's long-established preference for the stability of its franchises." A long-standing preference that within five years would change, as Baseball began encouraging such moves to "greener pastures." Lurie, who helped save the Giants from relocating in Toronto in 1977, was forced into accepting some $10 million less than his offer from the Tampa-St.Petersburg group, when he sold to a San Francisco syndicate headed by Peter Magowan, president and CEO of Safeway, Inc.

November 12

1923 — The New York Giants deal shortstop Dave Bancroft and outfielders Casey Stengel and Bill Cunningham to the Braves for outfielder Billy Southworth and pitcher Joe Oeschger. The trade was made by manager John McGraw to allow Bancroft to become manager of the Boston club. Bancroft was only 18 when he first became a professional and spent six seasons in the minors before joining the Phillies in 1915 and made his first World Series appearance in that rookie season. Before his career ended he would play in three more World Series with the Giants. Bancroft was best known for his defense and was rated as one of the better shortstops, often compared to Honus Wagner. As a switch hitter he hit .279 in his 16 years with the Phils, Giants, Boston and Brooklyn. He managed the Braves for four seasons without much success, never finishing out of the second division. Bancroft wrapped up his career as a player-coach back with the Giants in 1930 and was elected to the Hall of Fame n 1971.

November 13

1920 — The Pacific Coast League is hit hard with rumblings of gambling and conspiring to throw games – all of this on the heels of the Black Sox scandal in 1919. The league suspended first baseman W.B. Bouton and outfielders Bill Rumler and Harl V. Maggert for gambling and for conspiring to throw games during the 1919 season. Previously, the San Francisco Seals had released pitchers Tom Seaton and Case Smith for the good of the game. All five of the players were eventually barred from organized ball. Rumler, Maggert, and Seaton had played in the majors at various times during 1907-1917. Meanwhile, Gene Dale with Salt Lake City, and a former pitcher with the Cardinals and Reds (1911-1916) was expelled by the PCL for allegedly conspiring to throw games. Interestingly, Hal Chase, who was involved in gambling stories during his 15-year major league career, was barred from attending all Pacific Coast League games because of alleged attempts to seduce PCL players to throw games. Chase had finished his major league career with the Giants in 1919.

November 14

1985 — The Milwaukee Brewers release 39 year-old Rollie Fingers, bringing to a close his 17-year pitching career. That career would begin in 1968 with one game for Oakland and end after 944 pitching appearances, almost all of it out of the bullpen. Fingers started only 37 games and none after the 1973 season while pitching for the Athletics, San Diego, and the Brewers. He would finish as one of the all-time outstanding relief pitchers with 341 saves and a won-lost mark of 114-118 and an ERA of 2.90. Fingers (34) was the Rolaids Pitcher of the Year in 1977 (35 saves), 1978 (37 saves) and 1980 (23 saves with 11 wins) and was elected to the Hall of Fame in 1992.

November 15

1886 — In what is believed to be the first trade of reserved players ever completed takes place in the then-major league American Association. The St. Louis Browns send outfielder Hugh Nicol to the Cincinnati Red Stockings for catcher Jack Boyle and $400. Boyle was a rookie having played in only one game for Cincinnati and Nicol had played four seasons with St. Louis, making his big league debut with the National League Chicago White Stockings in 1881. Neither player could hit much — Boyle hit .253 in his 13 seasons with the Red Stockings, Browns, the Chicago Pirates (Players League) and the New York Giants and Philadelphia Phillies (National League). Nicol hit .235 in 10 years with Cincinnati, St. Louis and Chicago.

November 17

1953 — The Orioles officially become members of the American League for the second time in baseball history with the announcement of the transfer of the St. Louis Browns franchise to Baltimore. The Orioles had been members of the AL for two seasons (1901-1902) before the franchise was sold to New York interests in 1903 and became the Highlanders (Yankees). Professional baseball in Baltimore dates back to 1872, to the days of the Lord Baltimores in both the National Association and American Association. The team became the Orioles (named after the state bird of Maryland, the Baltimore Oriole) in 1883 and entered the National League in 1892. Baseball would not die following the move to New York and in 1903 the club would play in the minor leagues until 1954; the Eastern League 1903-1911, and the International League 1912-1953, with the exception of 1915 when the city fielded the Baltimore Terrapins in the outlaw Federal League.

November 18

1971 — Chicago Cubs owner P.K. Wrigley, in a published report in early September, threatened to fire his players instead of manager Leo Durocher. This led to another interesting development in Cubs history. In 1961 Wrigley had instituted the infamous College of Coaches instead of a manager to run his team, and that system remained in use through 1965. In 1963 he introduced the Athletic Director to baseball when he hired Air Force Colonel Robert V. Whitlow and gave him that title. With the Cubs in turmoil during the 1971 season, it was uncertain whether Wrigley would have Durocher back in 1972. The situation came to a head in a November 16 story in the Chicago *Sun-Times* when Durocher's third base coach, Peanuts Lowrey, was quoted as saying "I was surprised and ashamed by some of the stuff that was going on last season. Some of those guys [players] should have cried less and played ball more. If they fire Leo that means the players get his job and they'll be laughing up their sleeves." Two days later on this date Durocher's contract was renewed with another of Wrigley's unprecedented moves. To help appease the players, the Cubs hired former major league pitcher Hank Aguirre and gave him the unique title of "Information Services Coach." Aguirre would be in uniform, have a locker in the clubhouse and sit on the bench during games. He would be a uniformed public relations man between the manager and players. The buffer didn't work — Durocher would resign under pressure at the All-Star break.

November 20

1913 — When the San Francisco Giants finally got around to leaving Candlestick Park because of the wind, cold, and fog, it wasn't the first time a ballpark location fell by the wayside in the city for the same reasons. Following the 1906 San Francisco earthquake, the Seals began playing in their new ballpark called Recreation Park at 15th and Valencia streets in the warmest part of town. After several years, Seals co-owner J. Cal Ewing decided the city had outgrown the 11,000- seat stadium, and on this date in 1913 work began on a new 18,000-seat park at the foot of Lone Mountain, some two miles from the Pacific Ocean and near what is now the campus of the University of San Francisco. It would be the largest minor league park, not only in terms of seating capacity, but also in the size of the playing field – 340 feet down the lines and 400 feet to center.

Following a gala opening in May of 1916 that included a baseball boosters luncheon of 600 at the Palace Hotel, a parade down Market Street, the sale of 17,050 tickets to the opener, and the burial of a box of baseball relics under home plate, it was 'play ball' at Ewing Field. But it wasn't long before the afternoon fog started rolling in off the ocean almost every day when the games were in progress and most of the fans started remembering the sunshine at Recreation Park. Ewing Field was a complete failure as far as location was concerned and the Seals would return to Old Rec, as it was called, with an increase in seating capacity to 15,000 and there the team would remain until Seals Stadium opened in 1931. The "new-old" Ewing Field was used as a football stadium before being demolished to make way for a housing project. All that remains to remember — There Used to be a Ball Park Right Here – is a street called Ewing Terrace and the fog.

November 21

1933 — Chuck Klein, a future Hall-of-Famer, is traded by the Phillies after six seasons with Philadelphia to the Chicago Cubs. In return the Cubs get shortstop Mark Koenig, pitcher Ted Kleinhans, first baseman Harvey Hendrick and $65,000. This transaction marks the only time in history a team traded a player, by its own volition, following his Triple Crown season. The only other trade of a Triple Crown winner was forced upon the Philadelphia Athletics after Nap Lajoie won the crown in 1901. Lajoie, following his 1900 season with the Phillies had been lured to the A's for more money, and the Phillies sued for the return of the second baseman and eventually acquired an injunction against his playing for the Athletics. It wasn't until June of 1902 that the State Supreme Court ruled that Lajoie couldn't play for any Pennsylvania team other than the Phillies. As a result of this ruling the Athletics sold Lajoie to Cleveland.

1956 — Dodgers pitcher Don Newcombe captures the first-ever Cy Young Award. He led the majors with 27 wins and only seven losses. His earned run average was 3.06, allowing 219 hits in 268 innings, five shutouts, 139 strikeouts, and only 46 bases on balls. From 1956-1966 one Cy Young winner was selected for the major leagues – beginning in 1967 awards were given in each league.

November 22

1934 — Freddie Lindstrom is traded by Pittsburgh along with pitcher Larry French to the Cubs for outfielder Babe Herman and pitchers Guy Bush and Jim Weaver. Lindstrom's pro career began when he signed with Toledo of the American Association as a youngster, but Mudhens president Roger Bresnahan thought Lindstrom was too young to sit on the bench during a game. Toledo was doing so badly at the time (the club finished the 1922 season at 61-101) that manager George Whitted told Bresnahan he had to do something to help the team – "That kid's doing no good in the bleachers so I'm gonna stick him in the game whether you like it or not." Lindstrom was only 16 years old at the time and finished the season hitting .304. The third baseman/outfielder spent his first nine years in the majors with the Giants and the final four seasons of his 13-year career with the Pirates, Cubs and Brooklyn. Lindstrom (7) hit .311 in those 13 seasons and entered the Hall of Fame in 1976.

1954 — The Pittsburgh Pirates hit the jackpot in the winter draft when they pluck young Roberto Clemente off the Montreal International League roster. The property of the Brooklyn Dodgers, Clemente was being hidden from major league scouts, with limited playing time with the Royals, but Pirates' scouts Howie Haak and Clyde Sukeforth get credit for spotting the talents of the 20 year old who had played in only 87 games in 1954 with Montreal with only two homeruns, 12 runs batted in and a batting average of .257. It would be Clemente's only minor league season.

November 23

1943 — Commissioner Landis rules that Philadelphia Phillies owner William D. Cox is permanently banned from holding any office or employment in baseball for having bet on his own team. Cox had hired Bucky Harris as his manager in 1943, but by mid-season Harris and Cox had drifted apart, and on July 28 Harris was fired and replaced by Freddie Fitzsimmons. Harris, commenting on his dismissal said, "He's [Cox] a fine guy to fire me. He gambles on his own club." Following the commissioner's investigation, Landis said Cox had made "approximately 15 or 20 bets of $25 to $100 per game on his own club to win."

Financial losses were staggering during this period (because of the war) with major league teams losing almost a quarter of a million dollars. Hit hardest were the Phillies, who were forced to declare bankruptcy; the franchise was sold to the National League for $50,000. Commissioner Landis and National League president Ford Frick brokered the club's sale to Robert Carpenter, Sr., multimillionaire member of the DuPont family for $400,000. This sale would turn out to be one of the highlights, if not *the* highlight, in the history of the Philadelphia Phillies. Prior to the 1945 season with son Robert, Jr. now running the struggling club, the Phils held a contest for a new team nickname, offering a $100 War Bond and a season pass to the winner. 634 names were suggested and the winner was "Blue Jays" submitted by Mrs. Elizabeth Crooks who noted that the aggressive bird had the proper fighting spirit. Despite all of this, Phillies never went away – a fixture with the team since 1883 – the new uniform still carried "Phillies" across the chest while a Blue Jays patch was relegated to the left sleeve. The fans didn't buy the new name. Five years later the "Whiz Kids" won the National League pennant.

November 24

1953 — A meeting of the media is held in president Walter O'Malley's office on Montague Street to announce the new manager of the Brooklyn Dodgers. Chuck Dressen had been fired after losing the 1952 and 1953 World Series to the Yankees and still had the gall to demand a multi-year contract from O'Malley who abhorred anything more than a one-year pact. The leading candidate for the position was popular shortstop Pee Wee Reese but O'Malley stunned the gathering when he announced "This is Walter Alston, I've hired him as my manager to beat the Yankees next season." Neither the Dodgers nor Yankees made it to the World Series in 1954 but Alston, working on one-year contracts for the next 23 seasons, won seven pennants and four World Championships for Brooklyn and Los Angeles.

November 25

1941 — Shortstop Lou Boudreau, after two full seasons with Cleveland, is appointed manager of the Indians. At 24 years, four months and eight days old he becomes the youngest ever to start a season as a major league skipper. Boudreau was 22 when he began his big league career with the Tribe, leading the league in fielding in seven of his first eight years. In the winter of 1941-42, while serving as assistant basketball coach at his alma-mater, the University of Illinois, he applied for the managerial post left vacant by Roger Peckinpaugh, and following an interview with the Indians board of directors was awarded the post.

After nine seasons as player-manager, he had finished in the first division six times and won the World Championship in 1948. After his release following the 1950 season he signed with the Red Sox and was appointed Boston manager in 1952, holding that position for three seasons. He managed Kansas City

1955-57 then became a broadcaster for the Cubs in 1960. During that season Boudreau was pulled back to the field when owner Phillip Wrigley replaced Charley Grimm as his manager and Grimm took Boudreau's job in the booth. As a manager Boudreau finished with a win-percentage of .487, his playing career spanned 15 years with a batting average of .295, an American League batting championship in 1944 (.327) and the Most Valuable Player Award in 1948. Boudreau (5) was inducted into the Hall of Fame in 1970.

November 26

1935 — The National League takes over the bankrupt, last-place Boston Braves franchise after several failed attempts to sell the club. The league ultimately appoints Bob Quinn, former general manager of the Brooklyn Dodgers, as president.

1996 — Baseball owners, meeting in Chicago, ratify a collective bargaining agreement, ending nearly three years of labor unrest. Just 20 days earlier the owners had strongly rejected the agreement 18 votes to 12. This time around it was approved 26 to 4 with the White Sox, Cleveland, Kansas City, and Oakland casting the no votes. The agreement will run through October 2000 (later extended for one year). Among the highlights are revenue sharing among the clubs and a luxury tax system on team payrolls that exceeds set thresholds. Also, Interleague play is included and increases in minimum salary for players from $109,000 in 1996 to $150,000 in 1997 to $170,000 in 1998 and $200,000 in 1999. On December 5 the union votes to approve the contract and both parties sign the formal agreement on December 9.

November 27

1904 — The Pacific Coast League closes with Tacoma winning both halves of the split season of a 225 game schedule. The PCL, in its first year of operation, had only six teams, but five of the six won in excess of 100 games each. Tacoma (130), Los Angeles (119), Seattle (114), Oakland (116) and San Francisco (101). Only Portland failed to reach the century mark in wins but four of the circuit's six teams lost in triple-figures with only Tacoma (94) and Los Angeles (97) escaping the 100 mark. Tacoma beat Los Angeles four games to one in the playoffs with Los Angeles pitcher Doc Newton the league's best pitcher with a 39-17 .745 record. The Pacific Coast League grew out of the Pacific National League which operated in 1903 as an eight-team circuit consisting of Butte, Montana, Spokane,

Seattle, Portland, San Francisco, Tacoma and Helena, Montana. The last four teams mentioned disbanded on August 16 following a July 1 move of the Portland franchise to Salt Lake City. Over the next 94 years the PCL would lose eight of their former members to major league expansion or franchise moves: Los Angeles-Hollywood, San Francisco, Seattle, San Diego, Dallas-Fort Worth, Denver and Phoenix.

November 28

1927 — Pittsburgh trades Kiki Cuyler to the Chicago Cubs for infielder Sparky Adams and outfielder Floyd Scott. This move comes after Cuyler had spent his first seven seasons in the majors with the Pirates. He became a regular in 1924 hitting .354, .357 in 1925 and .321 in 1926. The beginning of the end of his Pittsburgh career was the 1927 season. Donie Bush took over as manager that season and one of his moves was to bat Cuyler second in the order, rather than his usual number three spot. Claiming he was not a disciplined hitter and unsuited to bat second, Cuyler, following a game in which he went hitless, blew up at Bush and the manager stated that he (Cuyler) had played his final game with Pittsburgh as long as Bush was manager. Bush held to his word despite Cuyler's .309 average at the time.

He had played in only 85 games prior to Bush's declaration and spent the entire 1927 World Series with the Yankees on the bench. If any ball player needed a nickname, it was Cuyler. Christened Hazen Shirley, he picked up his nickname in 1923 while playing centerfield for Nashville in the Southern Association. It began when his second base and shortstop teammates would shout "Cuy", indicating the centerfielder should make the catch. The fans picked up the cry and a Nashville sportswriter printed it out as "Kiki" in his game stories. Cuyler played 18 years in the majors with Pittsburgh, the Cubs, Cincinnati and Brooklyn hitting over .300 in ten of those seasons, finishing with a career .321 while leading the National League four years in stolen bases. As an outfielder with an outstanding arm he was one of the most graceful ever to play the game and was equally adept with his glove on ground balls as well as fly balls. Cuyler (3) was voted into the Hall of Fame in 1968.

November 29

1967 — Future Hall-of-Famer Luis Aparicio is traded by Baltimore with outfielder Russ Snyder and outfielder-infielder John Matias to the White Sox for infielder Don Buford and pitchers Bruce Howard and Roger Nelson. The little shortstop returns to the organization that signed him as a 20-year old from Venezuela. At that time, the White Sox and Cleveland were in a bidding war for his services, but Chicago won out when general manager Frank Lane informed Aparicio's agent to tell the owner of the Venezuelan winter league team (for whom the shortstop was playing): "That we will send no more players down there if we don't get Aparicio!" After two seasons in the minors the White Sox had the 1956 American League Rookie of the Year.

1971 — Cincinnati makes a landmark trade with Houston in acquiring second baseman Joe Morgan, pitcher Jack Billingham, third baseman Denis Menke and outfielders Cesar Geronimo and Ed Arbrister, in exchange for first baseman Lee May, as well as infielders Tommy Helms and Jimmy Stewart. The trade will immediately make the Reds a dominant team in the National League with Morgan the key in the trade. He joins a cast of players – Tony Perez, Dave Concepcion, Pete Rose, Johnny Bench and George Foster on a team that would become known as the Big Red Machine and go on to win five division titles and finish second three times, as well as playing in three World Series in Morgan's eight seasons with Cincinnati. Morgan was the personification of a winning player – batting .271 in his 22 major league seasons with Houston, the Reds, Giants, Phillies and Oakland. He hit 268 homeruns, drove in 1,133 runs while scoring 1,650, walking 1,865 times with 689 stolen bases. He had back-to-back Most Valuable Player Awards in 1975 and 1976 and racked up five Gold Glove Awards. Morgan (8) was voted into the Hall of Fame in 1990 in his first year of eligibility.

November 30

1999 — By an overwhelming 57-35 vote, Richie Philips, head of the union of baseball umpires since 1978, was ousted. The secret mail vote, conducted by the National Labor Relations Board, followed a tumultuous five months that included the union's mass resignation strategy that cost 22 members their jobs. Phillips was the target of dissidents who formed the Major League Umpires Independent Organizing Committee.

"And so I shall catch the fly"
Henry V, Shakespeare

"I'll catch it ere it comes to ground"
MacBeth, Shakespeare

Chapter Twelve

"I believe that baseball is a homeopathic cure for lunacy. It is a kind of craze in itself, and gives lunatics a new kind of craving to relieve them of the malady which afflicts their minds."

Dr. S.B. Talcott, superintendent of the State Lunatic Asylum in New York, from the *New York Clipper*, 1892.

December 1

1971 — Ernie Banks is released as a player by the Cubs; this ends his entire 19-year active major league career with Chicago as a first baseman-shortstop. He had been a player-coach since the 1967 season and continued with the organization in various coaching capacities through 1976. Banks, purchased in 1953 from the Kansas City Monarchs as a 22-year old for $25,000 and a little-known pitcher, would go on to be one of the most popular and productive players in Cubs history. With a batting average of .274, 512 homeruns and 1,636 runs batted in, he would lead the league in homeruns in 1958 and 1960 – hitting a total of 133 over that three-year period. He won one Gold Glove as a shortstop in 1960. Rarely missing a game, he was switched to first base in 1962. Banks (14) won back-to-back Most Valuable Player Awards in 1958 and 1959 and was inducted into the Hall of Fame in 1977 in his first year of eligibility.

December 2

1916 — Under pressure from the Players' Fraternity, the National Commission orders that injured players (later called the Disabled List) get full pay for the duration of their contracts. The injury clause previously allowed clubs to suspend players after 15 days pay.

December 3

1957 — Outfielder Larry Doby is traded by the Chicago White Sox to a team he would never play for – Baltimore. The Orioles moved Doby to Cleveland on April 1 before the opening of the 1958 season. This would be Doby's second stay with the Indians after spending his first nine seasons in the majors with the Tribe. In 1947 he was purchased from the Negro American League Newark Eagles when he was 22. He went on to rack up 13 seasons in the majors as a player then joined the coaching staff of the White Sox. In 1978 he finished Bob Lemon's term as manager for Chicago's final 87 games with a record of 37-50. Doby (14) wound up his American League career hitting .283 with 253 homeruns and was elected to the Hall of Fame in 1998.

December 4

1878 — Batting-order rules are altered making the first batter in the next inning follow the last batter in the previous inning. The old rule stated that the first batter in the next inning would follow the last player *retired* – should the inning end by retiring that base runner.

1906 — Despite winning the Class-B Connecticut State League pennant with a 72-53 record, the club falls on hard times and the franchise is sold at a sheriff's sale for $25.

1964 — Baseball approves a free agent draft at the annual winter meetings in Houston. A few months earlier the plan had been voted down when only eight National League and three American League teams favored the plan. This time, however, it was overwhelmingly approved. The former "first-year player rule" passed in 1958 was not working; it was anti-development, clogging major league rosters with young players not yet ready for the majors. Impetus was given to the new rule following the signing by the Los Angeles Angels of 21-year-old Rick Reichardt out of the University of Wisconsin for a bonus of $205,000 – exceeding the annual pay of many of the game's current stars.

The first draft pick in 1965, Rick Monday, was given a signing bonus of $104,000 by Oakland and even today it's obvious that major league owners still haven't learned fiscal responsibility. Signing bonuses have risen into the $1 million range and continue to rise over the $3 million mark. Payouts to unproven talent continued and records continue to be broken. With this precedent haunting the owners the draft in its present form has been under examination for years, but the only solution — stop spending — evidently is not on the owners' agenda.

December 5

1950 — Mel Ott, who had been associated with the Giants farm organization for the previous two seasons, is named manager of the Oakland Oaks of the Pacific Coast League. At 17 years old Ott had joined the New York club in 1926 and immediately became a pet project of manager John McGraw. McGraw refused to send him to the minors for fear Ott's unique batting style – the high leg kick — would be messed with by minor league managers. He was nursed along by

McGraw, playing in only 34 games his first season and 82 games in 1927 before becoming a fixture in the Giants outfield for the next 22 years. In 1942 he would succeed Bill Terry as the Giants player-manager and remain through 1948. Ott was the leading home run hitter in the National League in 1936, 1938 and 1942 and in three other seasons (1932-34-37) finishing in ties for the crown with Chuck Klein, Ripper Collins and Joe Medwick, respectively. He played in three World Series with an average of .295, hitting four homeruns. Ott (4) batted .304, with 511 homeruns, driving in 1,880 runs, 2,876 hits and 1,708 bases on balls. He was elected to the Hall of Fame in 1951.

1988 — Atlanta becomes the first team ever to select its own player in the Major League Rule 5 draft when it takes 19-year old pitcher Ben Rivera. Because of a clerical error, the Braves did not realize he would be eligible for the draft. Under rules of the draft, Rivera would have to clear waivers through the other 25 clubs before being farmed out by the Braves. Vice-president Paul Snyder said that Rivera, if claimed, would force Atlanta to keep him on the 25 man roster. However, Rivera was not claimed in March of 1989 and was sent to Class-A Durham in the Carolina League. Rivera would play in only eight games with the Braves in 1992 before being traded to the Phillies and eventually wound up in the Montreal organization with Triple-A Ottawa.

December 6

1968 — Major league club owners dismiss Commissioner William Eckert. The general is asked for his resignation on the final day of the winter meetings in San Francisco. To the surprise of everyone, Eckert immediately grants the request. The owners – particularly the younger ones – did not believe the general was strong enough to lead Baseball and were looking toward a more vigorous commissioner. Eckert had turned out to be a powerless leader totally without baseball knowledge and with no positive public image. The 59-year old general had served only three years and a month of his seven-year contract after succeeding Ford Frick, who had held the office for 14 years. Eckert was replaced on a pro-tem basis on February 4, 1969 by Bowie Kuhn; Kuhn later became permanent, serving until November 30,1984.

1990 — Shoeless Joe Jackson's signature is sold for $23,100 – the most ever paid for a baseball signature. The transaction took place at Leland's auction house in New York City. Jackson, who could not read or write, copied the signature from one written out by his wife. Hours later the signature was resold for an unknown amount.

1999 — ESPN-ESPN2 and Major League Baseball announce a new six-year contract beginning in the 2000 season. This settlement was the result of a lawsuit by Major League Baseball against the television giant for allegedly circumventing the current agreement, which was to run through 2002. Financial terms were not disclosed but the old agreement was an eight-year, $455 million package.

December 7

1980 — Commissioner Bowie Kuhn warns that club owners face heavy financial losses if salaries continue to escalate. In 1980 the average major league salary was $143,756, up from $113,558 in 1979. In Kuhn's final year as commissioner – 1984 – the owners had ignored the warning and the average had risen to $329,408.

December 8

1959 — With Branch Rickey going full-speed ahead in putting franchises together to start a third major league – the Continental League – the Baseball brass continues to soft pedal the probability of expansion. American League president Joe Cronin says expansion plans are indecisive and Rickey scores him for his indecisiveness by announcing that his league has awarded a franchise to Atlanta – other cities already announced in the fold for the proposed third league are New York, Houston, Denver, Minneapolis-St. Paul, and Toronto. However, the National League concurs with Cronin and the leagues announce that expansion cannot be considered for at least five years (1964). By December 22, 1959 the Continental League has all its franchises in the fold with the addition of Dallas/Fort Worth. Major League Baseball accepted the inevitable, and in 1961 the American League would expand and the National would follow in 1962.

1983 — Former third baseman for the Yankees, Dr. Bobby Brown, who later embarked on a successful medical career, becomes the sixth president of the American League succeeding Lee MacPhail. Brown served eleven years through 1994. By 1999 the offices of president in both the American and National Leagues would be eliminated and their duties absorbed by the commissioners' office.

December 9

1936 — The National League adopts a new design for home plate — it will have black beveled edges — and will be the first home plate change in 50 years. In earlier times, home base was constructed of iron, stone, marble or wood. In the mid-1880s the rubber home plate appeared. The refinement of employing rubber, which now seems natural, had evolved quietly. The idea belonged to Ed Keating, a left-handed pitcher with Baltimore in the major league American Association. In 1914 Keating was queried about his idea to use rubber. He answered the inquiry in unbelievable language, "Not only did I invent the rubber home plate, but I have invented various cycloidal, isoperimetrical and spiral catenaries." Keating pitched in only one game for the Orioles and lost it, allowing eleven runs. One of the contributing factors of his defeat was his inability to find home plate – he walked six batters. Incidentally, when the one-inch black bevel was added the width for a called strike remained at 17" – in other words if the ball crosses the plate on the black *only* it is NOT a strike!

1953 — Major league owners raise the minimum salary to $6,000.

1965 — In what can be called one of the worst trades in baseball history, Cincinnati trades former National League MVP Frank Robinson to Baltimore for pitchers Milt Pappas and Jack Baldschun and outfielder Dick Simpson. Reds general manager Bill Dewitt defends the transaction by labeling Robinson as "an old 30." In 1966 Robinson will win the Triple Crown with 49 homeruns, 122 RBI, an average of .316 and be voted the American League's Most Valuable Player. With the Reds, Pappas will go 12-11 with a 4.29 ERA, Baldschun 1-5, no saves with an ERA of 5.49 while Simpson hit .238 with four homers and 14 runs batted in. In the six seasons Robinson played for Baltimore the Orioles would win four pennants and two World Series.

December 10

1972 — The American League votes unanimously to adopt the designated hitter rule for a three-year experiment. In the December 1975 meeting the league will vote to permanently adopt the DH. However, the National League declines to go along with the AL. At the same time the major leagues adopt the save rule as an official statistic.

December 11

1928 — At the National League meeting, president John Heydler proposes the designated hitter for pitchers to improve and speed up the game. He contends fans are tired of seeing weak-hitting pitchers come to bat. The American League is against the proposal, but before commissioner Landis is forced to give the tie-breaking vote, Heydler withdraws the National League's offer.

1951 — One of baseball's all-time greats Joe DiMaggio announces his retirement at age 37.

December 12

1924 – Right-hander Stan Coveleski is traded by Cleveland to Washington for pitcher Byron Speece and outfielder Carr Smith. Coveleski had been with the Indians since 1916 following a three-game stint with the Athletics in 1912. During his 14-year major league career he was best known for his excellent control and devastating spitball. In 1925, the first year after his trade, he had his most productive season with a 20-5 record leading the league with an .800 winning percentage. Joining him in helping move the Nationals into the World Series was Walter Johnson — the two combining for 40 wins and only 12 losses. It was the second World Series for Coveleski as he went 3-0 in the 1920 fall classic for the Indians against Brooklyn with an ERA of 0.67 allowing only two walks. Coveleski finished his career with the Yankees in 1928. Born Stanislaus Kowalewski, he won 215 games and lost 142, giving up only 2.3 bases on balls per nine innings during his career. He was voted into the Hall of Fame in 1969.

1933 — Connie Mack, forced to unload some of his higher-salaried Philadelphia Athletic players during the depression, picks up $225,000 when he deals two future Hall-of-Famers, Mickey Cochrane and Lefty Grove. Cochrane is sent to Detroit and Grove to the Red Sox. Cochrane and catcher Johnny Pasek fetch $100,000; Cochrane immediately takes over as Detroit's player-manager. Grove is traded to Boston along with pitcher Rube Walberg and second baseman Max Bishop. The Athletics receive $125,000, pitcher Bob Kline and shortstop Rabbit Warstler. Over a 20-year period (1913-1933), because of financial difficulties, Mack would sell or trade six future Hall-of-Famers; those deals would realize over a half-million dollars.

1941 — Shortstop Arky Vaughan, following a brilliant ten years with the Pittsburgh

Pirates, is traded to Brooklyn for four players — second baseman Pete Coscarart, pitcher Luke Hamlin, catcher Babe Phelps, and outfielder Jimmy Wasdell. While with the Pirates Vaughan won the National League batting championship with .385 in 1935. He would play four years with Brooklyn, but spent three years on the voluntary retired list (1944-46) to tend to his ranch in California while his younger brother was in the service. Following his return to baseball he finished his 14 years in the majors with the Dodgers in 1947-48 and played his final year in the Pacific Coast League with the San Francisco Seals. Vaughan (21) batted .300 or better in 12 of his 14 seasons hitting .318 during his career and was voted into the Hall of Fame in 1985.

December 13

1922 — At the National League meeting the owner of the Brooklyn Dodgers, Charles Ebbets, proposes placing numbers on player's sleeves or caps. The proposal is left to each club to do as it wishes but none did so. In 1916 in the American League Cleveland became the first team to number sleeves but it never was adopted by other clubs.

December 14

1911 — Pittsburgh owner Barney Dreyfuss proposes that World Series participants be required to turn over one-fourth of their share of the gate to the league and divide it among the other clubs. Under the present system 60 percent of the gross went to the players, ten percent went to the National Commission (baseball's ruling body) and the rest to the two pennant winning clubs. This resolution marks the beginning of players receiving a percentage of the World Series money.

December 15

1900 — One of the oddest deals ever to involve two future Hall-of-Famers is pulled off by the New York Giants and Cincinnati Reds. One (Christy Mathewson) had never won a major league game and the other (Amos Rusie) would never win another. Mathewson, only 20 years old, had compiled a 20-2 record by July with Norfolk in the Virginia League and was purchased by the Giants for $2,000. For the remainder of the 1900 season with New York, he posted a 0-3 mark in six starts and was returned to the minors where he was promptly drafted by Cincinnati. At age 29 Rusie had already pitched eight years with the Giants even though he was a holdout the entire 1896 season and missed all of 1899 and 1900 while under suspension. Although he did not know it at the time, his career was all but over in 1898 when he hurt his arm. Making his first start for Cincinnati on April 8, 1901 following the trade from New York, Rusie was bombed 14-3 and after two more appearances went back to digging ditches at 30 years old. In the same season Mathewson would win 20 of his 373 career victories and become the first pitcher elected to the Hall of Fame. Rusie's official career figures depend on which record books are researched; his wins vary from 246 to 241 and his losses from 158 to 174. There is also a discrepancy in the number of games he won pitching at the old 50-foot distance — 92 or 106. He had some control problems –striking out 1,934 and walking 1,704 – and those figures also vary. Nonetheless, the "Hoosier Thunderbolt" was enshrined in the Hall of Fame in 1977.

1920 — The National League announces a statistic on the number of baseballs used during the 1920 season that points to the way the game is changing. 17,676 baseballs were used during the 1919 season but that figure jumped by more than 10,000 to 27,924 in 1920.

1932 — A joint meeting of National League and American League owners approve the concept of "chain store" baseball developed by the St. Louis Cardinals and outwardly supported earlier by owner William Wrigley of the Cubs. This concept by the Cardinals was the beginning of major league clubs owning outright, or having working agreements with numerous minor league teams to grow their own talent; it was the beginning of the Farm System. Interestingly, commissioner Kenesaw Mountain Landis strenuously objected to the farm system concept but for some reason did not pull rank on the owners to prevent it.

December 18

1920 — On his 34th birthday Ty Cobb signs to manage the Tigers. He replaces Hugie Jennings who resigned after 14 years to join John McGraw as assistant manager of the Giants. Cobb signs for $32,500 for the 1921 season and at the same time becomes the highest-paid player and probably Baseball's first millionaire, factoring in his wise investments, chiefly in General Motors and Coca-Cola. In six seasons as Tigers skipper he had a 479-444 .519 record, finishing second once, third twice, fourth once and sixth twice. Cobb had already won 12 batting titles and his talent and intensity while managing did not diminish. While player-manager he logged an average of 477 at-bats per season and totaled 1,044 hits for a bat mark of .365 (his career average was .367). It is interesting to note the many outstanding adversaries that managed against Cobb: Hugh Duffy, Frank

Chance, Johnny Evers, Eddie Collins, Kid Gleason, Tris Speaker, Miller Huggins, Connie Mack, George Sisler, and Bucky Harris.

December 19

1934 — The New York Yankees announce that three players are being sent outright to the San Francisco Seals and two others go on option to complete the deal for young outfielder Joe DeMaggio (that is how the press was spelling his name at the time). Floyd Newkirk, right-handed pitcher, who was with Newark (International League) and the Yankees the previous season; James Densmore, also a right-handed hurler, who performed for Sacramento (Pacific Coast League) and Eddie Farrell, infielder for the Newark Bears, become the property of the Seals. Ted Norbert, outfielder, farmed out to Binghamton (NY-PENN League) during the 1934 season and Leslie Powers, first baseman, who played with Sacramento, go on option. DiMaggio is scheduled to report to Newark the next fall to prepare for service with the Yankees. Newkirk's major league stay was limited to one game and one inning in 1934; Powers would reach the majors in 1938 playing in three games with the Giants and 19 games with the Phillies in 1939.

This transaction between the Yankees and San Francisco is one of greatest in the history of the game. DiMaggio's accomplishments ranked among the greatest in baseball during his 13 seasons with the Yankees. His career numbers were a .325 batting average, 361 homeruns and 1,537 runs batted in, leading the American League in each category twice (average .381-1939 and .352-1940 - homeruns 46-1937 and 39-1948 - RBI 125-1941 and 155-1948). One of his lesser-known accomplishments was the number of times he struck out in his career - 369 in 6,821 at bats. The "Yankee Clipper" (5) was the Most Valuable Player in the American League in 1939,1941, and 1947; he entered the Hall in 1955.

December 20

1926 — Frankie Frisch and pitcher Jimmy Ring are traded by the Giants to the Cardinals for Rogers Hornsby. Frisch had been John McGraw's captain and had sparked the Giants to four straight pennants (1921-24). However, the club dropped to second place in 1925 and fifth in 1926 and a breach developed between the manager and captain; two months after the season Frisch was gone. Both Hornsby and Frisch flourished in their new environs in 1927, The Rajah batting .361 for New York and The Fordham Flash .337 for the Cardinals. Frisch continued to be a big part of St. Louis' success in pennant-winning seasons of 1928, 1930-31. He would become player-manager in 1933, taking the Red Birds to the

World Championship in 1934. Frisch would spend 19 years as a player, five seasons as manager of the Cardinals, seven years as Pittsburgh skipper and three seasons as manager of the Cubs. During Frisch's career he hit .316, drove in 1,244 runs and stole 419 bases, winning the National League stolen base title twice, with 49 with Giants in 1921 and 48 with St. Louis in 1927. Frisch (3) appeared in eight World Series, was the National League Most Valuable Player in 1931 and was inducted into the Hall of Fame in 1947.

1940 — Connie Mack acquires controlling interest in the Athletics from the Shibe family for $42,000. This move comes following his 40th season as Philadelphia manager, the only skipper the team had ever had since the formation of the American League. Mack would remain as A's manager culminating his 50 years with the club in 1950. His total managerial career spanned 53 major league seasons – his first three years with Pittsburgh in 1894-1896.

December 21

1960 — Chicago Cubs owner P.K. Wrigley drops another of his infamous bombshells saying the Cubs will have no manager, but will use a college of coaches. The official announcement will not be made until January 12, 1961. This ill-fated system would last through 1965.

December 22

1915 — Major League Baseball offers to buy out the Federal League following two seasons of competition from the outlaw circuit. In the proposal, the American and National leagues would pay $600,000 for distribution to Federal League owners, take over the Federal players' contracts, absorb two Federal League franchises (one into each league), and reimburse some of those who invested in the defunct league. Ban Johnson, president of the American League, is opposed to the deal. Meanwhile, the Federal League Baltimore Terrapins, believing they are getting short-changed, go to court against the deal. The final agreement would not be ratified by all parties until January 3, 1916.

December 23

1975 — In a landmark decision, pitchers Andy Messersmith and Dave McNally are declared free agents by arbitrator Peter Seitz. Immediately following the decision, the chairman of the owners' Player Relations Committee, John Gaherin, is fired. On February 4, 1976 U.S. District Judge John W. Oliver upholds the arbitrator's decision.

December 24

1986 — Reggie Jackson inks his final contract after 21 years in the majors, signing on with the Oakland Athletics. Jackson, a free agent after five seasons with California, also had playing time with Baltimore and the Yankees. He joined the Athletics initially in 1967 as a rookie in their final year in Kansas City. In that first season he played in only 35 games hitting the first of his 563 homeruns. Jackson would lead the American League in homers in four seasons but had a clear-cut title in only 1973, hitting 32 the same season he received the league's Most Valuable Player Award. Oddly, he shared the homer crown with three different Milwaukee Brewers – George Scott, Ben Ogilvie and Gorman Thomas. Along with his 563 homeruns, Jackson (44), garnered 2,584 hits while batting only .262, along with 1,702 runs batted in and scoring 1,551 runs, all of which got him into the Hall of Fame in his first year of eligibility in 1993. He would also go down in the record books as the all-time strikeout leader, going down on strikes 2,597 times, the only player to strike out more than 2,000 times. However, the number of strikeouts against a player's record does not keep him out of the Hall of Fame. Among the top 12 career strikeout leaders, seven besides Jackson are in the Hall – Willie Stargell, Tony Perez, Lou Brock, Mickey Mantle, Harmon Killebrew, Willie McCovey and Mike Schmidt.

December 25

1989 — 61 year-old Billy Martin, former infielder and manager, is killed in an automobile accident in Johnson City, New York. Martin managed the Yankees five different times between 1978 and 1988, resigning once and fired the other four times. His managerial career, was to say the least, a stormy ride both on and off the field. Barroom and street fights, not only with "fans", but also with his own players. Martin suffered suspensions for ordering brush back pitches to his pitchers to throw at opposing batters, and lawsuits by umpires as well. He fought numerous battles with the front offices for failing to adhere to team policy and guidelines, as well as violating baseball and club protocol.

Martin and Yankees owner George Steinbrenner suffered through a ten-year love-hate relationship that ended for the last time June 23, 1988 when he was fired and left the Yankees for the fifth time as manager. A street fighter while growing up in Oakland, Martin is remembered as the same street fighter in baseball while managing the Yankees, Minnesota, Detroit, Texas and Oakland. He compiled a .553 winning percentage through 2,267 games.

December 26

1919 — Someone leaked the big news! Actually, it would be the first of two times the news got out concerning the sale of Babe Ruth by the Red Sox to the Yankees. Boston would confirm the deal on January 3rd and New York waited until two days later to do so. In the eyes of the Yankees it was not official until the Babe signed his contract. Ruth had threatened not to report unless New York doubled his $10,000 contract and received a $1,000 up-front bonus.

1934 — Matsutaro Shoriko, head of Yomiuri Newspapers, announces the official formation of Japan's first professional team, the Tokyo-based Yomiuri Giants. The team is made up of players signed to compete against the American all-star team. Professional league play, with six teams, does not begin until 1936.

December 28

1944 — John Kelly "Buddy" Lewis, one of the many major leaguers to serve in World War II, is awarded the Distinguished Flying Cross in honor of his precision flying over the Burma. Lewis, who spent his entire eleven playing years with the Washington Senators, had his career interrupted for three years when he entered the service in 1942. Following his discharge, the third baseman-outfielder returned for four more seasons and picked up where he left off, hitting .281 through 1949. His career batting average for the Senators was .297.

December 29

1933 — Yankees owner Jake Ruppert refuses to release Babe Ruth so he can become manager of the Cincinnati Reds.

1969 — The *New York Times* reports that Curt Flood will sue baseball and challenge the reserve clause. His suit would be officially announced January 19. 1970. Flood's Civil action was prompted by the October 16, 1969 trade that sent him from St. Louis to Philadelphia, and his subsequent refusal to report to the Phillies. The suit would not be settled until it reached the Supreme Court June of 1972. The Supreme Court sustained baseball's anti-trust exemption by upholding the reserve clause.

December 30

1926 — The *Chicago Tribune* breaks a story that the Detroit Tigers had thrown a 4-game series to the White Sox in 1917 to help Chicago win the pennant. This was a tough period for Judge Landis since he was in the midst of sorting out the gambling charges involving Ty Cobb and Tris Speaker. The charges in the Detroit-White Sox story were brought by Swede Risberg, one of the players expelled by Landis in the Black Sox scandal. Risberg claimed that in 1917, when Chicago was battling the Red Sox for the pennant, the Tigers "sloughed off" a September series with the White Sox and then were repaid with two games in 1919 after the White Sox had clinched the pennant and Detroit was in a third-place battle with the Yankees. After two days of hearings in January, which involved some of the greatest names in baseball being called to the witness stand, Landis completely absolved the Detroit and Chicago players of any wrong-doing. Later, on January 27, 1927 he would also clear Cobb and Speaker of gambling.

December 31

1914 — American League president Ban Johnson succeeds in his efforts to broker the sale of the New York Yankees to Colonel Jacob Ruppert and Cap Huston for $460,000.

1950 — The 1940s end as the only decade in major league history in which no new stadiums are built. The last to open was Cleveland Municipal Stadium in 1932. No new ballpark will be opened until County Stadium in Milwaukee in 1953.

1972 — Pittsburgh's star outfielder and future Hall-of-Famer Roberto Clemente dies in a plane crash. When Managua, Nicaragua was hit with an earthquake in late December, Clemente became active in raising relief funds for the victims. He was aboard a plane that left San Juan, Puerto Rico with supplies for the people of Managua; he was killed, along with four others, when the plane crashed off-shore.

1974 — The New York Yankees announce the signing of Catfish Hunter to a five-year contract as a free agent for $3.0 million even though it was reported that both San Diego and Kansas City came in with higher bids. Hunter's former boss, Oakland owner Charlie Finley, had failed to pay Hunter $50,000 of his $100,000 salary due on a deferred basis and payable to an insurance company as an annuity. The case had gone to arbitration and Hunter was declared a free agent. Hunter's contract with the Yankees called for a signing bonus of $1.0 million and a playing contract for each of the five years at $150,000 per season. At retirement he would receive a personal services contract for ten years totaling $500,000 plus attorney's fees ($200,000) and two 10-year, paid up life insurance policies for himself ($500,000) and his two children ($25,000) each.

"Within the ballpark, time moves differently, marked by no clock except the events of the game. This is the unique, unchangeable feature of baseball, and perhaps explains why this sport, for all the enormous changes it has undergone in the past decade or two, remains somehow rustic, unviolent, and introspective. Baseball's time is seamless and invisible, a bubble in which players move at exactly the same pace and rhythms as all their predecessors. This is the way the game was played in our youth and in our fathers' youth, and even back then – back in the country days – there must have been the same feeling that time can be stopped. Since baseball time is measured only in outs, all you have to do is succeed utterly; keep hitting, keep the rally alive, and you have defeated time. You remain forever young. Sitting in the stands, we sense this, if only dimly. The players below us – Mays, DiMaggio, Ruth, Snodgrass – swim and blur in memory, the ball floats over to Terry Turner, and the end of this game may never come."

Roger Angell, from the February 20, 1971 issue of *The New York.*

New York Herald
Oct. 25, 1845

BASE BALL PLAY—The subjoined is the result of the return match between the New York Base Ball Club and the Brooklyn players, which came off on the ground of the Brooklyn Star Cricket Club yesterday. Messrs. Johnson, Wheaton and Van Nostrand were the umpires.

NEW YORK BALL CLUB.	Hands out.	Runs.	BROOKLYN CLUB.	Hands out.	Runs.
Davis	2	4	Hunt	1	3
Murphy	0	6	Hines	2	2
Vail	2	4	Gilmore	3	2
Kline	1	4	Hardy	2	2
Miller	2	5	Sharp	2	2
Case	2	4	Meyers	0	3
Tucker	2	4	Whaley	2	2
Winslow	1	6	Forman	1	3
	12	37		12	19

Top: The first published Box Score, from *The New York Herald*, October 25, 1845.

Right: a modern box score, illustrating the growing complexity of box scores

Below: Shorts similar to those worn by the Hollywood Stars in the 1950s. See page 77.

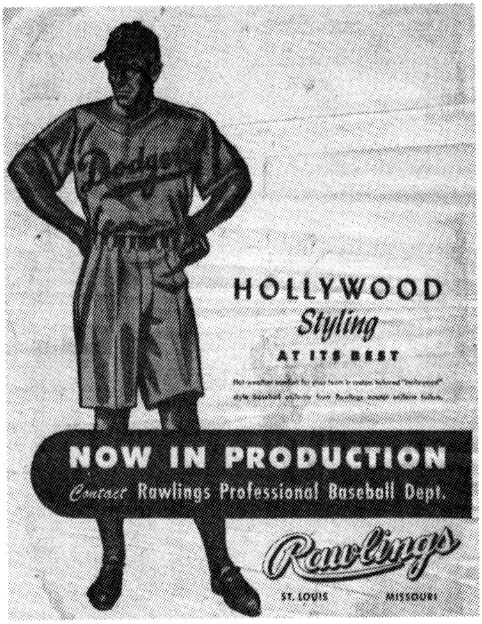

Cardinals 6, Expos 3 — September 27, 1998

Montreal Expos	AB	R	H	RBI	W	K	Avg.
W. Guerrero, 2b	5	1	2	0	0	0	.284
Jones, cf	5	0	1	0	0	0	.217
DeMay, lf	3	1	0	0	1	0	.239
Perez, lf	1	0	0	0	0	0	.236
V. Guerrero, rf	4	0	2	1	0	2	.324
Seguignol, rf	0	0	0	0	0	0	.262
Fullmer, 1b	4	0	1	0	0	1	.273
Barrett, c	3	0	1	1	1	1	.304
Andrews, 3b	3	0	1	0	1	0	.238
Cabrera, ss	4	1	1	1	0	0	.280
Thurman, p	2	0	0	0	0	0	.000
b-Vidro, ph	1	0	0	0	0	0	.220
Pavano, p	0	0	0	0	0	0	.158
d-McGuire, ph	1	0	0	0	0	1	.186
Telford, p	0	0	0	0	0	0	.250
Totals	36	3	9	3	3	5	
St. Louis Cardinals	**AB**	**R**	**H**	**RBI**	**W**	**K**	**Avg.**
McEwing, 2b-lf	3	2	2	0	0	0	.200
Drew, rf-cf	4	1	2	0	0	0	.417
McGwire, 1b	3	2	3	4	1	0	.299
Kelly, 2b	0	0	0	0	0	0	.216
Jordan, cf	4	0	0	1	0	1	.316
Little, rf	0	0	0	0	0	0	.083
Gant, lf	3	0	1	0	0	1	.240
King, p	0	0	0	0	0	0	.000
e-Lankford, ph	1	0	0	0	0	1	.293
Acevedo, p	0	0	0	0	0	0	.176
Tatis, 3b	4	1	1	1	0	1	.287
Ordaz, ss	4	0	0	0	0	0	.203
Morris, p	1	0	0	0	0	1	.069
a-DeShields, ph	1	0	0	0	0	0	.290
Frascatore, p	0	0	0	0	0	0	.167
c-Mabry, ph-lf-1b	2	0	0	0	0	0	.249
Marrero, c	3	0	0	0	0	1	.244
Lampkin, c	0	0	0	0	0	0	.231
Totals	33	6	9	6	1	6	

Montreal	0	0	2	1	0	0	0	0	0	—3	9	1
St. Louis	1	1	1	0	0	0	3	0	x	—6	9	2

a-flied out for Morris in the 4th. b-grounded into fielder's choice for Thurman in the 6th. c-grounded out for Frascatore in the 7th. d-struck out for Pavano in the 8th. e-struck out for King in the 8th.

E—Andrews (20), Tatis (12), Ordaz (13). LOB—Montreal 9, St. Louis 5. 2B—Barrett (2), Drew (3), Gant (17). HR—Cabrera (3) off Morris; McGwire 2 (70) off Pavano, Thurman; Tatis (8) off Thurman. RBI—V. Guerrero (109), Barrett (2), Cabrera (22), McGwire 4 (147), Jordan (91), Tatis (26). SB—Jordan (17). CS—McEwing (1). GIDP—W. Guerrero. Runners left in scoring position—Montreal 4 (Barrett, Andrews 2, Thurman); Cardinals 4 (Jordan, Gant, DeShields, Mabry). DP—St. Louis 1.

Montreal	IP	H	R	ER	W	K	NP	ERA
Thurman	5	6	3	3	1	3	82	4.70
Pavano (L 6-9)	2	3	3	3	0	2	32	4.21
Telford	1	0	0	0	0	1	14	3.86
St. Louis	**IP**	**H**	**R**	**ER**	**W**	**K**	**NP**	**ERA**
Morris	4	6	3	3	3	2	74	2.53
Frascatore (W 3-4)	3	3	0	0	0	2	34	4.14
King	1	0	0	0	0	1	13	3.53
Acevedo (S 15)	1	0	0	0	0	0	7	2.56

HBP—by Thurman (McEwing). WP—by Morris. Umpires—Home, Rieker; First, West; Second, Danley; Third, Gorman. Time—2:33. Attendance—46,110.

Index